D0207310

Malta
& Gozo

Carolyn Bain

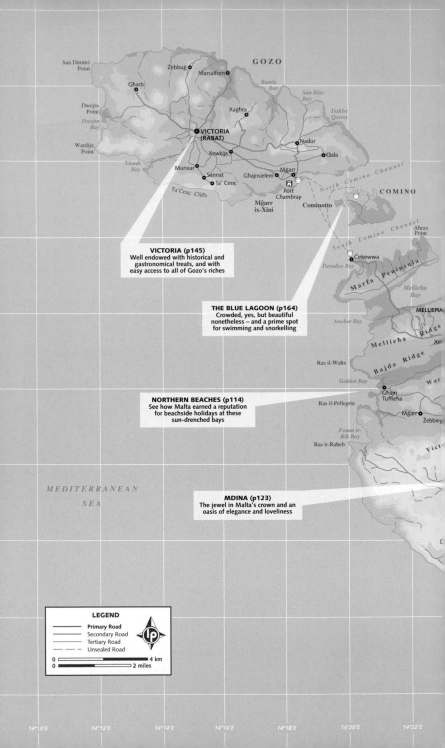

GOZO

San Dimitri Point

Zebbuġ

Marsalforn

Ramla Bay

San Blas Bay

Gharb

Dahlet Qorrot

Xaghra

Dwejra Point

Dwejra Bay

VICTORIA (RABAT)

Nadur

Wardija Point

Xewkija

Qala

Xlendi Bay

Munxar

Sannat

Ghajnsielem

Mġarr

North Comino Channel

COMINO

Ta' Cenc

Ta' Ċenċ Cliffs

Fort Chambray

Cominotto

North Comino Channel

Mġarr ix-Xini

Cominotto

South Comino Channel

Ahrax Point

VICTORIA (p145)
Well endowed with historical and gastronomical treats, and with easy access to all of Gozo's riches

Cirkewwa

Marfa Peninsula

Paradise Bay

Mellieħa Bay

THE BLUE LAGOON (p164)
Crowded, yes, but beautiful nonetheless – and a prime spot for swimming and snorkelling

MELLIEĦA

Anchor Bay

Xer

Mellieħa

Mellieħa Ridge

Ras il-Waħx

Bajda Ridge

Golden Bay

War

NORTHERN BEACHES (p114)
See how Malta earned a reputation for beachside holidays at these sun-drenched bays

Ras il-Pellegrin

Għajn Tuffieħa

Mġarr

Żebbieġ

Fomm ir-Rih Bay

Ras ir-Raħeb

Victi

MEDITERRANEAN SEA

MDINA (p123)
The jewel in Malta's crown and an oasis of elegance and loveliness

LEGEND

——	**Primary Road**
——	Secondary Road
——	Tertiary Road
– – –	Unsealed Road

0 _____ 4 km
0 _____ 2 miles

14°10'E 14°12'E 14°14'E 14°16'E 14°18'E 14°20'E 14°22'E

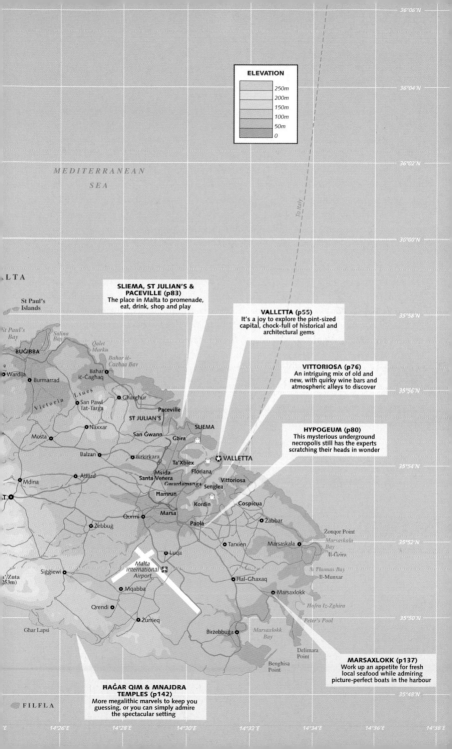

ELEVATION

250m
200m
150m
100m
50m
0

MEDITERRANEAN

SEA

To Italy

36°06'N
36°04'N
36°02'N
36°00'N
35°58'N
35°56'N
35°54'N
35°52'N
35°50'N
35°48'N

ᴸLTA

St Paul's
Islands

St Paul's
Bay

Salina
Bay

Qalet
Marku

Baħar iċ-
Ċagħaq Bay

BUĠIBBA

Wardija   Burmarrad

Baħar iċ-
ic-Ċagħaq

Għargħur

Victoria   Lines

San Pawl
Tat-Targa

Paceville

Mosta   Naxxar

ST JULIAN'S

San Ġwann

SLIEMA

Balzan   Birkirkara

Gżira

Attard   Ta'Xbiex

Mdina   Msida
Santa Venera

Floriana

VALLETTA

T.   Gwardamanġa

Ħamrun

Vittoriosa

Senglea

Qormi

Kordin

Cospicua

Marsa

Żebbuġ   Paola   Żabbar

Luqa   Tarxien   Marsaskala

Żonqor Point

Marsaskala
Bay

Il-Gżira

Siggiewi   Malta
International
Airport   Ħal-Għaxaq

St Thomas Bay

Il-Munxar

a'Żuta
(253m)   Mqabba   Marsaxlokk

Hofra Iz-Żghira

Qrendi   Peter's Pool

Żurrieq

Birżebbuġa   Marsaxlokk
Bay

Delimara
Point

Għar Lapsi

Benghisa
Point

FILFLA

**SLIEMA, ST JULIAN'S &
PACEVILLE (p83)**
The place in Malta to promenade,
eat, drink, shop and play

VALLETTA (p55)
It's a joy to explore the pint-sized
capital, chock-full of historical and
architectural gems

VITTORIOSA (p76)
An intriguing mix of old and
new, with quirky wine bars and
atmospheric alleys to discover

HYPOGEUM (p80)
This mysterious underground
necropolis still has the experts
scratching their heads in wonder

MARSAXLOKK (p137)
Work up an appetite for fresh
local seafood while admiring
picture-perfect boats in the harbour

**ĦAĠAR QIM & MNAJDRA
TEMPLES (p142)**
More megalithic marvels to keep you
guessing, or you can simply admire
the spectacular setting

14°26'E   14°28'E   14°30'E   14°32'E   14°34'E   14°36'E   14°38'E

Destination Malta & Gozo

From mysterious prehistoric temples to magnificent baroque architecture, celebratory feasts of rabbit to festas of noisy fireworks, or rattling yellow buses to colourful wooden fishing boats, this wee speck on the map offers plenty of unique charm. Malta is a fascinating microcosm of the Mediterranean, a sponge that has absorbed differing dollops of character from its neighbours and conquerors – listen to the local language to hear the North African and Arabic influences, sample the Sicilian-inspired cuisine on its menus, and note the legacies of 150 years of British rule. It is certainly an eclectic mix and there has been a long roll-call of rulers over the centuries, but be in no doubt, Malta is not just a notional outpost of Italy or a relic of colonial Britain. This diminutive island nation (all 316 sq km of it, comprising the main islands of Malta, Gozo and Comino) has a quirky character all its own.

In its recent past Malta has become known as a beach-holiday destination, and the sun and sea certainly justify such marketing. But there's much more to the country than that. What makes Malta a truly unique destination is that so much of its intriguing past is visible today – from 5000-year-old temples to immense 16th-century fortifications built by the Knights of St John, and museums dedicated to tales of WWII heroism. Couple the history, beaches and sunny climate with warm, friendly locals, character-filled villages, scenic landscapes, decent nightlife and first-class diving opportunities and you've got a pocket-rocket destination offering drawcards out of all proportion to its size.

JULIE

Valletta & Vittoriosa

MICHAEL GEBICKI

Cast your eye across Malta's Grand Harbour from the vedette (p80), Senglea

BETHUNE CARMICHAEL

Wander outside the former home of the Knights of St John at the Auberge de Castille (p66), Valletta

Lose yourself in the narrow laneways of Vittoriosa (p76)

MARK AVELLINO

CRAIG PERSHOUSE

Roman, Maltese and British history forge together to dazzle at the Maritime Museum (p76), Vittoriosa

Mdina & Marsaxlokk

EOIN CLARKE

History seeps from the stones on Villegaignon St (p123) in the peaceful citadel of Mdina

EOIN CLARKE

Slip through time at the ancient gate to Mdina (p123)

Boats dance to the ancient rhythms of the fishing village, Marsaxlokk (p137)

CRAIG PER

Gozo & Comino

Stroll with a special someone along the coast-hugging Ta'Cenc sea cliffs (p154), Gozo peninsula

JULIET COOMBE

Art, gold and guidance shine at Cathedral of the Assumption in Il-Kastell (p146), Victoria (Rabat)

CRAIG PERSHOUSE

Laze your way through another perfect day for swimming in the Blue Lagoon (p164) off Comino

MICHAEL GEBICKI

Ħaġar Qim

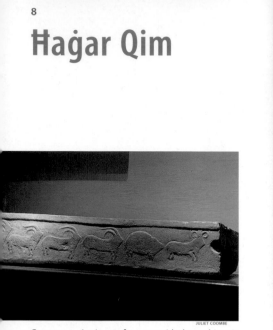

JULIET COOMBE

Cross centuries in one footstep with the prehistoric artefacts at the National Museum of Archaeology (p62), Valletta

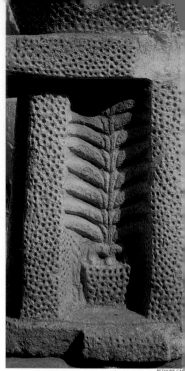

BETHUNE CARMICHAEL

Decode exquisite clues to the mystery of Ħaġar Qim (p142) and the solar alignments

Unearth another world at the temples of Ħaġar Qim (p142) in southeast Malta, which predate Egyptian pyramids

BETHUNE CARMICHAEL

Contents

Regional Map Contents

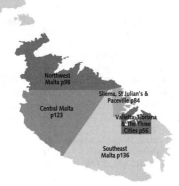

Gozo & Comino
p145

Northwest
Malta p98

Sliema, St Julian's &
Paceville p84

Central Malta
p123

Valletta, Floriana
& The Three
Cities p56

Southeast
Malta p136

The Author

CAROLYN BAIN

After travelling the four corners of Europe, Melbourne-born Carolyn still favours the southern region, and she happily dedicates a good deal of her time to the search for the perfect Mediterranean island. For Lonely Planet she has repeatedly visited Greece and Malta, among other destinations; for this book, it was back to tiny, sunny Malta for a spell of *pastizzi*, mad drivers, avoiding rabbit on the menu, and swotting up on the fascinating local history.

My Favourite Trip

For me, the best part of any trip to Malta is time spent on Gozo. I have fond memories of a previous visit, renting a 17th-century farmhouse in Xagħra (p160) and sitting by the pool with friends, sunning ourselves while winter had hit the rest of Europe. On this trip I was flying solo and was thrilled to hunt down a small apartment in the heart of Victoria (p145) – right next to the Basilica of St George, in fact. For the price of a cheap hotel room I had my own outdoor terrace, views over the square, and the perfect village at my doorstep. Days were spent checking out the sights of this lovely island (don't miss Xlendi p154, Dwejra p157 or Ramla Bay p163), but it was always a treat to come home.

LONELY PLANET AUTHORS

Why is our travel information the best in the world? It's simple: our authors are independent, dedicated travellers. They don't research using just the internet or phone, and they don't take freebies in exchange for positive coverage. They travel widely, to all the popular spots and off the beaten track. They personally visit thousands of hotels, restaurants, cafés, bars, galleries, palaces, museums and more – and they take pride in getting all the details right, and telling it how it is. For more, see the authors section on www.lonelyplanet.com.

Getting Started

Malta is a traveller-friendly country that provides holidays options for people on all budgets, and allows for more than just warm-weather, beach-going vacations – there's a good deal of history, culture and tradition to explore too, so a long weekend here in the low season could constitute a cheap and fun city break. The country is so small you could cover most of the highlights in just a few days.

Malta has a typically Mediterranean climate, with mild winters, hot, dry summers and some 300 days of sunshine. This means it's a year-round destination, so if you're planning to visit from most parts of Europe you should be able to find flights and package deals at any time of year. There aren't too many alternatives to Malta if you want to stay within Europe and still be sunbathing in November!

Winters are not at all unpleasant here, with an average of six hours of sunshine daily in January and daytime temperatures around 16°C. Sea temperatures around the islands range from 15°C in midwinter, to a balmy 25°C in August and September.

WHEN TO GO

See the climate chart (p170) for more information.

The peak season for travel to Malta is June to September, when many resort hotels are booked solid. However, daytime temperatures in July and August can reach more than 35°C – uncomfortably hot – and it's tough to find your own patch of sand or rock at any beach (or battle the crowds at attractions). Weather-wise, the best time to visit is spring (April to June) and autumn (September and October), though September still counts as high season in many hotels and the pleasant weather can sometimes be interrupted by a hot and humid wind, or rainfall. For water-babies, the sea temperature is considerably warmer in autumn than in spring.

In November and December you can expect daytime temperatures of 12°C to 18°C and a fair amount of sunshine between spells of rain showers (the total annual rainfall is low, at around 580mm, and it falls mainly between September and February). January and February are the coldest months, when a strong northeasterly wind (the *grigal*) makes conditions more unpleasant. Winds are a feature of Malta's weather (see p138). The stiff sea breeze is cooling in summer, but in winter the *grigal* can whip up

---

DON'T LEAVE HOME WITHOUT...

- Double-checking the visa situation (p178)
- Confirming what currency Malta is using – the lira or euro (p176)
- Prebooking your visit to the Hypogeum (p80) – limited spaces are available, and demand is high
- Sunscreen, sunglasses and a hat to protect you from the fierce summer sun
- A travel insurance policy (p174) specifically covering you for any planned 'high risk' activities, such as scuba diving
- A copy of your diving qualifications, or a snorkel and mask to help you better investigate Malta's underwater world (p44)
- Earplugs – handy if you find yourself in a hotel undergoing renovations or neighbouring one of the many construction sites around the country

the waves that pound across the harbour walls and occasionally disrupt the ferry service to Gozo. In spring and autumn the southeasterly *xlokk* (sirocco) sometimes blows in from North Africa, bringing humid and occasionally foggy conditions.

The main season for festas (feast days) is June to September, but if you want to catch a festa out of season, there's the Feast of St Paul's Shipwreck in Valletta on 10 February, and the Feast of the Immaculate Conception in Cospicua on 8 December.

Two of the liveliest and most popular events on the islands, marked by public holidays, are Carnival Week in early March and the L-Imnarja festival on 28 and 29 June. See p172 for more information on these events, plus details of how this nation of dedicated Catholics celebrates Christmas and Easter.

The Christmas–New Year period is a mini-high season in the middle of winter, when many Maltese emigrants return home to visit friends and family, and European tourists come looking for a spot of winter sunshine. Otherwise you can find some cheap flight and accommodation deals from November to March.

COSTS

If you're heading to Malta from North Africa (from Tunisia, for example), you'll find the prices quite steep. By European standards Malta is good value, although prices are steadily increasing and the authorities are behind a push to get more upmarket tourism down this way (hence a noticeable increase in the number of five-star hotels, and cruise liners dropping in to see the sights). Locals are worried about the potential impact on inflation the euro may have when it replaces the Maltese lira as the national currency (scheduled for 1 January 2008; see p176 for details).

If you budget on around Lm15 per day, you'll get pleasant hostel or guest-house accommodation, a simple restaurant meal, plenty of bus rides, and a decent street-side snack. If your accommodation has self-catering facilities and you cook your own meals, your costs will be even lower.

On around Lm25 a day, you can start to live it up in a hotel with air-con and a swimming pool (especially in the low season) and enjoy meals at better restaurants. Allow extra for car rental (average about Lm10 per day).

TRAVEL LITERATURE

Considering how many tourists Malta receives, it's somewhat surprising that there's nothing by way of travel literature. And the genre of dissatisfied/overworked/lovelorn cityslickers finding themselves/finding love/renovating a farmhouse (or all three) in regions like Provence or Tuscany has yet to encompass Malta (although Gozo seems a logical place to set one of these stories – there are plenty of interesting characters, and farmhouses to restore).

There are, however, a few writers who have relocated to or holidayed in Malta and subsequently used the islands and their turbulent history as a backdrop for their stories. *The Kappillan of Malta* by Nicholas Monsarrat is the best example – it's the classic English-language novel about Malta. Written in the early 1970s when the author was living in San Lawrenz, Gozo, it describes the experiences of the humble parish priest Dun Salvatore during WWII, interlaced with a potted history of Malta.

More gripping beach reading is provided by David Ball's novel, *The Sword and the Scimitar*. It's a sweeping adventure set in the 16th century, bringing to life characters from the Ottoman Empire and the Knights of St John against the dramatic backdrop of the Great Siege.

HOW MUCH?

Room in guesthouse Lm6-10 per person

Bus trip Lm0.20-0.50

Cup of coffee Lm0.60

Day hire of sun lounge Lm1.50

One hour internet access Lm1

See also the Lonely Planet Index, inside front cover.

TOP TENS

Planning on the Internet

The internet is loaded with sites that can help you plan a holiday in Malta. Here are some of our favourites; many more are mentioned throughout this book.

Malta Tourism Authority (www.visitmalta.com) Huge official site that makes a good first port of call in addition to the Lonely Planet site (lonelyplanet.com)

- Gozo (www.gozo.com) Great info if you're taking in Gozo too
- Maltese Islands (www.malteseislands.com) Nicely designed site with plenty of general information
- Malta Media (http://maltamedia.com) Bone up on issues making the headlines in Malta
- Malta Weather (www.maltaweather.com) Wondering what to pack? Check the 'Malta's Climate' section
- Heritage Malta (www.heritagemalta.org) Swot up on Maltese history and prioritise your sightseeing

- Restaurants Malta (www.restaurantsmalta .com) Plan to travel your tastebuds and expand your waistline
- About Malta (www.aboutmalta.com) If it's about Malta, you'll discover it on this comprehensive directory site
- Public Transport Association (www.apt .com.mt) Useful advice on getting from A to B courtesy of big yellow buses
- StarWeb Malta (www.starwebmalta.com) Labels itself 'Malta's first online concierge' and is home to listings in traveller-friendly categories

Must-See Historic Sites

Many parts of Malta feel like open-air museums. The most remarkable and mysterious sites date back 5000 years, but the era of the Knights of St John is the most fascinating, and resulted in some magnificent architecture and ripping yarns.

- Hypogeum, Paola – built between 3600 and 3000 BC (p80)
- Mdina – buildings from the 13th century (p123)
- Valletta's auberges and alleys – dating from the late 16th century (p55)
- Fortifications of Valletta & the Three Cities – defences from the mid-16th century (p65)
- Vittoriosa's Il Collachio – buildings from the 11th century (p78)

- Il-Kastell, Gozo – buildings from the 17th century (p146)
- St John's Co-Cathedral, Valletta – built in the 1570s (p60)
- Ħaġar Qim and Mnajdra Temples – built between 3600 and 3000 BC (p142)
- St Agatha's Crypt & Catacombs, Rabat – frescoes from the 12th century (p128)
- Ġgantija Temples, Gozo – built between 3600 and 3000 BC (p161)

Superlative Swimming Spots

It's not all history in Malta – the country built its holiday reputation on sunny weather and beaches. Just don't come here expecting miles of sand – there are only a handful of sandy stretches, and these get very busy. There are a number of rocky bays and coves that offer swimming and snorkelling in crystal-clear waters.

- Golden Bay (p114)
- Blue Lagoon, Comino (p164)
- Ramla Bay, Gozo (p163)
- Mellieħa Bay (p117)
- Għajn Tuffieħa Bay (p115)

- Ġnejna Bay (p116)
- Paradise Bay (p120)
- Għar Lapsi (p143)
- Peter's Pool (p137)
- Wied il-Għasri, Gozo (p159)

The British novelist Anthony Burgess was a tax exile in Malta for a brief spell at the end of the 1960s. He lived in a house in Lija, which became the fictional home of the 81-year-old protagonist in his masterly novel *Earthly Powers*.

Nicholas Rinaldi's novel *The Jukebox Queen of Malta* uses WWII Malta as a backdrop for his book – a love story between an American soldier and a girl called Melita. The book has been compared to *Captain Corelli's Mandolin* with its juxtaposition of island romance, local history and the senseless violence of war.

Itineraries
CLASSIC ROUTES

MALTA'S MAGIC   One Week

Malta's diminutive dimensions mean that you can squeeze a lot of sightseeing into a short time. But it's more fun to take it easy – take time to absorb the history from the stones of Valletta, Vittoriosa and Mdina, to cool off at swimming spots while exploring, or chill out at a view-blessed café. Your own car is an asset, otherwise base yourself in Valletta, Sliema, St Julian's or Buġibba for the easiest bus connections.

Begin by taking in **Valletta** (p55) – explore the narrow streets and walk around the fortifications. Feast your eyes on the views from the Upper Barrakka Gardens. On the second day explore the charms of **Vittoriosa** (p76) and **Senglea** (p80), towns not yet high on the tourist radar. On day three visit the **Tarxien Temples** and **Hypogeum** (p80) en route further south for a seafood lunch at **Marsaxlokk** (p137). On day four spend the morning at **Ħaġar Qim** and **Mnajdra temples** (p142) and the **Blue Grotto** (p141), and the afternoon in exquisite **Mdina** (p123) and **Rabat** (p128). Day five should be spent relaxing on a beach in the northwest (**Golden Bay**, p114, is glorious), recharging your batteries for some physical activity on day six – a clifftop walk, maybe a scuba-diving taster. End on a high with a day trip to Comino's spectacular **Blue Lagoon** (p164).

Few other countries can boast such concentrated history, architecture (and yes, beaches) in so tiny an area. Malta is perfect for travellers looking to take things easy for a week, do the rounds of the sights but not have to travel far.

GOZITAN DELIGHTS
Five Days to One Week

The island of Gozo is smaller than Malta (14km by 7km) and you might think a day here is all you'd need to whizz between villages and sights. But that wouldn't be doing Gozo justice – a slower sightseeing pace is necessary to appreciate the more relaxed way of Gozitan life. Plan your visit with culinary precision – for food-lovers, dining at some of Gozo's great restaurants should feature high on the agenda. The island is so small you could base yourself anywhere in order to follow this itinerary, particularly if you have your own set of wheels (recommended).

Ideally your trip should start with a day exploring **Victoria** (p145), wandering around majestic Il-Kastell and the laneways of Il-Borgo, then eating well somewhere like Maji Wine & Dine or It-Tmun Victoria. Spend day two walking, swimming and snorkelling at **Dwejra** (p157) after paying your respects at the grand **Basilica of Ta'Pinu** (p156). The **Xlendi waterfront** (p154) makes the perfect place for sundowner drinks. Begin day three with a visit to the temples and other attractions of **Xagħra** (p160), then spend the afternoon reclining on the red sands of the blue **Ramla Bay** (p163), the biggest beach on Gozo. Frock up for dinner at the highly acclaimed **Restaurant Ta'Frenċ** (p160) outside Marsalforn. Day four could be set aside for exploring around **Ta'Ċenċ** (p154) with its sunset views north, and for seeking out a lesser-known spot for swimming and snorkelling (nearby **Mġarr ix-Xini**, p153, is lovely). Spend day five visiting **Comino** (p164), discovering the tiny island on foot and swimming in crystal-clear water, then stop in for a beer at convivial Gleneagles in **Mġarr** (p153) after your boat ride back. There's five days covered – but why not allocate a week to Gozo, rent a lovely old farmhouse and spend a few days relaxing poolside?

Reset your clock to the relaxed pace of Gozo time. Malta's second island is pocket-sized and a pleasure to explore – take it in slowly to fully appreciate the character-filled villages, impressive landscapes and friendly locals, and set aside an afternoon for aquatic delights on tiny Comino.

Snapshot

These days it's hard to find a local newspaper *not* bemoaning Malta's declining tourist numbers, with editorials and letters to the editor suggesting just how to fix the problem. The number of tourists visiting Malta has been static or dropping for the last few years, with authorities 'confident' of a reversal, but few believing that figures will do anything but worsen. It's big, bad news for the country, with the potential to wreak havoc on the economy (see p34 for details on the importance of tourism to the local economy). Malta has certainly felt the squeeze from increased competition in the form of cheaper Med destinations (such as Croatia) and North African hotspots (Tunisia and Morocco, for example). Everyone hopes this trend might be reversed with the long-awaited advent of low-cost airlines servicing Malta from late 2006, making a holiday here more affordable. We can't help but think that there are bigger problems to be addressed in order to ensure visitors leave the island with a positive impression – problems such as the rampant, unchecked construction, neglect of heritage sites, pothole-ridden roads, abuse of the environment and the often shabby standards of service. See p42 for a long list of environmental challenges facing the country, including the political hot potato that is birdhunting.

Along with the worries of declining tourist numbers, locals face the very real anxiety of a new currency being implemented in the near future: if everything goes to plan, on 1 January 2008 the country will adopt the euro as its national currency. The fear most people share is that the changeover to euro will trigger price increases – this from a population already feeling the pinch in their back pocket from higher oil prices, which in Malta impacts the prices of everything from petrol to electricity and water.

Still, EU membership has brought rewards, and there is a sense among locals that the best is yet to come. EU funds are being channelled into a vast number of projects (improved roads and new heritage projects, to name a few that visitors will encounter), and there's an optimistic mood that EU membership will generate enormous opportunities for the younger generation.

Perhaps Malta's most pressing concern since joining the EU is the number of irregular immigrants that have landed on its shores, putting pressure on a small, crowded island and an unprepared population, triggering a nasty outbreak of racism. Poverty and conflict appear to be the root of the current mass migration from Africa to Europe along the major routes – into the Canaries and mainland Spain in the east, and into Malta and Italy in the heart of the Mediterranean. EU help is needed to help stem the tide, and to help Malta process, then repatriate or rehouse irregular immigrants. In 2005 just over 1800 Africans left Africa (most likely Libya) by boat and arrived in Malta (often by accident – most would prefer to reach Italy); in the first nine months of 2006, close to 1700 irregular immigrants made the dangerous journey. They are housed in very rudimentary detention centres (some for up to 18 months) while the authorities determine if they are eligible for refugee status (not easy to obtain) or are able to stay in Malta on humanitarian grounds. Those who are permitted to stay are moved to overcrowded open centres, and some are able to search for casual work, although there is little to be found. These irregular immigrants have won few local fans with their protests for better conditions. As seems to be the trend throughout Europe, right-wing xenophobic groups are gaining popularity in Malta, and a radical element has resorted to arson against those who help the migrants or vocally support their rights (Jesuits, lawyers, newspaper editors and journalists). It's an unfortunate and ugly side to the country.

FAST FACTS

Population: 400,000

Area: 316 sq km

Population density: 1266 people per sq km

Number of registered vehicles: 325,000

Number of mobile phone subscribers: 334,220

Inflation: 2.8%

Unemployment: 7.3%

Number of tourists annually: 1.16 million (around 465,000 from the UK)

Most popular name for males: Joseph (14,523 men named Joseph)

Most popular name for females: Mary (12,056 women named Mary – spot the trend?)

History

Malta has a fascinating history, and the island is crowded with physical and cultural reminders of the past, most of them easily accessible to visitors. The fossilised bones of animals found in Għar Dalam cave (p139) in the southeast suggest that Malta was once linked by a land bridge to Sicily and southern Europe. But Malta was not big enough to support a hunter-gatherer lifestyle, and the earliest evidence of human habitation – the remains of primitive farming settlements – has been dated to the period 5200 to 4000 BC. Neolithic pottery fragments unearthed at Skorba (p116) are similar to those found in Sicily.

THE TEMPLE BUILDERS

The Maltese Islands' oldest monuments are the megalithic temples built between 3600 and 2500 BC, the oldest surviving freestanding structures in the world. About 1000 years before the construction of the Great Pyramid of Cheops in Egypt, the people of Malta were manipulating megaliths weighing up to 50 tonnes and creating elaborate buildings that appear to be oriented in relation to the winter solstice sunrise (see the boxed text, p142).

No-one knows whether the temple builders evolved from the preexisting farming communities of Malta, or whether they arrived from elsewhere bringing their architectural skills with them. Rock-cut tombs found on a hillside near Xemxija and dated to before 4000 BC display a trefoil layout which may be a precursor to the three-lobed plan seen in the temples. The remains of around a dozen megalithic temples survive today, and some of them are remarkably well preserved. The best places to view these prehistoric marvels are at Tarxien (p81), south of Siġġiewi (p142) and on Gozo, near Xagħra (p161).

Whatever their origins, the temple people seem to have worshipped a cult of fertility. Archaeologists have found large numbers of figurines and statues of wide-hipped, well-endowed female figures – the so-called 'fat ladies' of Malta – that have been interpreted as fertility goddesses. These figures range in size from barely 10cm long to more than 1.5m, and the best examples can be seen at the National Museum of Archaeology in Valletta (p62).

The culmination of Malta's temple culture was the large temple complex at Tarxien and the subterranean burial chambers of the nearby Ħal Saflieni Hypogeum (p80). These sites appear to have been abandoned some time after 2500 BC and then taken over by a noticeably different Bronze Age culture. The new inhabitants cremated their dead and used the Tarxien temple site as a cemetery.

http://web.infinito
.it/utenti/m/malta_mega
_temples has everything
you ever wanted to know
about Malta's megalithic
temples, and then some.

PHOENICIANS & ROMANS

From around 800 to 218 BC, Malta was colonised by the Phoenicians and, for the last 250 years of this period, by Phoenicia's principal North African colony, Carthage. With their watchful eyes painted on the prow, the colourful Maltese fishing boats – the *luzzu* and the *kajjik* (check them out at Marsaxlokk, p137) – seem little changed from the Phoenician trading vessels that once plied the Mediterranean. The islands may have served as a Carthaginian naval base during the First Punic War against Rome (264–241 BC).

TIMELINE	c 5200 BC	c 3600–2500 BC
	Arrival of first known inhabitants (from Sicily)	Megalithic temples are built on Malta and Gozo

During the Second Punic War (218–201 BC) Rome took control of Malta before finally crushing Carthage in the Third Punic War (149–146 BC). The island was then given the status of a *municipium*, or free town, with the power to control its own affairs and to send an ambassador to Rome. However, there is evidence that Malta retained a Punic influence. The 1st-century BC historian Diodorus Siculus described the island as a Phoenician colony, and the biblical account of St Paul's shipwreck on Malta in AD 60 (see p101) describes the islanders as 'barbarous' (ie they did not speak the 'civilised' languages of Latin or Greek).

St Paul's shipwreck was certainly the most influential event of this period. According to tradition, during Paul's three-month stay both the Roman governor of Malta (later to become St Publius) and many of the islanders were converted to Christianity, making the Maltese one of the oldest Christian peoples in the world.

Malta seems to have prospered under Roman rule. The main town, called Melita, occupied the hilltop of Mdina but spread over an area around three times the size of the later medieval citadel. The excavated remains of town houses, villas, farms and baths suggest that the inhabitants enjoyed a comfortable lifestyle and occupied themselves with the production of olives, wheat, honey and grapes.

When the Roman Empire split into east and west in AD 395, Malta seems to have fallen under the sway of Constantinople. But very little is known of this period of Maltese history, when the islands seem to have been little more than a neglected Byzantine backwater.

ARABS & NORMANS

The rapid expansion of Islam in the 7th to 9th centuries saw an Arab empire extend from Spain to India. Arab armies invaded Sicily in 827 and finally conquered it in 878; Malta fell into Arab hands in 870. Both Malta and Sicily remained Muslim possessions until the end of the 11th century. The Arab rulers generally tolerated the Christian population, introduced irrigation and the cultivation of citrus fruits and cotton, and had a notable impact on Maltese customs and language. Apart from the names Malta and Gozo, which probably have Latin roots, there is not a single place name in the Maltese Islands that can be proved to predate the Arab occupation.

During the 11th century small groups of Norman adventurers from northern Europe arrived in Italy, formed allegiances with local leaders and set up a system of feudal lordships. One, Robert Guiscard, took over much of southern Italy and in 1060 his younger brother, Count Roger, captured Messina and used it as a base for the conquest of Sicily. It took 30 years of constant struggle, but by 1091 Count Roger had driven the Arabs out of Sicily. A year earlier, in 1090, he had captured Malta after a surprise attack. Tradition has it that, needing the support of the local people, Count Roger tore his red-and-white quartered banner in two and gave half to the Maltese contingent, thus inventing Malta's national flag.

For the next 400 years Malta's history was closely linked to Sicily's, and its rulers were a succession of Normans, Angevins (French), Aragonese and Castilians (Spanish). Malta remained a minor pawn on the edge of the European chessboard, and its relatively small population of downtrodden islanders paid their taxes by trading, slaving and piracy, and were repaid in

Get acquainted with 13 major museums and 14 heritage sites in Malta at www.heritagemalta .org, plus find out how to visit them.

The *luzzu* (traditional Maltese fishing boat) still carries the watchful 'Eye of Osiris' on its bow, a custom thought to date back more than 2500 years.

800–218 BC

Malta is colonised by the Phoenicians and then controlled by the Carthaginians

218 BC–AD 395

The Romans control Malta after their success in the Punic Wars

kind by marauding Turks and Barbary corsairs. During this period a Maltese aristocracy began to form, and a few of their elegant town houses survive in Mdina, Vittoriosa and Victoria. Their distinctive architectural style is referred to as Siculo-Norman (Sicilian-Norman), but it is almost entirely Sicilian – there is little if any Norman influence.

The marriage of the Catholic monarchs Ferdinand II of Aragon and Isabella of Castile led to the unification of Spain in 1479, and under their grandson, the Holy Roman Emperor Charles V, Malta became part of the vast Spanish Empire. One of the greatest threats to Charles' realm was the expanding Ottoman Empire of Süleyman the Magnificent in the east. Süleyman had driven the Knights of St John from their island stronghold of Rhodes between 1522 and 1523 (for information on the history of the Knights of St John see p22). When the Knights begged Charles V to find them a new home, he offered them Malta along with the governorship of Tripoli, hoping that they might help to contain the Turkish naval forces in the eastern Mediterranean. The nominal rent was to be two falcons a year – one for the emperor and one for the viceroy of Sicily (for more on falcons see the boxed text, p41).

THE KNIGHTS ARRIVE

Grand Master Philippe Villiers de L'Isle Adam (1530–34) of the Knights of St John was not particularly impressed by the gift of the Maltese Islands, which seemed to him barren, waterless and poorly defended. Neither were the 12,000 or so local inhabitants, who were given no say in the matter. Nor were the aristocracy, who remained aloof in their palazzi in Mdina. However, determined to make the best of a bad job and hoping one day to return to Rhodes, in 1530 the Knights decided to settle in the fishing village of Birgu (now Vittoriosa) on the south side of Grand Harbour and set about fortifying the harbour. Visitors can wander around Vittoriosa (p76) and admire the early auberges of the Knights.

In Rhodes, the Knights had developed into a formidable marine fighting force and had been a constant thorn in the side of the Ottoman Turks. Their expulsion allowed Turkish corsairs to roam the central Mediterranean at will, raiding and pillaging and carrying off Christians to serve as slaves or to hold for ransom. Short of funds and lacking any real support from European powers, the Knights became pirates themselves, attacking Turkish trading ships and raiding along the Barbary Coast of North Africa.

Their greatest adversary was Dragut Reis, the Turkish admiral, who invaded Gozo in 1551 and carried off almost the entire population of 5000 into slavery. Then in 1559 the Knights lost half their galleys in a disastrous attack on Dragut's lair on the island of Djerba off the Tunisian coast. With the power of the Knights at a low ebb, Süleyman the Magnificent saw an opportunity to polish off this troublesome crew once and for all, while at the same time capturing Malta as a base for the invasion of Europe from the south.

THE GREAT SIEGE OF 1565

Jean Parisot de la Valette (see the boxed text, p57) was Grand Master between 1557 and 1568. He was a stern disciplinarian and an experienced soldier who foresaw the threat of a Turkish siege and prepared for it well. Following the disaster of 1559, la Valette ordered the building of ditches and defensive

Malta Prehistory & Temples Renowned British archaeologist and scholar David H Trump has written the definitive guide to Malta's prehistory. This comprehensive book includes detailed visual treatment of 30 key sites.

AD 60   **395–870**

| St Paul is shipwrecked on Malta and brings Christianity to the population | Malta falls under Byzantine rule |

KNIGHTS OF ST JOHN

The Knights of who? This spiritual and military force was driven from its base in Rhodes in the early 16th century and made its new home in Malta in 1530. The knights played a starring role in Malta's development and you'll encounter references to them throughout the country, so some background info will come in handy.

Origins

The Sovereign and Military Order of the Knights Hospitaller of St John of Jerusalem – also known variously as the Knights of St John, the Knights of Rhodes, the Knights of Malta, and the Knights Hospitallers – had its origins in the Christian Crusades of the 11th and 12th centuries.

A hospital and guesthouse for poor pilgrims in Jerusalem was founded by some Italian merchants from Amalfi in 1070. The hospital, operated by monks, won the protection of the papacy in 1113 and was raised to the status of an independent religious order known as the Hospitallers. The Order set up more hospitals along the pilgrimage route from Italy to the Holy Land, and Knights who had been healed of their wounds showed their gratitude by granting funds and property to the growing Order.

Other Knights offered their services as soldiers to provide protection for pilgrims, and thus the Order's dual role of healing the sick and waging war on the enemies of Christ began to evolve. Knights of the Order kept the road to Jerusalem free of bandits. To kill an infidel was to win glory for Christ, and to die in battle in defence of the faith was to become a martyr in heaven.

When the armies of Islam recaptured the Holy Land in 1291, the Order sought refuge first in the Kingdom of Cyprus. In 1309 they acquired the island of Rhodes, planning to stay close to the Middle East in the hope of reconquering Jerusalem. But here they remained for over 200 years, building fortresses, auberges (hostels) and a hospital, and evolving from a land-based army into the most formidable naval fighting force the medieval world had ever seen.

Organisation

The Knights of St John were European noblemen who lived the lives of monks and soldiers. The objective of the Order was 'the service of the poor, and the defence of the Catholic faith'. The Order was financed by the revenue of properties and estates spread throughout Europe, which were either owned by members of the Order, or had been gifted to it.

The Knights' traditional attire was a hooded monk's habit, made of black camel hair with a white Maltese cross emblazoned on the breast. The distinctive eight-pointed cross is said to represent the eight virtues which the Knights strove to uphold: to live in truth; to have faith; to repent of sins; to give proof of humility; to love justice; to be merciful; to be sincere and wholehearted; and to endure persecution.

The Order comprised eight nationalities or langues (literally 'tongues' or languages) – Italy, France, Provence, Auvergne, Castile, Aragon, Germany and England. (The English langue was dissolved by King Henry VIII in 1540 following his breach with the Roman Catholic Church.) Each langue was led by a *pilier* (literally 'pillar'), and its members lived and dined together in an auberge, which operated a bit like an Oxford college or an American fraternity house. Each langue was assigned to a particular task or part of the city walls during battle (hence the Poste de France, the Poste d'Aragon etc on the walls of Vittoriosa), and each *pilier* had a specific duty – for example, the *pilier* of the Italian langue was always the admiral of the galley fleet.

870–1090	1090–1530
Malta is occupied by Arab rulers	Count Roger captures Malta and places the country under Norman control

The Order's properties and estates in Europe were managed by a network of commanderies and priories, often headed by older Knights who had retired from active service in the Mediterranean. Although the Knights were bound by vows of individual poverty, the Order as a whole was immensely wealthy. A Knight was required to bequeath four-fifths of his personal wealth to the Order.

Hospitals

The hospitals created by the Order – first in Jerusalem and the Holy Land, then in Rhodes and finally in Malta – were often at the leading edge of the development of medical and nursing science. Ironically, although the Knights had sworn to bring death and destruction to the 'infidel' Muslims, many of their medical skills and treatments were gleaned from the study of Arabic medicine.

The Sacra Infermeria in Valletta (built in the 1570s) had 600 beds – the Great Ward alone could hold 350 patients – and was famous throughout Europe. It was obliged to provide care for the sick of any race or creed, slaves included, though non-Catholics were put in a separate ward. Patients were nursed by the members of the Order even the Grand Master tended the sick at least once a week – and treated by physicians, surgeons and pharmacists. The hospital's plates and cutlery were made of solid silver 'to increase the decorum of the Hospital and the cleanliness of the sick' and basic rules of hygiene were observed.

The hospital was overseen by the Grand Hospitaller, a post traditionally filled by the *pilier* of the French langue. The Order's surgeons performed many advanced operations including trepanation, bladder-stone removal and cataract removal as well as more commonplace amputations and wound treatments.

From 1676 onwards the study of anatomy and human dissection was taken up. Anyone particularly interested in the medical services provided by the Knights should visit the Knights Hospitallers exhibition inside the Sacra Infermeria in Valletta (p65).

After Malta

Following the loss of their French estates and their expulsion from Malta by Napoleon in 1798, the Knights sought refuge first in Russia, where they were welcomed by Tsar Paul I, and later in Italy. After several years of uncertainty, they finally made their headquarters in the Palazzo di Malta (the former Embassy of the Hospitallers) in Rome.

In the late 19th and 20th centuries the Order rebuilt itself as a religious and charitable organisation. Now known as the Sovereign Military Order of Malta, it is an internationally recognised sovereign entity that mints its own coins and prints its own postage stamps. In effect, it's a state without a territory, although its properties in Rome enjoy extraterritorial status. It concerns itself largely with providing hospitals, medical supplies and humanitarian aid in regions stricken by poverty, war and natural disasters.

The Order now has diplomatic relations with 94 countries, has legations in several countries (including France, Germany, Belgium and Switzerland) and has been a permanent observer at the UN since 1994. It continues to work in the field of medical and social care and humanitarian aid.

The Order has an embassy in Malta (housed in the Cavalier of St John in Triq l-Ordinanza in Valletta), and since 1991 it has reoccupied its old home in the upper part of Fort St Angelo in Vittoriosa. Since 1988 the Grand Master has been Englishman Fra' Andrew Bertie.

1530	1565
The Knights of St John arrive after being given Malta by Emperor Charles V	The Knights are victorious over the Ottomans in the Great Siege of Malta

walls around the peninsulas of Birgu and Isla. Fort St Angelo on the tip of Birgu was rebuilt and strengthened, and Fort St Michael was built on Isla. A new fortress, Fort St Elmo, was constructed on the tip of the uninhabited Sceberras Peninsula.

The Knights' galley fleet was taken into the creek below Birgu, and a great chain was stretched across the harbour entrance between Fort St Angelo and Fort St Michael to keep out enemy vessels. Food, water and arms were stockpiled, and la Valette sent urgent requests for aid to the emperor, the pope and the viceroy of Sicily. But no help came. In May 1565, when an enormous Ottoman fleet carrying more than 30,000 men arrived to lay siege to the island, la Valette was 70 years old and commanded a force of only 700 Knights and around 8000 Maltese irregulars and mercenary troops.

Knights of St John –
www.orderofmalta
.org covers the long,
illustrious history of
the Knights, as well as
information
about present-day
knightly activities.

The Turkish force, led jointly by Admiral Piali and Mustafa Pasha, dropped anchor in the bay of Marsaxlokk, and its soldiers set up camp on the plain of Marsa. The entire population of Malta took refuge within the walls of Birgu, Isla and Mdina, taking their livestock with them and poisoning the wells and cisterns they left behind. The Turks took their time, digging out gun emplacements and setting up batteries, before beginning their campaign with an attack on Fort St Elmo, which guarded the entrance to both Grand and Marsamxett Harbours. The fort was small and held a garrison of only 60 Knights and a few hundred men. Mustafa Pasha was confident that it would fall in less than a week.

Dragut Reis, the wily old corsair who had always been the scourge of the Mediterranean sea lanes, was now, like la Valette, an old man. The 80-year-old ex-pirate was in the employ of Sultan Süleyman and arrived in Malta a few weeks into the siege to advise Mustafa and Piali. He was unhappy with their decision to concentrate first on the taking of St Elmo, but preparations were too far advanced to change plans. Dragut tirelessly went around the Turkish positions, inspiring his men and helping to set up batteries on Dragut Point and Ricasoli Point to increase the pressure on the tiny garrison. It was while setting up one such battery on Mt Sceberras that he was struck in the head by a splinter of rock thrown up by an enemy cannonball and retired, mortally wounded, to his tent.

Dragut's fears over the wisdom of besieging St Elmo were proved right. Despite continuous bombardment and repeated mass assaults on its walls, Fort St Elmo held out for over four weeks, and cost the lives of no fewer than 8000 Turkish soldiers before it was finally taken; not one of the Christian defenders survived. On receiving the news that the fort had been captured, old Dragut smiled, and died. Looking across at the looming bulk of Fort St Angelo from the smoke and rubble of St Elmo, Mustafa Pasha is said to have muttered, 'Allah! If so small a son has cost us so dear, what price shall we have to pay for so large a father?'

Hoping to intimidate the already demoralised defenders of Fort St Angelo, Mustafa Pasha ordered that several of the leading Knights should be beheaded and their heads fixed on stakes looking across towards Birgu. The Turks then nailed the decapitated bodies to makeshift wooden crucifixes and sent them floating across the harbour towards St Angelo. La Valette's response was immediate and equally cruel. All Turkish prisoners were executed and decapitated. The Knights then used their heads as cannonballs and fired them back across the harbour to St Elmo.

1566	1798–1800
Valletta is founded by the Knights' Grand Master Jean Parisot de la Valette	The French occupy Malta after Napoleon's conquest in 1798

Then began the final Turkish assault on the strongholds of Birgu and Isla. Piali's fleet moved from Marsaxlokk to Marsamxett Harbour to unload heavy artillery, and several ships were dragged across the neck of the Sceberras Peninsula – the entrance to Grand Harbour was still commanded by the guns of Fort St Angelo – to aid the ground forces with fire from the sea. Through the heat of summer, the Turks launched at least 10 massed assaults on the walls of Birgu and Isla, but each time they were beaten back. On 18 August, when a large section of wall was brought down and it looked as though the Turkish troops were on the verge of fighting their way into the town, Grand Master la Valette himself joined his Knights in the breach. The day was saved.

Turkish morale was drained by the long, hot summer, their increasing casualties, and the impending possibility of having to spend the entire winter on Malta (the Mediterranean sailing season traditionally ended with the storms of late September). The ferocity of their attacks decreased. Then on 7 September the long-promised relief force from Sicily finally arrived. Twenty-eight ships carrying some 8000 men landed at Mellieħa Bay and took command of the high ground around Naxxar as the Turks scrambled to embark their troops and guns at Marsamxett.

Seeing the unexpectedly small size of the relief force, Mustafa Pasha ordered some of his troops to land again at St Paul's Bay, while the rest marched towards Naxxar from Marsamxett. But the tired and demoralised Turkish soldiers were in no mood to fight these fresh and ferocious Knights and men-at-arms, and they turned and ran for the galleys now anchored in St Paul's Bay. Thousands were hacked to pieces in the shallow waters of the bay as they tried to escape. That night the banner of the Order of St John flew once again over the battered ruins of St Elmo, and in their churches the Knights and the people of Malta gave thanks for the end of the siege.

The part played in the Great Siege by the ordinary people of Malta is often overlooked, but their courage and resilience was a deciding factor in the Turkish defeat. The defence force was made up of some 5000 or 6000 Maltese soldiers. Local women and children contributed by repairing walls, bringing food and ammunition to the soldiers and tending the wounded. Although their names do not appear in the official accounts, local heroes like Toni Bajada – who has streets named after him in Valletta, St Paul's Bay and Naxxar – live on in Maltese legend. The date of the end of the siege, 8 September, is still celebrated in Malta as the Victory Day public holiday.

AFTER THE SIEGE

The Knights of Malta, previously neglected, were now hailed as the saviours of Europe. Money and honours were heaped on them by grateful monarchs, and the construction of the new city of Valletta – named after the hero of the siege – and its enormous fortifications began. Although sporadic raids continued, Malta was never again seriously threatened by the Turks. Süleyman the Magnificent died in 1566, and much of the Turkish fleet was destroyed by a magazine explosion in the Istanbul dockyards. What remained of Ottoman naval power was crushed at the Battle of Lepanto in 1571, a victory in which the galleys of the Order of St John played an important (and enthusiastic) part.

The Great Siege Marauding Muslims vs crusading Christians – a clichéd plotline, you have to admit. This is a page-turning account of the epic 1565 battle between the Ottoman Turks and the Knights of St John, by Ernle Bradford.

Malta Convoy More WWII drama. This book, by Peter Shankland and Anthony Hunter, describes the famous Operation Pedestal that succeeded in resupplying Malta at its lowest point in 1942.

1814	**1814–1964**
Malta is formally recognised as a British colony after British forces help drive the French from Malta in 1800	The British rule Malta, allowing varying levels of Maltese self-government

The period following the Great Siege was one of building – not only of massive new fortifications and watchtowers, but of churches, palaces and auberges. The military engineer Francesco Laparelli was sent to Malta by the pope to design the new defences of Valletta, and Italian artists arrived to decorate its churches, chapels and palazzi. An influx of new Knights, eager to join the now prestigious Order, swelled the coffers of the treasury.

The pious Grand Master Jean de la Cassière (1572–81) oversaw the construction of the Order's new hospital – the Sacra Infermeria (p65) – and the magnificent St John's Co-Cathedral (p60). The cathedral replaced the old Conventual Church of St Lawrence in Birgu (renamed Vittoriosa, or Victorious, after the siege). La Cassière's successor, Hugues Loubeux de Verdalle (1581–95), was more inclined to enjoy the privileges rather than the responsibilities of power and built himself the grandiose Verdala Palace near Rabat (p131).

Alof de Wignacourt (1601–22) initiated many worthy projects, including the construction of an aqueduct to bring water to Valletta from the hills near Mdina. In contrast, the decadent Antoine de Paule (1623–36) built the San Anton Palace (p133) as a summer retreat for hedonistic parties, an unchivalrous tendency which was to increase in the ensuing century. Grand Master Antonio Manoel de Vilhena (1722–36) adorned Malta with many magnificent buildings, including the Manoel Theatre (p64), Fort Manoel (p87) and the Palazzo de Vilhena (p125), but the long reign of the haughty Emanuel Pinto de Fonseca (1741–73), who considered himself on a level with the crowned heads of Europe, epitomised the change that had come over the Order. One glance at the portrait of Pinto in the museum of St John's Co-Cathedral in Valletta (p60) will reveal how far the Order had strayed from its vows of poverty, chastity and obedience.

With the Turkish threat removed, the Knights occupied themselves less with militarism and monasticism, and more with piracy, commerce, drinking and duelling. Although the Order continued to embellish Valletta, the Knights sank into corrupt and ostentatious ways.

Malte Tricolore – The Story of a French Malta 1798–1964 Didier Destremau, former French ambassador to Malta, has written a lighthearted, satirical history of Malta 'as it might have happened', had Napoleon not got the boot and the country remained under French rule.

NAPOLEON IN MALTA

In the aftermath of the French Revolution, Grand Master Emmanuel de Rohan (1775–97) provided money for Louis XVI's doomed attempt to escape from Paris. By the late 18th century around three-quarters of the Order's income came from the Knights of the French langue, so when the revolutionary authorities confiscated all of the Order's properties and estates in France, the Order was left in dire financial straits.

In 1798 Napoleon Bonaparte arrived in Malta aboard his flagship *L'Orient* at the head of the French Navy, on his way to Egypt to counter the British influence in the Mediterranean. He demanded that he be allowed to water his ships, but the Knights refused. The French landed and captured the island with hardly a fight – many of the Knights were in league with the French, and the Maltese were in no mood for a battle. On 11 June 1798 the Order surrendered to Napoleon. Although the French Knights were allowed to remain, the German Grand Master Ferdinand von Hompesch (1797–98) and the rest of the Order were given three days to gather what belongings they could and leave.

1853–56	1914–18
Malta is used as a base and supply station of the Royal Navy during the Crimean War	Malta serves as a military hospital during WWI

Napoleon stayed in Malta for only six days (in the Palazzo de Parisio in Valletta), but when he left, *L'Orient* was weighed down with silver, gold, paintings and tapestries looted from the Order's churches, auberges and infirmary. (Most of this treasure went to the bottom of the sea a few months later when the British Navy under Admiral Nelson destroyed the French fleet at the Battle of the Nile.) The French also abolished the Maltese aristocracy, defaced coats of arms, desecrated churches and closed down monasteries.

Napoleon left behind a garrison of 4000 men, but they were taken unawares by a spontaneous uprising of the Maltese people (see the boxed text, p125) and had to retreat within the walls of Valletta. A Maltese deputation sought help from the British, and a naval blockade was enforced under the command of Captain Alexander Ball, who was sympathetic to the islanders' aspirations. The French garrison finally capitulated in September 1800, but having taken Malta the British government was unsure what to do with it.

The Treaty of Amiens (March 1802) provided for the return of Malta to the Order of St John (then taking refuge in Russia and Naples), but the Maltese did not want them back and sent a delegation to London to petition the British to stay. Their pleas fell on deaf ears, and arrangements had been made for the return of the Order when war between Britain and France broke out again in May 1803. Faced with the blockade of European ports against British trade, the British government soon changed its mind regarding the potential usefulness of Malta. Even Admiral Nelson, who had previously dismissed the islands, wrote: 'I now declare that I consider Malta as a most important outwork…I hope we shall never give it up.'

While the latter stages of the Napoleonic Wars wore on, Malta rapidly became a prosperous entrepôt, and with the Treaty of Paris in 1814 it was formally recognised as a Crown Colony of the British Empire, with Lieutenant-General Sir Thomas Maitland as its first governor and commander in chief.

www.my-malta.com is a website chock-full of interesting articles. Click on the 'Our Rich History' section for a good overview and links to more detailed history pages.

CROWN COLONY

The end of the Napoleonic Wars brought an economic slump to Malta as trade fell off and little was done in the way of investment in the island. But its fortunes revived during the Crimean War (1853–56) when it was developed by the Royal Navy as a major naval base and supply station, and with the opening of the Suez Canal in 1869 Malta became one of the chief coaling ports on the imperial steamship route between Britain and India.

The early 19th century also saw the beginnings of Maltese political development. In 1835 a Council of Government made up of prominent local citizens was appointed to advise the governor and a free press was established. The constitution of 1849 allowed for eight elected representatives to partake in the government of Malta, but it was not until 1887 that the elected members constituted a majority.

In the second half of the 19th century vast sums were spent on improving Malta's defences and dockyard facilities as the island became a linchpin in the imperial chain of command. The Victoria Lines (see p99) and several large dry docks were built during this period. Commercial facilities were also improved to cater for the busy trade route to India and the Far East. In 1883 a railway was built between Valletta and Mdina (it was closed down in 1931). Between 1800 and 1900 the population of Malta doubled to 200,000.

1919	1921
Riots against British rule demonstrate a growing desire for self-government	A new constitution grants a limited form of self-government

THE BRITISH LEGACY

For 150 years, from 1814 to 1964, Malta was part of the British Empire. The legacy of British rule takes many forms, most noticeably in the fact that almost everyone speaks English as well as Malti. But there are many others – the Maltese drive on the left, and many of the vehicles on the road are vintage British models from the 1950s, '60s and '70s; the local football teams have typically British names like United, Hotspurs, Wanderers, Rangers and Rovers; cafés serve sausage, egg and chips and pots of tea; and beer is sold in pints and half-pints. Traditional items of British street furniture – red telephone boxes, red pillar boxes, and blue lamps outside police stations – persist in Malta, though they have largely disappeared from British towns. And conversations in Malti are liberally sprinkled with the English expression 'Awright?' and various other forms of 'Manglish'.

During WWI Malta served as a military hospital – it was known as the 'Nurse of the Mediterranean' – providing 25,000 beds for casualties from the disastrous Gallipoli campaign in Turkey. But prices and taxes rose during the war and the economy slumped. During protest riots in 1919, four Maltese citizens were shot dead by panicking British soldiers and several more were injured.

The Malta Story (1953) Surprisingly the only movie made about the dramatic WWII events in Malta. Men in spiffy uniforms fight dangerous battles, perform heroic acts and win hearts (of course). Stars Alec Guinness and Jack Hawkins.

The British government replied to the unrest by giving the Maltese a greater say in the running of Malta. The 1921 constitution created a diarchic system of government, with a Maltese assembly presiding over local affairs and a British imperial government controlling foreign policy and defence. The 1921 elections saw Joseph Howard of the Unione Politica (which later merged to become the Nationalist Party) take his place as the first prime minister of Malta.

The interwar years were marked by economic depression and political turmoil (the constitution was revoked in 1930 and again in 1933) and by growing tensions with Italy. Emigration became an increasingly attractive option, and many Maltese moved to Britain, Canada, the USA and Australia. Emigration to Canada and Australia increased after WWII, and today Australia has one of the largest Maltese communities in the world.

In 1930s Malta, Italian was the language of law and of polite conversation among the upper classes. Malti was the everyday language of the common people, and an increasing number could also speak English. Mussolini made the ridiculous claim that Malti was merely a dialect of Italian and that the Maltese Islands rightly belonged within his new Roman Empire. In 1934 Britain decreed that Malti would be the language of the law courts, and that henceforth Malti and English would be Malta's official languages.

FORTRESS MALTA

The day after Mussolini's Italy entered WWII, one of that country's first acts of war was to bomb Malta.

The outbreak of WWII found Britain undecided as to the strategic importance of Malta. The army and air force felt that the islands could not be adequately defended against bombing attacks from Sicily and should be evacuated. However, Winston Churchill (then First Lord of the Admiralty) insisted that possession of Malta was vital to Britain's control of supply lines through the bottleneck of the central Mediterranean. As a result of this indecision Malta was unprepared when Mussolini entered the war on 10 June 1940. The very next day Italian bombers attacked Grand Harbour.

1920s–30s	1940–43
Economic depression and political turmoil result in large numbers emigrating	Malta experiences heavy bombing and great hardship during WWII

The only aircraft available on the islands on 11 June were three Gloster Gladiator biplanes – quickly nicknamed *Faith*, *Hope* and *Charity* – whose pilots fought with such skill and tenacity that Italian pilots estimated the strength of the Maltese squadron to be in the region of 25 aircraft! (What remains of *Faith* can be seen in Malta's National War Museum, p63.) The Gladiators battled on alone for three weeks before squadrons of modern Hurricane fighters arrived to bolster the islands' air defences.

Malta effectively became a fortified aircraft carrier, a base for bombing attacks on enemy shipping and harbours in Sicily and North Africa. It also harboured submarines which preyed on Italian and German supply ships. These operations played a vital part in reducing the supplies of fuel and materiel to the Panzer divisions of Rommel's Afrika Korps, which were then sweeping eastwards through Libya towards British-held Egypt. Malta's importance was clear to Hitler too, and crack squadrons of Stuka divebombers were stationed in Sicily with the objective of pounding the island into submission.

Malta's greatest ordeal came in 1942, when the country came close to starvation and surrender. It suffered 154 days and nights of continuous bombing – in April alone some 6700 tonnes of bombs were dropped on Grand Harbour and the surrounding area. By comparison, at the height of London's Blitz there were 57 days of continuous bombing. On 15 April 1942 King George VI awarded the George Cross – Britain's highest award for civilian bravery – to the entire population of Malta. The citation from the king read: 'To honour her brave people I award the George Cross to the island fortress of Malta to bear witness to a heroism and devotion that will long be famous in history.' The award can be seen at the National War Museum in Valletta.

Just as Malta's importance to the Allies lay in disrupting enemy supply lines, so its major weakness was the difficulty of getting supplies to the island. At the height of the siege in the summer of 1942 the governor made an inventory of remaining food and fuel and informed London that if more supplies did not get through before the end of August then Malta would be forced to surrender. A massive relief convoy, known as Operation Pedestal, consisting of 14 supply ships escorted by three aircraft carriers, two battle-ships, seven cruisers and 24 destroyers, was dispatched to run the gauntlet of enemy bombers and submarines. It suffered massive attacks, and only five supply ships made it into Grand Harbour – the crippled oil tanker *Ohio*, with its precious cargo of fuel, limped in, lashed between two warships on 15 August. This date, the Feast of the Assumption of the Virgin Mary, led to the Maltese christening the relief ships 'The Santa Marija Convoy'.

In the words of Winston Churchill, 'Revictualled and replenished with ammunition and essential stores, the strength of Malta revived', and it was able to continue its vital task of disrupting enemy supply lines. The aircraft and submarines based in Malta succeeded in destroying or damaging German convoys to North Africa to the extent that Rommel's Afrika Korps was low on fuel and ammunition during the crucial Battle of El Alamein in October 1942, a situation that contributed to a famous Allied victory and the beginning of the end of the German presence in North Africa.

In July 1943 Malta served as the operational headquarters and air support base for Operation Husky, the Allied invasion of Sicily. By coincidence, the date

A Concise History of Malta It's no small feat to cover a country's past in under 300 pages. This book, by Carmel Cassar, is a readable introduction to Maltese history.

on which the Italian Navy finally surrendered to the Allies – 8 September – was the same as that on which the Great Siege had ended 378 years previously. As the captured enemy warships gathered in Marsaxlokk Bay, Admiral Cunningham, commander in chief of Britain's Mediterranean Fleet, cabled the Admiralty in London: 'Be pleased to inform their Lordships that the Italian battle fleet now lies at anchor under the guns of the fortress of Malta.'

For a better understanding of this tumultuous period in Maltese history, travellers should visit the National War Museum (p63) and Lascaris War Rooms (p64), which housed the headquarters and operations rooms of the Royal Air Force and Royal Navy. Both sights are in Valletta.

INDEPENDENT REPUBLIC

After 1943 Malta's role in the war rapidly diminished. WWII left the islands with 35,000 homes destroyed and the population on the brink of starvation. In 1947 the war-torn island was given a measure of self-government and a £30 million war-damage fund to help rebuilding and restoration. But the economic slump that followed Britain's reductions in defence spending and the loss of jobs in the naval dockyard led to calls either for closer integration with Britain, or for Malta to go it alone. On 21 September 1964, with Prime Minister Dr George Borg Olivier at the helm, Malta gained its independence. It remained within the British Commonwealth, with Queen Elizabeth II as the head of state represented in Malta by a governor general.

> When Malta gained independence in 1964 it was the first time since prehistory that the country had been ruled by the native Maltese and not by some outside power.

Borg Olivier's successor as prime minister in 1971 was the Labour Party's Dominic (Dom) Mintoff, whose name was rarely out of the news headlines in the 1970s. Mintoff was a fiery and controversial politician who was not afraid to speak his mind. During his period as prime minister (1971–84) Malta became a republic (in 1974, replacing the queen as head of state with a president appointed by parliament). In 1979 links with Britain were reduced further when Mintoff expelled the British armed services, declared Malta's neutrality and signed agreements with Libya, the Soviet Union and North Korea.

In 1987 the Nationalist Party assumed power under the prime ministership of Dr Eddie Fenech Adami, and won a second term with a landslide victory in 1992, when one of the party's main platforms was Malta's application to join the EC (European Community; now the EU). The 1996 general election saw the Labour Party, led by Dr Alfred Sant, narrowly regain power with a one-seat majority. One of its main policies was to suspend the country's application for full EU membership. However, in 1998, during a debate on development of the Vittoriosa waterfront into a marina for private yachts, Dom Mintoff, then 82 years old but still capable of causing controversy, crossed the floor of the house to vote with the opposition. A snap general election in September 1998 was effectively a vote of confidence in the Labour government. Labour lost, Fenech Adami's Nationalist Party was returned to power, and under the Nationalist Party, Malta's bid for EU membership was revived.

THE 21ST CENTURY

In 2002 Malta was formally invited to join the EU and in March 2003 the country voted in a referendum on the matter. Ninety-two percent of eligible voters cast their vote and, in a close result, just over 53% voted in favour of

1964	1974
Malta becomes independent, with Queen Elizabeth II still the head of state	Malta becomes a republic

EU membership. This pro-EU result was confirmed when Fenech Adami's Nationalist Party won a general election one month later, in April 2003. Malta became a member of the EU on 1 May 2004, and at the time of research was preparing for the adoption of the euro as the new national currency, scheduled for 1 January 2008.

In early 2004, upon reaching his 70th birthday, Fenech Adami resigned as Nationalist Party leader and retired from parliament. Soon after, he took on the figurehead position of president of Malta. Fenech Adami's deputy prime minister, Lawrence Gonzi, was elected leader of the ruling party and hence became the country's new prime minister. The next general election isn't due until August 2008, but may be called before that time.

As the Maltese prepare to enter the euro zone (see p176 for more information), they also confront a number of economic and social challenges, including over-development of the land and chronic environmental abuse, a decline in tourist numbers, and the recent wave of immigrants from northern Africa arriving by boat on Malta's shores and placing a strain on resources (and triggering an unpleasant outburst of racism among many locals). For more on these topical issues, see p18.

'In 2002 Malta was formally invited to join the EU'

2004	2005
Malta joins the EU	Around 1800 asylum-seeking irregular immigrants arrive on Maltese shores

The Culture

THE NATIONAL IDENTITY

When Malta gained its independence in 1964 it was the first time since prehistory that the islands had been ruled by the native Maltese, and not by some outside power. Since early in the 1st millennium BC Malta had been occupied successively by Phoenicians, Carthaginians, Romans, Byzantines, Arabs, Normans, Sicilians, the Knights of St John, the French and the British. All of these temporary powers have influenced Maltese culture to varying degrees, yet through all this time the population has managed to preserve a distinctive identity and a strong sense of continuity with the past. Despite an easy blend of Mediterranean and British culture in the islands today, there's still a strong feeling of tradition. The people remain fairly conservative in their outlook; the Catholic Church still exerts a strong influence, the church's buildings and parish activities remain at the core of village life, and family values are held in high regard.

The locals do talk about the slightly claustrophobic feeling of living in a tiny country with the population of a midsize regional town: on one hand, there's a great sense of community; on the other, a lack of privacy, and a tendency for gossip (everyone seems to know everyone else's business). People speak of 'six degrees of separation', but in Malta, given the small population, it's invariably two degrees – if I don't know you, I'm bound to know someone who does…

The Maltese are justifiably proud of their small country's historical importance and the local grit and determination (well demonstrated during WWII). Understandably, they have relished their independence since 1964 and the vast majority of the population takes great interest in political matters (one local spoke of a reverence for authority among many locals – perhaps a by-product of centuries of foreign rule, or of the strongly religious nature of the population). The people love discussing politics – a small population and the accessibility of politicians probably plays a large part. And the locals put their money where their mouth is too: voter turnout is very high (around 90%) but, interestingly, margins are usually very close – the country seems fairly evenly split on major issues.

The Maltese are friendly, laid-back and generally welcoming of tourists. As in most southern European countries, things can move slowly here, but this is tempered by an efficiency that may be a result of British rule. People are a little more reserved than you might expect for a Mediterranean country (in comparison to, say, Italians and Greeks) – again, this may be a direct result of the British influence.

Visitors will easily be able to observe the very Maltese quirks that have withstood globalisation and continue to make the country unique and fascinating – among them the language, the village festa, and the love of cars, sport, politics, fireworks and lotteries.

LIFESTYLE

Malta is a conservative country, with traditions and attitudes similar to those of southern Italy. Under the Maltese constitution, Roman Catholic Christianity is the official state religion and must be taught in state schools, but the constitution guarantees freedom of worship. Although its influence is waning, the Roman Catholic Church still plays an important part in everyday life. A Sunday Mass attendance census held in Malta in 2005 showed that just over half the population (52.6%) attend Mass on Sunday – a drop of

For aspiring anthropologists, Tarcisio Zarb's book, *Folklore of an Island – Maltese Threshold Customs*, covers Maltese traditions related to all of life's big occasions, including birth, puberty, marriage and death.

An estimated crowd of 100,000 people (one quarter of the population) attended the Mass celebrated by Pope John Paul II on his visit to Malta in 2001.

MALTI – A LINGUISTIC MELTING POT

The native language of Malta is called Malti (also called Maltese). Some linguists attribute its origins to the Phoenician occupation of Malta in the 1st millennium BC, but most link it to North African Arabic dialects. The language has an Arabic grammar and construction but is a melting pot of influences, laced with Sicilian, Italian, Spanish, French and English loan-words.

English is taught to schoolchildren from an early age, and almost everyone in Malta speaks it well. Many also speak Italian, helped by the fact that Malta receives Italian TV. French and German are also spoken, though less widely.

See also the Language chapter, p195.

---

around 11% in 10 years. Church ceremonies are still quite sombre affairs, full of tradition and reverence, and this may explain why many of the younger generation prefer not to attend every week. Still, baptisms, first communions, weddings and funerals continue to be celebrated in church (weddings in the parish where the bride was born), and the most important event in the calendar is the annual parish festa (p172), which is held on different dates, depending on the village. The sheer number of churches in the country is also a noticeable feature. Divorce and abortion are illegal; the possibility of divorce being legalised is a widely discussed issue, but seems unlikely. Still, family values are very important, as is the love of socialising common to southern European countries – Sunday in particular is the day to gather with family and friends and enjoy good food and company.

Statistically, the Maltese enjoy a good standard of living, low inflation (around 2% to 3%) and relatively low unemployment (around 7%). Schooling is compulsory between the ages of five and 16 and is provided free in state and church schools (church schools are subsidised by the government). A university education is also free to Maltese citizens and students receive an annual stipend. Statistics are only part of the equation – positive elements such as the warm climate, a strong connection to the land and a healthy sense of tradition and community also play their part in creating what to many might seem an enviably relaxed lifestyle. Dutch sociologist Professor Ruut Veenhoven (of Erasmus University in Rotterdam) created the World Database of Happiness, which includes the Happiness in Nations survey and compares happiness levels in 90 countries based on data collected between 1946 and 1992. According to the database, Malta is ranked the happiest country in the world in which to live (tied with Denmark and Switzerland). But can happiness really be measured? For those looking to unlock the secrets of happiness, the scientific explanations are at www1.eur.nl/fsw/happiness/.

WOMEN IN MALTA

Malta is the only country in Europe where divorce is not legal

Malta is a conservative country and, as in many staunchly Catholic, Mediterranean countries, women have been expected to stay at home to look after their children (or their elderly parents). Childcare costs are high, if childcare exists at all – there simply hasn't been the culture of paying for such a service in such a traditional, family-oriented society. The country consequently has an employment rate for women of only 34%, the lowest in the EU. Attempts to identify reasons why about 110,000 females of working age are not in employment are underway as part of an EU program, and plans will be made to make workforce reentry more accessible for women through improved education, vocational training, employment opportunities and the expansion of affordable childcare.

A study compiled in 2003 showed that the main reasons for women not working was to look after their families and because they were happy at home, taking care of the family. Moral imperatives, resistance by close family members and the overbearing pressure of household chores came a distant third, fourth and fifth as explanations. Moral imperatives is an interesting facet – reports indicate that women are pressured to go to work by governments, and pressured not to by the church. Among the more conservative members of Maltese society (and society in general), women who go out to work are not only seen as failing their families, but are also held responsible for most that is dysfunctional in modern society.

However, the statistics don't paint the full picture. Locals talk of low official wages spurring the creation of a parallel economy of cash work on the side. Second jobs are common (ie teachers giving private lessons, policemen working as house painters on their days off), and many qualified people work from home, in positions such as hairdressers and dressmakers – these are some reasons for such a low percentage of women in official employment.

> It is estimated that there are as many Maltese living abroad as there are in Malta.

ECONOMY

Malta produces only about 20% of its food needs, has limited fresh water supplies and has no domestic energy sources. Tourism is the most vital component of the island's economy, generating around a quarter of Malta's GDP. Recognising that Malta's traditional offerings of sun and sea are under siege from new and often cheaper competitors (such as North African or Eastern European destinations), the Malta Tourism Authority (MTA) and its private-sector partners are turning their attention to promoting niche products such as cultural tourism, family travel, diving holidays and meetings and conventions.

Over the past 10 years, investors, developers and international hotel chains have constructed over 30 five- and four-star properties, up from only five luxury hotels in 1996.

The country is otherwise dependent on foreign trade, ship building and repair, construction, and manufacturing (especially electronics and textiles).

> Malta is among the most densely populated countries in the world, with 1266 people per sq km (the comparable figure for the Netherlands, the secondmost populous country in the EU, is around 400).

POPULATION

Malta's population is around 400,000, with most people living in the satellite towns around Valletta, Sliema and Grand Harbour. Approximately 30,000 live on Gozo, while Comino has a mere handful of farmers in winter and a couple of hundred tourists in summer. Around 90% of the population lives in urban areas and only 10% in rural areas. Some 97% of the population is Maltese-born.

The number of foreigners residing in Malta has almost doubled in the past 15 years – but this number still only amounts to just under 3% of the population. The foreign community in Malta is predominantly British. Most foreigners live in Sliema and its surrounding modern suburbs. There is also a growing North African Muslim community of over 2000, who are married to Maltese nationals. Unfortunately, some racism exists, with occasional reports of owners of some bars and clubs periodically discouraging or prohibiting darker-skinned persons, especially of African or Arab origin, from entering their establishments. This racism has been more evident since the recent arrival on Maltese shores of many hundreds of irregular immigrants (see p18) from Africa.

> There are 359 Catholic churches in Malta, serving around 392,000 people – the 98% of Malta's population who are Catholic.

SPORT
Football (Soccer)

The Maltese are great football fans and follow the fortunes of local sides and international teams (especially British and Italian) with equal fervour; countless bars televise matches. The local football season runs from October till May, and there is a Maltese Premier League with 10 teams. League and international matches are held at the National Stadium at Ta'Qali, which is situated between Mosta and Rabat; results are reported in the local newspapers.

More information can be obtained from the website of the **Malta Football Association** (www.mfa.com.mt), which details the leagues, teams and fixtures. Another website, www.maltafootball.com, is also a good resource for information.

Water Polo

As the heat of summer increases, football gives way to water polo, with its season lasting from July till September. The fans who were shouting on the terraces now yell from the pool sides. Games are hard fought and physical, and it's worth trying to take in a match during your stay in Malta. The important clashes are held at the National Swimming Pool Complex on Triq Maria Teresa Spinelli in Gżira. Further information is available from the **Aquatic Sports Association** (☎ 2132 2884; www.asaofmalta.org).

Horse Racing

Horse racing is one of the Maltese Islands' most popular spectator sports, with race meetings held at the Marsa Racecourse, part of the Marsa Sports Complex outside Valletta (see p168), every Sunday from October to May. Races are mostly trotting – where the jockey rides a light two-wheeled gig drawn by the horse – and the betting is frantic. Some tour operators offer a day trip to the races (in season).

ARTS
Crafts

Malta is noted for its fine crafts – particularly its handmade lace, handwoven fabrics and silver filigree. Lace-making probably arrived with the Knights in the 16th century. It was traditionally the role of village women – particularly on the island of Gozo – and, although the craft has developed into a healthy industry, it is still possible to find women sitting on their doorsteps making lace tablecloths.

The art of producing silver filigree was probably introduced to the island in the 17th century via Sicily, which was then strongly influenced by Spain. Malta's silversmiths still produce beautiful filigree by traditional methods but in large quantities to meet tourist demand.

Other handicrafts include weaving, knitting and glass-blowing; the latter is an especially healthy small industry that produces glassware exported throughout the world. Head to Ta'Qali Crafts Village near Rabat (p129) or its smaller Gozitan equivalent, Ta'Dbieġi (p156) for the opportunity to see locals practising their craft and to buy souvenirs.

Literature

Pietro Caxaro's *Cantilena*, an epic poem composed in the mid-15th century, is the earliest known literary work in Malti but Italian remained the language of literature in Malta until the late 19th century. Important writers of this period include Ġan Anton Vassallo (1817–67) and Ġuże Muscat Azzopardi (1853–1927). *Inez Farruġ* by Anton Manwel Caruana (1838–1907), published in 1889, is considered to be the first literary novel written in Malti.

Probably the best-known and best-loved of Maltese writers is Carmelo Psaila (1871–1961). Under his pen name of Dun Karm he became Malta's national poet, movingly chronicling the island's sufferings in WWII. Anton Buttiġieġ (1912–83) was another important poet, who captured the essence

www.maltaculture.com
The Press & News section of the website of the Malta Council for Culture & the Arts is a great starting point for information about all sorts of forthcoming cultural events, including literary recitals, traditional folk music performances and lunchtime concerts.

LOCALS TO LISTEN OUT FOR...

■ **Joseph Calleja** is one of the most promising young tenors around today, winning international acclaim. Born in Attard in 1978, this guy has a voice that belies his tender years and he looks set for a long and illustrious career. Check out www.josephcalleja.com.

■ **Miriam Gauci** was born in 1958 and has since become the most successful Maltese soprano, enjoying an international career and reputation.

■ **Ira Losco**, born in Sliema in 1981, is a talented young singer-songwriter who has already been the best-selling artist in Malta for three consecutive years, and has supported artists such as Katie Melua and Elton John. Her most recent album, *Accident Prone,* is in her true pop-rock/alternative style and is a hit at home for its powerful guitars, edgy riffs and strong melodies. See www.iralosco.com.

---

of the Maltese landscape and the human relationship with nature in his lyric poetry and tightly written vignettes.

Among modern writers, the playwright and novelist Francis Ebejer (1925–93), who wrote in both Malti and English, stands out. His novels deal with the tensions between tradition and modernity. *For Rozina…a Husband* is a collection of short stories (in English) that attempt to capture the essence of Maltese village life. Oliver Friġġieri (b 1947), Professor of Maltese at the University of Malta, is Malta's best-known and most prolific living novelist.

Music

The Maltese are great music lovers and the *għana* (*ah*-na; folk song) is Maltese folk music at its most individual and traditional. A tribute to Malta's geographic location, *għana* verses are a mixture of a Sicilian ballad and the rhythmic wail of an Arabic tune, and were traditionally viewed as the music of the farmers, labourers and working classes. In its truest form, lyrics are created fresh each time and tell stories of village life and events in local history. The verses are always sung by men with guitar accompaniment.

Intrigued by *għana*? Read all about it (and listen to samples) at www.allmalta.com.

Some band clubs and bars, especially in the centre and south of Malta, organise *għana* nights or you might chance upon an impromptu *għana* in a rural bar. The St James' Cavalier Centre for Creativity in Valletta (p63) occasionally holds *għana* nights and you may see performances at various heritage events.

Etnika is a traditional folk group reviving ethnic Maltese musical forms and instruments. Their music, using traditional bagpipes, horns and drums, was once part of Malta's daily life, and was used in a variety of social contexts – from weddings to funerals. Etnika reinterpret this musical heritage for a contemporary audience and sometimes fuse it with *għana,* jazz and flamenco for a unique sound – you should be able to pick up a CD of their music at music stores throughout Malta. See also www.etnika.com.mt for information.

The highs! The lows! The bright outfits and big hair! Read all about Malta's performance at Eurovision over the years at www.eurovision malta.com.

Band music is one of the most popular traditions on the islands. Every town and village has at least one band club (sometimes two, and they are often engaged in strong rivalry). Bands play a vital role in the village festa and other open-air events.

There is also a strong modern music scene and live music is featured in many pubs and clubs. The Eurovision Song Contest may be derided in large parts of Europe but it is taken *very* seriously in Malta. Don't upset a local by mentioning Malta's worst-ever result at the 2006 competition (they came a dismal last) after the country came a close second in 2005.

Architecture

Malta's architectural heritage is dominated by two influences – the Knights of St John and the Roman Catholic Church. Together they created a distinctive variation of the baroque style of architecture that swept across Europe between the end of the 16th century and the 18th century.

The greatest Maltese architect of the 16th century was Gerolamo Cassar (1520–86). He was born in the fishing village of Birgu 10 years before the Knights of St John arrived from Rhodes, and he worked as an assistant to Francesco Laparelli, the military engineer who designed the fortifications of Valletta. He studied architecture in Rome and was responsible for the design of many of Malta's finest buildings, including the Grand Master's Palace, the façade of St John's Co-Cathedral, and many of the Knights' auberges.

The prolific architect Tommaso Dingli (1591–1666) created many of Malta's parish churches. His masterpiece is the Church of St Mary in Attard, which he designed when he was only 22 years of age. Lorenzo Gafa (1630–1704) designed many of the Maltese Islands' finest examples of Maltese baroque, among them the cathedrals of Mdina and Gozo.

Other important architects who also worked in the Maltese baroque style were Giovanni Barbara (Palazzo de Vilhena, Mdina; 1730), Giuseppe Bonnici (the Old Customs House, Valletta; 1747) and Domenico Cachia (the Auberge de Castile, Valletta; 1744).

In modern times, Malta's best-known architect is Richard England, a practising architect of international reputation, and also a sculptor, painter, photographer and poet. See www.richardengland.com.

Painting

As in architecture, Maltese art was much influenced by neighbouring Italy. Many Italian artists worked in Malta (most famously Caravaggio) and most Maltese artists went to study in Italy.

The greatest Maltese painter of the 17th century was Mattia Preti (1613–99). Preti was a painter from Calabria, Italy, who lived and worked in Malta for 30 years. In 1661 he was commissioned by Grand Master Rafael Cotoner to decorate the vault of St John's Co-Cathedral in Valletta (see p60). The 18 vivid scenes depicting events in the life of St John the Baptist – from Zachary

The website, www.angelfire.com/ma/architecture, has loads of information on the various eras of architecture in Malta, with good accompanying photographs and useful links.

5000 Years of Architecture in Malta, by Leonard Mahoney, provides comprehensive coverage of the topic, from Neolithic temples to the auberges of the Knights and beyond.

CARAVAGGIO IN MALTA

Michelangelo Merisi (1571–1610), better known by the name of his home town, Caravaggio, was a revolutionary Italian painter whose naturalistic representation of religious subjects replaced the traditional symbolism of 16th-century art. In particular, he introduced the bold use of shadow and selective lighting to dramatise his subjects.

He made his name in Rome with a series of controversial paintings, but also earned a reputation as a wild man, and numerous brawls and encounters with the law culminated in Caravaggio murdering a man during an argument over a tennis game. He fled Rome and went into hiding in Naples for several months. Then, towards the end of 1607, he moved to Malta.

In Malta, Caravaggio was welcomed as a famous artist and was commissioned to produce several works for the Knights of St John, including the famous *Beheading of St John the Baptist*, now on display in the oratory of the cathedral in Valletta (p61). In July 1608 he was admitted into the Order as a Knight of Justice, but only two months later he was arrested for an unspecified crime – it may be that news arrived of the murder he had committed – and he was promptly imprisoned in Fort St Angelo.

He escaped to Sicily, but was expelled from the Order and spent the next two years on the run. He created some of his finest paintings during this period, before dying of exhaustion and fever before the age of 38.

MALTA'S CHURCHES

The Maltese claim to be one of the oldest Christian peoples in the world, having been converted by St Paul after his shipwreck on Malta in AD 60. Maltese society remains deeply influenced by the Roman Catholic Church. Although local festas are a noisy and colourful expression of worship, church services are largely solemn experiences, full of reverence and Catholic ritual. If you are visiting a church, dress accordingly.

There are 64 Catholic parishes and 313 Catholic churches on Malta, and 15 Catholic parishes and 46 Catholic churches on Gozo. These range from full cathedrals down to tiny wayside chapels and were built between the 15th and 20th centuries. The main period of church-building in Malta took place after the arrival of the Knights of St John, in the 16th, 17th and 18th centuries. The oldest surviving church in Malta is the tiny medieval Chapel of the Annunciation at Ħal Millieri near Żurrieq (p141), which dates from the mid-15th century and is in Maltese vernacular style.

The 16th century saw the Renaissance style imported from Italy by the Knights, followed by the more elaborate forms of Maltese baroque which evolved throughout the 17th century and culminated in the design of St Paul's Cathedral in Mdina. The 19th and 20th centuries saw the addition of several large churches in the neogothic style, including St Paul's Anglican Cathedral in Valletta (1839–41) and the Church of Our Lady of Lourdes in Mġarr, Gozo (1924–75). Two huge rotundas were also built by public subscription: the Church of St Mary at Mosta (1833–60) and the Church of St John the Baptist (1951–71) at Xewkija on Gozo.

The following list includes some of Malta's most impressive examples of church and cathedral architecture.

St John's Co-Cathedral, Valletta (p60)

(1573–77; Gerolamo Cassar, interior by Mattia Preti) The austere Renaissance façade of St John's – the Conventual Church of the Order of St John from 1577 to 1798 – conceals a richly ornamental interior. The tombs of Grand Masters Nicolas Cotoner and Ramon Perellos in the Chapel of Aragon are floridly baroque.

Church of St Paul's Shipwreck, Valletta (p64)

(c 1580; Gerolamo Cassar, remodelled by Lorenzo Gafa in 1680) Don't be fooled by the largely 19th-century façade on Triq San Pawl – this is one of Valletta's oldest churches. The wooden statue of St Paul was carved in 1657 by Melchiorre Gafa, Lorenzo's brother, and is paraded through the streets on the festa day (10 February).

Church of St Mary, Attard (p133)

(1613–16; Tommaso Dingli) This is one of the finest examples of Renaissance-style architecture in Malta, built on a Latin cross plan with an elegant and restrained façade adorned with statues of the saints.

---

in the Temple to the beheading of St John – took five years to complete. Preti also designed the ornately carved decoration on the walls and pillars of the cathedral – a rich confection of gilded leaves, scrolls, flowers, Maltese crosses and coats of arms – and painted several of the altarpieces in the side chapels. Some of his best work can be seen in Valletta's National Museum of Fine Arts (p63). Preti was eventually accepted into the Order of St John and came to be known as *Il Cavalier Calabrese* – the Calabrian Knight.

Giuseppe Cali (1846–1930) was a portraitist and religious artist who painted altarpieces for parish churches and also created the murals in the Mosta Dome (p131).

Exhibitions by contemporary Maltese artists are regularly held in the Museum of Fine Arts in Valletta, and a great spot to check out what's happening on the local scene is the St James' Cavalier Centre for Creativity (p63).

Church of St Lawrence, Vittoriosa (p79)

(1681–97; Lorenzo Gafa) St Lawrence's occupies the site of a small church built by Count Roger in 1090. It was enlarged and taken over by the Knights of St John as their original conventual church in Malta in 1530 and houses relics brought from Rhodes, a silver processional cross, and a fine altarpiece by Mattia Preti showing the martyrdom of St Lawrence. The dome was rebuilt after being damaged by a bomb in 1942.

St Paul's Cathedral, Mdina (p124)

(1697–1702; Lorenzo Gafa) Designed by Gafa at the height of his career, this is probably the finest example of the Maltese baroque style (rather more restrained and less florid than the baroque of Italy). The cathedral occupies the site of a Norman church built in the 1090s, and there may have been a church here since the 4th century.

Cathedral of the Assumption, Victoria, Gozo (p146)

(1697–1711; Lorenzo Gafa) Gozo's cathedral is another fine example of Maltese baroque designed by Gafa. Lack of funds meant the dome was never built, but an 18th-century trompe l'oeil painting looks convincingly like one on the inside. The cathedral occupies the site of an older Norman church, and possibly of a Roman temple.

Church of Sts Peter & Paul, Nadur, Gozo (p162)

(1760–80; Giuseppe Bonnici) The extravagance of Bonnici's original design has been tempered by a more sober 19th-century façade, but the beautiful and ornate marble interior is pure baroque. The twin statues of its patron saints have given it the nickname iż-Żewġ (the pair, or the twins), and its festa (29 June) is one of the liveliest on the islands.

Church of Santa Maria, Mosta (p131)

(1833–60; Giorgio Grognet de Vassé) The circular design of this church, better known as the Rotunda or Mosta Dome, closely resembles that of the Pantheon in Rome, but it's the church's great dome – visible from most parts of Malta – that is its most notable asset. Inside is a lovely calming interior of blue, gold and white, and remarkable evidence of the hand of God (perhaps?) in a little piece of WWII history.

Church of St John the Baptist, Xewkija, Gozo (p154)

(1951–71; Joseph D'Amato) This huge rotunda was built with money and labour donated by the parishioners of Xewkija. It is the biggest church in the Maltese Islands, and can seat up to 4000 people.

Sculpture

Antonio Sciortino (1879–1947) was the leading Maltese sculptor of the 20th century. Born in Żebbuġ, he spent 25 years in Rome before returning to Malta and creating lively and thrusting compositions like the *Arab Horses*, which is displayed in the National Museum of Fine Arts in Valletta (p63). You can see other examples of his fine work outdoors in Valletta's public spaces.

Vincent Apap (1938–2003) also created many of the sculptures that adorn public spaces in Malta, notably the Triton fountain in the centre of the City Gate bus terminus between Valletta and Floriana.

At the Cathedral Museum in Mdina (p124) you can view a permanent display of the clever, contemporary olive-wood sculptures created by Anton Agius (b 1933).

Environment

THE LAND

The Maltese Islands cover a total area of only 316 sq km – less than the Isle of Wight in the UK or Martha's Vineyard in the USA. There are three inhabited islands – Malta, Gozo and Comino – and two uninhabited islets, Cominotto and Filfla. They lie in the central Mediterranean Sea, 93km south of Sicily, 290km east of Tunisia and 290km north of Libya.

There are no mountains on the islands. The highest point is Ta'Żuta (253m) on the southwest coast of Malta. This high plateau is bounded on the southwest by sea cliffs, and drops away gradually towards rolling plains in the south and east. Northwest Malta is characterised by a series of flat-topped ridges running generally northeast to southwest – the Victoria Lines escarpment, the Wardija Ridge, the Bajda Ridge, the Mellieħa Ridge and the Marfa Ridge – separated by broad valleys. The landscape of Gozo is greener than Malta and consists of flat-topped hills and terraced hillsides, with high cliffs in the south and west. The highest point is Ta'Dbieġi (190m) to the south of Għarb.

The soil is generally thin and rocky, although some valleys are terraced and farmed intensively. There are few trees and, for most of the year, little greenery to soften the stony, sun-bleached landscape. The only notable exception is Buskett Gardens (see p131), a lush valley of pine trees and orange groves protected by the imposing Dingli Cliffs of the south coast.

There is virtually no surface water and there are no permanent creeks or rivers. The water table is the main source of fresh water, but it is supplemented by several large desalination plants – a good 60% of all tap water is desalinated seawater, produced by means of a reverse osmosis operated by electricity. So please use water carefully while here (and you may prefer to drink bottled water).

Geology

Geologically speaking, the Maltese Islands are lumps of the Mediterranean sea bed that have been warped upward until they are poking above sea level. The warping was caused by the collision between the African tectonic plate to the south and the European plate to the north. This collision is ongoing and is also responsible for the volcanoes of Etna and Vesuvius, and for the earthquakes which occasionally strike southern Italy and Malta.

The rocks that make up Malta are between seven million and 30 million years old, and are layered one on top of the other. From the bottom up, there are four main layers – the Lower Coralline Limestone, the Globigerina Limestone, the Blue Clay and the Upper Coralline Limestone. The limestones are rich in fossils, especially at the junction between the Lower Coralline and Globigerina Limestones, where there is a huge concentration of fossil scallop shells and sand dollars (flat, disc-shaped relatives of sea urchins).

The Upper and Lower Coralline Limestones are hard and resistant to weathering – they form the great sea cliffs of southwest Malta and Ta'Ċenċ, and the crags that ring the flat tops of Gozo's hills. The golden-coloured Globigerina Limestone is softer and underlies much of central and eastern Malta. The sticky Blue Clay is rich in nutrients and is responsible for the more fertile soils of Gozo – you can see it in the cliffs west of Ramla Bay.

Local quarrymen refer to the easily worked Globigerina Limestone as *franka;* the harder-wearing coralline limestones are called *zonqor.* Both were widely used in the building of the islands' massive fortifications.

Malta, Gozo & Comino – Off the Beaten Track is an excellent resource by Nature Trust Malta that gives an overview of the Maltese environment (including its geology, flora and fauna). It also contains details and maps for walking tours.

Malta's built-up surface area stands at 22% (compared to the European average of 7%), and in an unpopular move the government announced in 2006 it will extend Malta's development boundaries by a further 2.4%.

WILDLIFE
Animals
The sparse vegetation supports little in the way of land-based wildlife – just a handful of rats, mice, hedgehogs, weasels and shrews. Rabbits have been hunted almost to extinction (the rabbit you'll see on menus has been bred). Geckoes and other lizards are fairly common – the dark green and red lizard *Lacerta filfolensis* is found only on the islet of Filfla – and there are three species of snake, none of them poisonous.

There are barely a dozen resident bird species, including sparrows, rock doves, linnets, corn buntings, herring gulls and the blue rock thrush – Malta's national bird, which appears on the 25c coin – but more than 150 species have been recorded as migrants and winter visitors (these are favourite targets for Maltese hunters, sadly).

The seas around Malta and Gozo are clean and clear, and support a rich and diverse marine fauna that attracts scuba divers from all over Europe. For more information, see p44.

Wildlife of the Maltese Islands edited by Joe Sultana & Victor Falzon is a large, comprehensive book that covers about 1000 species of plants and animals, all illustrated in colour.

Plants
Malta has little in the way of natural vegetation. Much of the island is cultivated and where it is not the land is often bare and rocky. The only extensive area of woodland is at Buskett Gardens (see p131), which is dominated by Aleppo pines.

The rough limestone slopes of the hilltops and sea cliffs support a typical Mediterranean flora of stunted olive, oleander and tamarisk trees, with growths of thyme, euphorbia, rosemary and brambles. Samphire, sea campion, spurge and saltwort can be found on the rocks beside the sea, and the rare parasitic plant *Cynomorium coccineus* is found at Dwejra on Gozo (see p157).

For botany buffs, www .maltawildplants.com is an incredibly comprehensive site describing in detail the wild flowering plants growing in Malta.

NATIONAL PARKS
Malta has no national parks – hardly surprising, given its diminutive size. In Central Malta you might see signs pointing to 'National Park' – these are in fact pointing to the national sports stadium at Ta'Qali!

There are two nature reserves that protect resident and migrating birdlife in Northwest Malta, managed by volunteers from Birdlife Malta – these are Is-Simar Nature Reserve (p114) at Xemxija, and Għadira Nature Reserve (p118)at Mellieħa Bay. Both are open to the public.

THE MALTESE FALCON

Falconry was the great passion of the Holy Roman Emperor Frederick II (1194 1250). He wrote a famous treatise on the subject, *De arte venandi cum avibus,* and chose as his emblem a peregrine falcon, the king of birds. He grew up in Sicily, and learned from his own experience that the finest peregrines came from Malta (the Maltese falcon is a subspecies of peregrine).

When Malta was given to the Knights of St John in 1530, the only condition attached was an annual rent of two Maltese falcons – one for the Spanish emperor and one for the viceroy of Sicily. Unfortunately, by the 1970s trapping and shooting had reduced these magnificent raptors to just one or two breeding pairs. There are occasional reports of peregrines – known as *bies* in Malti – being seen on the remote southwestern cliffs of Malta and Gozo, but there have been no confirmed sightings since the mid-1980s.

All this, of course, has nothing to do with Dashiell Hammett's famous detective story, *The Maltese Falcon.* If you've read the book you'll know that the eponymous black bird is actually a red herring.

ENVIRONMENTAL ISSUES

The combined pressures of population, land use and development, as well as pollution and the lack of protection of natural areas, have had a significant environmental impact on the islands. There is also a severe shortage of fresh water – the only natural supply comes from ground water, which is increasingly contaminated with nitrate run off from farmland. This has been eased slightly by the construction of several large desalination plants.

Air and noise pollution is caused by dust from uncontrolled building activity, the high concentration of cars, lorries and buses (many of them old) in the congested roads around Grand Harbour, and by discharges from coal-fired power stations and factories; this is contributing to many health problems, including the highest rate of asthma among children in Mediterranean countries. With such a small land area, disposal of rubbish in landfill sites is also increasingly problematic, although the authorities are increasing the number of sites where people can take recyclables.

Newspaper reports indicate that the state of the roads, increasing urbanisation, traffic congestion and low levels of cleanliness in urban areas are the environmental issues generating high levels of dissatisfaction in visitors to Malta (and these concerns are shared by most locals, too). There is recognition that these negatives are playing a part in Malta's declining tourist numbers (letters to the editor are full of the message to 'clean up our act'), but there doesn't seem the push to do much about these issues and the government is showing hardly any initiative. In 2006 the government decided to instead extend Malta's development boundaries, a very unpopular move. During the past few years Malta has witnessed a massive increase in speculative property development, to such an extent that one in every four houses is vacant. This in a country that has a high population density and few green areas. Developers are also busy proposing huge new tourism, residential and/or marina developments in what little countryside that remains (eg Ta'Ċenċ and Ħondoq ir-Rummien on Gozo). In a continued move to lure cashed-up residents and travellers, there are also proposals for golf courses (at Ta'Ċenċ and close to Golden Bay) – crazy in a country that already has a high-standard golf course, but has so little countryside and fresh water. Meanwhile, the country's true assets – its heritage and cultural sites – continue to be neglected.

Recent world events have also highlighted Malta's lack of natural resources. Tensions in the Middle East have led to higher oil prices, and Malta – as elsewhere – has felt the pinch. Oil is needed here to generate power and water (via desalination plants) and utility bills have risen alarmingly. Moreover, the population seems inexplicably attached to its cars (quite baffling in such a tiny country). The government has begun investigating energy options for the future, and is evaluating the possibilities of installing a cable between Malta and a neighbouring country to be able to purchase electricity through the European grid, as well as the installation of a pipeline or gas storage plant in order to introduce gas as another source for the generation of electricity. There is also early talk of wind farms having some potential.

Bird Hunting

One of the favourite Maltese sports is shooting or trapping anything that flies. Bird shooting is still a popular pastime in Malta, and one of the more unpleasant aspects of the islands for many foreign visitors. The shooters will take a potshot at almost anything that flies – from a sparrow to a swift – though the main prey are turtledoves and quail. Shooters' hides can be seen in the quieter corners of the countryside and the crack of shotguns is a common accompaniment to an evening walk in these areas.

With 53 cars per 100 inhabitants, Malta has one of the highest number of cars in the EU on a per-capita basis (and the lowest number of road fatalities), plus the least amount of land on which to drive them.

The Blue Flag (www .blueflag.org) program grants recognition to beaches and marinas worldwide that demonstrate high environmental standards and good sanitary and safety facilities. Malta plans to implement the Blue Flag criteria to its beaches by mid-2008.

Flimkien għal Ambjent Aħjar is a brand-new pressure group, concerned about the threats to Malta's heritage and environment. The name means 'Together for a Better Environment', and the website, www .ambjentahjar.org, details the group's mission and the issues worth fighting for.

Bird netting is also very popular – the rickety little towers of stones and metal poles you see in the Maltese countryside are for supporting the drop-nets and for holding cages containing decoy birds. Greenfinches are a popular prey and you can often see them being bought and sold at the markets in Valletta. Conservative estimates are that around half a million birds are shot or trapped in Malta each year – but we also came across reports that put this number at six million. The truth probably lies in the middle of these extremes, at around three million – a phenomenal amount for such a small country. Most birds are shot or trapped while migrating between Africa and Europe in the spring and autumn.

Laws were introduced in 1980 designating a closed season for shooting and trapping, protecting many bird species (especially migrants), and making shooting and trapping illegal in certain protected areas. They include Ghadira Nature Reserve at Mellieħa Bay, Is-Simar Nature Reserve in Xemxija, Filfla island, Buskett Gardens, the Ta' Qali area and Gozo's Ta' Ċenċ cliffs. However, these laws are regularly flouted and poorly policed (in September 2006, for example, hunters attempted to break into Ghadira, but the intervention of a watchman on duty prevented this).

The closed season for shooting is 22 May to 31 August (the shortest in Europe) – but these dates are routinely ignored by hunters. BirdLife Malta (www.birdlifemalta.org), a large organisation of bird-lovers, is seeking a ban on spring hunting and trapping as well as a stop to hunting at sea, but it faces an uphill battle – the hunters are a large and powerful lobby group (estimated at around 20,000) that has actively opposed government measures to curb their activities by resorting to violence and extreme vandalism. In a country where electoral victories usually involve very small margins, political parties want to keep hunters on side, even going in to bat for them against EU authorities.

EU laws prohibit bird hunting and bird trapping in spring; Malta is the only EU member state that still allows hunting during the spring season, invoking a derogation (exemption of sorts) allowed under the EU's Birds Directive. The derogation permits hunting for just two bird species (turtle-dove and quail) on condition that rigid rules are adhered to. But in order to operate the derogation, Malta has to justify its position every year by sending a report to the commission. The bureaucratic toing and froing between authorities gives some hope to bird-lovers, as the EU is making it increasingly hard for Malta to justify its claims that hunting should continue. There is hope that eventually Malta will step into line with the rest of Europe and bring in bans, but rest assured that hunters will not give in without a fight (and even if bans are introduced, their adherence to them is unlikely). Things could get ugly (well, uglier).

www.birdlifemalta .org is an excellent website belonging to an active organisation of bird-lovers (not shooters) whose main aim is the protection of birds and their habitat.

Fatal Flight: Maltese Obsession with Killing Birds A thought-provoking account by Natalino Fenech of the massacre of millions of migrating birds that takes place each year in Malta.

Diving & Snorkelling

The Maltese Islands – and Gozo in particular – offer some of the best scuba diving in Europe and have many advantages for divers (especially beginners), including a pleasant climate, warm, clear water, a wide range of interesting dive sites (caves, reefs, wartime wrecks) – many of them accessible from the shore – and a large number of dive schools with qualified, professional, multilingual instructors. There are also sites perfect for experienced open-water and cave divers.

Most schools in Malta offer courses that lead to qualifications issued by one or more of the internationally recognised diving bodies – the most common being Professional Association of Diving Instructors (PADI) courses. The websites of these organisations offer general information about diving and dive qualifications, plus details of accredited diving schools in Malta:

British Sub-Aqua Club (BSAC; www.bsac.co.uk)
Confédération Mondiale des Activités Subaquatiques (CMAS; www.cmas.org)
Professional Association of Diving Instructors (PADI; www.padi.com)

The average sea temperature in Malta is above 20°C from June to October. The average temperature in June is 21°C, in August it is 25.5°C, and in October it's 22°C.

DIVING
Requirements

If you want to learn to dive in Malta, there are a few things required of you, not the least of which is the ability to swim. Restrictions on minimum age are at the instructor or operator's discretion, but operators generally advise that 10 years of age is the youngest they will teach; note that those under 18 must have written parental consent. Some dive schools operate 'Bubblemaker' programmes designed to introduce kids aged eight and nine to breathing underwater.

Medical bureaucracy has been relaxed a little in recent times. All persons registering at a dive centre are now required to fill out a self-assessment medical questionnaire to show that they are medically fit to dive. If this questionnaire highlights any medical condition that may restrict your diving practices, you will be requested to have a medical examination, and a physician will determine your fitness. The medical can be organised by the dive school, usually at a cost of around Lm6 to Lm8. You should also heed medical warnings and not fly within 24 hours of your last dive. Your last day in Malta should be spent reacclimatising to sea-level pressures.

Qualified divers wishing to lead their own groups must do so through a licensed dive centre. The instructor will first have to register with a dive centre, presenting an instructor qualification and a current copy of an annual medical examination by a doctor specialising in diving medicine.

SHINING THE SPOTLIGHT ON GOZO

Recent EU funding has been channelled toward promoting diving as a niche tourism market for Gozo. The island will be promoted in the international media as a top diving destination. As well a few practical issues will be addressed, including the setting up of a decompression chamber at Gozo General Hospital (in the past divers had to be airlifted to Malta's main hospital for treatment). To add to the catalogue of dive sites off Gozo's shores, in August 2006 two vessels were scuttled off Xatt l'Aħmar (west of Mġarr) to create an artificial dive-site, landing in a perfect position on the seabed 35m underwater. The location was chosen in part because it is sheltered from the strong prevailing winds that can make popular sites such as Dwejra and Marsalforn inaccessible.

Courses & Qualifications

Most schools offer a 'taster course' or 'beginner's dive', which begins with one or two hours of shore-based instruction on the workings of scuba equipment and safety procedures. You will then be introduced to breathing underwater in a pool or shallow bay and will end up doing a 30-minute dive in the sea. A beginner's course should cost around Lm15 to Lm20.

A so-called 'resort course' gives you shore-based instruction plus four to six open-water dives accompanied by an instructor and costs Lm50 to Lm70. These courses do *not* result in an official qualification.

A course that will give you an entry-level diving qualification (CMAS One-Star Diver, PADI Open Water Diver, BSAC Ocean Diver) should take three to five days and it should cost between Lm130 and Lm150.

For certified divers, guided dives usually cost Lm10 to Lm15 for one dive (including all equipment), but multi-dive packages are a better option, costing around Lm65 to Lm80 for six dives (gear included). Transport to dive sites may be included in these packages, but if you're staying in Malta, boat trips to Gozo or Comino will often be an additional cost (this varies depending on your location).

Unaccompanied diving is possible for those in possession of a minimum qualification of a CMAS two-star or PADI advanced certificate; a six-day dive pack that includes use of cylinder, weight belt and unlimited air fills costs around Lm35.

DIVE SCHOOLS

There are more than 40 dive school operators in Malta. The majority are members of the **Professional Diving Schools Association** (PDSA; www.pdsa.org.mt), an organisation dedicated to promoting high standards of safety and professionalism.

The following dive schools all offer a similarly comprehensive menu of PADI-, BSAC- or CMAS-approved training and education courses, guided diving and the rental of scuba equipment to experienced divers. Some are based at large resorts; many can organise packages covering diving, accommodation and possibly airport transfers and car rental, should you require them.

Note that Nautic Team Diving Centre in Marsalforn, Gozo, specialises in diving for people with disabilities.

Guide to Shore Diving the Maltese Islands, by Peter G Lemon, is a well-researched guide to 36 dive sites, with aerial photographs, good underwater plans and detailed text (but no details of boat dives).

Sliema & St Julian's Area

Aquarrigo Scuba Diving Centre (Map p86; ☎ 2133 0882; www.planetsea.net; Preluna Beach Club, Triq it-Torri, Sliema)

Diveshack (Map p86; ☎ 2133 8558; www.divemalta.com; ix-Xatt Ta'Qui-Si-sana, Qui-Si-sana, Sliema)

Divewise (Map p88; ☎ 2135 6441; www.divewise.com.mt; Westin Dragonara Complex, St Julian's)

Northwest Malta

Buddies Dive Cove (Map p100; ☎ 2157 6266; www.buddiesmalta.com; 24/2 Triq il-Korp Tal-Pijunieri, Buġibba)

Dive Deep Blue (Map p100; ☎ 2158 3946; www.divedeepblue.com; 100 Triq Ananija, Buġibba)

Meldives Dive School (☎ 2152 2595; www.meldives.info; Tunny Net Complex, Mellieħa Bay)

Paradise Diving (☎ 2157 4116; www.paradisediving.com; Paradise Bay Hotel, Ċirkewwa)

Subway Scuba Diving School (Map p100; ☎ 2157 0354; www.subwayscuba.com; Triq il-Korp Tal-Pijunieri, Buġibba)

Gozo

Atlantis Diving Centre (Map p158; ☎ 2156 1826; www.atlantisgozo.com; Atlantis Hotel, Triq il-Qolla, Marsalforn)

Calypso Diving Centre (Map p158; ☎ 2156 1757; www.calypsodivers.com; Triq il-Port, Marsalforn)

Frankie's Gozo Diving Centre (☎ 2155 1315; www.gozodiving.com; Triq Mġarr, Xewkija)

Moby Dives (☎ 2155 1616; www.mobydivesgozo.com; Triq il-Gostra, Xlendi Bay)

Nautic Team Diving Centre (Map p158; ☎ 2155 8507; www.nauticteam.com; cnr Triq il-Munġbell & Triq ir-Rabat, Marsalforn)

St Andrews Divers Cove (☎ 2155 1301; www.gozodive.com; Triq San Ximun, Xlendi)

Comino

Comino Dive Centre (Map p164; ☎ 2157 0354; www.cominodivecentre.com; Comino Hotels, Comino)

Safety

Speedboat and ferry traffic can be quite heavy, especially in peak summer months and in the Gozo Channel area. For their own protection, divers are required to fly the code-A flag or use a surface-marker buoy.

Divers should ensure that their travel insurance policy covers them for diving. Some policies specifically exclude 'dangerous activities', which can include scuba diving.

Malta's public general hospital is **St Luke's Hospital** (Map p84; www.slh.gov.mt; Triq San Luqa, Gwardamanġa), near Pietà (southwest of Valletta), and there is a decompression chamber here. Staff at the hospital can be contacted for any diving incidents requiring medical attention on ☎ 2123 4765 or ☎ 2123 4766. Divers on Gozo have previously been transferred by helicopter to Malta in the case of an emergency, but a decompression chamber should be in operation at Gozo's **General Hospital** (Map p146; ☎ 2156 1600; Triq l-Arċisqof Pietru Pace, Victoria) by the time you read this.

Top Diving & Snorkelling Spots

NORTHWEST MALTA

Ahrax Point (average depth 7m, maximum depth 18m) Caverns and a tunnel opening up to a small inland grotto with good coral growth. Suitable for all levels of diving experience. Shore dive. Can also be viewed by snorkelling.

Anchor Bay (average depth 6m, maximum depth 12m) Not much to see in the bay itself, but around the corner are good caves. Suitable for all levels of diving experience. Shore dive.

Ċirkewwa Arch (average depth 15m, maximum depth 36m) Underwater walls and a magnificent arch, where divers can encounter a variety of fish and sometimes seahorses. Suitable for all levels of diving experience.

Marfa Point (average depth 12m, maximum depth 18m) Large dive site with caves, reefs, promontories and tunnels. Can be accessed from the shore. Decent snorkelling opportunities.

St Paul's Islands (multiple sites, average depths 6m to 12m, maximum depth 25m) Popular dive sites with a wreck between the shore and inner island, a reef on the eastern side of the northernmost island, and a valley between the two islands. Suitable for all levels of diving experience. The wreck can be accessed from the shore.

Tugboat Rozi (average depth 30m, maximum depth 36m) A boat deliberately sunk in 1991 as an underwater diving attraction and now colonised by thousands of fish.

VALLETTA AREA

Carolita Barge (average depth 12m, maximum depth 22m) Possibly mistaken for a submarine, this barge was hit by a torpedo in 1942 and sank immediately. Well preserved and home to groper and octopus. Popular training site for divers and therefore busy. Suitable for all levels of diving experience. Shore dive.

Sidebar notes:

www.visitmalta.com/en/diving has loads of stuff, including safety regulations, marine life, dive operators and an interactive map with the country's best dive sites.

Click on 'Diving sites of the Maltese Islands' at www.locationmalta.com/theme/diving and browse through extensive notes on 34 dive locations on Malta, Comino and Gozo.

Diving Around Gozo is available in English and in German. Author Klaus-Thorsten Tegge details 15 of the best shore dives from Gozo, coupled with good travel information for Gozo-bound travellers. Tegge also has useful information at www.dive-gozo.com.

TOP DIVING & SNORKELLING SPOTS ON MALTA

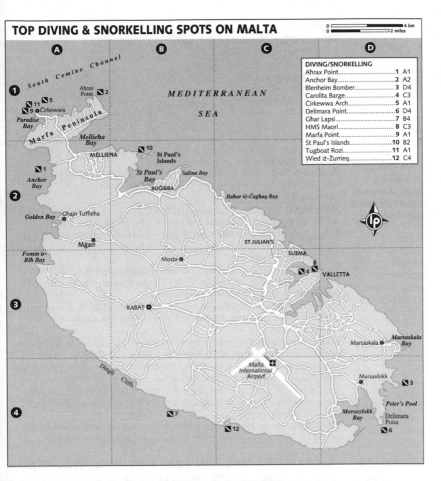

DIVING/SNORKELLING	
Ahrax Point.....................1	A1
Anchor Bay.....................2	A2
Blenheim Bomber...............3	D4
Carolita Barge..................4	C3
Ċirkewwa Arch...................5	A1
Delimara Point..................6	D4
Għar Lapsi.......................7	B4
HMS Maori......................8	C3
Marfa Point.....................9	A1
St Paul's Islands................10	B2
Tugboat Rozi....................11	A1
Wied iż-Żurrieq.................12	C4

HMS Maori (average depth 13m, maximum depth 18m) Below Fort St Elmo is the wreck of the HMS *Maori*, sunk in 1942. Silted up, but home to fish and octopuses. Suitable for all levels of diving experience. Shore dive.

SOUTHEAST MALTA
Blenheim Bomber (average depth 42m, maximum depth 42m) Exciting dive to explore the well-preserved wreck of a WWII bomber, with engine and wings intact. For experienced divers only.

Delimara Point (average depth 12m, maximum depth 25m) Usually excellent visibility for divers, with vertical cliffs and many caverns. Varied and colourful flora and fauna. Suitable for all levels of experience. Shore dive.

Għar Lapsi (average depth 6m, maximum depth 15m) Popular training site for divers. Safe, shallow cave that winds through the headland. Shore dive, reasonable snorkelling and suitable for all levels of experience.

Wied iż-Żurrieq (average depth 9m, maximum depth 30m) Close to the Blue Grotto. Underwater valley and labyrinth of caves. Shore dive, reasonable snorkelling and suitable for all levels of experience.

GOZO

Billinghurst Cave (average depth 20m, maximum depth 35m) Long tunnel leading to a cave deep inside the rock, with a multitude of coloured sea sponges. There's very little natural light (torch required). For experienced divers only.

Blue Hole & Chimney (average depth 20m, maximum depth 45m) The Blue Hole is a natural rock formation and includes a large cave plus a fissure in the near-vertical wall. Popular, busy site. Shore dive, excellent snorkelling and suitable for all levels of experience.

Coral Cave (average depth 25m, maximum depth 30m) Huge semicircular opening with a sandy bottom, where divers can view varied and colourful flora and fauna. Shore dive.

Malta is popular with underwater photographers due to the clarity of its waters. Natural colours can be captured on film without the use of a flash, even at a depth of 10m to 12m.

Crocodile Rock (average depth 35m, maximum depth 45m) Rocky reef between the shore and crocodile-shaped rock off the west coast. Natural amphitheatre and deep fissures. Shore dive, decent snorkelling and suitable for all levels of experience.

Double Arch Reef (average depth 30m, maximum depth 45m) Site characterised by a strange formation, with an arch dividing two large openings in the rock. Prolific marine life. For experienced divers.

Fessej Rock (average depth 30m, maximum depth 50m) A prominent column of rock. Vertical wall dive descending to 50m amid large schools of fish. A very popular deep-water dive.

Fungus Rock (average depth 30m, maximum depth beyond 60m) Dramatic underwater scenery with vertical walls, fissures, caverns and gullies. Good site for underwater photography and suitable for all levels of diving experience.

Reqqa Point (average depth 25m, maximum depth beyond 70m) Near-vertical wall cut by fissures, caves and crevices. Large numbers of small fish, plus groups of amberfish and groper if conditions are favourable. Shore dive and good snorkelling.

San Dimitri Point (average depth 25m, maximum depth beyond 60m) Lots of marine life and exceptional visibility (sometimes exceeding 50m). Good snorkelling and suitable for all levels of experience.

Ta'Ċenċ (average depth 25m, maximum depth 35m) Sheltered bay – access is by 103 steps from car park of nearby hotel. Canyon with large boulders, plus cave. Good marine life, but visibility can occasionally be poor. Good spot for night dives. Shore dive and suitable for all levels of experience.

Wied il-Għasri (average depth in cave 12m, maximum depth 30m) A deep winding cut in the headland makes for a long, gentle dive. May view seahorses in the shallows. Cave with a huge domed vault and walls covered in corals. Can be done as a shore dive. Very good snorkelling and suitable for all levels of experience.

Xatt L'Aħmar (average depth 9m, maximum depth 30m) Small bay, excellent for observing a large variety of fish including mullet, groper, sea bream, octopus and cuttlefish. Shore dive, OK

TOP DIVING & SNORKELLING SPOTS ON GOZO & COMINO

DIVING/SNORKELLING
Billinghurst Cave..................(see 9)
Blue Hole & Chimney...............1 A1
Blue Lagoon.......................2 C2
Coral Cave........................3 A2
Crocodile Rock...................(see 3)
Double Arch Reef..................4 B1
Dwejra...........................5 A1
Fessej Rock.......................6 B2
Fungus Rock.......................7 A2
Lantern Point.....................8 C2
Reqqa Point.......................9 B1
San Dimitri Point................10 A1
Santa Marija Bay.................11 C2
Santa Marija Cave................12 C2
Ta'Ċenċ..........................13 B2
Wied il-Ghasri...................14 A1
Xatt L'Ahmar.....................15 B2
Xlendi Cave & Reef...............16 A2
Xwieni Bay.......................17 B1

RESPONSIBLE DIVING

The popularity of diving is placing immense pressure on many sites – over 40,000 divers a year visit the Maltese Islands. Please consider the following tips when diving and help preserve the ecology and beauty of Malta's underwater world:

- Avoid touching living marine organisms with your body or dragging equipment across the rocks.
- Be conscious of your fins. Even without contact the surge from heavy fin strokes can damage delicate organisms.
- Practise and maintain proper buoyancy control. Make sure you are correctly weighted and that your weight belt is positioned so that you stay horizontal. If you have not dived for a while, have a practice dive in a pool before taking to the sea. Be aware that buoyancy can change over the period of an extended trip: initially you may breathe harder and need more weight; a few days later you may breathe more easily and need less weight.
- Take great care in underwater caves. Spend as little time within them as possible as your air bubbles may be caught within the roof, leaving previously submerged organisms high and dry. Taking turns to inspect the interior of a small cave will lessen the chances of damaging contact.
- Resist the temptation to collect or buy shells or other remains of marine organisms. Aside from the ecological damage, taking home marine souvenirs depletes the beauty of a site and spoils the enjoyment of others. The same goes for marine archaeological sites (mainly shipwrecks). Respect their integrity; some sites are protected from looting by law.
- Ensure that you take home all your rubbish and any litter you may find as well. Plastics in particular are a serious threat to marine life.
- Resist the temptation to feed fish. You may disturb their normal eating habits, encourage aggressive behaviour or feed them food that is detrimental to their health.
- Minimise your disturbance of marine animals. Never ride on the backs of turtles.

snorkelling and suitable for all levels of experience. Two vessels were scuttled here in August 2006 to create an artificial dive-site.

Xlendi Cave & Reef (average depth 6m, maximum depth 25m) Easy cave dive in shallow water and popular with beginners. Brightly coloured cave walls. Rocky headland dips steeply to the sea. An abundance of flora and fauna. Shore dive, OK snorkelling.

COMINO

Blue Lagoon (average depth 6m, maximum depth 12m) Easy site to the north of the sheltered lagoon, very popular with divers and snorkellers, plenty of boat traffic. Shore dive. Suitable for all levels of experience.

Lantern Point (average depth 30m, maximum depth 45m) Very popular dive site. Dramatic dive down a vertical wall. Rich fauna and an abundance of colour. OK snorkelling.

Santa Marija Cave (average depth 7m, maximum depth 10m) Large cave and cavern system, and one of the most popular sites for cave dives. An abundance of fish in the area. Very good snorkelling and suitable for all levels of experience.

SNORKELLING

If you don't fancy scuba diving, you can still sample the delights of the underwater world by donning mask, snorkel and fins and exploring the rocks and bays around Malta's coastline. The only qualification necessary is the ability to swim. You can usually rent or buy the necessary equipment from hotels, lidos (recreational facilities with a swimming pool) and watersport centres in all the tourist areas.

Top snorkelling spots are off Comino and Gozo and include the **Blue Lagoon** and the crags and caves east of **Santa Marija Bay** on Comino; the cave-riddled coastline at **Dwejra**; the long, narrow inlet at **Wied il-Għasri** off Gozo; and along the salt pan rocks west of **Xwieni Bay** near Marsalforn on Gozo.

MALTA'S MARINE LIFE

Malta's location in the narrows between Sicily and North Africa, far away from the pollution of major cities and silt-bearing rivers, means that its marine life is richer than in many other parts of the Mediterranean.

Dive Sites of Malta, Gozo & Comino by Lawson and Leslie Wood is a comprehensive guide with details on marine life, plus a very helpful star-rating system grading the diving and snorkelling at each of the 80-odd sites reviewed.

Invertebrates such as brightly coloured bryozoans, cup corals, sea anemones, sponges, starfish and sea urchins encrust the underwater cliffs and caves around the shores of Malta and Gozo. The countless nooks and crannies in the limestone provide shelter for crabs, lobsters, common octopuses and white-spotted octopuses. By night, cuttlefish graze the algal beds below the cliffs.

Most divers who visit Malta hope to catch sight of a seahorse. The maned seahorse is fairly common around the Maltese coast, preferring shallow, brackish water. They grow up to 15cm in length and feed on plankton and tiny shrimps. They mate for life and display an unusual inversion of common male and female reproductive roles. Using her tube-like ovipositor, the female deposits her eggs in a brood pouch in the male's abdomen where they are fertilised. Here the eggs develop and finally hatch before the male 'gives birth' by releasing the live brood into open water.

Migratory shoals of sardine, sprat, bluefin tuna, bonito, mackerel and dolphin fish – known in Malti as *lampuka*, and a local delicacy – pass through the offshore waters in late summer and autumn. Swordfish are fairly common all year round. Sea bream, sea bass, groper, red mullet, wrasse, dogfish and stingray frequent the shallower waters closer to shore, where moray and conger eels hide among the rocks and venture out at night to feed on octopus and fish.

The seas around Malta are known among shark-watchers as one of the 'sharkiest' spots in the Med. In April 1987 a great white shark caught by local fisherman Alfredo Cutajar off Filfla was claimed to be a world record at 7.13m in overall length. However, later investigations brought the accuracy of the original measurements into doubt (still, be it 7m or 7.13m, it's still *big*!). Photographs of the shark – including some of Alfredo with his head in the (dead!) shark's mouth – can be bought in souvenir shops at Wied iż-Żurrieq (p141).

Other shark species known to haunt Maltese waters include the blue, thresher and mako. However, bathers and divers should not be unduly alarmed. Shark sightings in inshore waters are extremely rare. Indeed, the great white is considered to be an endangered species, and the decrease in its numbers is thought to have resulted from dwindling stocks of tuna, its main food source.

The loggerhead turtle is another endangered species that is occasionally sighted in Maltese waters, but the lack of secluded, sandy beaches means that they do not nest on the Maltese Islands. The common dolphin – known as *denfil* in Malti – and the bottlenose dolphin are fairly common in Maltese waters and are occasionally seen from cruise boats and dive boats.

Food & Drink

Like Malti, Maltese cuisine is influenced by the many foreign cultures that have ruled the country in its long history. The food is rustic and meals are generally based on seasonal produce and the fisherman's catch.

Malta is not known as a destination for gourmets, but the food is generally good and cheap. The most obvious influence is Sicilian, and most cheaper restaurants serve pasta and pizza; there are also upscale places serving more creative Italian specialities. English standards (eg grilled chops, roast with three veg) are also commonly available, particularly in tourist areas. If you tire of the meat-fish-pasta-pizza menus, you'll also find Chinese restaurants, a few Indian eateries and an increasing number of Japanese and Thai places.

Food-lovers, don't eat out without the *Definitive(ly) Good Guide to Restaurants in Malta & Gozo*. It's updated annually and includes reviews of 150 of Malta's best restaurants. Available from most major bookshops (Lm4); information is also online at www .restaurantsmalta.com.

STAPLES & SPECIALITIES
Snacks

Ġbejniet You'll either love or hate this small, hard, white cheese traditionally made from unpasteurised sheep's or goat's milk. They are dried in baskets and often steeped in olive oil flavoured with salt and crushed black peppercorns.

Ħobż Freshly baked Maltese bread is delicious. It is made in a similar manner to sourdough bread, using a scrap of yesterday's dough to leaven today's loaves.

Ħobż biż-żejt This is another traditional snack – slices of bread rubbed with ripe tomatoes and olive oil until they are pink and delicious, then topped with a mix of tuna, onion, capers, olives, garlic, black pepper and salt.

Ftira Bread baked in a flat disc and traditionally stuffed with a mixture of tomatoes, olives, capers and anchovies.

Pastizza (plural *pastizzi*) The traditional Maltese snack is the *pastizza*, a small parcel of flaky pastry filled with either ricotta cheese or mushy peas. A couple of *pastizzi* make for a tasty – if somewhat high-fat – breakfast or afternoon filler. You'll probably pay around Lm0.10 for one, so they're also great for budget travellers. They're available in most bars or from special takeaway *pastizzerija* (usually hole-in-the-wall places in villages – follow your nose).

FINE FOOD VENUES IN MALTA

We've enjoyed some fabulous meals in Malta (and quite a few uninspiring ones). Here are our restaurant picks for top nosh.

Ambrosia (Valletta, p69) Offers a warm welcome and top use of fresh local produce.

Bed (St Julian's, p92) Playful Portomaso option, with nightclub-esque décor and (surprisingly) a Korean menu.

Fusion Four (Valletta, p69) A hidden gem in the capital, big on innovative fusion flavours.

Ir-Rizzu (Marsaxlokk, p138) Fabulously fresh seafood, straight off the local fishing boats.

It-Tmun Victoria (Gozo, p150) Stylish Gozitan option wooing locals and visitors with creative choices.

Kitchen (Sliema, p92) Award-winning chef presides over a modern menu.

Restaurant Ta' Frenċ (outside Marsalforn, Gozo, p160) Voted Malta's best restaurant, deserving the high praise.

Tal-Familja (Marsaskala, p140) Generous portions, friendly service and a huge menu of traditional Maltese dishes.

Zest (St Julian's, p93) Funky décor and an inspiring menu of treats from East and West.

If you're keeping it casual, you can't go past:

Avenue (Paceville, p93) A cheap-and-cheerful crowd-pleaser.

Café Jubilee (Valletta, Gzira, p69; Victoria, p94; Gozo, p150) Old-world décor, cosy nooks and a budget-friendly menu of easy edibles.

Il Gattopardo (Mdina, p127) A gorgeous Mdina setting and interesting Greek-inspired fare.

Mill Room (Victoria, Gozo, p150) A quirky laneway find for lunch in Victoria.

Ta'Rikardu (Victoria, Gozo, p149) Perfect platters of farm-fresh local produce in the picturesque Il-Kastell.

Trabuxu (Valletta, p69) Perfect spot in the capital for vino and colourfully presented platters.

Soups

Aljotta A delicious fish broth made with tomato, rice and lots of garlic.
Kusksu Soup made from broad beans and small pasta shapes, often served with a soft fresh *ġbejniet* floating in the middle.
Minestra A thick soup of tomatoes, beans, pasta and vegetables, similar to Italian minestrone.
Soppa tal-armla The so-called 'widow's soup' (possibly named because of its inexpensive ingredients) is traditionally made only with components that are either green or white. Basically a vegetable soup, it contains cauliflower, spinach, endive and peas, poured over a poached egg, a *ġbejniet* and a lump of ricotta cheese.

www.aboutmalta.com/FOOD_and_DRINK (case-sensitive address) gives links to topics in the Food and Drink category, from a site purely about Kinnie soft drink to recipes for octopus.

Main Dishes

Braġioli These are prepared by wrapping a thin slice of beef around a stuffing of breadcrumbs, chopped bacon, hard-boiled egg and parsley, then braising these 'beef olives' in a red wine sauce.
Fenek *Fenek* (rabbit) is *the* favourite Maltese dish, whether fried in olive oil, roasted, stewed, served with spaghetti or baked in a pie (*fenek bit-tewm u l-inbid* is rabbit cooked in garlic and wine, *fenek moqli* is fried rabbit, *stuffat tal-fenek* is stewed rabbit). See Celebrations, opposite
Kapunata A Maltese version of ratatouille made from tomatoes, capers, eggplant and green peppers – it goes well with grilled fish.
Qarabali Baby marrows – particularly good baked, stuffed with minced beef and parsley, or made into a creamy soup.
Ravjul/ravjuletti Maltese variety of ravioli (pasta pouches filled with ricotta, parmesan and parsley).
Timpana A rich pie filled with macaroni, cheese, egg, minced beef, tomato, garlic and onion, *timpana* is a Sicilian dish not dissimilar to Greek *pastitsio*.
Torta tal-lampuki The local fish speciality is *torta tal-lampuki*, or *lampuki* pie. *Lampuka (Coryphaena hippurus)* – plural *lampuki* – is known in English as dolphin fish, dorado or *mahi-mahi*. It is delicious simply fried in olive oil, but the traditional way to prepare it is to bake it in a pie with tomatoes, onions, black olives, spinach, sultanas and walnuts. *Lampuki biz-zalza pikkanti* is *lampuki* in a piquant sauce.

UK-based bespoke tour company Tabona & Walford (www.tabonaandwalford.com) offers a week-long tour of Malta that combines cooking with walking and sightseeing.

Sweets

Kannoli Believed to have originated in Sicily, *kannoli* is a tube of crispy, fried pastry filled with ricotta and sometimes sweetened with chocolate chips or candied fruit.
Mqaret Diamond-shaped pastries stuffed with chopped, spiced dates and deep-fried.
Qubbajt Maltese nougat, flavoured with almonds or hazelnuts and traditionally sold on festa (feast) days.
Qagħħ tal-għasel Honey or treacle rings made from a light pastry, served in small pieces as an after-dinner accompaniment to coffee.

25 Years in a Maltese Kitchen is a glossy hardcover book that will whet your appetite for Maltese specialities. It's by Pippa Mattei and contains easy-to-follow recipes from *aljotta* (traditional fish soup) to stuffed zucchini.

DRINKS
Nonalcoholic Drinks

Good Italian coffee – espresso and cappuccino – is widely available in cafés and bars, and in the main tourist areas you'll find a cup of strong British tea, heavy on the milk and sugar.

Cold soft drinks are available everywhere. Kinnie – its advertising signs are all over the place in Malta – is the brand name of a local soft drink flavoured with bitter oranges and aromatic herbs. It slips down nicely when mixed with rum or vodka.

Alcoholic Drinks

Maltese bars serve up every kind of drink you could ask for, from pints of British beer to shots of Galliano liqueur. The good locally made beers, Cisk Lager and Hopleaf Ale, are cheaper than imported brews.

The main players on the local wine scene are **Camilleri Wines** (www.camilleriwines.com), **Emmanuel Delicata** (www.delicata.com), **Marsovin** (www.marsovin.com) and **Meridiana**

THE TASTE FOR THE GRAPE

When Malta joined the EU in 2004, it said goodbye to government levies charged on sales of foreign wine. Wine became cheaper, sales grew (by an estimated 25%), and wine bars started popping up all over the country. Some of these wine bars are simply cafés that have added 'wine bar' to their name and a few bottles to their menus, while other places have embraced the culture surrounding wine-drinking and gone the whole hog, with lengthy lists of imported and locally produced drops, available by the glass or bottle. Some newly opened restaurants have made a feature of an attached bar. And it seems no wine bar is complete without a menu of platters – local nibble-worthy produce such as sausage, olives, cheese and sundried tomatoes feature prominently. You'll no doubt find a favourite of your own, but recommended options include Trabuxu (p69) in Valletta, Del Borgo and Il-Forn (p79) in Vittoriosa, The Bar at Balluta Bay in Sliema (p94), Gigi's Concept Café (p93) on Spinola Bay in St Julian's, Portovino (p92) in the Portomaso Complex and Grapes Wine Bar (p150) in Gozo's Victoria. These all make a good alternative to English- or Irish-styled pubs or noisy Paceville nightclubs, and are frequented by a mature crowd as well as young local hipsters.

(www.meridiana.com.mt). These companies make wine from local grapes and also produce more expensive 'special reserve' wines – merlot, cabernet sauvignon, chardonnay and sauvignon blanc – using imported grapes from Italy. The result can be surprisingly good and the quality is improving all the time.

Maltese liqueurs pack a punch and make good souvenirs. Look out for Zeppi's liqueurs concocted from local honey, aniseed or prickly pear. Gozo-produced *limunċell* (a variant on the lemon-flavoured Italian *limoncello*) is delicious and there are orange and mandarin variants too.

CELEBRATIONS

A *fenkata* is a big, communal meal of rabbit, usually eaten in the country-side. It supposedly originated as a gesture of rebellion against the occupying Knights, who hunted rabbits and denied them to the local population. The most important *fenkata* is associated with the L-Imnarja harvest festival at the end of June, when hundreds of people gather at Buskett Gardens to eat rabbit, drink wine, sing folk songs and dance all night (see p131). *Fenkata* is also eaten on special occasions, with family and friends taking over a country restaurant for an afternoon of celebration. A number of village bars and small restaurants specialise in preparing a *fenkata* for large parties of merrymakers – these places are mainly concentrated in the off-the-tourist-track areas in northern Malta (in the village of Baħrija for example). Your hotel or a friendly local could also recommend a favourite; see also the review for Bobbyland Restaurant (p130), Il-Barri (p116) and Valletta's Rubino (p69).

WHERE TO EAT & DRINK

Many travellers to Malta opt for packages that include breakfast and dinner at their hotel. This is a pity, as it means they don't get the chance to experience some of the great dining establishments in Malta, don't sample the local specialities or enjoy the views from scenically situated eateries, and never get the chance to chow down on rabbit with the locals. We recommend you opt only for a bed and breakfast arrangement and get out and travel your tastebuds in Malta. That said, many of Malta's finest restaurants are actually inside the four- and five-star hotels – and these are all open to the public.

Restaurants

Restaurants usually open for lunch between noon and 3pm, and for dinner between 7pm and 11pm. Many fine-dining restaurants open only in the

The Food & Cookery of Malta by Anne and Helen Caruana Galizia is the definitive guide to Maltese cuisine, packed with recipes and information on local ingredients.

OVERCHARGING

Beware the scourge of overcharging! A growing number of upmarket restaurants have introduced an odious 'cover charge' of between Lm0.50 and Lm1 per person – somewhat acceptable if it means that bread and the like are free with your meal, but a rather cheeky way of making money if not. And some places don't even advertise on the menu that they charge diners such a fee – it just appears on the bill.

Overcharging tourists appears to be a nasty habit in some restaurants that have no written menu. The idea of preparing meals based on whatever's fresh at the market is a good one when done well, and a few places in Valletta offer this. However, wherever you travel, it's always a good idea to beware of places that overcharge non-locals, who can't really argue because prices are not written anywhere. Our advice is to always ask prices upfront. The same advice applies when buying from kiosks that don't display their prices – and don't be afraid to walk away if the price seems high. And double-check your change from such establishments (learned from experience!).

---

evening; conversely, some of Valletta's best eateries open only for lunch. Many restaurants open only six days a week, but days of closure vary (Sunday and Monday are popular – call ahead to find out if a place is open).

Cafés
Cafés are usually open all day. Some such as Café Jubilee in Valletta (p69), Gżira (p94) and Victoria (p150) and Café Juliani (p94) and neighbouring Gigi's Concept Café (p94) in St Julian's, morph from daytime café to night-time café-bar, staying open till after midnight, serving alcohol and snacks.

Breathe easier – in 2004 Maltese authorities introduced a ban on smoking in all enclosed public places, including restaurants and bars.

Quick Eats
Look out for hole-in-the-wall *pastizzerijas* selling authentic *pastizzi* and other pastries – two central ones are on Triq San Pawl in Valletta (p70). Also try decent snacks from the many kiosks at Valetta's City Gate bus terminus.

VEGETARIANS & VEGANS
Vegetarians are reasonably well catered for, vegans less so. Some restaurants offer meat-free dishes as main courses, and most offer vegetarian pizza and pasta options (these usually include egg and/or dairy ingredients). Seafood eaters will have greater options. Alternatively, vegetarians and vegans can make a beeline for the local Chinese or Indian restaurant for a greater selection of dishes. It's best to steer clear of off-the-beaten-track village restaurants that specialise in rabbit – the menu will most likely also feature lamb, beef and quite possibly horse, and you'll go away hungry and disheartened.

Mona's just the kind of in-the-know local we'd want pointing us in the right gastronomical direction. Check out her spot-on restaurant reviews at www.planet mona.com before making dinner plans.

EATING WITH KIDS
Like most Mediterranean cultures, the Maltese love children. (See p170 for more information on visiting Malta with children.) Generally speaking, babies and children are made welcome almost everywhere in the world of eating out, the exception to this may be upmarket establishments such as the Carriage (p69) in Valletta or Zest (p93) and Barracuda (p92) in St Julian's. But then you'll encounter somewhere like the elegant Ta'Frenċ) outside Marsalforn on Gozo that welcomes babies and children and even offers a children's menu. Many restaurants offer highchairs and perhaps a kids' menu, or at least dishes that will appeal to kids (pasta, pizza etc). If in doubt, it pays to call ahead.

The most child-friendly restaurants include the Avenue (p93) in Paceville, Piccolo Padre and Paparazzi in St Julian's (p93) and Tal-Familja (p140) in Marsaskala.

Valletta

Few places can lay claim to the title of Europe's tiniest capital (well, maybe Liechtenstein's Vaduz, but let's not trifle with details here). Valletta is Malta's Lilliputian capital, measuring all of 600m by 1000m – you won't wear out too much shoe leather seeing the sights of the city, but you will come to appreciate its sheer compactness and the ease of exploring. You may also come to love its history-filled streets, squares and alleys, sometimes dilapidated but always charming, and its idiosyncratic quirks – a colourful row of overhanging first-floor balconies, a hulking bastion as a reminder of a turbulent past, a collection of bright yellow and orange buses, a shopfront that could be a relic of 1930s Britain.

When Valletta was built by the Knights of St John in the 16th and 17th centuries, its founder decreed that it should be 'a city built by gentlemen for gentlemen', and it retains much of its elegance to this day. But that's not the capital's only quote-worthy quote: when Unesco has named Valletta a World Heritage site, it described it as 'one of the most concentrated historic areas in the world', and who are we to disagree?

Still, when you tire of all the history in and around Valletta, there are the treats you'd expect of most European capitals, albeit on a teensy scale (this capital has a population of only 7000). Good restaurants, bars and theatre can be enjoyed here, but don't expect Valletta to be buzzing all night – it's far too small for that sort of action, but that's a large part of its charm.

HIGHLIGHTS

- Exploring the nooks and crannies of **Valletta**, admiring the monuments and soaking up the history

- Checking out the view that puts the grand in Grand Harbour, from the **Upper Barrakka Gardens** (p66)

- Treading lightly on the magnificent marble floor of **St John's Co-Cathedral** (p60)

- Admiring the womanly curves of the 'fat ladies' at the **National Museum of Archaeology** (p62)

- Asking the unanswerable questions (who? why? how?) at the remarkable **Hypogeum** (p80) – book ahead!

- Exploring Vittoriosa's charming **Il Collachio** (p78), followed by a cruise of **Grand Harbour** (p77) in a *dgħajsa* (traditional oar-powered boat)

VALLETTA

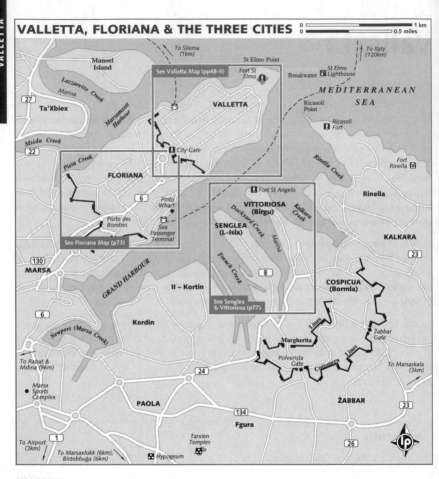

VALLETTA, FLORIANA & THE THREE CITIES

HISTORY

Before the Great Siege of 1565, the Sceberras Peninsula was uninhabited and unfortified, except for Fort St Elmo at its furthest point. Fearing another attack on Malta by the Turks, Grand Master la Valette (of the Knights of St John) began the task of financing and building new fortifications and a new city on what was then just a barren limestone ridge.

The foundation stone of Valletta was laid on 28 March 1566. Around 8000 slaves and artisans toiled on the slopes of Sceberras, levelling the summit, cutting a drainage system into the bedrock and laying out a regular grid of streets – Valletta was to be the first planned city in Europe, with buildings tall enough to shade the streets from the hot sun, and straight streets to allow cooling sea breezes to circulate. A great ditch – 18m deep, 20m wide and nearly 1km long – was cut across the peninsula to protect the landward approach, and massive curtain walls and bastions were raised around the perimeter of the city.

Spurred on by the fear of a Turkish assault, the Knights completed the fortifications in only five years. With the defences in place, the new city was bestowed with churches, palaces, residential streets and, of course, a hospital.

Valletta was considered a masterpiece of architecture and town planning and today it remains one of Europe's finest and most distinctive cityscapes.

The threat of a Turkish attack in 1634 prompted Grand Master Antoine de Paule to begin the construction of a second line of landward defences, the Notre Dame Ditch, about 1km southwest of Valletta's Great Ditch. These were designed by the Italian engineer Pietro Paolo Floriani, who gave his name to the town (Floriana) that grew up within these walls in the 18th century.

ORIENTATION

Valletta and its suburb, Floriana, occupy the long finger of the Sceberras Peninsula that divides Grand Harbour to the south from Marsamxett Harbour to the north. City Gate bus terminus (Malta's main bus station) lies between the two towns.

Valletta is barely a kilometre long and 600m wide, with a regular grid of narrow streets confined within its massive medieval fortifications. The main street, Triq ir-Repubblika (Republic St), runs in a straight line northeast from City Gate (adjacent to City Gate bus terminus) to Fort St Elmo, passing through Misraħ l-Assedju l-Kbir (Great Siege Sq), Misrah ir-Repubblika (Republic Sq) and Pjazza San Ġorġ (St George's Sq).

Two other major streets run parallel to Repubblika – Triq il-Merkanti (Merchants' St) two blocks to the southeast, and Triq l Ifran (Old Bakery St) two blocks to the northwest. Triq ir-Repubblika and Triq il-Merkanti roughly follow the spine of the peninsula, and side streets fall steeply downhill on either side. The main sights, St John's Co-Cathedral and the Grand Master's Palace, are on Triq ir-Repubblika within 500m of City Gate.

Street signs in Valletta are in both Malti and English. Note that houses are numbered in sequence along one side of the street, and then back in the opposite direction along the other side, which means that No 20 can sometimes be across the street from No 200.

Maps

Most maps of the Maltese Islands include an inset street plan of Valletta. Half a dozen different tourist maps of Valletta can be bought cheaply from the souvenir shops and bookshops on Triq ir-Repubblika. You can pick up free street maps of Valletta and Floriana at the tourist information office, as well as free brochures detailing walking tours of Valletta, Floriana and the Three Cities.

INFORMATION
Bookshops

Most major attractions also have a shop selling a range of Malta books, maps and souvenirs.

Agenda (☎ 2125 2117; Embassy Complex, Triq Santa Luċija)

Aquilina (☎ 2123 3774; www.maltabook.com; 58 Triq ir-Repubblika) A very good selection of history books, travel guides, reference and fiction; most are available to buy online.

Newsstand (Triq il-Merkanti) A wide range of British, German and Italian newspapers and magazines is available from this hole-in-the-wall place near the Auberge d'Italie.

Sapienzas (☎ 2123 3621; 26 Triq ir-Repubblika) Another excellent selection of history books, travel guides, reference and fiction.

Cultural Centres

Valletta and the surrounding area house a number of cultural centres, which offer exhibitions, lectures, language courses and cultural events.

THE FOUNDER OF VALLETTA

Jean Parisot de la Valette (1494–1568) was a French nobleman from Provence. He joined the Order of St John at the age of 20 and served it faithfully for the rest of his life, holding the title of Grand Master from 1557 until his death. He was a hardened fighter who had been captured by Barbary pirates in 1541 and spent a year as a galley slave and was a natural leader whose greatest achievement was the defence of Malta against the Turks in the Great Siege of 1565.

In the aftermath of the Great Siege, la Valette immediately set about the fortification of the Sceberras Peninsula and the construction of a new city. Three years later, with the streets of Valletta already laid out, he suffered a stroke and died in August 1568 at the age of 73. His tomb in the crypt of St John's Co-Cathedral bears a Latin inscription which translates as: 'Here lies Valette, worthy of eternal honour. He who was once the scourge of Africa and Asia, and the shield of Europe, whence he expelled the barbarians by his holy arms, is the first to be buried in this beloved city, whose founder he was.'

VALLETTA

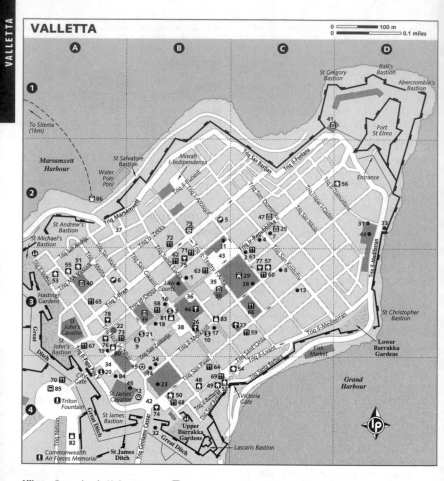

VALLETTA

Alliance Française de Malte (Map p73; ☎ 2123
8456; http://site.voila.fr/alliancefr.mt; 108 Triq San Tumas,
Floriana)
British Council (☎ 2122 6377; www.britishcouncil
.org/malta; Exchange Buildings, Triq ir- Repubblika,
Valletta)
German-Maltese Circle (☎ 2124 6967; www
.germanmaltesecircle.org; Messina Palace; 141 Triq San
Kristofru, Valletta)
Italian Cultural Institute (☎ 2122 1462; www
.iicmalta.org; Pjazza San Ġorġ, Valletta)
Russian Centre for Science & Culture (☎ 2122
2030; 36 Triq il-Merkanti, Valletta)

Emergency
Malta Police headquarters (Map p73; ☎ 2294 2190;
Pjazza San Kalcidonju, Floriana)

Police station (☎ 2122 5495; Triq Nofs in-Nhar,
Valletta) Opposite the site of the old Opera House.

Internet Access
Ziffa (☎ 2123 4007; www.ziffa.net; 194 Triq id-Dejqa;
per hr Lm1; ☼ 9am-11pm Mon-Sat, 9am-10pm Sun)
Plenty of computers, fast internet access and good rates for
overseas phone calls.

Medical Services
Royal Pharmacy (☎ 2125 2396; 271 Triq ir-Repubblika)
Central pharmacy open during shopping hours.

Money
There are plenty of places to change money
and cash travellers cheques on and near Triq
ir-Repubblika in Valletta.

Bank of Valletta (cnr Triq ir-Repubblika & Triq San Ġwann; 8.30am-2pm Mon-Thu, 8.30am-3.30pm Fri, 8.30am-12.30pm Sat) Foreign exchange machine and ATMs.

HSBC (15 Triq ir-Repubblika & 32 Triq il-Merkanti) Foreign exchange machine and ATMs.

Travelex (20 Triq ir-Repubblika; 8.30am-1pm & 2-5.30pm Mon-Fri, 9am-1pm Sat) Currency exchange bureau.

Post
Main Post Office (Pjazza Kastilja; 8.15am-3.45pm Mon-Fri, 8.15am-12.30pm Sat) Found under the St James' Cavalier, opposite the Auberge de Castille.

Tourist Information
Heritage Malta (2295 4000; www.heritagemalta .org; Old University Buildings, Triq il-Merkanti) Head office of the organisation entrusted with managing the national museums and heritage sites of the Maltese Islands. The

office distributes information on sites under their management and hosts occasional art exhibits.

Tourist Information Branch (2369 6073; Malta International Airport, arrivals hall; 10am-9pm)

Tourist Information Office (2123 7747; Misraħ il-Ħelsien; 8.30am-6pm Mon-Sat, 8.30am-2pm Sun, closed public holidays) In the City Arcade, immediately on the right as you enter Valletta through City Gate.

Travel Agencies
National Student Travel Service (NSTS; 2558 8000; www.nsts.org; 220 Triq San Pawl) Specialises in student and youth travel; can arrange budget holiday packages, water-sports facilities and English-language courses (for more information see p166).

SMS Travel & Tourism (2123 2211; www.sms travel.net; 311 Triq ir-Repubblika) A good general agency, offering excursions, guided tours, currency exchange and plane and ferry tickets.

VALLETTA

VALLETTA STREET NAMES

It's helpful to know the names of Valletta's main streets in both Malti and English, as many maps feature only one language or the other, and many businesses advertise in English and use the English street name.

Triq id-Dejqa	Strait St	Triq Melita	Melita St
Triq il-Merkanti	Merchants' St	Triq Nofs in-Nhar	South St
Triq ir-Repubblika	Republic St	Triq San Ġwann	St John's St
Triq it-Teatru l-Antik	Old Theatre St	Triq San Pawl	St Paul's St
Triq iz-Zekka	Old Mint St	Triq San Zakkarija	St Zachary's St
Triq l'Arċisqof	Archbishop St	Triq Sant'Orsla	St Ursula's St
Triq l-Ifran	Old Bakery St	Triq Santa Luċija	St Lucija's St

SIGHTS
St John's Co-Cathedral

Malta's most impressive church, **St John's Co-Cathedral** (☎ 2122 0536; Triq ir-Repubblika; adult/child Lm1.50/free; ⏰ 9.30am-4.30pm Mon-Fri, 9.30am-12.30pm Sat, last admission 30 min before closing, closed Sun, public holidays & during services) was designed by the architect Gerolamo Cassar and built between 1573 and 1578 as the conventual church of the Knights of St John. It took over from the Church of St Lawrence in Vittoriosa as the place where the Knights would gather for communal worship. It was raised to a status equal to that of St Paul's Cathedral in Mdina – the official seat of the Archbishop of Malta – by a papal decree of 1816, hence the term 'co-cathedral'.

The façade is rather plain, and framed by twin bell-towers – a feature that has been copied by almost every church in Malta – but the interior is a colourful treasure house of Maltese baroque. The nave is long and low and every wall, pillar and rib is encrusted with rich ornamentation, giving the effect of a dusty gold brocade – the Maltese Cross and the arms of the Order (a white cross on a scarlet background) can be seen everywhere. The floor is a vast patchwork quilt of colourful marble tomb slabs in black, white, blue, red, pink and yellow, and the vault is covered in paintings by Mattia Preti (see the boxed text, p37) illustrating events from the life of St John the Baptist. The altar is dominated by a huge marble sculpture of the baptism of Christ, with a painting, *St John in Heaven*, by Preti above it.

There are six bays on either side of the nave, eight of which contain chapels allocated to the various langues (or divisions, based on nationality) of the Order of St John and dedicated to the patron saint of the particular langue. The first bay you'll encounter upon entering and walking to your right is the **Chapel of Germany**.

Opposite is the **Chapel of Castille & Portugal**, with monuments to Grand Masters Antonio Manoel de Vilhena and Manuel Pinto de Fonseca. This is followed by the **Chapel of Aragon**, the most splendid in the cathedral. The tombs of the brothers – and consecutive Grand Masters – Rafael and Nicolas Cotoner compete for the title of most extravagant sculpture.

The last bay in this aisle, past the **Chapel of Auvergne**, contains the **Chapel of the Blessed Sacrament** (also known as the Chapel dedicated to the Madonna of Carafa), closed off by a pair of solid silver gates. It contains a 15th-century crucifix from Rhodes and keys of captured Turkish fortresses.

Opposite is the dark and moody **Chapel of Provence**, containing the tombs of Grand Masters Antoine de Paule and Jean Lascaris Castellar. The steps at the back lead down to the cathedral **crypt** (usually closed to the public), where the first 12 Grand Masters of Malta – from 1523 to 1623 – are interred. The reclining effigies include Jean Parisot de la Valette, hero of the Great Siege and the founder of Valletta, and his English secretary Sir Oliver Starkey, the only man below the rank of Grand Master to be honoured with a tomb in the crypt. Darker still is the **Chapel of the Holy Relics** (also known as the Chapel of the Anglo-Bavarian Langue), which contains a wooden figure of St John that is said to have come from the galley in which the Knights departed from Rhodes in 1523.

The austere **Chapel of France**, with a Preti altarpiece of St Paul, was stripped of its baroque decoration in the 1840s. Preti's painting,

The Mystic Marriage of St Catherine, hangs in the **Chapel of Italy**, looking down on a bust of Grand Master Gregorio Carafa.

Visitors to the cathedral should note that they are requested to dress appropriately for a house of worship – shawls can be provided at the ticket office. Stiletto heels are not permitted, to protect the marble floor. Flash photography is also banned.

CATHEDRAL MUSEUM

The first bay in the south aisle of St John's gives access to the **Cathedral Museum** (☎ 2122 0536; admission included in cathedral ticket price; ⏰ 9.30am-4.30pm Mon-Fri, 9.30am-12.30pm Sat, last admission 30 min before closing, closed Sun, public holidays & during services). The first room is the Oratory, built in 1603 as a place of worship and for the instruction of novices. It is dominated by the altarpiece the *Beheading of St John the Baptist* (c 1608) by Caravaggio, one of the artist's most famous and accomplished paintings. The executioner – reaching for a knife to finish off the job that his sword began – and the horrified Salome with her platter are depicted with chilling realism. On the east wall hangs *St Jerome,* another of Caravaggio's masterpieces.

The rest of the museum houses collections of vestments, 16th-century choral books and a collection of Flemish tapestries depicting Bible scenes and religious allegories. The tapestries were based on drawings by Rubens, and were commissioned by Grand Master Ramon de Perellos, whose escutcheon appears on each panel.

Grand Master's Palace

The 16th-century **Grand Master's Palace** (Pjazza San Ġorġ, visitor entrance on Triq il-Merkanti), once the residence of the Grand Masters of the Knights of St John, is today the seat of Malta's parliament and the official residence of the Maltese president.

There are two VIP entrances on Pjazza San Ġorġ, but these are not for general public admission. The right-hand arch leads to **Prince Alfred's Courtyard**, where two stone lions guard a doorway leading to the Great Hall (now occupied by Malta's parliamentary House of Representatives) and a clock tower built in 1745 marks the hours with bronze figures of Moorish slaves striking gongs. The left-hand arch leads into **Neptune's Courtyard**, named for the 17th-century bronze statue of the sea-god that stands there.

From the public entry on Triq il-Merkanti it is possible to visit the **Armoury** (☎ 2124 9349; adult/child Lm2/0.50; ⏰ 9am-5pm) and the **State Apartments** (☎ 2124 9349; adult/child Lm2/0.50; ⏰ 10am-4pm Fri-Wed); note that the State Apartments are closed from time to time when official state visits are taking place.

Heritage Malta conducts guided tours (included in the cost of admission) of the Armoury and the apartments at 10.30am, 12.30pm and 2.30pm daily; tours and times are not set in stone, so it may be worth making advance enquiries.

The **Armoury** is now housed in what was once the Grand Master's stables. The armour and weapons belonging to the Knights were

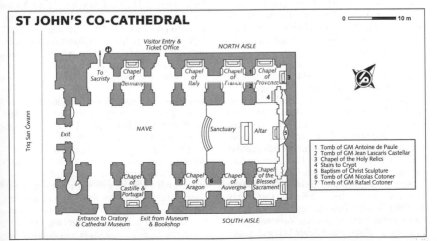

ST JOHN'S CO-CATHEDRAL

0 ———— 10 m

Triq San Ġwann

Visitor Entry & Ticket Office

NORTH AISLE

To Sacristy

Chapel of Germany

Chapel of Italy

Chapel of France

Chapel of Provence

Exit

NAVE

Sanctuary

Altar

Chapel of Castille & Portugal

Chapel of Aragon

Chapel of Auvergne

Chapel of the Blessed Sacrament

Entrance to Oratory & Cathedral Museum

Exit from Museum & Bookshop

SOUTH AISLE

1 Tomb of GM Antoine de Paule
2 Tomb of GM Jean Lascaris Castellar
3 Chapel of the Holy Relics
4 Stairs to Crypt
5 Baptism of Christ Sculpture
6 Tomb of GM Nicolas Cotoner
7 Tomb of GM Rafael Cotoner

VALLETTA

VALLETTA IN...

Two Days

Get the day started with alfresco coffee and *pastizzi* at **Caffe Cordina** (p70) then educate yourself on the country at the **Malta Experience** (p65). Spend the day wandering Valletta's history-loaded streets – be sure to pop in to major attractions such as **St John's Co-Cathedral** (p60), the **Grand Master's Palace** (p61) and the **National Museum of Archaeology** (below), then rest your legs at the view-enriched **Upper Barrakka Gardens** (p66). On the second day, take a tour of the **Hypogeum** (p80) – be sure to prebook – then spend the afternoon exploring the nooks and crannies of the intriguing **Three Cities** (p75) area. Take in an evening show in Valletta at **Manoel Theatre** (p64) or **St James' Cavalier Centre for Creativity** (p71).

Four Days

Shake and add water to the two-day itinerary, then stir in the following: see the **Wartime Experience** (p65) and visit the **National War Museum** (opposite) to learn of WWII heroism and hardships in Malta. For a change of scenery, stroll around **Floriana** (p73) and head down to **Pinto Wharf** (p75) for a leisurely waterfront meal. The next day, explore further afield – take a bus to **Mdina** (p123), **Marsaxlokk** (p137) or the **northern beaches** (p114), or go by ferry across to bustling **Sliema** (p83).

once stored at the Palace Armoury (now the Great Hall used by the parliament), and when a Knight died they became the property of the Order. The current collection of over 5000 suits of 16th- to 18th-century armour is all that remains of an original 25,000 suits – Napoleon's light-fingered activities, over-enthusiastic housekeeping by the British and general neglect put paid to the rest.

Some of the most interesting pieces are the breastplate worn by la Valette, the beautifully damascened (steel inlaid with gold) suit made for Alof de Wignacourt, and the captured Turkish sipahi armour. A second room contains displays of weapons, including crossbows, muskets, swords and pistols. To overcome the dearth of exhibit labelling, admission now includes a self-guided audio tour (available in six languages).

A staircase past the Armoury entrance provides access to the **State Apartments**. Only a few rooms are open to the public, depending on what is currently being used. The long **Armoury Corridor**, decorated with trompe l'oeil painting, scenes of naval battles, blue colours and the portraits and escutcheons of various Grand Masters, leads to the **Council Chamber** on the left. It is hung with 17th-century Gobelins tapestries gifted to the Order in 1710 by Grand Master Ramon Perellos. They feature exotic scenes of Africa, India, the Caribbean and Brazil, including an elephant beneath a cashew-nut tree; an ostrich, cassowary and flamingo; a rhino and a zebra being attacked by a leopard; and a tableau with palm trees, a tapir, a jaguar and an iguana.

Beyond lie the **State Dining Room** and the **Supreme Council Hall**, where the Supreme Council of Order met. It is decorated with a frieze depicting events from the Great Siege of 1565, while the minstrels' gallery bears paintings showing scenes from the Book of Genesis. At the far end of the hall a door gives access to the **Hall of the Ambassadors**, or Red State Room, where the Grand Master would receive important visitors, and where the Maltese president still receives foreign envoys. It contains portraits of the French kings Louis XIV, Louis XV and Louis XVI, the Russian empress Catherine the Great, and several Grand Masters. The neighbouring **Pages' Room**, or Yellow State Room (despite the abundance of greenish tones), was used by the Grand Master's 16 attendants, and now serves as a conference room.

National Museum of Archaeology

Housed in the Auberge de Provence, the **National Museum of Archaeology** (☎ 2122 1623; Triq ir-Repubblika; adult/child Lm1/0.25; ☿ 9am-5pm) is well worth a visit, despite the fact that it is still undergoing renovation and expansion (long past its scheduled completion date). At the time of research only the galleries on the ground floor (detailing the early Neolithic and Temple periods, c 5200 to 2500 BC) were open, but new exhibitions should be opening upstairs sometime in 2007, and these will explore the

Bronze Age, Phoenician and Roman culture and the medieval period up to the modern period (c 2500 BC to AD 1800s).

In the downstairs galleries you can see the beautiful and often mysterious objects that have been found at Malta's prehistoric sites, along with displays showing the technology used to build Malta's prehistoric temples, and the evolution of temple design from simple stone huts to the elaborate layout of Ġgantija. There is also a very good model of the Hypogeum on display.

The exhibits include female figurines found at Ħaġar Qim, the so-called 'fat ladies' (no offence, girls) – perhaps representing a fertility goddess – with massive rounded thighs and arms, but tiny, doll-like hands and feet, wearing a pleated skirt and sitting with legs tucked neatly to one side. The so-called *Venus de Malta*, also from Ħaġar Qim, is about 10cm tall and displays more realistic modelling, possibly of a pregnant woman. Best of all is the *Sleeping Lady*, found at the Hypogeum and dating from around 3000 BC – here the well-endowed Venus is seen lying on her side with her head propped on one arm, apparently deep in slumber.

Heritage Malta conducts one-hour guided tours of the museum at 10am and 2pm Tuesday and Thursday, 10am and 11.30am Sunday; the tours are free with admission and are a great way to learn about the prehistoric temple-building period, especially if you plan to visit the Hypogeum or any of the megalithic temples scattered around Malta. Tours and times are not set in stone, so it may be worth making advance enquiries.

National Museum of Fine Arts

Occupying Admiralty House, Malta's **National Museum of Fine Arts** (☎ 2122 5769; Triq Nofs in-Nhar; adult/child l m1/0.25; ☉ 9am-5pm) is a baroque palazzo that was used as the official residence of the admiral commander-in-chief of the British Mediterranean Fleet from the 1820s until 1961. Lord Louis Mountbatten also had his headquarters here in the early 1950s.

The museum's collection of paintings – mostly Italian and Maltese – ranges from the 15th to the 20th century, and there are some fine examples of 17th- and 18th-century Maltese furniture.

Begin your explorations upstairs and to the left (note the church silver and sculptures en route). Highlights include rooms 12 and 13,

which display works by Mattia Preti (see p37). Look out for the dramatic *Martyrdom of St Catherine,* doubting Thomas poking a finger into Christ's wound in *The Incredulity of St Thomas,* and St John the Baptist dressed in the habit of the Knights of St John.

Downstairs, room 14 contains portraits of several Grand Masters by the 18th-century French artist Antoine de Favray, including one of the imperious Manoel Pinto de Fonseca. Room 18 has scenes of Malta by 19th-century British artists, including poet Edward Lear, and a wonderful watercolour depicting a Grand Harbour scene, painted by Turner in 1830 – the museum's pride and joy. Interestingly, Turner never visited Malta, and the work is based on scenes painted by another artist. Room 19 has many 19th-century scenes of Valletta.

Heritage Malta conducts guided tours (free with admission) of the museum at 11am and 2pm Tuesday and Thursday; tours and times can change, so it may be worth making advance enquiries.

National War Museum

Commemorating the country's ordeal during WWII, Malta's **National War Museum** (☎ 2122 2430; Triq il-Fontana; adult/child Lm1/0.25; ☉ 9am-5pm) is housed in the northwest corner of Fort St Elmo. The collection of relics, photographs and equipment includes the Gloster Gladiator biplane called *Faith* (minus wings), the jeep *Husky* used by General Eisenhower, and the wreckage of a Spitfire and a Messerschmitt Me-109 fighter aircraft recovered from the sea bed. The pictures of bomb damage in Valletta give some idea of the amount of rebuilding that was needed after the war. Pride of place goes to the replica George Cross medal that was awarded to the entire population of Malta in 1942.

Heritage Malta conducts guided tours of the museum at 11am and 2pm daily; tours are free with admission; tours and times are not fixed, so enquire in advance.

St James' Cavalier

The St James' Cavalier has undergone a remarkable transformation from a 16th-century fortification into a bright, modern arts centre. Inside the **St James' Cavalier Centre for Creativity** (☎ 2122 3200; www.sjcav.org; Triq Nofs in-Nhar; admission free; ☉ 10am-9.30pm) are a couple of exhibition spaces (with a bias towards the contemporary art scene), a theatre-in-the-round where live music and theatre performances are held and a cinema showing arthouse films. It's worth stopping in to check out the interesting interior and to grab a programme of what's on.

Manoel Theatre

The 600-seat **Manoel Theatre** (☎ 2124 6389; www .teatrumanoel.com.mt; 115 Triq it-Teatru l-Antik), Malta's national theatre, was built in 1731 and is one of the oldest theatres in Europe. Take an entertaining guided tour (conducted in English, French, Italian and German) to see the restored baroque auditorium with its gilt boxes and huge chandelier. Tours begin at 10.30am, 11.30am and 2.30pm Monday to Friday, and 1.30pm Saturday. Tickets cost Lm1.70 and include admission to the theatre's small museum. See above for information on the theatre's programme of performances.

Fort St Elmo

At the furthest point of Valletta and guarding the entrance to both Marsamxett and Grand Harbours is **Fort St Elmo**, named after the patron saint of mariners. Although now much altered and extended, this was the fort that bore the brunt of Turkish arms during the Great Siege of 1565. It was built by the Knights in 1552 to guard the entrances to the harbours on either side of the Sceberras Peninsula. The courtyard outside the entrance to the fort is studded with the lids of underground granaries.

Today Fort St Elmo is home to Malta's police academy and is open to the public only for historical reenactments, held at 11am on most Sunday mornings except during the peak summer period from mid-July to late September. **In Guardia** (☎ 2123 7747; adult/child Lm2/0.50) is a colourful and photogenic military pageant in 16th-century costume, which includes a cannon-firing demonstration that will clear the wax from your ears. **Alarme!** (☎ 2123 7747; adult/child Lm2/0.50) is a reenactment of a military encounter between French and Maltese troops. Inquire about dates for these shows at the tourist office.

Church of St Paul's Shipwreck

In AD 60 St Paul was shipwrecked on Malta and brought Christianity to the population. The moody **Church of St Paul's Shipwreck** (Triq San Pawl, enter from Triq Santa Luċija; admission free, donations welcome; ☉ 9am-7pm) dates from the 16th century and houses many treasures, including a

dazzling gilded statue of St Paul, carved in Rome in 1650s and carried shoulder-high through the streets of Valletta on the saint's feast day (10 February). There's also a golden reliquary containing some bones from the saint's wrist, and part of the column on which he is said to have been beheaded in Rome (see the boxed text, p38, for more information).

Lascaris War Rooms

WWII history boffins should make time to visit the **Lascaris War Rooms** (☎ 2123 4936; adult/child Lm1.75/0.85; ☉ 9.30am-4pm Mon-Fri, 9.30am-12.30pm Sat & Sun). These chambers, hewn out of the solid rock beneath Lascaris Bastion, housed the headquarters of the Allied air and naval forces during WWII, and were used as the control centre for Operation Husky, the Allied invasion of Sicily in 1943.

The rooms are a little tricky to find. Your best option is to walk south from Pjazza Kastilja along Triq Girolamo Cassar and look for the path on the right (signposted) that leads down into the Great Ditch beneath St James' Bastion and doubles back under the road to the entry. Once inside, you take a self-guided audio tour through the operations rooms. You'll need to use your imagination to fill these deserted control rooms and corridors with the clatter of typewriters, the crackle of radio transmissions and the hushed urgency that must have permeated the air during major operations.

Casa Rocca Piccola

The 16th-century palazzo **Casa Rocca Piccola** (☎ 2122 1499; www.casaroccapiccola.com; 74 Triq ir-Repubblika; adult/child Lm2.50/free) is the elegant family home of the Marquis de Piro. The marquis has opened part of the palazzo to the public and guided tours on the hour (10am to 4pm Monday to Saturday) give an unique insight into the privileged lifestyle of the aristocracy.

Toy Museum

Opposite Casa Rocca Piccola is the small **Toy Museum** (☎ 2125 1652; 222 Triq ir-Repubblika; adult/child Lm1/free; ☉ 10.30am-3.30pm Mon-Fri, 10.30am-1pm Sat & Sun), housing an impressive private collection of model planes and boats from the 1950s, as well as Matchbox cars, farmyard animals, train sets and dolls. The collection is generally in glass display cabinets, so this place is better suited to nostalgic adults than hyperactive ankle-biters.

Audiovisual Shows & Exhibitions

The **Wartime Experience** (☎ 2122 2225; Triq Santa Luċija; adult/child Lm2.20/1.50) is a worthwhile 45-minute show made up of archive film from WWII, which movingly records the ordeal suffered by the Maltese during the siege of 1940 to 1943. It's shown at the Embassy Cinemas (p71) inside the Embassy Complex daily at 10am, 11am, noon and 1pm.

The **Malta Experience** (☎ 2124 3776; www.themaltaexperience.com; Triq il-Mediterran; adult/child Lm3.50/1.75) is a somewhat pricey 45-minute audiovisual presentation that provides a good introduction to Malta, especially for first-time visitors. The film is available in 13 languages; it showcases the country's long history and highlights many of its scenic attractions. Screenings begin on the hour from 11am to 4pm Monday to Friday, and from 11am to 1pm on weekends and public holidays (with an extra 2pm show from October till June).

The Malta Experience is screened in the basement of the Mediterranean Conference Centre, which is housed in the **Sacra Infermeria**, the 16th-century hospital of the Order of St John. Here surgeons performed advanced operations as well as the more routine amputations and treatment of war wounds. See the boxed text, p22, for more details. A pretty lacklustre **Knights Hospitallers exhibition** (☎ 2124 3840; Triq it-Tramuntana; adult/child Lm1.85/0.90; 9.30am-4.30pm Mon-Fri, 9.30am-4pm Sat & Sun), with an entrance across the street from the Malta Experience, records the achievements of these medieval medics.

One heavily promoted exhibition is the **Great Siege of Malta & the Knights of St John** (☎ 2124 7300; www.greatsiege.com.mt; Misraħ ir-Repubblika; adult/child Lm3.50/2.75; 10am-last admission 4pm), beside the entry to the Bibliotheca. It advertises a 'state-of-the-art 3D walk-through adventure' but quite frankly doesn't live up to the hype. For the steep admission fee you get a 45-minute, sometimes-tedious self-guided audio tour through re-creations of battle scenes from the 1565 siege.

WALKING TOUR

The walk outlined here follows the outer fortifications of Valletta and offers great views of Marsamxett Harbour, Sliema, Grand Harbour and the Three Cities. Climbing the town's steep stairs is a good way of working up a thirst before retiring to the shade of a café for a well-earned drink. The route described can

WALK FACTS

Start City Gate
Finish Triq ir-Repubblika
Distance approx 3.5km
Duration 2 hours

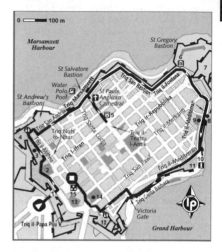

be completed in about 1½ to two hours, but if you spend some time at all the sights detailed here, it could take a half-day or more.

Begin at **City Gate (1)** – hold your breath and go up the (grotty, smelly) stairs on the left immediately inside the gate. These lead to the bridge above City Gate, with a good view along Triq ir-Repubblika in one direction, and across the chaotic but colourful bus terminus to Floriana in the other.

Head northwest along Triq il-Papa Piju V, past **St John's Cavalier (2)**, which today houses the Embassy of the Order of St John. Continue along Triq il-Mithna to **St Michael's Bastion (3)**. Nip into **Hastings Gardens (4)** here for a panorama over Marsamxett Harbour to Sliema and Manoel Island.

Descend steeply via Triq San Andrija and a flight of steps to Triq San Marku and continue straight on to Triq Marsamxett, the main road that runs along the top of the city walls and affords views of the mammoth Tigné Point construction underway in Sliema. Head past the water polo pool on the shore below and look out for the steep staircase of Triq it-Teatru l-Antik on the right, beneath the prominent spire of St Paul's Anglican

DIY CAPITAL BUS TOUR

Fancy a cheap, quick, DIY bus tour of the capital? Bus 98 is a circular route departing City Gate on the hour from 7am to 6pm. It does a clockwise loop around the bastions of Valletta and through Floriana, so you can take in harbour views, Fort St Elmo and Pinto Wharf (encompassing the start of the new Valletta waterfront development). You'll see the periphery of the capital from the bus, but you'll need to 'fill in the gaps' on foot. A complete bus circuit takes around 15 to 20 minutes; the fare is all of Lm0.15.

Cathedral. A stiff climb leads up to **Manoel Theatre** (5; p64), built in 1731 and one of the oldest theatres in Europe.

Continue along Triq Marsamxett and around the walls of the Poste D'Angleterre and Poste de France. Drop in to the **National War Museum** (6; p63) to learn of WWII heroism, then continue past **Fort St Elmo** (7; p64), which bore the brunt of Turkish attacks during the Great Siege of 1565.

A little further along Triq il-Mediterran lies the entrance to the **Malta Experience** (8; p65), an audiovisual presentation that provides a potted history of Malta. The show screens in the basement of the 16th-century hospital of the Order of St John, the **Sacra Infermeria** (9; p65), now a conference centre. There's an exhibition here on the history of the medical care given by the Knights.

About 200m past the Sacra Infermeria the road forks, and on the left is a small park and a tall pillared cupola. This is the **Siege Bell Memorial (10)**, which commemorates those who lost their lives in the convoys of 1940 to 1943. Take the right hand fork in the road (still Triq il-Mediterran) past the entrance to **Lower Barrakka Gardens (11)**, which contains a little Doric temple commemorating Sir Alexander Ball, the naval captain who took Malta from the French in 1800.

Continue along Triq Santa Barbara, a charming tree-lined street (rare in these parts) with views over the harbour to the Three Cities. Cross the bridge above Victoria Gate and head through a sun-trap of a square, usually home to a handful of café tables, beside the Grand Harbour Hotel. Turn left and climb up steep Triq il-Batterija to reach the **Upper Barrakka Gardens**

(12). The balcony here provides a magnificent panorama of Grand Harbour and the creeks and dockyards of Vittoriosa and Senglea. Time your visit to coincide with the firing of the noon-day gun (a cannon fired at noon daily).

From the gardens continue to Pjazza Kastilja. On your left are the high walls of the **St James' Cavalier (13**; p63) which now houses interesting exhibition spaces, a theatre and cinema. Pause to admire the façade of the **Auberge de Castille (14)** on your right, designed by the architect Andrea Belli in 1741. It adorns a 16th-century building that was once the home of the Spanish and Portuguese langue of the Knights of St John, but now houses the offices of the Maltese prime minister (not open to the public).

Head straight along Triq Nofs in-Nhar towards Triq ir-Repubblika, passing the cracked steps and shattered column stumps of the ruined **Royal Opera House (15)** on your left. This once imperious building was built in the 1860s, but was destroyed during a German air raid in 1942. Its gutted shell has been left as a reminder of the war and is rather unceremoniously used as a car park while controversy rages as to what should be done with the site. The most recent proposal is to transform the ruins into a permanent open-air performance space.

From here you can continue your explorations of the capital by turning right and heading down the main street, Triq ir-Repubblika, home to the bulk of Valletta's major attractions. Taking any side street off this main thoroughfare can quickly take you away from crowds and into the heart of workaday Valletta.

VALLETTA FOR CHILDREN

Valletta is a treasure trove of history and architecture – but, let's face it, there are not too many kids who get excited over such grown-up subjects. It's likely that your young offspring will enjoy walking along the city walls and taking in the great views, scenically situated gardens, café-filled squares and vaulted cellar restaurants of Valletta, but there are few attractions in the capital designed specifically for children. Older kids should enjoy the Malta Experience (p65) and historical reenactments at Fort St Elmo (p64), and younger kids may delight in some of the gory scenes depicted in exhibitions such as the Great Siege of Malta & the Knights of St John (p65) or the Knights Hospitallers (p65) – but it's unlikely that much of the history lessons will sink in.

FESTIVALS & EVENTS

See p172 for details on some of the country's foremost festivals, most of which include events staged in and around the capital.

SLEEPING

Except for a couple of notable exceptions, accommodation in Valletta is depressingly lacklustre. Despite this (and the fact that there are only a handful of options here), the capital still gets our vote for best place in Malta to be based if you're more interested in history and culture than a beach holiday. The main museums and attractions are within easy walking distance, and buses depart from the City Gate terminus to all parts of the island.

Many places offer discounts on stays of seven days or longer – it's worth asking. Some also offer half-board and full-board options: these are usually reasonable value, but you're better off with the freedom to visit the eateries of your choice.

Valletta guesthouses are from another era – you won't find internet bookings or TV rooms here. In the midrange category there are two OK hotel options, and two shabby but well-located hotels crying out for a facelift. Where prices are listed 'per person', these are based on two people sharing a room; guesthouses rarely charge a single supplement, but hotels often do. Valletta's only top-end hotel is technically in Floriana, just outside the city walls, but it's a mere hop, step and jump from the capital.

Budget

Coronation Guesthouse (☎ 2123 7652, 9940 6080; 10E Triq M A Vassalli; B&B per person with shared bathroom Lm5-6) The warmth of the welcome here and the bargain prices should help overcome any concerns you may have with the occasionally problematic plumbing. Rooms (with washbasin; bathrooms are shared) are bright and airy and simply furnished; try for one with Marsamxett views. We were assured by amiable Charlie, the owner, that new plumbing and a guest kitchen were in the pipeline.

Midland Guesthouse (☎ 2123 6024; 255 Triq Sant'Orsla; B&B per person with shared bathroom Lm6) Down the hill from the polished Asti Guesthouse is another elegant old townhouse. The neat rooms here are very pleasant, spread over three floors, and have washbasin and homely, older-style décor.

our pick Asti Guesthouse (☎ 2123 9506; http://mol net.mt/asti; 18 Triq Sant'Orsla; B&B per person with shared

bathroom from Lm7) You'll get a taste of old-school Valletta charm here plus the best-value accommodation in town. This classy, 350-year-old townhouse features huge, airy guest rooms and gleaming shared bathrooms. The bargain prices give little indication of its simple elegance – breakfast is served in a cheery plant-filled room with vaulted ceiling and chandelier. Up the stairs on various levels are nine large rooms, each with two or three beds, fuss-free wooden furniture and washbasin. Plants, wall hangings and ornaments adorn the halls, lending a warm and homely feel.

Other options, in a pinch:

Le Bonheur Guesthouse (☎ 2123 8433; bonheurmalta@hotmail.com; 18 Triq I-Inġinieri; B&B per person Lm6) Aging place at the top of the town, where the building's bones hint at a grander era. Rooms come with washbasin and, bizarrely, a shower in the corner of the room (you'll need to know your travel companion well!). Toilets are shared.

YMCA (☎ 2124 0680; www.ymcahomeless.org; reception at 178 Triq il-Merkanti; dm Lm3) Only for open-minded budget travellers with a social conscience. The local YMCA does a great job working with the homeless and disadvantaged who reside here; one floor of this temporary shelter, known as Dar Niki Cassar, is given over to cramped dorm accommodation for travellers. Kitchen and bathrooms are communal. Reception is at the YMCA office drop-in centre; the hostel itself is located elsewhere. To protect the privacy of residents, the YMCA prefers travellers to contact the office first for exact details of the location.

Midrange

British Hotel (☎ 2122 4730; www.britishhotel.com; 40 Triq il-Batterija; s/d Lm14/20, with sea view Lm16/25; ☒) Large parts of the 2005 movie *Munich* were filmed in Malta, and when location scouts wanted a 1970s-styled hotel, they chose the British – and barely needed to do a thing to it. The décor in the foyer, TV room and bar is so dated it might now be considered retro-cool. The hotel has its fans and its detractors – on the plus side it's affordable and well located, and enjoys great views over the Three Cities. The minuses: it's looking quite shabby and is a real rabbit warren; the rooms are basic and lacking in charm; you'll pay a deposit for *everything* (hairdryer, iron, electrical adaptor, air-con remote – air-con is Lm3 per day). However, it's worth paying extra for a view.

Castille Hotel (☎ 2124 3677/8; www.hotelcastille malta.com; Pjazza Kastilja; B&B per person Lm16.50-20; ☒) Castille has a number of points in its favour – not least its cheerful front-desk staff and grand position, in an old palazzo next to the ornate 16th-century Auberge de Castille. The hotel's small lobby and lounge make a good first impression, while guest rooms have a more faded charm and feature heavy Italianate furnishings and some questionable colour combos. The décor would certainly benefit from an upgrade, but in-room facilities include air-con and satellite TV; decent-sized single rooms are available for solo travellers (no supplement). Request a room at the front of the building for better light and views of the square below. One bonus of staying here is the fun cellar pizzeria, La Cave (opposite), and the rooftop restaurant for breakfast or dinner with a view over Grand Harbour.

Osborne Hotel (☎ 2124 3656; www.osbornehotel.com; 50 Triq Nofs in-Nhar; d Lm28-34; ✂ ☎) The Osborne deserves some credit for breathing much-needed life into the hotel scene, with newly renovated rooms on its lower floors. The plan is eventually to renovate each of the five floors, but this may be a slow process. Shame, really, because – as things stand – the best views are on the top floors, the best rooms on the lower floors. The lower-level 'superior' rooms feature pale streamlined furnishings and decent storage space, plus flatscreen TVs as a mark of modernity. As you move up the building, the furniture grows darker and the fittings more dated. Still, air-con and cable TV are standard, views on request… And despite the anonymity of the rooms (superior or not), there's some character in the ground level. The small reception area is flanked by a restaurant and classy bar and lounge. On the 6th floor there's a roof terrace with city views and a tiny splash pool.

our pick Valletta G-House (☎ UK +44 (0)781 3988 827; www.vallettahouse.com; Triq it-Tramuntana; apt per week UK£380-410) You'll need to book early to snare time at this sumptuous, adults-only apartment, and note that prices are in UK pounds and rentals are generally only on a weekly basis. The artistic owner, a Maltese guy based in London, has restored a 16th-century, character-filled townhouse to offer wonderfully romantic self-catering accommodation within its limestone walls. Entry is at street level and the entrance area doubles as a small sitting room, with TV and DVD (classic movies provided). Downstairs is a rustic, low-ceilinged cellar kitchen and a small, modern bathroom. On the first level is the

apartment's definite *pièce de résistance* – the large and luxe bedroom, which includes a sitting area, traditional Maltese enclosed balcony and striking floor tiles. Books, CDs, artwork, tapestries, fresh flowers and fine linen round out the picture beautifully. Prices include airport transfers and a welcome basket of local produce.

If everywhere else is full, you might want to consider the tired **Grand Harbour Hotel** (☎ 2124 6003; www.grandharbourhotel.com; 47 Triq il-Batterija; B&B per person Lm10), with much the same pros and cons as the nearby British Hotel.

Top End

Le Meridien Phoenicia Hotel (Map p73; ☎ 2122 5241; www.phoenicia.lemeridien.com; The Mall, Floriana; r from Lm90/120 low/high season; ✂ ☐ ☎) This grand old dame feels like a relic from another era. Built in the late 1930s, it is one of Malta's classiest hotels and takes up some prime real estate, only a minute's walk from Valletta's City Gate. Step away from the chaos of the bus terminus and up the garden path to be ushered in to an oasis of calm. The summery décor of the elegant guest rooms conjures up a more tropical climate; a higher rate gets you views of Marsamxett Harbour or the city walls of Valletta. First-class facilities include 24-hour room service, free car parking (a boon in this traffic-clogged neighbourhood), a business centre and a magnificent seven-acre garden with minigolf course, kids' play area and heated outdoor pool. There's an old-world club bar, a fine-dining restaurant and a more casual brasserie on site.

EATING

Valletta is essentially a business district, and there are many restaurants and cafés that are open at lunchtime but closed in the evenings. Still, there are a growing number of quality places in which to enjoy dinner and a relaxed evening drink.

Restaurants

La Sicilia (☎ 2124 0659; 1a Triq San Gwann; snacks & meals Lm0.50-6; ☷ 8am-5pm Mon-Fri) You're sure to find something to fill a rumbling tum at this tiny, unpretentious eatery, which spills out onto a little sun-trap of a square. There are lots of hearty Italian pasta dishes (under Lm3), grilled meats and fish, plus burgers, omelettes and salads. The setting is lovely and the prices are easy on the wallet.

La Cave (☎ 2124 3677; Pjazza Kastilja; meals Lm2-4; ☽ lunch & dinner) In a 400-year-old cellar beneath Castille Hotel, this busy restaurant churns out crunchy pizzas big enough for two – the pizza Maltija is topped with goat's cheese, olives and Maltese sausage. There's also a good assortment of pasta dishes (and a few salad options best avoided), and you can wash your food down with a selection of local wine – you might need more than one bottle though, as service can be slow.

Blue Room (☎ 2123 8014; 59 Triq ir-Repubblika; dishes Lm2-7; ☽ lunch & dinner) A few readers think this place has gone downhill, but on our most recent visit we found the aromatic duck as tasty as we did first time around. The polished service and attractive interior still score points, as does the menu – this is one of very few places in the capital not offering pizza and/or pasta. There are vegetable and rice/noodle dishes at the lower end of the price scale, and seafood and sizzling hotplates if you want to lash out. The Lm0.75 cover charge does sting, however.

Trabuxu (☎ 2122 3036; cnr Triq Nofs in-Nhar & Triq d-Dejqa; dishes Lm2.50-4; ☽ lunch Tue-Fri, dinner Tue-Sun) The name means 'corkscrew' and this intimate little cellar passes itself off as a wine bar, but we like it equally for its superbly presented meals. The short menu offers pâté, dips and other colourful platters perfect for wine-time grazing, but also all-to-yourself dishes such as a first-rate vegie lasagne. Local wines by the glass are a pleasing Lm0.90.

Papannis (☎ 2125 1960; 55 Triq id Dejqa; mains Lm3-6; ☽ lunch Mon Sat, dinner Fri & Sat) This cosy bistro combines a good-looking menu of pasta, risotto and seafood with cheerful, friendly service. The traditional soup (Lm1.30) is a hearty, rustic delight, full of local sausage, beans and vegies, so you can feel virtuous when you order another glass of local wine (Lm0.95) and move on to the tiramisu.

Carriage (☎ 2124 7828; 22/5 Valletta Bldgs, Triq Nofs n-Nhar; mains Lm3-7; ☽ lunch Mon-Fri, dinner Fri & Sat) A consistently polished performer, but considered expensive by local standards. Come for the good-value lunch deal (Lm8 for three courses, including a glass of wine), when your fellow diners could include local power-lunchers or a Japanese tour group. Entry is through a nondescript office building next door to Cocopazzo, and the restaurant is on the top floor enjoying a great Marsamxett view.

Ambrosia (☎ 2122 5923; 137 Triq I-Arċisqof; mains Lm3-7.50; ☽ lunch & dinner Mon-Sat) A close contender for our favourite Valletta restaurant. The standards here are high and the welcome is warm (the chef might just pop by to see how you enjoyed your meal). The blackboard menu changes daily; on it you'll find Mediterranean dishes making great use of fresh local produce, produced according to the Slow Food philosophy (eg spaghetti with sea urchins, goat's cheese soufflé, a salad of grilled Gozo asparagus).

Rubino (☎ 2122 4656; 53 Triq I-Ifran; mains Lm4-6; ☽ lunch Mon-Fri, dinner Tue & Fri) Rubino earns rave reviews for reinventing Maltese cuisine while staying true to its roots. There's no menu, just a selection of the day's dishes depending on seasonal produce and local tradition. Leave room for dessert – the house speciality, cassata siciliana, is particularly recommended. Tuesday night is usually *fenkata* (a communal meal of rabbit) night, for which bookings are advised.

our pick Fusion Four (☎ 2122 5255; cnr Triq il-Papa Piju V & Triq San Ġwann Kavalier; mains Lm5.50-7; ☽ lunch Mon Fri, dinner Tue Sat) For us, this stylish, well-hidden restaurant is the culinary highlight of the capital. It houses a small bar, funky furnishings, a dining room under vaulted ceilings and perfect, private courtyard. Icing on the cake is a small but innovative menu of fusion dishes such as sweet chilli prawn cakes, chicken breast in a red Thai curry, or pancetta-wrapped pork fillet on a bed of red apples. Finish with a delectable white chocolate and honeycomb mousse.

Cafés

282 Coffee Garden (☎ 2122 2111; 282 Triq ir-Repubblika; snacks & meals Lm0.50-3; ☽ breakfast & lunch) This place is right in the thick of things. It's a little touristy but nicely done – the upstairs area with comfy rattan chairs and greenery (take) offers respite from the bustling main street below. Don't look for surprises in the 'classic hits' menu: pasta, pizza, salads, sandwiches, cakes.

Café Jubilee (☎ 2125 2332; 125 Triq Santa Luċija; snacks & meals Lm1-3.50; ☽ 8am-1am Mon-Thur, Fri & Sat 8am-3am) A feel-good place you can drop in to anytime, for bacon and eggs or breakfast the Maltese way (coffee and a *pastizza*), a lunchtime baguette, or a simple dinner of salad, pasta or risotto. It's a convivial continental-style bistro, with low lighting, cosy nooks and poster-plastered walls. It's also a good option for a late-night drink.

Caffe Cordina (☎ 2123 4385; 244 Triq ir-Repubblika; snacks & meals Lm1-4; ☟ breakfast & lunch) There's some prime people-watching on Misraħ ir-Repubblika, where several cafés command the ranks of tables around the statue of Queen Victoria. The oldest (and busiest) option is Caffe Cordina, established in 1837 and now a local institution. You have the choice of waiter service at the tables in the square or inside, or joining the locals at the zinc counter inside for a quick caffeine hit. And be sure to look up; the ceiling is exquisitely painted. Excellent for savoury pastries and decadent sweets, and there's a gelati counter out front.

Quick Eats

The major fast-food outlets are near the top of the town, but cheaper and tastier fare can be found at the kiosks beside City Gate bus terminus. Millennium (the first kiosk on your right after you exit City Gate) sells hot *pastizzi* (small parcels of flaky pastry filled with either ricotta cheese or mushy peas) for Lm0.10 each; next door, the Dates Kiosk sells traditional *mqaret* for Lm0.07 – these are delicious pastries stuffed with spiced dates and deep-fried.

Follow your nose to a couple of friendly, hole-in-the-wall places on Triq San Pawl where you can pick up a fresh hot *pastizza* for loose change (Lm0.08) from around 7.30am Monday to Saturday. Agius Confectionery & Pastizzerija is opposite the Church of St Paul's Shipwreck at No 273, while Carmelo Azzopardi Pastizzerija is at No 310.

Self-Catering

Wembley Store (305 Triq ir-Repubblika; ☟ 7.15am-7pm Mon-Fri, 7.45am-7pm Sat) This store has a limited selection of groceries (tinned and dried food).

There's also a **fresh produce market** (Triq il-Merkanti; ☟ 7am-1pm Mon-Sat) behind the Grand Master's Palace, where you can buy fruit, vegetables and deli items upstairs, and fish, meat and poultry on the ground level. Homesick Brits might want to visit the well-stocked food section of **Marks & Spencer** (Triq id-Dejqa; ☟ 9am-7pm Mon-Sat).

DRINKING

The Pub (☎ 7980 7042; 136 Triq l-Arċisqof; ☟ from 11.30am) Fans of the late British actor Oliver Reed might want to raise a glass to their hero in this succinctly named watering hole. This is the homely little hostelry where the wild man of British film enjoyed his final drinking session before last orders were called forever in 1999. It's a tiny, tucked-away place, but worth visiting for the memorabilia on the walls and to read of Reed's heavy drinking visits during the filming of *Gladiator*.

Maestro e' Fresco (☎ 2123 3801; 8 Triq Nofs in-Nhar; ☟ from 5.30pm Tue-Sun) A couple of inviting bars lure after-work locals and visitors to the southern end of town. The Maestro was a music shop from 1842 to 2001; these days it offers up snacks, brews and live music to help you celebrate the coming of the weekend (usually acoustic stuff on Friday, old classics on Saturday).

Trabuxu (☎ 2122 3036; cnr Triq Nofs in-Nhar & Triq id-Dejqa; ☟ from 7pm Tue-Sun) On the same street as the Maestro is Trabuxu, whose name means 'corkscrew'. This cosy spot is decorated with great B&W shots and musical instruments, and its menu includes perfect platters to accompany much wine quaffing. Local and international wines are on offer.

Labyrinth (☎ 2122 0499; 44 Triq id-Dejqa; ☟ Wed-Sun night) Nightowls will enjoy the dimly lit hidey-holes of Labyrinth, a cool and cavernous bistro/wine bar/club, offering edibles and DJ entertainment. Somewhat fittingly, it's tucked away in a seedy-by-night alley a block north of Triq ir-Repubblika; there are plenty of nooks and crannies at street level and below in which to nurse a drink or whisper sweet nothings into someone's ear.

Castille Wine Vaults (☎ 2123 7707; Pjazza Kastilja; ☟ from 9pm Thu-Sun) It's a shame about the limited opening hours of this fabulously situated café-bar. It's underneath the stock exchange building, accessed by walking down some steps and a long low-lit passageway. In the dining area you can snack on panini and platters of Maltese delicacies, cheese, seafood or dips, plus learn about and sample some very good local drops of wine (Lm2.75 for four wines).

Other good drinking dens include **Café Jubilee** and **Fusion Four**. There's also plenty of action (restaurants and bars) at the new Pinto Wharf waterfront development (p75), where cruise ships dock under Valletta's bastions in Floriana, or you might like to go further afield and check out Vittoriosa's terrific wine bars (p79).

ENTERTAINMENT

For years Valletta has seemed half-dead after 8pm, its streets hushed and empty after the business folk and day-trippers have left, and those seeking any form of nightlife automatically headed to Paceville (p95). But there's been something of a revival in recent years, and Valletta is now home to a handful of café-bars where you can eat, drink and be merry among in-the-know locals – you just need to know where to look. These places tend to draw an older crowd, and closing times vary depending on how busy the venue is. Only Labyrinth passes for anything resembling a nightclub in Valletta, so the overseas students and early-20-somethings usually head to Paceville, and if that's more your scene you can take a night bus. Bus 62 runs from Valletta to Paceville (Lm0.50, every half-hour) until around 1am on Friday and Saturday nights year-round, and until 2.30am every night from mid-June to mid-September (the last bus from Paceville to Valletta in these summer months is at 3am).

See Drinking, opposite, for reviews of bars. Maestro e' Fresco hosts live music on Friday and Saturday nights; Labyrinth parties into the wee hours with local DJs providing the soundtrack. Another good venue for more formal musical performances is the St James' Cavalier Centre for Creativity – check the newspapers or pick up a programme at the centre.

See p75 for information about **Tom Bar**, a popular gay bar not far outside Valletta, and p79 for information about the closest casino to Valletta, on the Vittoriosa waterfront.

Theatre

Manoel Theatre (☎ 2124 6389; www.teatrumanoel.com .mt; 115 Triq it-Teatru l-Antik) This beautiful place is Malta's national theatre, and the islands' principal venue for drama, concerts, opera, ballet, and the much-loved Christmas pantomime. The performance season runs from October to May, and during these months there are popular lunchtime concerts every Wednesday at 1pm (Lm2). Check the website for details of the programme, or pick one up at the **booking office** (☎ 2124 6389; cnr Triq l-Ifran & Triq it-Teatru l-Antik; ☼ 9am-1pm & 5-7pm Mon-Fri, 10am-noon Sat, plus 90min before performances). Guided tours of the Manoel Theatre are also offered (see p64).

The **St James' Cavalier Centre for Creativity** (☎ 2122 3200; www.sjcav.org; Triq Nofs in-Nhar; ☼ 10am-9.30pm) also stages intimate performances in its theatre-in-the-round.

Cinemas

Embassy Cinemas (☎ 2122 2225; www.embassycomplex .com.mt; Triq Santa Luċija; tickets adult/child, Lm2.35/1.50, adults before 5pm weekdays, Lm2), inside the Embassy Complex, shows the latest mainstream releases from Hollywood.

The **St James' Cavalier Centre for Creativity** (☎ 2122 3200; www.sjcav.org; Triq Nofs in-Nhar; tickets adult/child, Lm2/1; ☼ 10am-9.30pm) has a cinema screening alternative and arthouse films on a nightly basis.

SHOPPING

There are small shopping centres, souvenir shops and a range of UK high-street fashion labels all along or just off Triq ir-Repubblika, but little of interest to visitors looking for a purchase that's uniquely Maltese. Triq Santa Lucija, behind Misraħ ir-Repubblika, is home to a number of jewellery stores offering silver filigree – the most popular souvenir here is a silver eight-pointed Maltese Cross on a chain.

Malta Crafts Centre (☎ 2122 4532; Misraħ San Ġwann) This place has a small range of locally produced crafts, including glassware, ceramics, jewellery and lace.

Gio Batta Delia (☎ 2123 3618; 307 Triq ir-Repubblika) Behind a photogenic façade close to City Gate, this browse-worthy store sells the big names in fine chinaware and glass (eg Wedgwood, Meissen) alongside more Malta-specific treasures such as prints, pottery and old lace.

A crowded **street market** (Triq il-Merkanti; ☼ around 7am-1pm Mon-Sat) set up between Triq San Ġwann and Triq it-Teatru l-Antik sells mainly clothes, shoes, watches and jewellery, pirated CDs and computer games. The **Monti** (St James' Ditch; ☼ Sun) is a much bigger market selling similar items, just south of the City Gate bus terminus.

GETTING THERE & AWAY
Air

See the Transport chapter (p180) for information on flights from Malta International Airport at Luqa, 8km south of Valletta.

Most airline offices are found at the airport, although some airlines also have offices in Valletta.

Air Malta (☎ 2124 0686; Misraħ il-Helsien; ☼ 8.30am-5pm Mon-Fri) Near the tourist office.

British Airways (☎ 2124 2233; 20/2 Triq ir-Repubblika; ☼ 8.30am-1pm & 2.30-5.30pm Mon-Fri) Above the Travelex office.

Boat

The **Marsamxetto ferry service** (☎ 2346 3862) provides a quick, easy way to travel between Valletta and Sliema. The crossing costs Lm0.40 each way and takes about five minutes. There are departures every hour (every half-hour from 10am to 4pm) daily in both directions, beginning at around 8am and finishing at around 6pm (slightly earlier on Sundays). To reach the ferry departure point in Valletta, follow Triq San Marku all the way to the north, then under the overpass and down to the water.

Ferries depart from Sliema on the hour and half-hour, and from Valletta at a quarter past and quarter to the hour.

Bus

All bus routes lead to Valletta. **The City Gate bus terminus** is the source of services to all parts of the island – it's chaotic, to say the least, but seems to work. For information on routes, fares and timetables, inquire at the Public Transport Authority kiosks dotted around the terminus, and see p186 for a map and more details.

GETTING AROUND
To/From the Airport

Bus 8 runs between the airport and the City Gate terminus in Valletta, passing through Floriana on the way – the fare is Lm0.20, and the journey takes about 40 minutes. The airport bus stop is immediately outside the entrance to the departures hall. Ignore any taxi drivers who tell you that the bus stop is a 20-minute walk away, or that the bus won't be along for another hour – they're just touting for business.

You'll find a taxi information desk in the airport arrivals hall and you can organise and pay for your taxi there. The set fare for a taxi from the airport to Valletta or Floriana is Lm6.50.

To/From the Sea Passenger Terminal

It's not terribly straightforward to travel between Valletta and the **Sea Passenger Terminal** next to the developing Pinto Wharf in Floriana. If you're travelling with Virtu Ferries from Sicily, it's probably best to arrange a transfer with them when booking your passage. Otherwise, bus 98 (Lm0.15, hourly until 6pm) stops about 300m away, and you can take a sightseeing stroll.

If you decide to walk to Valletta, you face a steep climb (not a great choice if you're carrying luggage). There are two options: follow the waterfront northeast, under the Lascaris Bastion, then veer left and climb the steps up at Victoria Gate. At the top of the stairs you'll be greeted by La Sicilia restaurant (p68). Alternatively, walk northeast along the waterfront then take a sharp left up It-Telgħa Tal-Kurċifiss (Crucifix Hill). Halfway up you'll encounter Il Taraġ Tal-Kalkara (Kalkara Steps) – climb these to reach the war memorial; from here it's a few minutes' walk north to Valletta's City Gate. Allow at least 15 minutes for either journey.

As at the airport, there's a taxi information kiosk on Pinto Wharf where you organise and pay the set rate for your taxi journey up-front. The cheapest fare (to an address in Valletta or Floriana) is a ridiculously overpriced Lm4. The *karrozzin* (traditional horse-drawn carriage) drivers loitering here will charge considerably more (there are plenty of reports of newly arrived tourists, unfamiliar with the local currency, paying extortionate prices).

There is talk of reestablishing a 'vertical connection' to link the harbour area with Valletta's Upper Barrakka Gardens, via a panoramic lift. This is a great idea but, this being Malta, the project could take years to see the light of day.

Car & Motorcycle

A car is more of a hindrance than a help in Valletta. The streets around City Gate are clogged with cars, buses and taxis most of the day, and cars without a resident's permit are not allowed to park in Valletta – instead you must use the big underground car park in Floriana, which is just southwest of the bus station and charges Lm2 for 4½ hours or more.

Public Transport

Bus 98 makes a clockwise circuit of Valletta from City Gate to Fort St Elmo along the outer road that follows the top of the city walls (Lm0.15), but walking is generally the fastest and easiest way to get about.

See p190 for information about the horse-drawn *karrozzin*, which offer rides around town, and p190 for tips on local taxis for horseless rides. There is a taxi rank just outside City Gate.

AROUND VALLETTA

FLORIANA

pop 2550

The suburb of Floriana, immediately southwest of the capital, grew up in the 18th century within the landward defences of Valletta. The northern part is taken up with government buildings and offices, while the south side is mostly residential.

The broad avenue formed by Vjal ir-Re Edwardu VII (King Edward VII Ave) and Triq Sarria runs southwest from City Gate bus terminus for 500m, dividing the government buildings of Beltissebḣ to the northwest from the long, open rectangle of Pjazza San Publiju (St Publius Sq) to the south. The main street of Floriana, Triq Sant'Anna (St Anne's St), lies two blocks south of the square. The main traffic route from Valletta to the rest of Malta exits from the southwest end of Triq Sant'Anna.

The most exciting thing to happen to Floriana in recent times is the Pinto Wharf redevelopment (also known as the Valletta Waterfront), on the southeast side of Floriana, just beneath the capital's fortifications. It's where a growing number of cruise ships dock, and it sits alongside the Sea Passenger Terminal, where passenger ferries arrive and depart. At the time of research transport links to the area were poor; see opposite for details of walking routes between Valletta and the wharf.

Street signs in Floriana are usually in Malti only.

Walking Tour

Begin at the City Gate bus terminus and walk southwest along the central garden strip between Vjal ir-Re Edwardu VII and Triq Sarria. The **monument to Christ the King (1)**, opposite Le Meridien Phoenicia Hotel, commemorates the International Eucharistic Congress held in Malta in 1913.

Cross Triq l-Assedju l-Kbir and continue along **Il-Mall (2)**. Now occupied by tree-lined gardens, the 400m-long mall was laid out in the 17th century on the orders of Grand Master Lascaris, so that the younger Knights might play at pall-mall (an ancestor of

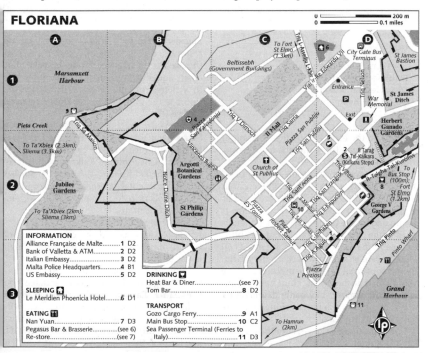

FLORIANA

0 ————— 200 m
0 ————— 0.1 miles

INFORMATION
Alliance Française de Malte	**1** D2
Bank of Valletta & ATM	**2** D2
Italian Embassy	**3** D2
Malta Police Headquarters	**4** B1
US Embassy	**5** D2

SLEEPING
Le Meridien Phoenicia Hotel	**6** D1

EATING
Nan Yuan	**7** D3
Pegasus Bar & Brasserie	(see 6)
Re-store	(see 7)

DRINKING
Heat Bar & Diner	(see 7)
Tom Bar	**8** D2

TRANSPORT
Gozo Cargo Ferry	**9** A1
Main Bus Stop	**10** C2
Sea Passenger Terminal (Ferries to Italy)	**11** D3

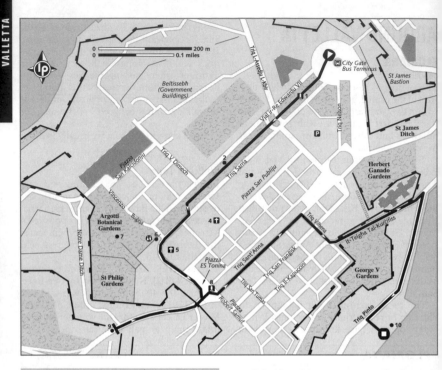

WALK FACTS

Start City Gate bus terminus
Finish Pinto Wharf
Distance approx 2km
Duration 1 hour

croquet), in the forlorn hope that this might keep them from the temptations of wine, women and gambling.

The long open space on the south side of the mall is Pjazza San Publiju. The circular slabs that stud its paved surface are the lids of underground **granaries (3)**. The square is dominated by the **Church of St Publius (4)**, dedicated to the patron saint of Floriana. Publius was the Roman governor of Malta in AD 60 when St Paul was shipwrecked on the island. He was converted to Christianity and became Malta's first bishop. The church was built in the 18th century, and badly damaged by WWII bombs. Its rich red interior and ornate ceiling are worth a look.

Continue along Triq Sarria to the circular **Sarria Chapel (5)**, built in 1678 and designed

and decorated by Mattia Preti (undergoing restoration at the time of research). Across the street is the **Wignacourt Water Tower (6)**, part of an aqueduct system that brought water to Valletta from the central hills. Beside the tower is the entrance to the **Argotti Botanical Gardens (7)**.

Follow the street round to the left past the Sarria Chapel and downhill to the **Lion Fountain (8)**, and turn right on the main road out of town. A five-minute walk along this busy stretch of road leads to the **Porte des Bombes (9)**, an ornamental gateway dating from 1697 to 1720 that once formed part of the Floriana Lines fortifications.

Pass through it to admire its decorations – reliefs of cannons and the coat of arms of Grand Master Perellos, under whose reign it was built.

Return to the Lion Fountain and then continue straight on along the grand, arcaded Triq Sant'Anna. This will lead you back towards Valletta, but a side-trip right down Triq Vilhena and left along It-Telgħa Tal-Kurċifiss (Crucifix Hill) will take you to **Pinto Wharf (10)**, also know as the Valletta Waterfront, which is a great place for a wander and a drink at one of the many restaurants.

Eating & Drinking

Le Meridien Phoenicia Hotel (p68), by City Gate, is home to a couple of restaurants.

Pegasus Bar & Brasserie (☎ 2291 1084; The Mall, Le Meridien Phoenicia Hotel; mains Lm4-7; ⏰ lunch & dinner) This relaxed setting offers upmarket café fare, with the menu including locally influenced Med dishes like grilled swordfish or *limoncello panna cotta*. There's also a lounge in the lobby serving all-day sandwiches and snacks (right down to scones for a civilised afternoon tea).

Tom Bar (☎ 2125 0780; 1 It-Telgha Tal-Kurċifiss; ⏰ from 8.30pm Tue-Sun year-round) It's not the most likely location for one of Malta's prime gay nightspots, but this two-storey bar is very popular, especially among older gays, who prefer it to Paceville's offerings. Tom offers upstairs for chilling out and downstairs for dance music.

Getting There & Away

Floriana is just a five-minute walk from Valletta. All buses to and from Valletta also pass through Floriana. The **main bus stop** on Triq Sant'Anna has an information board displaying the various route numbers and destinations.

There are two ferry terminals in Floriana. The daily **Gozo cargo ferry** (used primarily by trucks) departs the Sa Maison wharf at Pieta Creek in Marsamxett Harbour (p189), while passenger ferries to/from Sicily dock at the **Sea Passenger Terminal** by Pinto Wharf (p184). Pinto Wharf is also where cruise liners moor when in town.

THE THREE CITIES

This trio of towns, Vittoriosa, Senglea and Cospicua, are close-knit working communities largely dependent on their dockyards for employment. They are surprisingly off the tourist radar and – for now, at least – they offer a welcome escape from the commercial hustle of Valletta and Sliema.

The controversial Cottonera waterfront 'regeneration project' (www.cottonerawaterfront.com) has seen the opening of a chi-chi casino at Vittoriosa, as well as a marina for so-called 'superyachts', plus the construction of some very out-of-place modern residential apartments. Plans for a new five-star hotel seems to have stalled, so the land (by the casino) remains fenced and vacant. While it's hoped that projects such as these will bring

---

PINTO WHARF

Opened in mid-2005, Pinto Wharf (also known as the Valletta Waterfront; www.vallettawaterfront .com) is the much-heralded development of a formerly run-down dockside area. Developers transformed old warehouses into a fashionable area for dining, drinking, shopping and promenading, and an important new venue for festivals and concerts. It's a good-looking revamp too, with 250-year-old stone warehouses from the era of the Knights prettied up with doors and window shutters painted in bright primary colours. The view is a bit mixed – the fortresses of the Three Cities combine with the cranes of the dockyards to provide a somewhat industrial panorama (if it's not blocked by a huge cruise ship).

Sure, the shops down here are geared toward the cashed-up passengers of the cruisers that dock at the wharf (local craft outlets offering glass, ceramics and jewellery), but the restaurants and bars have been embraced by the locals, and you'll find families and groups taking up plenty of tables on the tree-lined promenade.

As far as food goes, there are half-a-dozen venues competing for your custom – it's worth a stroll to peruse the menus and prices of each, and to see if there are outside tables available. **Heat Bar & Diner** (☎ 2124 2400; mains Lm2-8; ⏰ lunch & dinner) promotes itself as an American-styled diner but the menu features all the usual Maltese suspects. It's more popular as a bar and nightclub and stays open late. **Nan Yuan** (☎ 2122 5310; dishes Lm2-6; ⏰ lunch & dinner Tue-Sun) is slightly incongruous given the setting, but offers a menu of Cantonese specialities. **Re-store** (☎ 2122 5000; snacks & meals Lm1-5; ⏰ lunch & dinner) offers decent café fare such as sandwiches, pasta and take-away ice creams.

Sadly, public transport links to the wharf are pretty dismal; see p72 for walking routes between Valletta and the waterfront.

WHAT'S IN A NAME?

The Three Cities were originally named Birgu, L-Isla and Bormla, but their names were changed after the Great Siege of 1565. Birgu became Vittoriosa (Victorious), L-Isla became Senglea (after Grand Master Claude de la Sengle), and Bormla became Cospicua (as in conspicuous courage). Local people and some road signs still use the old names, and all three together are often referred to as 'The Cottonera', a reference to the Cottonera Lines – the landward fortifications surrounding the Three Cities that were built in the 1670s at the instigation of Grand Master Nicolas Cotoner.

employment and prosperity to a formerly neglected area, there is a danger of diluting the character and charm of the area in the rush to embrace development and attract wealthy locals and tourists.

The best place for tourist information on the area is from the *dghajsa* boat **information kiosk** on the Vittoriosa waterfront (opposite). There are no hotels or guesthouses in the Three Cities, but the number of eating and drinking venues is growing.

History

When the Knights of St John first arrived in Malta in 1530, they made their home in the fishing village of Birgu, on a finger of land on the south side of Grand Harbour, overlooking the inlet (now known as Dockyard Creek) that was called the Port of the Arab Galleys. Here they built their auberges and repaired and extended the ancient defences. By the 1550s, Birgu (Fort St Angelo) and the neighbouring point of L-Isla (Fort St Michael) had been fortified, and Fort St Elmo had been built on the tip of the Sceberras Peninsula. Bormla, at the head of Dockyard Creek, was not fortified until the 17th century.

From this base, the Knights withstood the Turkish onslaught during the Great Siege of 1565 (see p21 for more on this battle), but in the years that followed, they moved to their new city of Valletta across the harbour. During WWII, the Three Cities and their surrounding docks were bombed almost daily throughout 1941 and 1942, and suffered terrible damage and bloodshed. Today they offer an untouristy welcome escape from Valletta and Sliema.

Vittoriosa

pop 3035

Atmospheric Vittoriosa is only 800m long and 400m at its widest, so it's hard to get lost – but aimlessly wandering its old, plant-filled alleys makes for a pleasant diversion. However, street signs are in Malti, while most tourist maps are in English only, which can be confusing. From the Poste de France, Triq il-Mina l-Kbira (Main Gate St) leads to the town's main square, Misraħ ir-Rebħa (Victory Sq). From the square, the marina and Maritime Museum are downhill to the left, while Triq San Filippu (St Philip's St) leads on towards Fort St Angelo at the tip of the peninsula.

There's good information on Vittoriosa at www.cittavittoriosa.com.

SIGHTS & ACTIVITIES

Inquisitor's Palace

The **Inquisitor's Palace** (☎ 2182 7006; Triq il-Mina l-Kbira; adult/child Lm2/0.50; ♨ 9am-5pm) was built in the 1530s and served as law courts until the 1570s, when it became the tribunal (and prison) of the Inquisition, whose task it was to find and suppress heresy.

The palace is now the home of the **National Museum of Ethnography**, which focuses on the religious values in Maltese culture up to the present day. In addition to the display areas in the tribunal room and prison complex, there is a permanent exhibition on the impact of the Inquisition on Maltese society.

Maritime Museum

The old naval bakery, built in the 1840s, now houses Malta's **Maritime Museum** (☎ 2166 0052; Vittoriosa Waterfront; adult/child Lm2/0.50; ♨ 9am-5pm). Well-displayed exhibits include Roman anchors, traditional Maltese fishing boats, models of the Knights' galleys and British naval vessels. There are also displays of old navigational instruments, log books and signal books.

Heritage Malta conducts guided tours of the museum (included in the cost of admission) at 11am daily. Their tour times can change, so check ahead.

Fort St Angelo

The tip of the Vittoriosa peninsula has been fortified since at least the 9th century, and before that it was the site of Roman and Phoenician temples. The Knights took over

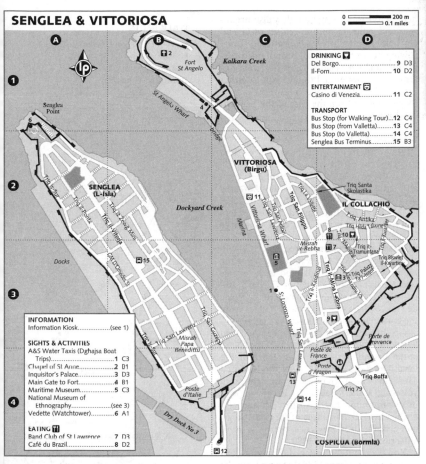

SENGLEA & VITTORIOSA

0 ——— 200 m
0 ——— 0.1 miles

DRINKING 🍷
Del Borgo...............................**9** D3
Il-Forn................................**10** D2

ENTERTAINMENT 🎭
Casino di Venezia................**11** C2

TRANSPORT
Bus Stop (for Walking Tour)...**12** C4
Bus Stop (from Valletta)........**13** C4
Bus Stop (to Valletta).............**14** C4
Senglea Bus Terminus...........**15** B3

INFORMATION
Information Kiosk................(see 1)

SIGHTS & ACTIVITIES
A&S Water Taxis (Dghajsa Boat
Trips)....................................**1** C3
Chapel of St Anne.................**2** B1
Inquisitor's Palace.................**3** D3
Main Gate to Fort.................**4** B1
Maritime Museum.................**5** C3
National Museum of
Ethnography.....................(see 3)
Vedette (Watchtower)............**6** A1

EATING 🍴
Band Club of St Lawrence **7** D3
Café du Brazil.......................**8** D2

the medieval fort in 1530 and rebuilt and strengthened it – Fort St Angelo served as the residence of the Grand Master of the Order until 1571 and was the headquarters of la Valette during the Great Siege.

Further defences were added in the late 17th century by the talented engineer Don Carlos Grunenberg, whose florid coat-of-arms still sits above the gate overlooking St Angelo Wharf.

The British took over the fort in the 19th century, and from 1912 until 1979 it served as the headquarters of the Mediterranean Fleet, first as HMS *Egmont* and from 1933 as HMS *St Angelo*. The upper part of the fort, including the Grand Master's Palace and the 15th-century **Chapel of St Anne**, is now occupied by

the modern Order of St John. The remainder of the fort is officially closed to visitors due to its poor state of repair, but access through the gate above St Angelo Wharf is usually pretty straightforward and you can wander around parts of the site, an unusual mixture of medieval fortress and abandoned 20th-century officers' mess. The fort is in the early stages of what promises to be a long rehabilitation project.

Harbour Cruises

At the waterfront, in front of the Freedom Monument, is a kiosk belonging to **A&S Water Taxis** (☎ 2180 6921; www.maltesewatertaxis.com; ⏰ 9am-5pm, or until dark in summer). The friendly guys here dispense maps of the Three Cities and offer helpful tourist information; they also organise good-value 35-minute cruises of Grand Harbour in a restored *dghajsa* (traditional rowing boat or water taxi; pronounced diesa) for Lm3 per person. These boatmen can also act as a water taxi to take you to either Senglea (Lm0.60) or Valletta (Lm1.50; deposits you not far from the base of the Lascaris Bastion).

WALKING TOUR

Begin at the bus stop at the corner of Triq San Lawrenz (St Lawrence St) and Triq 79. Cross the road towards the Poste d'Aragon and enter the bastion through the **Advanced Gate (1)**, inscribed with the date 'MDCCXXII' (1722) and a relief of crossed cannons. Here you'll find a café, and next door is a large WWII air-raid shelter open to the public as the **Malta at War Museum (2**; adult/child Lm1.50/0.75; 10am-4pm Mon-Sat). Cross the bridge over the moat, which has been planted with orange trees and is now the Coronation Gardens, and pass through the Couvre Porte into the Poste de France (there's a good view of Senglea from the battlement up the ramp to the left).

Go through Porte de Provence and head left along Triq il-Mina l-Kbira, past the **Church of the Annunciation (3)** on your left and the **Inquisitor's Palace (4**; p76), now the National Museum of Ethnography, on your right, until you reach **Misraħ ir-Rebħa (5**; Victory Sq) with its two monuments: the Victory Monument, erected in 1705 in memory of the Great Siege; and a statue of St Lawrence, patron saint of Vittoriosa, dating from 1880.

You'll definitely notice the magnificent building dating from 1888 that stands on the eastern side of the square and is home to the Band Club of St Lawrence. Note its striking wooden balcony.

From the square head east on Triq Hilda Tabone (Britannic St, by Café du Brazil), then take the first left (Triq Santa Skolastika, or St Scholastica St) towards the massive blank walls of the **Sacra Infermeria (6)**, the first hospital to be built by the Knights on their arrival in Malta. It now serves as a convent. After it, go down a stepped alley (signposted Triq il-Miratur) and walk along the wall's perimeter. The ramp descending into a trench in front of the Infermeria leads to the **Bighi Sally Port (7)**, where the wounded were brought by boat to the infirmary under the cover of darkness during the Great Siege.

WALK FACTS

Start cnr Triq San Lawrenz & Triq 79
Finish base of Fort St Angelo
Distance approx 2km
Duration 1½ hours

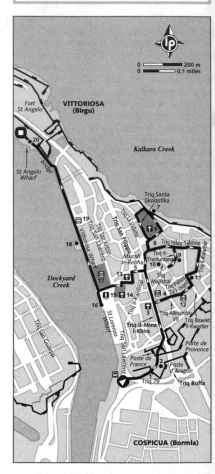

After doing a circuit of the Sacra Infermeria head back onto Triq Hilda Tabone. To your right lies a small maze of charming alleys, collectively known as **Il Collachio (8)**, with some of the oldest surviving buildings in the city. Wander up Triq it-Tramuntana (North St) to the so-called **Norman House (9)** at No 11 (on the left) and look up at the 1st floor. The twin-arched window, with its slender central pillar and zigzag decoration, dates from the 13th century and is in a style described as Siculo-Norman (similar windows survive in Il-Kastell on Gozo). Also in this area are the first auberges built by the Knights in the 16th century – the **Auberge d'Angleterre (10**; Triq il-Majjistral), the auberge of the English Knights, now serves as the local library.

At the far end of Triq Hilda Tabone turn right along Triq il-Kwartier (Barrack St), and bear right at the corner of the imposing **Armoury (11)**. Turn left and then right along Triq Palazz Ta'l-Isqof (Bishop's Palace St) past the **Bishop's Palace (12)**, built in 1542. Return to Triq il-Mina l-Kbira and turn right to again reach Misraħ ir-Rebħa.

From the square, to explore the waterfront area turn left into the nearby chapel where the little **Oratory of St Joseph (13)** contains relics of Grand Master la Valette, and continue down past the **Church of St Lawrence (14)**. Built on the site of an 11th-century Norman church, St Lawrence's served as the conventual church of the Knights of St John from 1530 until the move to St John's Co-Cathedral in Valletta (see the boxed text, p38, for more information on its history).

At the foot of the hill, pass to the left of the large building across the street. The palm and cactus garden on the left contains the **Freedom Monument (15)**, which commemorates the departure of the last British forces in Malta in 1979. Bronze figures show a bugler playing the 'Last Post' as his comrade lowers the flag, and a British sailor saying goodbye to a Maltese girl while, rather unromantically, shaking her hand.

Head to the waterfront, where you'll encounter a **kiosk (16**; p77) dispensing tourist information and offering cruises of Grand Harbour. Continue along the waterfront past the interesting **Maritime Museum (17**; p76), housed in the old naval bakery, and you'll reach the **marina (18)**, filled with flash boats, and a **casino (19**; right) in 17th-century buildings that were once the Knights' Treasury, the Captain-General's Palace, and a hostel for galley captains. At the far end of the quay you can cross the bridge over the moat and follow a path beyond St Angelo Wharf to the rocky point beneath the walls of **Fort St Angelo (20**; p76), where old cannons serve as bollards and the remains of WWII gun installations can be seen.

From the wharf, you can retrace your steps back along the waterfront. You can opt for a *dgħajsa* cruise or taxi service (see above), head left up to the cafés of Misraħ ir-Rebħa, or continue walking south to make your way to Senglea (see below for a walking tour of the area).

EATING & DRINKING

There are limited daytime eating options in Vittoriosa, but your choices increase in number and quality of an evening. Time your explorations for late afternoon, then head to one of the wine bars that have sprung up. Café du Brazil and the Band Club of St Lawrence provide opportunities for a casual drink and offer limited lunch selections on Misraħ ir-Rebħa.

Il-Forn (☎ 2182 0379; 27 Triq it-Tramuntana; snacks & meals Lm2-5; ☒ 7.30pm-1am Tue-Sun) This alluring art gallery and wine bar in Il Collachio (almost opposite the Norman House) has plenty of fabulously colourful art by the Austrian-born owner of the bar on display. It's well worth a look, and you can enjoy traditional snacks and local wines in one of the courtyards.

Another excellent choice is **Del Borgo** (☎ 2180 3710; 36 Triq it-Torri ta'San Ġwann; mains Lm3-7; ☒ from 7.30pm daily, plus lunch Sun), a surprisingly sophisticated restaurant and wine bar in a side street not far from the main gates into Vittoriosa.

ENTERTAINMENT

Casino di Venezia (☎ 2180 5580; Vittoriosa waterfront; ☒ 2pm-4am Mon-Thu, 2pm-5am Fri-Sat, noon-4am Sun) Vegas meets Venice: travellers looking for a chance to make (or blow) some holiday dough should head to this ritzy casino beside the marina and part of the (stalled) Cottonera waterfront redevelopment. Visitors must be aged at least 18 to enter (25 for Maltese citizens), be smartly dressed and carry a passport or ID card. A shuttle service is offered from some hotels – call the casino to inquire. Casinos in Malta draw many gamblers from Sicily, which doesn't have any casinos of its own.

GETTING THERE & AWAY

Buses 1, 4 and 6 from Valletta will take you to the **bus stop** on Triq 79 beneath the Poste d'Aragon; bus 2 goes all the way to Misraħ ir-Rebħa. One of these four route options departs Valletta for Vittoriosa at least every 15 to 20 minutes; the fare on all services is Lm0.20.

VALLETTA

Bus 627 runs hourly until 3pm from Buġibba via Sliema to the Three Cities (Lm0.50) and on to Marsaxlokk.

Senglea
pop 3500
Senglea is even more difficult to get lost in than Vittoriosa, as the streets form a grid pattern. The town was pretty much razed to the ground during WWII, and little of historic interest remains, but there are great views of Valletta and Vittoriosa, and the little **vedette** (watchtower) at the tip of the peninsula is one of the classic sights of Malta.

WALKING TOUR
From the bus stop in the square outside the fortifications, walk up the ramp and pass through the gate at the Poste d'Italie, and continue along Triq il-Vitorja (Victory St). At the first square is the **Church of Our Lady of Victory (1)**, which was completely rebuilt after WWII. Follow Triq il-Vitorja all the way to the **Church of St Philip (2)**, and follow the road right and then left (Triq iż-Żewġ Mini, or Two Gates St) to reach Safe Haven Gardens at the tip of the peninsula. The **vedette (3)** here is decorated with carvings of eyes and ears symbolising watchfulness, and commands a view to the west over the whole length of Grand Harbour and the southern flank of Valletta – check out the view of the new Pinto Wharf development too.

Immediately on your left as you leave Safe Haven Gardens is a staircase down to Triq is-Sirena. Follow this street as it descends to the quayside. Follow the waterfront, with its moored *dghajsas* and impressive views of Vittoriosa, back to the starting point. There are a couple of reasonable restaurants along the quay.

Towards the end of the quay the road passes under the bastion, and a walkway goes around the outside beneath the so-called **Gantry House (4)**. This was where the galleys of the Knights of St John were moored while their masts were removed using machinery mounted on the wall above the walkway.

GETTING THERE & AWAY
Bus 3 runs between Valletta and the central square in Senglea bus terminus every half-hour or so (Lm0.20). (Get off at the bus stop just outside the fortifications if you wish to do the walking tour outlined on above.)

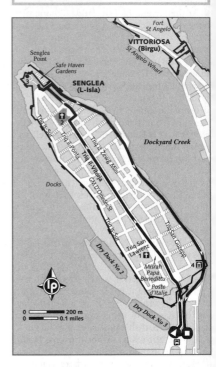

Alternatively, catch bus 1, 2 4 or 6 to Vittoriosa and get off at Dry Dock No 1 (at the head of Dockyard Creek), walk back up the hill and turn right. It's a 15-minute walk from the main gate at Vittoriosa around to the main gate at Senglea.

HYPOGEUM & TARXIEN TEMPLES
The suburb of Paola, about 2km southwest of Cospicua, conceals two of Malta's most important prehistoric sites. The **Hal Saflieni Hypogeum** (☎ 2180 5019, 2182 5579; Triq iċ-Ċimiterju; adult/child Lm4/2) is an incredible underground necropolis, discovered during building work in 1902. It consists of halls, chambers and passages hewn out of the living rock and covering some 500 sq metres; it is thought to date from around 3600 to 3000 BC, and an estimated

7000 bodies may have been interred here. Excellent 50-minute tours of the complex are available daily at 9am, 10am, 11am, 1pm, 2pm, 3pm and 4pm. Note that the tours aren't suitable for children aged under six.

Tours start with a brief introductory exhibition and multilingual film focusing on the temple-building people and the Hypogeum's relationship to Malta's overground temple sites. Touring the site is a fascinating experience, but leaves you with more questions than it does answers about the ancient civilisation responsible for the Hypogeum's construction – who were they, what exactly did they do here, and where did they go? (See p19 for more on Malta's temple builders.)

Carbon dioxide exhaled by visiting tourists was doing serious to damage the delicate limestone walls of the burial chambers of the Hypogeum, and it was closed to the public for 10 years, reopening in mid-2000. It has now been restored with Unesco funding and reopened in 2000; its microclimate is now strictly controlled to ensure its conservation. For this reason, the maximum number of visitors to the site is 70 per day – tickets are understandably in demand, and you can't just turn up to the site and expect to join the next tour (although it's astounding how many people roll up under this impression). Prebooking is *essential* (usually at least two weeks before you wish to visit, or up to a month in advance for busy periods such as summer's peak, Easter and Christmas). Tickets are available in person from the Hypogeum and the Museum of Archaeology in Valletta (p62), or online (www.heritagemalta.org; info@heritagemalta .org). If you're desperate, you might decide to try your luck for cancellations – you'll have to turn up before the first scheduled tour. Some readers have reported success with this method, but it's far from guaranteed.

The **Tarxien Temples** (☎ 2169 5578; Triq it-Templi Neolitiċi; adult/child Lm1/0.25; ◷ 9am-5pm), pronounced tar-*sheen*, are hidden up a back street several blocks east of the Hypogeum – keep your eyes peeled, as the entrance is inconspicuous. These megalithic structures were excavated in 1914 and are thought to date from between 3600 and 2500 BC. There are four linked temples, built with massive stone blocks up to 3m by 1m by 1m in size, decorated with spiral patterns and pitting, and reliefs of animals including bulls, goats and pigs. The large statue of a broad-hipped female figure was found in the right-hand niche of the first temple. Heritage Malta conducts guided tours of the Tarxien site (included in the cost of admission) at 9.30am, 11.30am and 3.30pm daily. Their times are not fixed, so enquire in advance. This is another heritage site promising big things – the construction of a sleek new visitors centre is scheduled for completion by 2008.

Getting There & Away

Dozens of buses pass through Paola, stopping at various points around the main square, Pjazza Paola. Buses 1, 2, 3, 4 and 6 between Valletta and the Three Cities stop at the northern end of the square (look for landmarks such as the police station out the front of the prison). Buses 8, 11, 15 and 27 stop on the eastern side of the square, by the large Church of Christ the King (to return to Valletta, catch a bus from the western side of the square).

From the main square, the Hypogeum is a five-minute walk, the Tarxien Temples are 10 minutes.

FORT RINELLA

Built by the British in the late 19th century, **Fort Rinella** (Map p56; ☎ 2180 9713; Triq Santu Rokku, Kalkara; adult/child/family Lm3/1.50/6; ◷ 10am-5pm), 1.5km northeast of Vittoriosa, was one of two coastal batteries designed to counter the threat of Italy's new ironclad battleships. The batteries (the second one was on Tigné Point in Sliema) were equipped with the latest Armstrong 100-ton guns – the biggest muzzle-loading guns

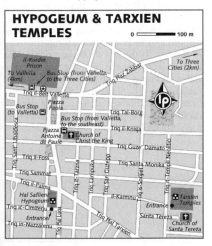

HYPOGEUM & TARXIEN TEMPLES

0 ▭▭▭▭ 100 m

Il-Kordin Prison
To Valletta (4km)
To Valletta (4km)
Bus Stop (from Valletta, to the Three Cities)
To Three Cities (2km)
Triq Ħaż-Żabbar
Triq Il-Belt Valletta
Bus Stop (to Valletta)
Pjazza Paola
Triq Tal-Borġ
Bus Stop (from Valletta, to the southeast)
Pjazza Antoine de Paule
Church of Christ the King
Triq Il-Knisja
Triq Il-Foss
Triq Sant' Ubaldeska
Triq Guże' Damato
Triq Sammat
Triq Il-Lazzra
Triq Santa Monika
Triq San Ġużepp
Triq It-Templi Neolitiċi
Triq Il-Palma
Hal Saflieni Hypogeum
Triq Il-Limpuka
Il-Karmnu
Tarxien Temples
Triq Ic-Cimiterju
Entrance/Triq in-Nazzarenu
Triq Ħal Tarxien
Entrance
Santa Tereza
Church of Santa Tereza

MOVIE-MAKING IN MALTA

From the road to Fort Rinella visitors have a good view of the huge water tanks of the Mediterranean Film Studios (not open to the public). There's not a lot to see, but these are the biggest film-production water facilities in Europe – the two main water tanks have a clear horizon behind them, allowing directors to create the illusion that on-screen characters are miles out to sea. Water scenes from such films as *The Spy Who Loved Me* (1977), *Raise the Titanic* (1980), *White Squall* (1996), *U-571* (2000) and *The League of Extraordinary Gentlemen* (2003) were shot here.

But it's not just the water tanks that have drawn film crews to Malta. The country's fortresses have long been popular with location scouts – the basement and casemates of Fort St Elmo were used for the Turkish prison scenes in the 1978 film *Midnight Express*, and Fort St Elmo has doubled as locations in Marseille and Beirut in more recent productions. Also out near Fort Rinella is Ricasoli Fort (also closed to the public), where a large portion of the 2004 Trojan War epic *Troy* was filmed on specially crafted sets. Scenes from another sandals-and-swords blockbuster, *Gladiator* (2000), were also filmed here. More recently it was transformed into a Palestinian refugee camp in the controversial 2005 film *Munich*.

Comino's St Mary's Tower appears in *The Count of Monte Cristo* (2002), a film that features various locations in the Maltese Islands (including Mdina and Vittoriosa), while the Blue Lagoon provides a great backdrop to a dire film, *Swept Away* (2002), starring Madonna and produced by her husband, Guy Ritchie.

In recent years Malta doubled for most of the Mediterranean and Middle Eastern locales (including Israel, Lebanon, Cyprus, Greece and Italy) in Steven Spielberg's 2005 movie *Munich* (look out for Malta's distinctive yellow buses in a number of scenes), and Maltese locations were chosen for a handful of flashback scenes involving the murderous albino monk in the 2006 film, *The Da Vinci Code*.

There are some good websites to check out if you're interested in learning more: see **Mediterranean Film Studios** (www.mfsstudios.com), the **Malta Film Commission** (www.mfc.com.mt) and the website of the **Malta Tourism Authority** (www.visitmalta.com) – click on 'What to See', and then the 'Malta Movie Map' icon. Although much of the movie map hasn't been updated in years, the 'latest news' section is reasonably up-to-date.

Be sure to keep your eyes peeled and ask around if you want to know what film sets (and stars) you might stumble across as you travel around the country.

---

ever made. Their 100-ton shells had a range of 6.4km and could penetrate 38cm of armour plating. The guns were never fired in anger, and were retired in 1906. Fort Rinella has been restored by a group of amateur enthusiasts from the **Malta Heritage Trust** (www.wirtartna.org) and is now one of Malta's most interesting military museums. Guided tours given by volunteers dressed as late-19th-century soldiers, including historical re-enactments, are held at 2.30pm daily (you'll pay an additional Lm2 on top of the entry price to join one of these tours).

Getting There & Away

To get to Fort Rinella, take bus 4 from Valletta or the Three Cities; departures leave from Valletta at half-past the hour from 9.30am to 4.30pm and then drop you off out the front of the fort. If the bus drops you only as far as the Mediterranean Film Studios, face the water and head to your left – after about 10 minutes you should see a Union Jack flying from the fort. For a small fee you can also call the fort and arrange a direct pick up from your accommodation (Lm1).

Sliema, St Julian's & Paceville

Malta's cool crowd flocks to this area to promenade, eat, drink, shop and party. As well as being a local playground for the cashed-up, it's where many tourists base themselves, among the growing number of high-rise hotels, apartment blocks, shops, restaurants, bars and nightclubs. There's little by way of old-school tourist attractions here (no museums, historic sites or churches of note), but there's plenty of opportunity for a harbour cruise, swim, long lunch or big night, plus good transport links to Valletta and other points of the island.

The seaside suburb of Sliema was once the preserve of the Maltese upper classes, a cool retreat from the heat and bustle of Valletta. The waterfront streets have lost their local charm as they sprout concrete monoliths in the shape of hotels and apartments blocks, but the back streets remain largely residential and a Sliema address is still something of a status symbol in Maltese society.

Cosmopolitan St Julian's, north of Sliema, has also been the focus of much recent tourist development, with five-star hotels and apartment complexes rising along the rocky shoreline (notably at Portomaso and St George's Bay). Paceville is the heart of St Julian's – it's pretty shabby and quiet by day but comes to life after dark, when it lives up to its title as the country's nightlife capital. This is where many of Malta's English-language schools are located, so you'll hear a variety of languages and accents, and see lots of groups of students hitting the bars instead of the books.

HIGHLIGHTS

- Enjoying the early-evening people parade along Sliema's **waterfront promenade** (p85)
- Alfresco wining and dining on **Spinola Bay** (p93), Malta's gastronomic epicentre
- Seeing how the other half lives at **Portomaso** (p92), while travelling your taste buds in one of the complex's restaurants
- Bar-hopping and letting yourself get messy on a big night out in **Paceville** (p95)
- Living high on the hog in one of the area's fab **five-star hotels** (p90), especially if you've managed to snare a bargain rate
- Taking to the waters on a **cruise** (p87) out of Sliema, to enjoy history, snorkelling, coastal panoramas or whatever takes your fancy

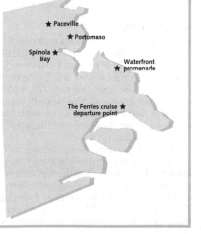

★ Paceville
★ Portomaso
Spinola ★ Bay
Waterfront ★ promenade
The Ferries cruise ★ departure point

SLIEMA, ST JULIAN'S & PACEVILLE

(map labels) St George's Bay · Dragonara Point · See St Julian's & Paceville Map (p88) · Il-Qaliet · Paceville · Portomaso · ST JULIAN'S · To Buġibba (9km); St Paul's Bay (10km) · MEDITERRANEAN SEA · St Julian's Bay · See Sliema Map (p86) · Spinola Bay · St Julian's Tower · Triq it-Torri · Balluta Bay · Pool · Il-Fortizza · SLIEMA · Triq Manwel Dimech · Triq Birkirkara · GŻIRA · Qui-Si-Sana · The Ferries · Tigné Point Development (under construction) · Dragut Point · Triq Tas-Sliema · Gżira Hotels · Sliema Creek · Tigné Fort · Café Jubilee · Triq Forti Manoel · Triq ix-Xatt (The Strand) · St Elmo Point · University of Malta · Manoel Island · Fort Manoel · Harbour · Fort St Elmo · Triq Mikiel Anton Vassalli · Triq D'Argens · Lazzaretto Creek · Lazzaretto di San Rocco · Marina · Pool · VALLETTA · TA'XBIEX · UK & Netherlands Embassies · Australian Embassy · Marsamxett · Ix-Xatt Ta'Xbiex Marina · Msida Creek · Pietà Creek · FLORIANA · City Gate · GRAND HARBOUR · To Birkirkara (1.5km); Rabat (7km) · MSIDA · St Luke's Hospital · PIETÀ · To Valletta (2km)

ORIENTATION

Sliema occupies the peninsula to the north of Valletta, from which it is separated by the thin stretch of water of Marsamxett Harbour. The main thoroughfare on the south side of the peninsula is the coast-hugging Triq ix-Xatt (commonly known as 'the Strand'), which continues south along the Gżira waterfront and around the Ta'Xbiex Peninsula to the marina at Msida.

The focal point of Sliema, known as the Ferries, is at the northeastern end of the Strand, where you'll find the bus terminus and the ferry to Valletta, along with plenty of operators offering harbour cruises. From here Triq it-Torri (Tower Rd) strikes north across the neck of the peninsula, then follows the

coastline west past St Julian's Tower to Balluta Bay and St Julian's.

St Julian's (San Ġiljan) lies between Balluta Bay and St George's Bay, facing out onto the Mediterranean Sea. The compact grid of streets packed with pubs and clubs to the north of Spinola Bay between Triq San Ġorġ and Triq id-Dragunara is known as Paceville (patchy-ville). North of St Julian's lies St George's Bay, home to a number of large upmarket hotels.

Maps

Most maps of the Maltese Islands include a handy inset street plan of this area. Pick up free street maps at the tourist information office.

INFORMATION
Emergency
Police Station (Map p86; ☎ 2133 0502; cnr Triq Manwel Dimech & Triq Rudolfu, Sliema)
Police Station (Map p88; ☎ 2133 2196; Triq San Ġorġ, St Julian's) Close to McDonald's, on Spinola Bay.

Internet Access
MelitaNet (Map p88; ☎ 2133 7557; Triq Ball, Paceville; per hr Lm1; 🕒 24hr) Large internet café inside the Tropicana Hotel. Also offers good-value rates for international calls.
CyberSurf (Map p86; ☎ 2134 2063; 38 Triq ix-Xatt, Sliema; per hr Lm1; 🕒 10am-late) Close to the corner of Triq Manwel Dimech.
Magic Kiosk (Map p86; ☎ 2133 5653; cnr Triq ix-Xatt & Triq it-Torri, Sliema; per hr Lm1; 🕒 10am-10pm) Also offers good rates for international calls.

Medical Services
St Luke's Hospital (☎ 2124 1251, emergency 112; www .slh.gov.mt; Triq San Luqa, Gwardamanġa) Malta's public general hospital is near Pietà (about 3km southwest of Valletta); to get there take bus 75. The long-delayed opening of Malta's large new hospital, Mater Dei, was scheduled and rescheduled for 2007. Mater Dei is in Tal-Qroqq, about 3km west of Valetta near the University of Malta.

Money
There are plenty of banks and ATMs throughout the area. Paceville in particular has plenty of money-exchange offices, catering to tourists and foreign students.
Travelex Sliema (Map p86; Il-Piazzetta, Triq it-Torri; 🕒 8.30am-1.30pm & 2-5.30pm Mon-Fri, 9am-1pm Sat); Paceville (Map p88; Bay Street Complex; 🕒 10am-10pm)

Post
Post Office Sliema (Map p86; 118 Triq Manwel Dimech; 🕒 7.30am-12.45pm Mon-Sat) Paceville (Map p88; Triq Elija Zammit; 🕒 7.30am-12.45pm Mon-Sat)

Tourist Information
Tourist Information Office (Map p88; ☎ 2138 1392; Palazzo Spinola; 🕒 generally 8am-12.30pm & 1.15-5pm Mon-Fri) Enter from Triq Ross. The complex opening hours involve closing for lunch, and sometimes closing at 2pm in the high season. Unhelpfully, it's closed Saturday, Sunday and public holidays.

DANGERS & ANNOYANCES
The tidal wave of alcohol and testosterone that swills through the streets of Paceville on weekends occasionally overflows into outbreaks of violence. Some people also find that the noise levels in and around Paceville at night are high enough to be a nuisance. Unless you plan to party the night away, you may prefer to seek accommodation in a quieter part of town.

SIGHTS
Sliema
There's really not a lot to see in Sliema itself, but there are good views of Valletta from Triq ix-Xatt (the Strand), especially at dusk as the floodlights are switched on. Triq ix-Xatt and Triq it-Torri make for a pleasant waterfront stroll, with plenty of bars and cafés in which to quench a thirst. In the evenings these streets fill up with promenading families out for their daily *passeggiata* (evening stroll) and joggers and dog-walkers doing their thing.

There are two towers on Triq it-Torri. **St Julian's Tower** is one of the network of coastal watchtowers built by Grand Master de Redin in the 17th century. **Il-Fortizza** was built by

---

TIGNÉ POINT DEVELOPMENT
Tigné Point (Map p84), a promontory east of Sliema, was one of the sites where the Turkish commander Dragut Reis ranged his cannons to pound Fort St Elmo into submission during the Great Siege in 1565 (p21). The tip of the peninsula is still known as Dragut Point. This whole area is currently undergoing massive redevelopment, with construction of residential apartments set around large pedestrianised areas. It's anticipated that there will be new restaurants, shops and sporting grounds as part of the development – completion isn't likely until sometime in early 2008. The previously neglected Tigné Fort, built in 1792 by the Knights of St John, will be restored and possibly used as a gallery or museum. When the Tigné Point revitalisation is complete, the same developers will turn their attention to the neglected Manoel Island (p87) – so expect big things there too (although possibly not until 2012 or later). If you're interested in all the goings-on, or are in the market for Maltese real estate, check out www.tignepoint.com and www.midimalta.com.

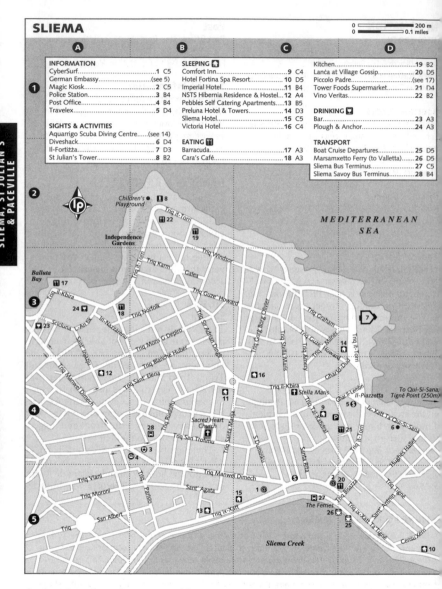

SLIEMA

0 ———————— 200 m
0 ———————— 0.1 miles

INFORMATION
CyberSurf.................................1 C5
German Embassy.............(see 5)
Magic Kiosk.............................2 C5
Police Station..........................3 B4
Post Office..............................4 B4
Travelex..................................5 D4

SIGHTS & ACTIVITIES
Aquarrigo Scuba Diving Centre......(see 14)
Diveshack.................................6 D4
Il-Fortizza................................7 D3
St Julian's Tower........................8 B2

SLEEPING
Comfort Inn..............................9 C4
Hotel Fortina Spa Resort.............10 D5
Imperial Hotel..........................11 B4
NSTS Hibernia Residence & Hostel...12 A4
Pebbles Self Catering Apartments....13 B5
Preluna Hotel & Towers...............14 D3
Sliema Hotel.............................15 C5
Victoria Hotel...........................16 C4

EATING
Barracuda...............................17 A3
Cara's Café..............................18 A3

Kitchen...................................19 B2
Lanča at Village Gossip................20 D5
Piccolo Padre......................(see 17)
Tower Foods Supermarket.............21 D4
Vino Veritas.............................22 B2

DRINKING
Bar.......................................23 A3
Plough & Anchor.......................24 A3

TRANSPORT
Boat Cruise Departures................25 D5
Marsamxetto Ferry (to Valletta).....26 D5
Sliema Bus Terminus...................27 C5
Sliema Savoy Bus Terminus...........28 B4

the British in the 19th century and has now been taken over by TGI Friday's, an American restaurant chain.

Sliema's **beaches** are mostly shelves of bare rock, making clambering in and out of the sea sometimes a little bit awkward. In places along Triq it-Torri and at Qui-si-Sana, square pools have been cut into the soft limestone – these

were made for the convenience of leisure-loving upper-class Maltese ladies, but have since fallen into some disrepair. For sun and water seekers, there are better facilities at the private **lidos** scattered along the coast, including swimming pools, sun lounges, bars and water sports; admission costs are around Lm2 to Lm3 per day.

Around Sliema

Sliema merges southward into the suburb of Gżira. A short bridge gives access to **Manoel Island**, most of which is taken up by boat-building yards and the dilapidated ruins of Fort Manoel. The island was used as a quarantine zone by the Knights of St John, and the shell of their 17th-century plague hospital, the **Lazzaretto di San Rocco**, can still be seen on the south side – it served as an isolation hospital during WWI and was last used during an epidemic in 1936. **Fort Manoel** was built in the early 18th century under Grand Master Manoel de Vilhena, and suffered extensive bomb damage during WWII, when nearby Lazzaretto Creek was used as a submarine base. The overgrown island is scheduled for long-overdue development, but not for a while yet (see the boxed text, p85).

Ta'Xbiex (pronounced tashb-*yesh*), to the south of Manoel Island, is an upmarket area of gracious villas, mansions and embassies, with yacht marinas on either side.

St Julian's

Amid the heaving bars and packed restaurants of central St Julian's lies the elegant **Palazzo Spinola**, built for the Italian knight Rafael Spinola in the late 17th century. Surrounded by a walled garden (the entrance is on Triq il-Knisja), it now houses an elegant and expensive restaurant and the tourist office. Another aristocratic residence that's found a new lease of life is **Villa Dragonara**, set on the southern headland of St George's Bay. Built in the late 19th century for the Marquis Scicluna, a wealthy banker, it's now occupied by the Dragonara Casino (p95).

Paceville is the place to get messy – it's the in-your-face cluster of pubs, clubs and restaurants that forms the focal point for the wilder side of Malta's nightlife. This is party-all-night and sleep-all-day territory, but there is new upmarket development going on all around – notably the ultraposh **Portomaso apartment and marina complex** on the site of the old Fort Spinola (featuring a five-star hotel, boutique marina and upmarket apartments) and the newish **InterContinental** hotel. The tourist authorities are trying to push Malta's image upmarket, but Paceville is likely to retain its raucous, rough-and-ready atmosphere for some time to come.

Most of the **beaches** around St Julian's are of the bare rock or private lido variety (the five-star hotels offer beach clubs and water sports), but there is a genuine, if crowded, sandy beach at the head of St George's Bay.

ACTIVITIES
Water Sports

Traditional touristy stuff like banana rides, paragliding and paddle boats are available at most of the private lidos along the shore. Many also offer waterborne activities, including windsurfing, water-skiing, motorboating, snorkelling and scuba diving. **Yellow Fun Watersports** (Map p88; ☎ 2373 4366; www.yellowfunwatersports.com) operates from the Portomaso marina, behind the Hilton hotel, and offers a huge menu of activities, including jet-ski rental, yacht charter, self-drive boats, water taxis to Sliema, Valletta or Vittoriosa, and trips to Gozo and Comino.

Boat Trips

The average price for a 1½ to two-hour cruise taking in Marsamxett and Grand Harbours costs Lm6.50, but you may find smaller operators with cheaper rates. Cruise touts line the waterfront at the Ferries in Sliema (from where most cruises depart), and on the other side of the road from them are tour agencies offering island-wide excursions. All these agents can book you on the tours offered by the major operators listed here; prices for half- and full-day cruises usually include hotel transfers.

Captain Morgan Cruises (☎ 2346 3333; www.captainmorgan.com.mt) has a boat trip for every traveller's taste and pocket, while **Alliance Cruises & Tours** (☎ 2133 2165; www.alliancecruises.com) offers a smaller programme of boat tours out of Sliema. **Hera Cruises** (☎ 2133 0583; www.herayachtmalta.com) organises sailing adventures, including the option of snorkelling and/or diving instruction. See p191 for price and itinerary details of these three operators.

Jeep Safaris & Bus Tours

As well as its extensive programme of boat trips, **Captain Morgan Cruises** (☎ 2346 3333; www.captainmorgan.com.mt) runs popular 4WD jeep safaris exploring the more remote parts of Malta and Gozo. **Alliance Cruises & Tours** (☎ 2133 2165; www.alliancecruises.com) also offers land tours, including bus tours to major landmarks and a jeep safari to get off the beaten track. See p191 for details of the offerings of both companies.

SLIEMA, ST JULIAN'S & PACEVILLE

Diving

There are several dive operators in the area that can help you explore Malta's excellent dive sites (see p46). These include the following:

Aquarrigo Scuba Diving Centre (Map p86; ☎ 2133 0882; www.planetsea.net; Preluna Beach Club, Triq it-Torri, Sliema) At the lido of the Preluna Hotel & Towers.

Diveshack (Map p86; ☎ 2133 8558; www.divemalta .com; Ix-Xatt Ta'Qui-si-Sana, Qui-si-Sana, Sliema)

Divewise (Map p88; ☎ 2135 6441; www.divewise .com.mt; Westin Dragonara Resort, St Julian's)

SLEEPING

Most of the accommodation in the area is aimed squarely at the package holiday and luxury hotel market, but you'll find that there

are some bargains to be had during the low season. Very few hotels offer parking for guests (except for the more upmarket places on large grounds). You may find street parking hard to come by.

Budget

SLIEMA

The following hotels are all located on the Sliema map (Map p86).

NSTS Hibernia Residence & Hostel (☎ 2133 3859; www.nsts.org; Triq Mons G Depiro; dm Lm3.70-5.10; tw studio Lm9-14; 🖳) Malta's only true hostel, the Hibernia is perfect for those after quality budget accommodation and a ready-made crowd (it's popular with English-language students). As well as a comprehensive roll-call o facilities inside this modern, seven-storey building (laundry, internet café, breakfast room–cafeteria, TV lounge, rooftop sun terrace, good security), there's a choice of sleeping options. Shoestringers can camp out in the single-sex dorm sections, where three to four bedrooms (each with six to eight beds) share bathrooms and a generous kitchen-dining area. Long-stayers or travellers after more privacy can choose a studio or apartment in the 'residence'. These sleep up to four and have their own kitchenette and ensuite. From Valletta, take bus 62, 64, 66 or 67 to Balluta Bay and walk 300m up Triq Manwel Dimech; Triq Mons G Depiro is on the left.

Comfort Inn (☎ 2133 4221; www.comfortinnmalta .com; 29 Triq tal-Katidral; B&B per person Lm6-8.50; 💻) A budget gem in the heart of Sliema. Behind its eye-catching terracotta exterior, this homely, family-run guesthouse offers 12 spick-and-span rooms (connected each level by a lift), each with sunny yellow décor, simple furnishings and an en suite. Family-friendly rooms can sleep up to four; prices includes a buffet breakfast. On the ground level is a TV lounge where guests can socialise; on the roof is a sun terrace where you can take in the busy streetscapes below.

Pebbles Self Catering Apartments (☎ 2131 1889; www.maltaselfcatering.com; 89 Triq ix-Xatt; d Lm14-20; 💻 💻) Handy to the bus terminus and the ferry to Valletta is this complex of great-value studio apartments. They are not for the claustrophobic – don't expect a lot of living space, but do expect some bang for your buck:

all studios have a private bathroom, kitchenette, phone and cable TV (the most expensive studios enjoy a sea view). At ground level is a café-bar, and on the roof is a sun terrace. Air-con is via a user-pays system.

PACEVILLE

Tropicana Hotel (Map p88; ☎ 2133 7557; www.tropicana .com.mt; Triq Ball; B&B per person Lm6; 💻 💻) Dirt-cheap and in the heart of Paceville, this hotel has small, dark but clean rooms (with facilities including private bathroom, air-con and cable TV). It also has out-of-date décor, stained carpets and the aroma of stale tobacco, but it's a good place to meet other travellers, and if all you're after is a bed to crash in who can argue with the price?

Midrange

SLIEMA

The following hotels are all located on the Sliema map (Map p86).

Sliema Hotel (☎ 2132 4886; www.sliemahotel.com; 59 Triq ix-Xatt, Sliema; s Lm10-20, d Lm16-35; 💻) It's nondescript and lacks the pulling power of a swimming pool or sun terrace, but this central hotel has friendly service and represents excellent value. The rooms are standard issue, but they are large, spotless and comfy; it's worth paying the extra for front rooms with a balcony and sea views towards Valletta.

Imperial Hotel (☎ 2134 4093; www.imperialhotel malta.com; Triq Rudolfu; s Lm11.50-20, d Lm17-32; 💻 💻) Things move rather slowly at the Imperial, in keeping with the old-world interior (it dates from 1865) and older patrons. It's tucked away in the heart of residential Sliema, and inside you'll be impressed by the lobby's chandelier and grand sweeping staircase. The rooms don't live up to the high standards set downstairs, but they're comfortable and well equipped (you'll pay more for a garden/pool view and a balcony). Facilities include a courtyard garden and restaurant. There's good disabled access.

Preluna Hotel & Towers (☎ 2133 4001; www .preluna-hotel.com; 124 Triq it-Torri; B&B per person Lm17- 26; ☒ ☐ ☒) Malta's tallest hotel commands views along the coast, attracting plenty of Euro holidaymakers. The attractive lobby and obliging staff create a good first impression; rooms are small but bright and fresh, and facilities are exhaustive (health spa, private beachfront lido, dive school and choice of bars and restaurants). Superior rooms aren't all that much better than standard rooms but are worth it for the sea view and balcony.

GŻIRA

Many of Sliema's waterfront hotels have seen better days. There are better-quality midrange options a few minutes' walk west of Sliema, on the waterfront in neighbouring Gżira. It's best to opt for sea-view rooms at the following hotels, which are located on the Sliema, St Julian's & Paceville map (Map p84).

Waterfront Hotel (☎ 2133 3434; www.waterfrontho telmalta.com; Triq ix-Xatt, Gżira; s Lm21-36, d Lm32-47; ☒) Built in 2000, the Waterfront has a modern interior that makes it look newer that it is. The nautically themed lobby, blue-and-white rooms and rooftop pool and terrace with excellent views make this a great midrange choice. Wi-fi access throughout is a bonus.

Also recommended:

Hotel Bayview (☎ 2132 0216; www.bayviewmalta .com; 143 Triq ix-Xatt, Gżira; s/d from Lm12/18 low season, Lm20/30 high season, apt from Lm20/34 low/high season; ☒) Offers rooms, studios with kitchenette, and one- and two-bedroom apartments.

Hotel Kennedy Nova (☎ 2134 5480; www.kenne dynova.com; 116 Triq ix-Xatt, Gżira; s Lm15.50-33, d Lm21-48; ☒)

PACEVILLE

The following two hotels are located on the St Julian's & Paceville map (Map p88).

our pick **Hotel Valentina** (☎ 2138 2232; www.ho telvalentina.com; Triq Schreiber; s/d Lm10/16 low season, Lm20/32 high season; ☒) Prices at split-personality Valentina are shockingly reasonable. There's a boutique-y feel about the place, but just what the 'design story' is depends on your room number: older rooms have a handsome, rustic feel; newer rooms have clean, contemporary lines and splashes of vivid colour. The dichotomy exists on the ground floor too – sign in at reception in the bright modern half and take breakfast in the older stone quarters. There's a mixed crowd of young and old, English and Italian, and a surprising number of solo travellers taking advantage of easily the best-value option in this neck of the woods (an area crawling with pricey five-stars and shabby student digs). Rooms aren't huge but then neither are the prices, and facilities include air-con, satellite TV and minibar.

Ir-Rokna Hotel (☎ 2138 4060; www.roknahotel.com; Triq il-Knisja; s/d Lm13/18 low season, Lm17/26 high season; ☒) Stay within spitting distance of the treats of Portomaso, but a long way from the Hilton price-tag. You're also close to the nightlife, but far enough away to not suffer with noise. Ir-Rokna is decent value, and while the rooms are timeworn and bland, the service is friendly, and the hotel is home to Malta's oldest (and, many claim, its finest) pizzeria.

Top End

There are lots of four- and five-star properties here (primarily around Paceville). Competition to fill rooms can be tough, so there are often special offers and internet deals to bring down the rates quoted here (especially outside July and August). It pays to shop around and ask what special rates are available.

THAI MASSAGE?

Chao Praya Thai Massage & Spa (Map p88; ☎ 2137 8666; 52 Triq il-Wilga, Paceville; ☽ 9am- 10pm Mon-Sat, 9am-7pm Sun) is a small, surprising piece of Thailand in downtown Malta – from the smell of Tiger Balm as you enter the shopfront to the Thai chatter of the staff. Prices are not direct from Thailand, however – a half-hour massage is Lm8, a full hour costs Lm12, but the benefits to legs sore from sightseeing or clubbing are invaluable. You can also submit to foot massages, reflexology, manicures and pedicures. It's a real contrast to the swish day spas of the area's megahotels.

SLIEMA

These two hotels are located on the Sliema map (Map p86).

Victoria Hotel (☎ 2133 4711; www.victoriahotel.com; Triq Gorġ Borg Olivier; r Lm33-44, ste Lm53-74; 🅿 🖳 🌐) In a quiet location away from the seafront, this refined hotel has the feel of a gentlemen's club, with its lobby and bar full of dark wood and leather club sofas. The masculine feel carries through to the mahogany furniture of the well-equipped guest rooms (if that sounds too heavy, opt for a room with softer furnishings in blue tones). If you're looking to live it up, next door to the hotel, and under its management, is Palazzo Capua, a spectacularly restored palazzo that's home to five luxurious duplex suites – the rich décor and facilities here will have you plotting to move in permanently.

Hotel Fortina Spa Resort (☎ 2346 0000; www .hotelfortina.com; Triq ix-Xatt Ta'Tigné; full board per person from Lm40/60 low/high season; 🅿 🖳 🌐) The Fortina subscribes to the 'bigger is better' philosophy, with 700 beds, seven restaurants, seven swimming pools (yes, seven) and oodles of distractions for guests. The brand-spanking new five-star tower is pitching squarely for the spa traveller, with 'world-first therapeutic spa bedrooms' (from Lm100 per person per night – ouch!). These are oversized guest rooms with therapeutic baths and detox capsules for your own private spa experience – possibly not as gimmicky as it sounds if all you want from your holiday is to de-stress, but we think there are better places in Malta to blow that kind of money. There's a mind-boggling array of rates, depending on room type, and a hundred different supplements; prices listed here include all meals and drinks.

ST JULIAN'S

These and the following Paceville hotels are located on the St Julian's & Paceville map (Map p88).

Hotel Juliani (☎ 2138 0000; www.hoteljuliani.com; 12 Triq San Gorġ, Spinola Bay; r from Lm55; 🅿 🖳 🌐) In an industry dominated by megahotels, the 44-room Juliani scores points for introducing Malta to the boutique hotel concept. That it's superbly located (inside a restored seafront townhouse), houses top-notch eateries and is heavily design-driven means its overall satisfaction score sheet is high. The reception is in the ground-level Café Juliani

(p94), whose soft, calming colour scheme sets the tone. In the guest rooms you can enjoy more chic surrounds, with chocolate brown shades and pale blue accents. It's worth paying extra for a room with a sea view (these come with a Jacuzzi), but there's no beating the views from the rooftop pool and terrace, all gleaming white tiles and glass. The hotel overlooks Spinola Bay, bustling away as one of the country's culinary epicentres. The hotel itself is home to two innovative restaurants, Zest (p93) and Mezè (p93).

Le Meridien St Julian's (☎ 2133 000; www.stjulians .lemeridien.com; 39 Triq il-Kbira, Balluta Bay; r from Lm80; 🅿 🖳 🌐) The paint was barely dry when we visited Malta's newest five-star hotel, high above Balluta Bay. If you're driving, take Trejqet il-Bajja off the waterfront; for visitors on foot, the entry from Balluta Bay takes you past a few boutiques, and you can catch the lift to reception on the 3rd floor. Le Meridien is a shiny new temple to upmarket travellers; the décor follows clean contemporary lines and makes strong use of rich, warm colours (in the guest rooms too). There's great attention to detail and all the pretty accoutrements you'd expect. The rooftop pool and terrace, blissful beauty spa and great onsite dining options make this a winner.

PACEVILLE

Hilton Malta (☎ 2138 3383; www.malta.hilton.com; Portomaso; r from Lm118/138 low/high season; 🅿 🖳 🌐) This seriously swish hotel allows you an insight into the privileged world of Malta's moneyed classes: yes, that's a chichi private marina down below, filled with shiny motorboats. And yes, the ever-expanding, 12.5-hectare Portomaso complex is home to some outstanding boutiques, bars and restaurants alongside the designer apartments. The hotel itself certainly won't have you going without – it's home to a half-dozen restaurants too, plus private beach club, water sports, three outdoor swimming pools, gymnasium and beauty spa. You probably won't spend too much time in your room, but rest assured that it will be extremely comfortable when you do, and from the balcony you'll be able to take in either a Mediterranean or a marina view. Although the hotel seems a playground for cashed-up grown-ups, families are looked after too, with both kids' activities and baby-sitters available.

Also recommended, with all the five-star bells and whistles:

Westin Dragonara Resort (☎ 2138 1000; www
.westinmalta.com; Triq id-Dragonara; r from Lm90;
❄ ☐ ☎) A vast, 300-room complex on Dragonara
Point, complete with casino.

InterContinental Malta (☎ 2137 7600; www.malta
.intercontinental.com; Triq Santu Wistin; r from Lm110/130
low/high season; ❄ ☐ ☎) If it's good enough for the
Emirates flight crew, it's good enough for us. Right in the
heart of the action.

EATING
Restaurants
SLIEMA

The following restaurants are located on the Sliema map (Map p86).

Lanca at Village Gossip (☎ 2133 8743; cnr Triq ix-Xatt
& Triq Bisazza; mains Lm1-7; ☽ lunch daily, plus dinner in
summer) One of Sliema's loveliest options, this corner eatery has a character-filled rustic interior covered with old signs and bric-a-brac, or you can opt for alfresco dining under a vine-covered terrace. Service is attentive, the setting is lovely and the menu pleasing, but given what other places charge, we think Lm5 is too much to pay for a simple bowl of pasta at lunchtime.

Piccolo Padre (☎ 2134 4875; Triq il-Kbira; mains Lm2-
5; ☽ dinner) Beneath the Barracuda (right), this casual, family-friendly pizzeria is almost always crowded – try to snare a coveted table on an enclosed balcony overlooking the sea. Pizzas are crunchy and tasty – the house

speciality is decorated with tomato, mozzarella, Maltese sausage and Gozo cheese. Also available are good pasta options, salads and burgers, plus a kids' menu for little pizza fans.

Vino Veritas (☎ 2132 4273; 59 Triq Sir Adrian Dingli;
mains Lm3-6) Justifiably popular with both locals and tourists, convivial Vino Veritas has well-priced salad, pasta and pizza options, and also has decent veg selections. Try the house specialities: home-made ravioli, with fillings such as artichoke hearts, swordfish, salmon, porcini mushrooms or veal. There's a kids' menu too.

Kitchen (☎ 2131 1112; 210 Triq it-Torri; mains Lm3-9;
☽ lunch Wed-Sun, dinner nightly) On a none-too-interesting stretch of the promenade, the Kitchen's owner-chef (named national chef of the year for 2006) whips up some exemplary Med-fusion dishes in a smart, simple setting. Mouthwatering mains include fresh salmon fillet topped with a sundried tomato crumble, followed by desserts such as Belgian chocolate truffle cake.

Barracuda (☎ 2133 1817; 195 Triq il-Kbira; mains Lm4-
8; ☽ dinner) It's a pretty harsh name for what is in fact an oh-so-elegant restaurant, set in the drawing room of an early-18th-century seaside villa on the western fringes of Sliema. Enjoy the tasteful décor, water views, professional service and a menu of carefully prepared Italian and Mediterranean dishes, with the fish and seafood reliably first-rate.

You're bound to find a restaurant to take your fancy at the **Hotel Fortina Spa Resort** (see

---

PARTAKING OF PORTOMASO

There are loads of stellar eating and drinking options at the Portomaso complex. If you enter from street level (Triq il-Knisja), go down the steps towards the marina and you'll pass half a dozen eateries – all have outdoor terraces, with heaters making alfresco dining more appealing in the cooler months. First up are **Zen**, offering quality Japanese cuisine, and **Trattoria Don Antonio**, serving seafood and pasta. Next level down is **Buffalo Bill's**, a steakhouse with Wild West décor (check out the saddle-topped bar stools) and huge pulling power for dedicated carnivores. Opposite is **Caesar's**, working hard to be all things to all people, from 9am breakfasters to 2am late-night snackers. Next to Caesar's is the clubby and sophisticated **Portovino** wine bar, with more than 500 tipples to choose from, accompanied by cigars or a platter of cheese.

Finally come our top picks, favourites for their great décor, out-of-the-ordinary menus and waterside tables; it's especially atmospheric down here by night. The kooky name of **the Bed** (☎ 2138 3227; dishes Lm2.50-5; ☽ lunch & dinner) stands for Beverages, Entertainment & Dining, but nowhere is there a hint of the Korean cuisine served up. It must be a bugger to keep clean, but the all-white décor and soft colourful lights create quite an impact. Opposite is **Le Souk** (☎ 2138 3200; mains Lm3-5; ☽ lunch & dinner), candlelit by night with a menu of Moroccan food – with plenty of *tajines* (Moroccan meat and vegetable stews). There's great attention to detail, right down to the low outdoor tables with cushions and hookah pipes.

91), with seven to choose from. Hibiki offers
apanese cuisine, Can Thai prepares Chinese
and Thai specialities, and Sa Re Ga Ma serves
up Indian dishes. There are also a couple of
options for closer-to-home Mediterranean
concoctions.

ST JULIAN'S

These and the following Paceville restaurants
are located on the St Julian's & Paceville map
(Map p88).

The St Julian's and Paceville area is Malta's
gastronomic heartland, and while there are
plenty of places cranking out so-so meals,
you shouldn't need to look hard to find some
gems. Fertile hunting grounds include Spinola
Bay and the sleek Portomaso complex (opposite). At the former you should angle for an
outdoor table and bay view; at the latter you
can travel your taste buds – from Italian to
Japanese, Moroccan and even Korean.

Paparazzi (☎ 2137 4966; 159 Triq San Ġorġ, Spinola
Bay; mains Lm2.50-7; ☺ lunch & dinner) The sunny
terrace here is a prime people-watching spot,
with a fine view of Spinola Bay. Fight your
way through the huge portions on the big,
cheeky, crowd-pleasing menu. It's child- and
veg-friendly too.

Mezè (☎ 2138 8000; 12 Triq San Ġorġ; set menus per
person Lm6-7; ☺ dinner) Part of the stylish trio of
eateries at Hotel Juliani, basement-level Mezè
has low lighting, mosaics, an inviting bar area
and a menu of 30 share-worthy treats. Come
with a group and partake of small plates of
Mediterranean and Middle Eastern–inspired
delectables; the themed 'chef's selections' take
the hard work out of ordering. In summer
(mid-June to mid-September) Mezè relocates
to Hotel Juliani's lovely rooftop, with a smaller
menu of fresh local seafood.

Zest (☎ 2138 8000; 12 Triq San Ġorġ; mains Lm6-8;
☺ dinner Mon-Sat) More culinary magic awaits
upstairs from Mezè (accessible via the external
staircase from ground level). Zest features a
monochrome décor with vibrant splashes of
colour and one of Malta's most interesting
menus. The theme is 'East meets West', so
you can choose from the West (continental)
section of the menu (seared salmon, lamb
loin), or the East (Asian) section – perhaps
Peking duck, beef teppanyaki or spicy Viet-
namese chicken salad. There's also a decent
selection of sushi, and great desserts (try the
orange-blossom crème brûlée). Bookings are
advised; leave small kids at home.

PACEVILLE

Avenue (☎ 2131 1753; Triq Gort; mains Lm1.25-6; ☺ lunch
Mon-Sat, dinner nightly) Thanks to its enduring
popularity, the ever-expanding Avenue now
takes up half the block and can seat around
300 diners. Even with this capacity it's always bustling – that's no doubt because of
its cheery décor, crowd-pleasing menu and
great-value prices. It's perfect for families,
groups, students and travellers; simple meals
of meat and fish, plus huge portions of pizza
and pasta, keep the fans happy.

Paranga (☎ 2137 7600; St George's Bay; snacks & meals
Lm2.50-8; ☺ lunch & dinner Tue-Sun) On a wooden
deck built over the water's edge, right on the
only sandy beach in the neighbourhood, this
new and stylish outfit (run by the InterContinental hotel) offers plenty of cocktail options
and a full menu of pizza, pasta, seafood etc.
A winning option for a sunny afternoon or
sundowners.

Mongolian Barbeque (☎ 2137 0831; Triq il-Wilġa;
lunch/dinner Lm4/5.25; ☺ lunch & dinner) You really
shouldn't leave here hungry either, thanks
to the budget traveller–friendly 'all-you-can-
eat' deals. Inside this streamlined restaurant,
you choose your raw produce from a buffet
(meat/seafood/tofu, plus vegies and a sauce to
accompany), and then have these cooked to
order in front of you (rice, noodles or couscous included). You can revisit the buffet as
often as you like.

Hugo's Lounge (☎ 2138 2264; Triq San Ġorġ; meals
Lm4-6; ☺ lunch & dinner) If you're hungry, Hugo
lets you choose from a menu of well-executed
Asian food – sushi, Thai soups and curries,
noodles and stir-fries – in his fashionable
lounge, full of brown leather. Merely thirsty?
Pull up a pew for cocktails and snacks at the
bar, or recline on the sofas in the alfresco area
on Paceville's party street.

Cafés

Cara's Café (Map p86; ☎ 2134 3432; 249 Triq it-Torri,
Sliema; snacks & sweets Lm0.20-1.30; ☺ 9am-1am) The
savoury section of the menu at Cara's won't
take up much of your time – it's tiny, comprising quiche, pastizzi (ricotta- or pea-filled flaky
pastries) and various toasted sandwiches. It's
all about the sweets here, and there are dozens
of ways to get your sugar rush, from profiter-
oles to apple strudel and tiramisu to ice-cream
sundaes. There's a large outdoor area where
you can have a late-night drink among the
fairy lights.

Café Jubilee (Map p84; ☎ 2133 7141; 209 Triq ix-Xatt, Gżira; snacks & meals Lm1-3.50; ⏰ 8am-1am, weekends to 3am) If you're on a good thing, stick to it. A third branch of this café (which is also in Valletta and Victoria on Gozo) has opened in Gżira, a few minutes' walk from Sliema, opposite Manoel Island. There's the same great French-bistro feel, with cosy booths, quirky décor, wines by the glass and a comprehensive menu of easy edibles.

Gigi's Concept Café (Map p88; ☎ 2135 9865; 23 Triq San Ġorġ, Spinola Bay; snacks & meals Lm1-5; ⏰ lunch & dinner) Gigi's concept is not that revolutionary, but it is mighty appealing: café by day, wine bar by night, then throw in some funky artwork (familiar if you've visited Il-Forn in Vittoriosa, p79), interesting décor and windows opening onto the street. It's open until 1am and has a good-looking wine list; there's also a side room with internet connections.

Café Juliani (Map p88; ☎ 2138 8000; 12 Triq San Ġorġ, Spinola Bay; snacks & meals Lm2.50-4; ⏰ 7am-11pm) From the chic décor (blues, greens and neutrals) to the comfy couches, water feature and smooth tunes being played, this place oozes understated style. There's a modern menu of platters, wraps, baguettes, salads and sushi, plus decadent sweets, and it's a wi-fi hot spot too.

Quick Eats

You'll have no trouble finding the big multinational chains in St Julian's and Paceville. There are numerous fast-food eateries in the streets of Paceville, open late and serving snacks to quell the hunger and soak up the alcohol. Look out for places serving up hot *pastizzi* or pizza slices. A decent option for late-night munchies is **Ed's Easy Diner** (Map p88; Triq id-Dragunara), where you can get burgers, hot dogs and kebabs for around the Lm1 mark.

Self-Catering

For self-caterers **Tower Foods Supermarket** (Map p86; 46 Triq il-Kbira, Sliema; ⏰ 8am-7.30pm Mon-Sat) sells a wide range of groceries, frozen foods and fresh fruit and veg. Other well-stocked options include **Dolphin Supermarket** (Map p88; Triq il-Wilga, Paceville; ⏰ 8am-7pm Mon-Sat) and **Arkadia Foodstore** (Map p88; Triq il-Knisja, Paceville; ⏰ 8am-8pm Mon-Sat).

DRINKING

This area has a bar for everyone, from the teenage clubber to the old-age pensioner. Paceville is the place for full-on partying, with wall-to-wall bars and clubs in the area around the northern end of Triq San Ġorġ (where it turns into the steps of Triq Santa Rita), while the St Julian's and Sliema waterfronts have everything from slick wine bars to traditional British pubs. Check out the nightclub venues listed on opposite, as these are also popular drinking dens. Many of the restaurants and cafés listed under Eating in this chapter would also be ideal for a cold beer, cocktail or glass of wine – consider Mezè and neighbouring Gigi's Concept Café on Spinola Bay in St Julian's, Hugo's Lounge in the heart of Paceville, Paranga on St George's Bay, Café Jubilee in Sliema, and Portovino, Bed and Le Souk at Portomaso.

Plough & Anchor (Map p86; ☎ 21 334 725; 263 Triq it-Torri, Sliema) The Plough offers cheap pub grub and a cosy bar downstairs crammed with maritime paraphernalia. This is a decent option for a drink earlier in the night if you're en route from Sliema to Paceville, but if you're simply after a nightcap (or ice-cream sundae) as you head back to your hotel, consider Cara's Café (p93).

Bar (Map p88; ☎ 21 337 349; www.thebarmalta.com; 32 Balluta Bldgs, Triq il-Kbira, St Julian's) Housed in a beautifully ornate building not far up from the church on Balluta Bay, the Bar has a low-key profile on the bar scene and is frequented by in-the-know locals. It's a good choice for wining and reclining, serves great snacks, and has DJs spinning tunes after 11pm.

7 Rooms Terrace Bar (Map p88; ☎ 2137 5331; Triq id-Dragunara, Paceville) Sophisticates (or those who came to Malta but were secretly hoping to holiday somewhere like Bali) will get a kick out of 7 Rooms, with wooden gazebos curtained and set about white sofas and cushions in an open-air setting. It's all lit by candles and fairy lights – very romantic and very Far East.

Muddy Waters (Map p88; ☎ 2137 4155; www.muddywatersbar.net; 56 Triq il-Kbira, St Julian's) On Balluta Bay, Muddies has a great jukebox, rock DJs on Friday and Saturday, and live rock bands on Sunday nights – when things can get pretty rowdy and the tables may act as dance floors. It's a favourite of the student crowd.

City of London (Map p88; ☎ 2133 1706; 193 Triq il-Kbira, St Julian's) Right by Muddies, this tiny pub is packed on weekends and there's a great party atmosphere. It's popular on the gay scene, but everyone is welcome, and there's a nicely mixed crowd of expats, locals and students.

More pub action can be found at **Ryan's Irish Pub** (Map p88; ☎ 2135 0680; Spinola Bay), high up overlooking the action on Spinola Bay, or **O'Casey's Irish Pub** (Map p88; ☎ 2137 3900; Triq Santu Wistin, Paceville), beneath Hotel Bernard in the heart of Paceville's clubland. Both Ryan's and O'Casey's are pretty much what you'd expect of an Irish theme bar anywhere in the world – crowded, lively, friendly and well stocked with cold Guinness. They also screen live football games. Want something harder than Guinness? **Qube** (Map p88; ☎ 2137 1944; www.qubemalta.com; Triq Santa Rita, Paceville) bar and nightclub has 30 types of flavoured vodkas, plus vodka jellies and shooters – pass the bucket….

ENTERTAINMENT
Nightclubs
There are loads of clubs concentrated at the northern end of Triq San Ġorġ in Paceville (where it turns into Triq Santa Rita), but their names come and go with the seasons. Speaking of seasons, this area is pumping and jam-packed most nights of the week in the high season (June to September), but you won't experience the same level of action in the low season (although weekends year-round are definitely classified as party-time). The places listed here are all on the St Julian's & Paceville map (Map p88).

The best advice is to wander this area, check out the offerings and see what takes your fancy (the right crowd, the right music, free entry or no need to queue, drinks promotions etc). Families might prefer Paceville's cinema and 10-pin bowling alley.

You should pick your times to party. Locals tell us that Paceville nightlife is the reverse of the expected order of things (ie that the younger crowd has the stamina to stay out late and the oldies head home early). Here, the under-21s are out and partying before midnight, then head home early to mum; that's when it's the older crowd's turn (after 1am they have the clubs to themselves).

Axis (☎ 2138 2767; www.axis.com.mt; Triq San Ġorġ, Paceville) Malta's biggest and best nightclub (and one that's managed to stand the test of time) houses three separate clubs (commercial house is usually served up) and seven bars providing party space for over 3000 punters. There's normally an entrance fee of around Lm3.

BJ's (☎ 2137 7642; Triq Ball, Paceville) An offbeat club featuring live music nightly (primarily

jazz, but also soul, blues and rock), BJ's draws a more mature crowd than most of its neighbours.

Fuego (☎ 2138 6746; www.fuego.com.mt; Triq Santu Wistin, Paceville) Get hot and sweaty dancing up a storm at this very popular indoor-outdoor salsa bar – head first to its free salsa-dancing classes (Monday to Wednesday from 8.30pm) then show off your new moves to the Latin grooves. The open terraces (covered and heated in winter) are full of people checking each other out – there's something of a meat-market atmosphere, but it's friendly, fun and not too sleazy.

Havana (☎ 2137 4500; www.havanamalta.com; 82 Triq San Ġorġ, Paceville) Free entry, six bars and a mixed menu of R&B, soul and commercial favourites keep the crowds happy here. There are lots of students and tourists chatting each other up, but plenty of locals too.

Places (☎ 2137 8055; www.places.com.mt; Triq Ball, Paceville) Places claims to be the 'home of Maltese club culture', and it's a good place to get your bearings if you take the subject seriously. It's strictly house here – room one is smaller and offers funky and vocal house; room two is kept pumping with house and hard house.

Casinos
Dragonara Casino (Map p88; ☎ 2138 2362; www.dragonara.com; entry from Triq Dragunara; ☺ 10am-6am Mon-Thu, 24hr Fri-Sun) Out on the point beyond the Westin Dragonara Resort, this casino is housed in a 19th-century mansion that, appropriately enough, once belonged to a wealthy banker. The minimum age for tourists is 18 (25 for Maltese citizens) and you'll need your passport or ID card to get in. The dress code is 'smart casual' (no shorts or jeans after 8pm). There's also a courtesy bus that offers free transport to the casino from all areas – call to arrange pick-up.

Cinemas

Eden Century Cinemas (Map p88; ☎ 2371 0400; www
.edencinemas.com.mt; Triq Santu Wistin) This large complex has 16 screens (on both sides of the road)
showing first-run films. Adult tickets cost
Lm2 in the afternoon, Lm2.85 after 5pm. See
the website or local newspapers for movie
details and screening times. All films are in
English (foreign films are in their original
language, with English subtitles).

Ten-Pin Bowling

Eden Super Bowl (Map p88; ☎ 2138 7398; www.eden
leisure.com/superbowl; Triq Santu Wistin; adult/child per game
Lm1.50/1.20, shoe hire Lm0.50; ☼ 10am-11pm) Great for
a rainy day or to amuse the kids, this complex
(across the road from the cinema ticket office)
offers a 20-lane tenpin bowling alley to pass
the time.

SHOPPING

Sliema's Triq ix-Xatt and Triq it-Torri together comprise Malta's prime shopping
area. In among the tourist tat are some decent shoe stores and clothing labels, although
there's little that's original – you won't need
to look too hard to find the big British and
European highstreet labels: the likes of Zara,
Marks & Spencer, Dorothy Perkins, Next,
Diesel, Topshop, Bhs, Oasis, Accessorize and
Monsoon. Other decent hunting grounds
include the **Bay Street Complex** (Map p88; Triq Santu
Wistin, Paceville) and the **Luxe Pavilion** and **Portomaso Shopping Complex** (Map p88; Triq il-Knisja), at
either end of the Portomaso complex. As
the name suggests, the Luxe Pavilion houses
some high-end boutiques trading in luxury
items, including perfume, jewellery, leather
goods, designer clothing and accessories.
The latter complex hosts the Glass House,
which sells locally produced glass pieces,
and Space, a contemporary art gallery that
shows and sells interesting works by local
artists.

GETTING THERE & AWAY
Bus

Buses 62, 64, 66 and 67 run regularly between Valletta and Sliema, St Julian's and
Paceville (bus 66 continues on to the hotels
of St George's Bay). The Sliema terminus is at

the Ferries on the waterfront, the St Julian's,
Paceville terminal is off Triq Elija Zammit.
Buses 60 and 63 go from Valletta to the Savoy
terminus off Triq Rudolfu in Sliema (near
the post office). All journeys cost Lm0.20.
There is a late-night service (bus 62) that operates from Paceville to Valletta via St Julian's,
Sliema and Gżira on Friday and Saturday
nights year-round (last bus departs Paceville
at 1.30am) and nightly from mid-June to mid-
September (last bus at 3am) – all fares are the
one price of Lm0.50.

Direct bus services to and from the area –
avoiding Valletta – include the following (all
fares one way Lm0.50; all routes stop at the
Ferries in Sliema, St Julian's and Paceville):

65 – to Mosta, Ta'Qali Crafts Village and Rabat

70 – along the coast to the Buġibba terminus

627 – runs between Buġ's and Sliema

645 – to St Paul's Bay, Mellieħa town, Mellieħa Bay, and
the Gozo Ferry at Ċirkewwa

652 – to Buġibba then to Għajn Tuffieħa and Golden Bay

Car

If you decide to rent a car, bear in mind that
finding a place to park in this area is a real
nightmare.

Ferry

The **Marsamxetto ferry service** (Map p86; ☎ 2346
3862) crosses frequently between Sliema and
Valletta. The crossing costs Lm0.40 each way
and takes only about five minutes, with frequent departures (see p72).

GETTING AROUND

Wembleys (Map p88; ☎ 2137 4141 or for taxi 2137 4242;
www.wembleys.net; 50 Triq San Ġġ's) provides a reliable 24-hour radio taxi service (similar to the
UK's minicabs). Rates are generally cheaper
than official taxi rates (to Valletta is Lm5, to
the airport Lm7, to the Gozo ferry Lm11).
Wembleys can also arrange car hire – the
smallest costs Lm17 for one day in the high
season (Lm10.50 per day for rentals of six
to 10 days), Lm13.50 for one day in the low
season (reduced to Lm8 for six- to 10-day
hire).

There's a busy taxi rank catering to the late-
night crowd close to the intersection of Triq
San Ġġ and Triq il-Wilga in Paceville.

Northwest Malta

If you've been distracted by Malta's ancient sites and historic cities, you may have started to wonder where the beaches are hiding. It's in the northwest of Malta that visitors will discover how the country received its reputation for bucket-and-spade holidays. Beach bums should make a beeline for Mellieħa Bay for facilities and water sports laid on thick, or either Għajn Tuffieħa Bay or Ġnejna Bay for something more low-key and a chance to hang out with the locals. Scenic Golden Bay offers a choice midway between those two extremes, and is now home to one of Malta's loveliest five-star hotels. Just be aware that there's little chance of finding solitude on any patch of sand or rock during the high season – locals and visitors will all be looking to escape the heat. In the low season, however, you may well get to experience those picture-perfect images the tourist brochures are so fond of. Or you could always go looking for peace, solitude and natural beauty *under* the water – the rocky shores of the north boast some of the country's best diving outside Gozo.

Many of the country's large resorts – Buġibba, Qawra, St Paul's Bay (three neighbouring towns that have more or less blurred into one conglomeration of hotels) and Mellieħa Bay – are in the northwest, but the list of drawcards extends beyond facilities-laid-on holiday hot spots. The northwest offers noteworthy activities, including diving and water sports, of course, but also bird-watching and horse riding, good coastal walking in the region's remote corners, and Malta's best family-fun attractions.

NORTHWEST MALTA

HIGHLIGHTS

- Squeezing yourself into a wetsuit to explore the local marine life, scuba diving off the **Marfa Peninsula** (p120)
- Fulfilling every kid's dream and swimming with dolphins at **Mediterraneo Marine Park** (p98)
- Enjoying **Golden Bay** (p114) at your doorstep from a five-star suite at the new hotel here
- Feasting your eyes on the magnificent coastal views from the wild headland of **Ras il-Qammieħ** (p120)
- Making the long climb down to the near-empty **Għajn Tuffieħa Bay** (p115) on a quiet spring day
- Letting the locals know that you prefer your bird life alive, not hunted down, by supporting the beautiful birds of **Għadira Nature Reserve** (p118)

NORTHWEST MALTA

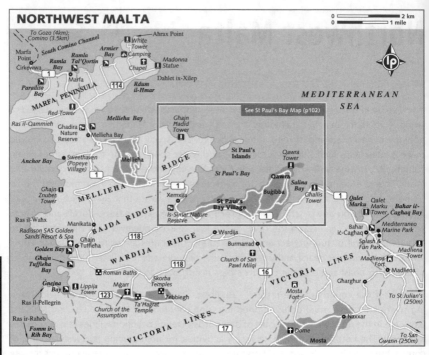

BAĦAR IĊ-ĊAGĦAQ

Baħar iċ-Ċagħaq (*ba*-har eetch *cha*-ag; also known, less tongue-twistingly, as White Rocks) lies halfway between Sliema and Buġibba. It has a scruffy rock beach and a couple of hugely popular family-friendly attractions.

The waterlogged **Splash & Fun Park** (☎ 2137 4283; www.splashandfun.com.mt; adult/child Lm7/4; ☼ 9am-5pm April-Oct, to 9pm Jul–mid-Sep) has undergone an expansion and rejuvenation to justify the price hike – it's now home to the largest wave pool in Europe, constantly pumping 1.5m artificial waves. There's also a safe kids' area with plenty of tunnels and spray jets, fibreglass waterslides, and a 240m-long 'lazy river' you can coast down on a rubber tube. There are plenty of sun lounges, a restaurant and the requisite number of ice-cream parlours. It's a fun day out, but potentially pricey, as food can't be brought into the park; from July to mid-September you pay less if you visit after 3pm (adult/child Lm4/2.50), outside these months there's a decent-value family pass costing Lm16. Note that a combined ticket for this park and Mediterraneo Marine Park is Lm12/7.50 per adult/child.

Next door, the well-organised **Mediterraneo Marine Park** (☎ 2137 2218; www.mediterraneo.com.mt; adult/child Lm6.50/4.50; ☼ 10am-5pm) is home to a group of performing Black Sea dolphins, rescued from an old Soviet marine park that went bust. The dolphins go through their routine at 12.30pm and 4.30pm daily, preceded by a sea-lion show (11.30am and 4.30pm), and a performing parrot show (10.30am and 2.30pm). The cost of admission includes viewing of all shows. Other kid-friendly attractions include a seal enclosure, a reptile house and a playground and kiddies' amusement rides. Also on offer through the marine park is the chance to swim with dolphins, under the guidance of their carers. This costs Lm45 per person (including admission to the park) and is very popular, so advance bookings are necessary (note that the minimum age for the dolphin swim is eight).

On Qrejten Point, west of Baħar iċ-Ċagħaq Bay, is **Qalet Marku Tower**, one of several 17th-century watchtowers along this coastline.

To get to Baħar iċ-Ċagħaq, take bus 68 from Valletta (Lm0.20), bus 70 south from Buġibba (Lm0.50) or bus 70 or 645 north from Sliema (Lm0.50).

BUĠIBBA, QAWRA & ST PAUL'S BAY
pop 8375

St Paul's Bay is named after the saint who was shipwrecked here in AD 60 (see the boxed text, p101). The unattractive sprawl of Buġibba and Qawra, on the eastern side of the bay, is the biggest tourist development in Malta.

This is the heartland of the island's cheap-and-cheerful package-holiday trade, and it's absolutely mobbed in summer. It's full of hotels, bars and so-so restaurants – fine if you want a week or so of beer-fuelled, sun-filled hedonism, but rather lacking in local charm (and almost devoid of attractions). Still, there are some points in its favour, number one being that it is affordable, especially in the low season when there are some real accommodation bargains and the swimming areas are not so crowded. Just don't expect the same level of after-dark action during this quieter period.

Orientation

The tourist towns of Buġibba and Qawra (*aow*-ra) occupy the peninsula on the eastern side of St Paul's Bay. Buġibba merges westward into the fishing village of St Paul's Bay (San Pawl il-Baħar in Malti). The smaller resort of Xemxija lies at the head of the bay on the west shore, about 3.5km from Buġibba. St Paul's Islands guard the northwestern point of the bay.

The main coast road from Valletta and Sliema to Mellieħa and the Gozo ferry bypasses Buġibba, Qawra and St Paul's Bay village.

Information

BOOKSHOPS
Agenda (Map p100; ☎ 2157 4866; 91 Dawret il-Gżejjer, Buġibba) Sells foreign newspapers and magazines and a good range of English-language books.

EMERGENCY
Police Station (Map p100; ☎ 2157 6737; Triq it-Turisti, Buġibba)

INTERNET ACCESS
9-Ball Café (Map p100; ☎ 2158 6091; Triq it-Turisti, Buġibba; per hr Lm1; ☯ 8am-midnight) Large cybercafé in a café-cum-snooker hall, close to the bus station.
Browsers (Map p100; ☎ 2158 5082; Triq Kavetta, Buġibba; per hr Lm1; ☯ 10am-1.30am) Scanning and printing facilities, cheap international telephone calls, and a bar upstairs.
Mirabelle's (Map p100; ☎ 2157 0917; Triq Bajja, Buġibba; per hr Lm1; ☯ 10am-late) There's an internet café next door to Mirabelle's Restaurant (the entrance is on Misraħ il-Bajja).

MONEY
HSBC (Map p100; Misraħ il-Bajja, Buġibba) Full bank services plus a 24-hour foreign exchange machine and an ATM.
Travelex (Map p100; Triq Bajja, Buġibba; ☯ 9am-1.30pm & 2-5.30pm Mon-Fri, 9am-1pm Sat) Currency-exchange bureau not far from Misraħ il-Bajja (Bay Sq).
Travelex (Map p100; Dawret il-Gżejjer, Buġibba; ☯ 9am-1.30pm & 2-5.30pm Mon-Fri, 9am-1pm Sat) Another branch, near the entrance to the Dolmen Resort Hotel.

POST
Just Jase (Map p100; Dawret il-Gżejjer, Buġibba) Sub-post office in a souvenir shop.

THE VICTORIA LINES

Built by the British in the late 19th century, the Victoria Lines were supposedly built to protect the main part of the island from potential invaders landing on the northern beaches, but they didn't see any military action and some historians think they were commissioned simply to give the British garrisons something to do. The fortifications were named after Queen Victoria's Diamond Jubilee in 1897.

The lines run about 12km along a steep limestone escarpment that stretches from Fomm ir-Riħ in the west to Baħar iċ-Ċagħaq in the east and are excellent for country walking. There is still some talk of a heritage trail being developed along the lines, but little sign of the talk being put into action. If you're interesting in doing some independent exploration, try to get hold of *The Victoria Lines*, edited by Ray Cachia Zammit. A guide to the site, it includes a foldout map and is available in the better bookshops in Valletta.

Three forts – Madliena Fort, Mosta Fort and Binġemma Fort – are linked by a series of walls, entrenchments and gun batteries. The best-preserved section – the Dwejra Lines – is north of Mdina.

BUĠIBBA

Primera Hotel	**24**	C2
Sea View Hotel	**25**	C1
Sunseeker Holiday Complex	**26**	C1
EATING		
Bombay Palace	**27**	C1
Cherry Tree	**28**	B2
Gillieru	**29**	A2
La Krepree	**30**	B1
Mongolian Barbeque	**31**	C1
Ta'Pawla	**32**	D1
Trolees	**33**	D1
Venus	**34**	C2
Wagon Steakhouse	**35**	C3
DRINKING		
Corner Pocket Bar	(see 3)	
Fat Harry's	**36**	C2
Grapevine Pub & Restaurant	**37**	C2
Rookies Sports Bar & Grill	**38**	C2
Victoria Pub	(see 40)	
ENTERTAINMENT		
Amazonia	(see 11)	
Empire Cinema Complex	**39**	B3
Miracles	**40**	C1
Oracle Casino	(see 20)	
Zoo Bar	**41**	B3
TRANSPORT		
Bus Station	**42**	D1
Taxi Rank	**43**	C1

INFORMATION		
9-Ball Café	**1**	D1
Agenda	**2**	B1
Browsers	**3**	C2
HSBC Bank	**4**	C1
Just Jase (Sub-Post Office)	**5**	B1
Mirabelle's Restaurant	**6**	C2
Police Station	**7**	D1
Post Office	**8**	D1
Travelex	**9**	D1
Travelex	**10**	C2
SIGHTS & ACTIVITIES		
Amazonia Beach Club	**11**	C1
Buddies Dive Cove	**12**	C2
Captain Morgan Cruises – Underwater		
Safari Departures	**13**	A1
Captain Morgan Ticket Office	**14**	B1
Church of St Paul's Bonfire	**15**	A2
Dive Deep Blue	**16**	C2
Subway Scuba Diving School	**17**	C2
Yellow Fun Watersports	(see 11)	
SLEEPING		
Buccaneers Guesthouse	**18**	B2
Cape Inch Hotel	**19**	D1
Dolmen Resort Hotel	**20**	D1
Gillieru Harbour Hotel	**21**	A2
Grand Hotel Mercure San Antonio	**22**	D1
Howard Johnson Mediterranea Hotel & Suites	**23**	A2

Post Office (Map p100; Triq it-Turisti, Buġibba; 8am-1.30pm Mon-Sat year-round, plus 4.30-8pm Jun-Sep) By the entrance to the Grand Hotel Mercure San Antonio.

TRAVEL AGENCIES
You'll be tripping over travel agencies in Buġibba, especially in the area around Misraħ il-Bajja. All can help organise excursions, activities, car rental and so on.

Dangers & Annoyances
Plenty of holidaymakers to Buġibba complain of aggressive timeshare touts, who approach tourists on the main drag and can get abusive and aggressive if you express no interest. The best advice is to ignore them – *don't* get lured back to a hotel on the promise of a free gift.

Sights & Activities
There's not much to see in Buġibba except acres of painted concrete and sunburnt flesh, and not much to do other than stroll along the spruced-up promenade, lie around in the sun, go swimming or get towed around the bay on a variety of inflatable objects. There are a number of private lidos (recreational facilities) lining the waterfront (on both the east and west side of the peninsula), many offering sun lounges, water sports, swimming pools and café-bars (for a fee), and a newly constructed small sandy beach just east of Misraħ il-Bajja. Another option is to head for the harbour at the exotically named Plajja Tal'Bognor (Bognor Beach) and get away from it all on a **boat trip** (opposite).

On the ground floor of a new apartment complex, the new **Malta Classic Car Collection** (Map p102; ☎ 2157 8885; www.classiccarsmalta.com; Triq it-Turisti, Qawra; adult/child Lm2.75/1.75; ☷ 9.30am-6pm Mon-Fri, 9.30am-12.30pm Sat) is a temple to one man's love of cars. The privately owned collection of mint-condition vehicles (cars and motorbikes) includes plenty of 1950s and '60s British- and Italian-made classics, and it's not merely the domain of rev-heads. It's all bright and shiny and very well done.

The old fishing village of St Paul's Bay, now merged with Buġibba, has retained something of its traditional Maltese character and has a few historical sights. The 17th-century **Church of St Paul's Bonfire** (Map p100) stands on the waterfront to the south of Plajja Tal'Bognor, supposedly on the spot where the saint first scrambled ashore. A bonfire is lit outside the church during the festival of St Paul's Shipwreck (10 February).

Built in 1609, the **Wignacourt Tower** (Map p102; ☎ 2122 5222; Triq it-Torri; adult/child Lm0.50/free; ☷ 9.30am-12.30pm Mon-Sat) was the first of the towers built by Grand Master Wignacourt. It guards the point to the west of the church, and houses a tiny museum with exhibits on local fortress history, including a small selection of guns and armour.

West again, near the fishing-boat harbour at the head of the bay, is **Ghajn Rasul** (Apostle's Fountain; Map p102), where St Paul is said to have baptised the first Maltese convert to Christianity. On the festival of Sts Peter and Paul (29 June), people gather at the fountain before taking fishing boats out to St Paul's Islands, where they hear Mass beneath a large white **statue of St Paul** (Map p102) that was erected in 1845.

BOAT TRIPS & WATER SPORTS

Most **Captain Morgan Cruises** (Map p100; ☎ 2346 3333; www.captainmorgan.com.mt) operate out of Sliema, but there are Buġibba departures for an hour-long 'underwater safari' in a glass-bottomed boat exploring the marine life around St Paul's Islands. Underwater safaris set off at 10.30am, noon, 1.30pm and 3pm Monday to Saturday from May to October, departing from Plajja Tal'Bognor, and tickets cost Lm5.95/4.50 per adult/child.

Plenty of smaller operators offer tours from the jetty at Plajja Tal'Bognor. A 90-minute trip taking in St Paul's Bay (including the islands) and Salina Bay may cost as little as Lm2; some operators offer trips from St Paul's Bay to Comino for around Lm5. Head down to the jetty area to see what's available.

ST PAUL IN MALTA

The Bible (Acts 27–8) tells how St Paul was shipwrecked on Malta (most likely around AD 60) on his voyage from Caesarea to stand trial in Rome. The ship full of prisoners was caught in a storm and drifted for 14 days before breaking up on the shore of an unknown island. All aboard swam safely to shore, '…and when they were escaped, then they knew that the island was called Melita'.

The local people received the shipwrecked strangers with kindness and built a bonfire to warm them. Paul, while adding a bundle of sticks to the fire, was bitten by a venomous snake – a scene portrayed in several religious paintings on the island – but suffered no ill effects. The Melitans took this as a sign that he was no ordinary man.

Act 28 goes on to say that Paul and his companions met with 'the chief man of the island, whose name was Publius; who received them, and lodged them three days courteously', during which time Paul healed Publius' sick father. The castaways remained on Melita for three months before continuing their journey to Rome, where Paul was imprisoned and sentenced to death.

According to Maltese tradition, Paul laid the foundations of a Christian community during his brief stay on the island. Publius, who was later canonised, was converted to Christianity and became the bishop of Malta and later of Athens. The site of the shipwreck is traditionally taken to be St Paul's Islands. The house where Publius received the shipwrecked party may have occupied the site of the 17th-century church of San Pawl Milqi (St Paul Welcomed) on the hillside above Burmarrad, 2km south of Buġibba, where excavations have revealed the remains of a large Roman villa and farm. The site can be visited by appointment with Heritage Malta; phone ☎ 2295 4000 or email info@heritagemalta.org.

NORTHWEST MALTA

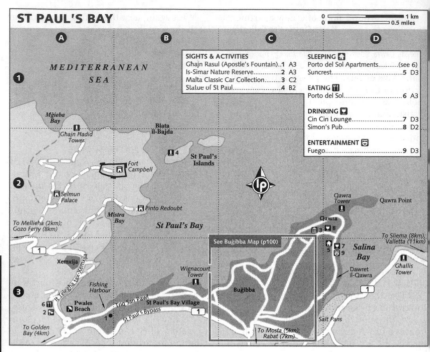

SIGHTS & ACTIVITIES
Ghajn Rasul (Apostle's Fountain)..1 A3
Is-Simar Nature Reserve.................2 A3
Malta Classic Car Collection.........3 C2
Statue of St Paul.............................4 B2

SLEEPING
Porto del Sol Apartments...........(see 6)
Suncrest.......................................5 D3

EATING
Porto del Sol.................................6 A3

DRINKING
Cin Cin Lounge..............................7 D3
Simon's Pub...................................8 D2

ENTERTAINMENT
Fuego..9 D3

Yellow Fun Watersports (Map p100; ☎ 2355 2570; www.yellowfunwatersports.com; Dawret il-Gżejjer, Buġibba) operates from the Amazonia Beach Club in front of the Oracle Casino and offers powerboat trips to the Blue Lagoon on Comino. Trips leave daily at 10.30am and 11am, returning at 3pm; the cost is Lm5 per person. Yellow Fun can also arrange boat charter, sea-taxi service, fishing trips and showers of watersports fun, such as waterskiing, jet skiing, canoeing, windsurfing and paragliding.

DIVING
There are several dive operators in Buġibba that can help you explore the excellent nearby dive sites (p46) or sites around the Maltese Islands. These include the following:
Buddies Dive Cove (Map p100; ☎ 2157 6266; www .buddiesmalta.com; 24/2 Triq il-Korp Tal-Pijunieri, Buġibba)
Dive Deep Blue (Map p100; ☎ 2158 3946; www.dive deepblue.com; 100 Triq Ananija, Buġibba)
Subway Scuba Diving School (Map p100; ☎ 2157 0354; www.subwayscuba.com; Triq il-Korp Tal-Pijunieri, Buġibba)

Sleeping
Most accommodation around St Paul's Bay is taken up by package-holiday companies from April to October, so book in advance if you want to stay in summer. In the low season (November to March) you can get some good deals, especially for stays of a week or more (although many smaller establishments may close during this period). There is very little by way of small and intimate hotels, except in the budget category. Most hotels are large and have good facilities (pool, restaurant etc), but are impersonal and often have dated, super-bland décor – you get what you pay for here. They usually offer a choice of hotel rooms or self-catering studios and apartments; the latter are usually good value as you'll get a larger room (to accommodate a kitchen/kitchenette and dining area) and you can cut costs by preparing your own meals. Half- and full-board arrangements are available at most guesthouses and hotels, but the food is rarely anything to write home about. There are supplements for solo travellers, sea views and for stays of less than three days at many hotels.

BUDGET

The following budget and midrange hotels are located on the Buġibba map (Map p100).

Buccaneers Guesthouse (☎ 2157 1671; www.buccaneers.com.mt; Triq Ġulju, Buġibba; B&B per person Lm6; ☪ Apr-Oct; ☒ ☒) This friendly, well-run guesthouse has surprisingly decent rooms at a bargain price (if you're on a shoestring budget, the princely sum of Lm7.50 gets you dinner, bed and breakfast). Rooms are large, clean and well-equipped – all with phone, air-con and private shower and washbasin (toilets are shared). There's a sun terrace on the roof with a newly-installed small pool, and a lively bar and restaurant downstairs.

Sea View Hotel (☎ 2157 3105; seaview@waldonet.net.mt; cnr Dawret il-Gżejjer & Triq il-Imsell, Buġibba; B&B per person Lm5.50/8.75 low/high season; ☒) Small-fry in comparison to the big boys in town, this budget hotel is on the promenade northeast of Misraħ il-Bajja and is open year-round. It's home to tiny, rather basic rooms, but all have balconies and bathroom, and there's a small pool too, with terrace and bar. You'll pay for extras such as a TV and/or a fridge in your room, a sea view, or for one-night stays.

MIDRANGE

Sunseeker Holiday Complex (☎ 2157 5619; www.sunseekerholidaycomplex.com; Trejqet il-Kulpara, Buġibba; 1-bedroom apt Lm65/100 low/high season; ☒) Tucked one block back from the waterfront in what feels like a quietish location, this central complex has indoor and outdoor pools, a gym, sauna, Jacuzzi and handy minimarket. On offer are one- to three-bedroom self-catering apartments for weekly lets (although shorter stays are welcome); all have ceiling fans (no air-con), kitchenette and lounge area. Apartments with families in mind sleep up to seven. Low-season prices (November to April) are good value, but you'll pay extra to have a TV or phone in your apartment.

Howard Johnson Mediterranea Hotel & Suites (☎ 2157 8759; www.hojomed.com.mt; Triq Buġibba, St Paul's Bay; hotel B&B per person Lm8/20 low/high season; 1-bedroom apt Lm19/40 low/high season; ☒ ☒ ☒) HJ offers more of the same in terms of hotel rooms and spacious self-catering studios and apartments (one-/two-bedroom sleeping up to four/six), but the rustic décor is a cut above the other places listed in this category, with plenty of polished timber, arched windows, full kitchens and attention to detail. There is a rooftop pool and gym, a restaurant and a

good location high above the bay close to St Paul's Bay village.

Also recommended if you are travelling in summer and struggling hard to find accommodation:

Primera Hotel (☎ 2157 3880; www.primerahotel.com; cnr Triq il-Korp Tal-Pijunieri & Triq Bajja, Buġibba; B&B per person from Lm6/12 low/high season; ☒ ☒) Bang in the heart of Buġibba. Don't expect luxury, but it's not too bad an option for the low price.

Cape Inch Hotel (☎ 2157 2025; www.capeinchhotel.com; cnr Triq it-Turisti & Triq il-Merluzz, Buġibba; B&B per person Lm8/18 low/high season; ☒) Something of an oddity in Buġibba – a small (25 rooms), family-run, old-style hotel opposite the bus station, and without a pool.

Gillieru Harbour Hotel (☎ 2157 2720; gillieru@vol.net.mt; Triq il-Knisja, Buġibba; B&B per person Lm9/20 low/high season; ☒ ☒) Adjacent to Gillieru seafood restaurant; has decent rooms (despite the threadbare bedspreads) and a good pool and terrace above the restaurant.

TOP END

Suncrest (Map p102; ☎ 2157 7101; www.suncresthotel.com; Dawret Il-Qawra, Qawra; s/d/ste from Lm25/35/45 low season, Lm35/50/65 high season; ☒ ☒) This vast hotel takes up a good stretch of the Qawra waterfront facing Salina Bay and is the biggest hotel in Malta, with 453 rooms. The lobby is a pastiche of classic '80s décor, with marble, mirrors and gold, but the facilities are excellent and the clientele is diverse (the brochure is printed in six European languages). There are plenty of restaurants, bars and a nightclub, and guests have free use of swimming pools, beachside lidos and a summer water-sports centre. Rates quoted here are for the cheapest (inland) rooms – you'll pay extra for a sea view. Suites are a good option, with a spacious lounge/dining area (no kitchen, however).

Dolmen Resort Hotel (Map p100; ☎ 2355 2355; Triq il-Merluzz, Buġibba; www.dolmen.com.mt; s/d from Lm29/38 low season, Lm43/56 high season; ☒ ☒ ☒) Another huge hotel, this one with the selling points of a casino and its very own prehistoric temple incorporated into the grounds. It's on the waterfront about 200m northeast of Misraħ il-Bajja (with its entrance at the end of Triq il-Merluzz), and boasts all the creature comforts you would expect of a four-star hotel, and then some – four outdoor swimming pools (one solely for kids), sports facilities, a health spa, an excellent beach club and a bevy of bars and restaurants. It draws a mixed international clientele, from Euro-package families to older, gambling-focused travellers.

Grand Hotel Mercure San Antonio (Map p100; ☎ 2158 3434; www.accorhotels.com; Triq it-Turisti, Buġibba; s/d Lm33/44 low season, Lm45/60 high season; ⊠ 🖳 🏊) The Med-themed whitewashed exterior and colourful, light-filled lobby effortlessly create the best first impression of any hotel in the neighbour-hood. The high standards carry through to the restaurants, pool and garden areas and well-kitted-out rooms, simply furnished with terracotta tiles and cheery green fabrics. For our money, the best option in town.

Eating

Buġibba is awash with cheap eating places, many offering 'full English breakfast' and 'typical English fish and chips', as well as piz-zas, burgers and kebabs. But there's a reason-able selection of other cuisines and a few good Maltese places too. All of the places listed here are in Buġibba and located on the Buġibba map (Map p100).

Ta'Pawla (☎ 2157 6039; Triq it-Turisti; mains Lm2-6; ☾ lunch Mon-Sat, dinner nightly) Buġibba may make you feel you're visiting an English seaside resort (but with better weather), but you can get a taste of good, authentic Maltese cuisine in the cute farmhouse interior of this busy little place op-posite the San Antonio hotel. A set three-course Maltese menu is only Lm4.75. On the menu are local classics like rabbit in garlic and octopus stew, but there's also a good assortment of stock-standard pizza, pasta, steak and seafood (or roast beef with gravy, if you must).

Cherry Tree (☎ 9982 6667; Triq il-Korp Tal-Pijunieri; mains Lm2-6.50; ☾ lunch & dinner) New for summer 2006, Cherry Tree pleases all-comers in its various incarnations (bar, restaurant, lounge). There are sought-after alfresco tables, comfy lounges and a more upmarket restaurant section (all dramatic black with red-leather booths). Snacks are available all day, plus there's a decent menu of well-priced salads, risotto, pasta and pizza.

Bombay Palace (☎ 2157 4457; Triq il-Ħalel; dishes Lm3-6; ☾ lunch & dinner) Escape pizzas and pasta to explore favourites of the subcontinent. Veg-etarians and curry lovers will be happy with the 'classic hits' menu – beef or lamb vindaloo, chicken korma, tandoori lamb chops and various biryanis. Octopus balti adds a bit of Maltese colour to the menu.

Wagon Steakhouse (☎ 2158 0666; Empire Cinema Complex, Triq il-Korp Tal-Pijunieri; mains Lm3.50-9; ☾ din-ner) There's some heavy-duty cowboy in the rich, warm décor here and a menu to please

the most discerning carnivore. The Montana mixed platter features chicken breast, beef fil-let, pork fillet and kangaroo meat – for when too much meat is never enough; there's some greenery by way of a salad buffet. Needless to say, there's little joy for vegetarians here.

Gillieru (☎ 2157 3480; 66 Triq il-Knisja; mains Lm4-8; ☾ lunch & dinner) Gillieru enjoys a five-star loca-tion on a terrace overlooking the harbour. The building is designed to resemble the front of a ship – sit at a window and you'll feel you're on a cruise liner. The restaurant has been around for decades (the décor shows this) and is a local institution famed for its unadventurous but fresh seafood dishes (prawns, lobster, grilled swordfish, calamari). There are good choices for nonseafood-eaters too.

Mongolian Barbeque (☎ 2157 4072; Dawret il-Gżejjer; lunch/dinner Lm4/5.25; ☾ dinner Tue-Sun, lunch Sun) A funky modern dining room with sea views and a novel, budget-friendly menu. For your money you get to choose raw produce from a buffet (meat, fish, vegies and a sauce to ac-company), and then have it cooked to order in front of you (rice, noodles or couscous included). You can revisit the buffet as often as you like, making this place perfect for those 'so hungry you could eat a horse' occasions.

Venus (☎ 2157 1604; cnr Triq Bajja & Gandoffli; mains Lm6-8.50; ☾ dinner) Venus is an oasis of class in a neighbourhood swimming in fast-food places and tourist restaurants. There's a bright and so-phisticated interior and the modern menu adds an imaginative twist to traditional ingredients – try the salmon and coriander or Thai beef salad, followed by roast rabbit with garlic and star anise or marinated Moroccan chicken.

The Buġibba promenade is lined with jewel-lery and souvenir stores and some very touristy eateries, but there is a decent array of ice-cream kiosks, and a good (unsigned) creperie. **La Krepree** (☎ 2157 1517; 165 Dawret il-Gżejjer; crepes Lm0.80-1.90; ☾ noon-midnight), perfect for an inex-pensive late-night snack (sweet or savoury).

SELF-CATERING

There are minimarkets everywhere, including inside some large accommodation providers and fruit-and-veg vans set up Monday to Sat-urday on the corner of Triq it-Turisti and Triq il-Merluzz, close to the bus station. Probably the best-stocked supermarket is **Trolees** (Triq il-Merluzz, Buġibba; ☾ 7.30am-9pm Mon-Sat, to 7pm Sun).

(Continued on page 113)

Path to megalithic temple ruins (p143) in Mnajdra

Entrance to Ħaġar Qim temple complex (p142)

JULIET COOMBE
Locals walking the streets of Valletta (p55)

Vedette (watchtower; p80),
Senglea

NEIL WILSON

CRAIG PERSHOUSE
In Guardia pageant at Fort St Elmo (p64), Valletta

Locals in a Rabat square (p128), central Malta

PATRICK BEN L

CRAIG PERSHOUSE

Luzzu (boats) in the fishing village of Marsaxlokk (p137)

Streets of Valletta (p55)

BETHUNE CARMICHAEL

PATRICK BEN LUKE SYDER

Nun shopping at a vegetable shop in Gozo (p144)

Baroque flourish in Valletta (p55)

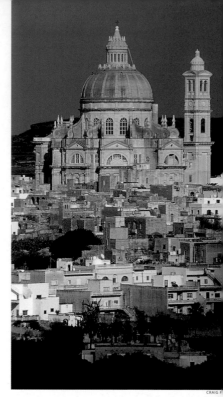

Rotunda (p154), Xewkija, Gozo

Auberge de Castille (p66), Valletta

Grand Master's Palace (p61), Valletta

MARK AVELLINO

CRAIG PERSHOUSE

Façade of building on Pjazza San
Pawl in Mdina (p123)

Mosta Dome (p131), Mosta, central Malta

EOIN CLARKE

MARK PEARSON/ALAMY

Diving in Gozo (p48)

Ta'Ċenċ sea cliffs (p154), Gozo

DONALD C. & PRISCILLA ALEXANDER EASTMAN

Arch of Blue Grotto (p141) at Wied iż-Żurrieq, southeast Malta

Diving in Dwejra (p157), Gozo

JACK SULLIVAN/ALAMY

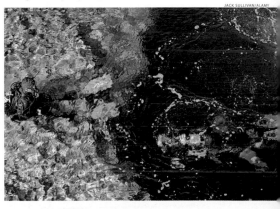

Sea urchin shells (p50)

CAROLE HEWER/ALAMY

ROUGH GUIDES/ALAMY

Bar in St Julian's (p94)

Street café (p69) in Valletta

JOHN ST

(Continued from page 104)

Drinking

Take your pick from the dozens of bars along Triq it-Turisti and the streets around Misraħ il-Bajja (particularly Triq Sant'Antnin). There are two species of bar in Buġibba. There's the 'typical British pub', with names like the Victoria or the Red Lion, drawing tourists looking for the comforts of home. Here you can down pints of bitter, play darts and sing along with the karaoke machine. Then there are bars for the younger party crowd where the mission for the evening is to get sloshed and maybe get lucky. The bars catering to the boozy crowd come alive in the high season and vary from year to year – but it shouldn't take you too long to find them. Don't expect the same level of hedonism in the low season.

Fat Harry's (Map p100; ☎ 2158 1298; Triq Bajja, Buġibba) Fat Harry's belongs firmly to the first category. It's a central English-style pub doing all-day traditional pub grub like fish and chips, and offering plenty of draught beer, outdoor tables for people-watching and, inside, live sports on the big screen or live entertainment.

Rookies Sports Bar & Grill (Map p100; ☎ 2157 4550; www.rookiesmalta.com; Triq Sponoż, Buġibba) Fourteen TVs and three giant screens televise sports from around the world at this large and popular American-style sports bar. There are also regular live bands and a wide range of international beers (and meals) to get you going.

Grapevine Pub & Restaurant (Map p100; ☎ 2157 2973; Triq il-Korp Tal-Pijunieri, Buġibba) The Grapevine is of Irish persuasion, as evidenced by the Guinness on tap, among other things. There are good pizzas and snacks, plus the ubiquitous TV screens broadcasting sports, and regular live bands.

Simon's Pub (Map p102; ☎ 2157 7566; www.simonspub .com; Triq it-Turisti, Qawra) Simon's got a two-room shrine to Elvis going on. He's clearly a huge fan of the King – so are we, so we love this place. There's live entertainment every night – stop in on Friday for the highlight, the Elvis tribute. Cheesy fun, thankyouverymuch.

Cin Cin Lounge (Map p102; ☎ 9949 6577; Dawret il-Qawra, Qawra) Along the seafront, opposite the Suncrest hotel and among touristy cafés and pizzerias, you'll find the new Cin Cin Lounge, part of the wine bar craze that's sweeping through Malta. It's a grown-up option for those looking for something more that just a pub, with tables, sofas and a seafront terrace, plus a menu of platters, snacks and salads.

Victoria Pub (Map p100; ☎ 2157 1355; Misraħ il-Bajja, Buġibba) On Buġibba's main square, this pub has a sign out the front boldly claiming to be 'Malta's No 1 karaoke venue' – consider yourself warned. There's karaoke every night for up-for-anything holidaymakers who wouldn't dare sing along back home.

Corner Pocket Bar (Map p100; ☎ 2158 5082; Triq Kavetta, Buġibba) A great after-dark spot, this bar has something for everyone – karaoke, DJs, big screens for sports coverage, pool tables and video games. It's above Browsers, a large internet café.

Cherry Tree (Map p100; ☎ 9982 6667; Triq il-Korp Tal-Pijunieri, Buġibba) This stylish new place has fast become a hot spot for beers, wines or cocktails, with live entertainment on Friday and Saturday nights and a big screen for sports events.

Entertainment

NIGHTCLUBS

Fuego (Map p102; ☎ 2138 6746; Dawret il-Qawra, Qawra) Due to the enormous popularity of the first Fuego in Paceville, a sister salsa bar opened in Qawra. With its unique music policy (DJs playing pure and commercial Latin music), free entry, free salsa dancing classes (8.30pm to 10.30pm Thursday and Friday), tequila specials and open terraces (covered and heated in winter), this place is sizzling!

Miracles (Map p100; ☎ 2157 1034; Misraħ il-Bajja) Near the Victoria Pub, Miracles (formerly Caesar's) is a mainstream nightclub playing summer anthems for the holidaymakers – it's open nightly in high season, spilling out into Buġibba's main square.

Zoo Bar (Map p100; ☎ 2157 1714; www.zoobarmalta .com; Triq il-Ħġejjeġ) The slogan painted on the bright purple exterior of this drinking den – 'party all night or go home' – seems pretty redundant. If you choose the former option, there are free snacks to keep you drinking and in the party mood.

Amazonia (Map p100; ☎ 2355 2461; www.amazonia malta.com; Dawret il-Gżejjer) This pumping summer club is at the lido opposite the Dolmen Resort Hotel and is popular with tourists and locals happy to kick on all night to cool tunes in a lush waterfront setting.

CASINOS

Oracle Casino (☎ 2157 0057; www.oraclecasino.com; admission free; ☉ 10am-4am) Buġibba's casino is smaller and less formal than the other two casinos on the island (at St Julian's, p95, and Vittoriosa, p79). It's part of the Dolmen Resort Hotel (enter via Dawret il-Gżejjer) and open daily until the wee small hours. The minimum age is 18 for visitors (25 for Maltese citizens). The dress code is 'smart casual' and you'll need your passport or ID card.

CINEMAS
Empire Cinema Complex (☎ 2158 1787; www .empirecinema.com.mt; Triq il-Korp Tal-Pijunieri) These cinemas show first-run movies. Tickets cost Lm2.50/1.50 adult/child (Lm2 for adults before 5pm weekdays).

Getting There & Away
There is a central taxi rank on Misraħ il-Bajja in Buġibba.

Buġibba bus station is on Triq it-Turisti near the Dolmen Resort Hotel. Buses 49 and 58 run frequently between Valletta and Buġibba (one way Lm0.23).

Direct bus services to/from Buġibba (avoiding Valletta) include the following (all fares one way Lm0.50):

No 45/49 – late-night bus linking Buġibba with Paceville (nightly from mid-Jun to mid-September; last bus from Paceville is at 3am; the rest of the year the service operates Friday & Saturday only, with the last bus around 1.30am)

No 48 – to Mellieħa town, Mellieħa Bay and Ċirkewwa (for the Gozo ferry)

No 70 – to St Julian's and Sliema

No 86 – to Mosta, Ta'Qali Crafts Village and Rabat

No 427 – to Mosta, Attard, Paola (for the Hypogeum and Tarxien temples) and Marsaxlokk

No 627 – to St Julian's, Sliema, the Three Cities and Marsaxlokk

No 652 – north to Għajn Tuffieħa and Golden Bay, or south to Sliema and St Julian's

XEMXIJA
The small, south-facing village of Xemxija (shem-*shee*-ya), on the north side of St Paul's Bay, takes its name from *xemx*, meaning sun in Malti. There are a couple of private lidos along the waterfront, but Pwales Beach at the head of St Paul's Bay is just a narrow strip of gravelly sand. The town itself is desperately in need of some TLC – along the main road is a collection of derelict buildings creating a serious eyesore.

Back from the water is **Is-Simar Nature Reserve** (Map p102; ☎ 2134 7646; www.birdlifemalta.org; admission free, donations welcome; ⏰ 12.30-4.30pm Sun Nov-May), opened in 1995 on a marshy patch of neglected land and managed by BirdLife Malta volunteers on behalf of the government. As with the Għadira Nature Reserve at Mellieħa Bay (p118), it's wonderful to see this commitment to Malta's natural assets and an area where local and migratory bird life is protected from hunters. Over 180 bird species have been recorded at the site.

At the foot of the hill on the main road is **Porto del Sol** (Map p102); ☎ 2157 3970; portosol@maltanet .net; It Telegħa tax-Xemxija; mains Lm4-6.50; ⏰ lunch & dinner Mon-Sat, lunch Sun Oct-May), a family-run restaurant with views of the bay from its large picture windows. The service is top-notch and it's popular with locals for its fresh seafood and local dishes. Above the restaurant are 18 self-catering apartments, ranging from two-person studios (Lm8/15 low/high season) to two-bedroom apartments that sleep up to four (Lm14/20 low/high season). The spotless, no-frills apartments are spacious and bargain priced; all have private bathroom and fan (no air-con or TV), and most have a kitchenette and balcony with bay views.

About 300m west of the roundabout at the top of the hill in Xemxija a minor road leads to **Mistra Bay** (Map p102), which has another tiny, gravelly beach and a tourist restaurant. It's not very pretty and the bay itself is filled with fish-farm pens, but there's good swimming and snorkelling off the rocks. There's also good hiking along the coast beyond the **Pinto Redoubt** (Map p102), a 17th-century gun battery at the far end of the bay.

GOLDEN BAY & GĦAJN TUFFIEĦA
The fertile Pwales Valley stretches 4km from the head of St Paul's Bay to Għajn Tuffieħa (ayn too-*fee*-ha, meaning 'Spring of the Apples') on Malta's west coast. Here, two of Malta's best sandy beaches draw crowds of sun-worshippers. **Golden Bay** – the sand is more grey-brown than golden – is the busier and more developed of the two beaches, with cafés, water sports and boat trips, and a huge new hotel rising above the shoreline. There is talk of a golf course being built behind the Radisson hotel – a proposal firmly opposed by environmental groups.

Borg Watersports (☎ 2157 3272) is on the shoreline in front of the hotel, offering rental of snorkelling gear, sailboards, jet skis, speedboats, pedalos and canoes, as well as the chance to go parasailing (Lm14) or waterskiing (Lm8).

From Golden Bay, you can take a worthwhile cruise with **Charlie's Discovery Speedboat Trips** (☎ 9948 6949; mattnick@onvol.net). Charlie is a knowledgeable guide who will take you south from Golden Bay, to view rugged cliffs and visit the bays and grottoes that indent the northwest coast, including Għajn Tuffieħa, Ġnejna (p116) and Fomm ir-Riħ (tricky to get to on land – see p130). The one-hour trips leave at noon and 2.30pm daily and cost Lm4/2.50 per adult/child. Look out for Charlie and his boat on the northern part of the beach, or ask at Munchies Bar-Pizzeria on the sand. Charlie also operates a trip every day at 4pm from April to October to Comino's Blue Lagoon – a great chance to visit this beautiful spot and take a swim after most of the crowds have left. This trip costs Lm6/3.50 per adult/child.

Landlubbers don't miss out though. Behind the beach (well signposted) is **Golden Bay Horse Riding** (☎ 2157 3360; ☽ 8am-8pm), offering enjoyable one- and two-hour rides on fields overlooking the northwest beaches (but marred by the sight of so many bird hunters in the area). A one-/two-hour ride costs Lm6/9. All levels of experience are welcome, and free transport to the stables can be arranged for riders staying in the island's north. Advance booking is preferred.

Around the headland and to the south, guarded by a 17th-century watchtower, is **Għajn Tuffieħa Bay**. It's reached via a long flight of 186 steps from a car park beside the derelict Old Riviera Hotel, which is slowly sliding downhill towards the sea. The 250m strip of red-brown sand, backed by slopes covered in acacia and tamarisk trees, is more attractive than its neighbour; sun lounges can be hired here.

There are good coastal walks south to Ġnejna Bay and north to Anchor Bay.

Sleeping & Eating

ourpick Radisson SAS Golden Sands Resort & Spa (☎ 2356 1000; www.goldensands.malta.radissonsas.com; Golden Bay; r from Lm50/80 low/high season; ☒ ☒ ☒) Did Malta really need another five-star megahotel? The answer, quite clearly, is 'yes'. We were impressed at every turn by this shiny new three-tower, 10-storey hotel, chock-full of facilities and standing guard over one of Malta's loveliest beaches. The hotel opened in late 2005 and everything is in pristine condition (and in generous proportions). The standard

rooms are spacious and welcoming; fluffy robes, fancy toiletries and buffet breakfast are provided. The next notch up in accommodation comprises roomy one-bedroom suites with a separate lounge, and then there's the 'Heavenly Collection', and it's here that we fell in love – these are slick, contemporary apartments with a private deck and outdoor spa, plus a gadget-filled kitchen and indoor Jacuzzi. The most stressful thing about the Radisson experience is determining whether to spend your days at the private section of beach, by one of the pools, in the day spa, or at one of the numerous restaurants or bars. Hey, life's tough.

Apple's Eye Restaurant (☎ 2158 1042; meals Lm2-4), on a terrace overlooking Golden Bay, this place peddles an uninspiring menu of tourist fare (burgers, pizzas etc). It's better to come here just for a drink, as many of the locals do. On the beach are a number of cafés and kiosks selling snacks and drinks to parched and hungry sunbathers.

Your best bet for a meal is to brush the sand off your feet and head to one of the Radisson's shiny new options – the fab outdoor terrace of **Mokka Lobby Bar & Terrace** (snacks & meals Lm1-5, ☽ 8am-11pm) for coffee, cake and light meals, or the cheery, aqua-coloured **Agliolio** (mains Lm3-7; ☽ lunch & dinner), with an appealing Med-flavoured menu heavy on pizza, pasta and salads. Options increase of an evening, with **Essence** (☎ 2356 1000 ext 1920; mains Lm6.75-9.50; ☽ dinner), the number one pick for a fancy-pants dinner – the six-course set menu (Lm16, or Lm24 with wine) could be the way to go; bookings are recommended. The hotel is home to a decent number of bars too, poolside and indoors.

At Għajn Tuffieħa Bay there's a kiosk selling drinks and ice creams at the top of the steps leading down to the beach, and you're usually able to buy drinks on the beach without having to complete the marathon climb.

Getting There & Away

By car from Buġibba (or anywhere on Malta's east coast), turn south at the roundabout at the western end of St Paul's-Buġibba Bypass (towards Manikata). Otherwise, catch bus 652 from Buġibba or Sliema (Lm0.50 from either destination), or bus 47 from Valletta (Lm0.23).

Note that the car-park attendant at Għajn Tuffieħa Bay will expect a small payment upon your departure – Lm0.25 is sufficient.

NORTHWEST MALTA

MĠARR & AROUND

The village of Mġarr (mm-jarr), 2km to the southeast of Għajn Tuffieħa (and not to be confused with Mġarr on Gozo), would be unremarkable were it not for the conspicuous dome of the famous **Egg Church**. The Church of the Assumption was built in the 1930s with money raised by local parishioners, largely from the sale of locally produced eggs. Across the village square from the church is the **Mġarr Shelter** (☎ 2157 3235; Triq il-Kbira; adult/child Lm1/0.50; ☺ 9am-2pm Tue-Sat, 10-11.30am Sun), used by locals during the WWII bombings of Malta (enter through Il Barri restaurant). You can only imagine the long uncomfortable hours spent down here in the humidity, 12m underground, but to show that life went on under such tough conditions, there are rooms on display that served as classrooms and hospitals.

The site of the **Ta'Ħaġrat Temple** (☎ 2123 9545; Triq San Pietru; adult/child Lm2/0.50; ☺ 9.30-11am Tue), dating from around 3600 to 3300 BC and the earliest temple building in Malta, is concealed down a side street near the police station (on the road towards Żebbiegħ), but it's hardly worth seeking out. The site is fenced off and there is little to see except a few tumbled stones. The **Skorba Temples** (☎ 2123 9545; Triq Sant'Anna; adult/child Lm2/0.50; ☺ 11.30am-1pm Tue), in the neighbouring village of Żebbiegħ, are slightly more interesting, but probably only to archaeology enthusiasts. The excavation of the site was important in providing evidence of village habitation on Malta in the period between 4500 and 4100 BC (earlier than the temple-building period), now known as the Skorba Phase. Fragments of pottery and figurines found on the site are displayed in the National Museum of Archaeology in Valletta (p62).

A minor road leads west from Mġarr past the ornate early-19th-century **Zammitello Palace** – originally a manor house, and now a wedding and function hall – to **Ġnejna Bay**. The red-sand beach is backed by terraced hillsides and enjoys a distant view of the Ta'Ċenċ cliffs on Gozo. There is good swimming off the rocks on either side of the bay, and kiosks and water sports on the beach itself. The **Lippija Tower** on the northern skyline makes a good target for a short walk.

On the road between Mġarr and Għajn Tuffieħa are the fenced remains of the **Roman Baths**. There are only scant remnants of floor mosaics, the fire-bricks beneath the caldarium (hot room), and the stone toilet seats from the latrine, but the site is closed to the public.

Il-Barri (☎ 2157 3235; Triq il-Kbira; mains Lm2.50-6.50) is on the village square in Mġarr, close to the Egg Church. It's a favourite local venue for a *fenkata* – whole fresh rabbit served in a casserole, either fried in garlic or in a wine gravy, or stewed with pork belly and potatoes to really harden the arteries (Lm11.85 for a whole rabbit, which serves three, or Lm3.95 for a single portion). There are also grilled steaks, lamb chops and king prawns, plus Maltese-as-they-come local favourites such as *aljotta* (fish broth), quail, horsemeat and *braġioli* (a thin slice of beef wrapped around a stuffing of breadcrumbs, chopped bacon, hard-boiled egg and parsley, then braised in a red-wine sauce).

Bus 47 runs from Valletta to Golden Bay via Mġarr (Lm0.23).

MELLIEĦA

pop 6540

The sprawling, rapidly developing town of Mellieħa (mell-*ee*-ha) perches picturesquely atop the ridge between St Paul's Bay and Mellieħa Bay. Because of its distance from the beach, Mellieħa escaped the tidal wave of development that blighted Sliema and Buġibba in the early days of Malta's package-holiday boom. Although there are now several large hotels in town, Mellieħa today exudes a certain atmosphere of exclusivity, and is home to some high-class restaurants. A 15-minute walk leads down the steep hill to **Mellieħa Bay** (also known as Għadira Bay), the biggest and best sandy beach in the Maltese Islands. It's also, predictably, one of the most popular.

Orientation & Information

Triq Ġorġ Borg Olivier – Mellieħa's slender main drag – runs north–south along a narrow gorge in the limestone plateau of the Mellieħa Ridge, and descends via a series of hairpin bends towards Mellieħa Bay. The older part of the town lies to the west of this street, with the Church of Our Lady of Victory at the northern end. Newer houses, luxury villas and apartments spread along the ridge to the east. Buses in both directions stop on the main street, below the church. The main road to Ċirkewwa and the Gozo ferry bypasses Mellieħa to the south and west.

The **Bank of Valletta** (Triq Ġorġ Borg Olivier) and **HSBC Bank** (Triq il-Kbira) both have central

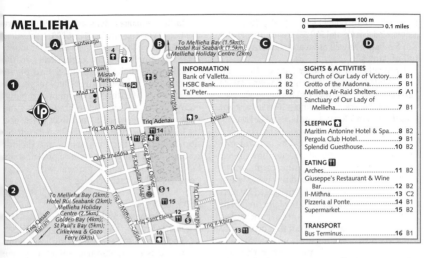

MELLIEĦA

INFORMATION
Bank of Valletta..........................1 B2
HSBC Bank..................................2 B2
Ta'Peter.......................................3 B2

SIGHTS & ACTIVITIES
Church of Our Lady of Victory.....4 B1
Grotto of the Madonna...............5 B1
Mellieħa Air-Raid Shelters..........6 A1
Sanctuary of Our Lady of
    Mellieħa.....................................7 B1

SLEEPING
Maritim Antonine Hotel & Spa.....8 B2
Pergola Club Hotel......................9 B1
Splendid Guesthouse.................10 B2

EATING
Arches......................................11 B2
Giuseppe's Restaurant & Wine
    Bar..12 B2
Il-Mithna..................................13 C2
Pizzeria al Ponte.......................14 B1
Supermarket..............................15 B2

TRANSPORT
Bus Terminus.............................16 B1

branches with ATMs. **Ta'Peter** (☎ 2152 3537; 45 Triq Ġorġ Borg Olivier; per hr Lm1; ☽ 10am-2pm & 6pm-late Tue-Sun) is a bar and café with 1970s décor and a few computers for Internet access.

Sights & Activities
MELLIEĦA
The **Church of Our Lady of Victory** sits prominently on a rocky spur overlooking Mellieħa Bay. Stairs lead down on the eastern side of the church to a little pedestrian plaza beside the **Sanctuary of Our Lady of Mellieħa** (☽ 8am-noon & 5-7pm), which has been a place of pilgrimage since medieval times. Its walls are covered with votive offerings; the fresco of the Madonna above the altar is said to have been painted by St Luke.

Across the main street from the shrine, a gate in the wall and a flight of steps lead down to the **Grotto of the Madonna** (☽ 8am-6pm), another shrine dedicated to the Virgin. It is set deep in a cave lit by flickering candles, beside a spring with waters that are reputed to heal sick children. Baby clothes hung on the walls are votive offerings given in thanks for successful cures.

As you approach the sanctuary from the main street, steps to the left lead up to the entrance to the **Mellieħa air-raid shelters** (☎ 2152 1970; Triq il-Madonna tal-Għar; adult/child Lm1/0.25; ☽ 9am 3.30pm Mon Sat), dug by hand to shelter the town's population from WWII bombs. It's one of the largest underground shelters in Malta, with a depth of 12m and a length of around 500m. Visitors tour a marked route

through the narrow corridors; mannequins have been placed in some rooms in order to re-create the scene.

MELLIEĦA BAY
Mellieħa Bay really is family-holiday turf, but not exclusively so. The warm, shallow waters of Mellieħa Bay are great for swimming and safe for kids, so the sea gets almost as crowded as the sand. Add the water-skiers, rental canoes, banana rides, parasailing boats and the fact that the reliable northeasterly breeze blowing into the bay in summer makes it ideal for windsurfing, and you begin to realise that Mellieħa Bay is not the place to get away from it all. Still, there are good summertime facilities, including sun beds (per day Lm1.50) and umbrellas (Lm2.50) for rent, windsurfing and kite-surfing gear for hire, and numerous kiosks serving drinks and snacks.

Boat and sailboard rental is available from the striking **Adira Sailing Centre & Lido** (☎ 2152 3190; www.adirasailingcentre.com.mt) at the beach's northern end. Sailboards can be hired from Lm5/18 for one/four hours; rental of an easy-to-sail Laser Pico dinghy costs Lm14/25 for one/four hours.

At the southern edge of the bay is the **Tunny Net Complex**, with restaurants and a few shops, a lido, a water-sports operator open from April to October (parasailing, ringo rides on rubber tubes, jet skis for hire, canoes and paddle boats etc), and a diving operator: **Meldives Dive School** (☎ 2152 2595; www.meldives. info). If you're not after sea-based activities, there's a small **ten-pin bowling alley** (adult/child per game incl shoe hire Lm1.95/1.55) inside the Hotel Riu Seabank, as well as an amusement arcade full of games.

Ironically, on the other side of the road from Malta's busiest beach is **Għadira Nature Reserve** (☎ 2134 7646; www.birdlifemalta.org; admission free, donations welcome; ☺ 10.30am-4.30pm Sat & Sun Nov & Feb-May, 9.30am-3.30pm Sat & Sun Dec-Jan, closed Jun-Oct). This area of shallow, reedy ponds surrounded by scrub is an important resting area for migrating birds (over 200 species have been recorded at the site). The name, pronounced aa-*dee*-ra, means 'marsh', and this was Malta's first national nature reserve, managed by passionate volunteers of BirdLife Malta on behalf of the government. Visitors are accompanied for a walk along a nature trail that eventually leads to a bird-watching hide, and it's wonderful to visit an area in Malta where bird life is respected and admired in its natural habitat, rather than hunted and trapped.

Sleeping

MELLIEĦA

Splendid Guesthouse (☎ 2152 3602; www.splendid malta.com; Triq il-Kappillan Magri; s/d with shared bathroom Lm10.50/17, with bathroom Lm12.50/19; ☺ Apr-Oct; ✖ ☐) This pleasant, affordable guesthouse is at the southern end of town in a residential area, a few minutes' walk from the main street. The spick-and-span guest rooms have plain, no-frills furnishings, and all rooms have a private shower and washbasin (some have full en suite). Rates include breakfast in the cheerful breakfast room–bar area, and there's a sunbathing terrace on the rooftop. The friendly owners also have self-catering apartments available, and a large villa sleeping up to 11.

Pergola Club Hotel (☎ 2152 3912; www.pergolahotel .com.mt; Triq Adenau; hotel B&B per person Lm6/17 low/high season, 2-person studio Lm12/30 low/high season, 4-person apt Lm18/45 low/high season; ✖ ☐ ☎) Across the bridge from the main road is the Pergola, offering comfortable if unremarkable hotel rooms and self-catering apartments (entry is at the top of the steps). The views from the sun terraces towards the church are lovely. There is also a health spa, an indoor pool and a children's play area, plus the obligatory choice of bars and restaurants. Studios and apartments are very good value, especially for families (note that studio/apartment prices given here are per room, not per person); low-season rates are a bargain.

Maritim Antonine Hotel & Spa (☎ 2152 0923; www .maritimmalta.com; Triq Ġorġ Borg Olivier; B&B per person from Lm15.50/31 low/high season; ✖ ☐ ☎) The glossy Antonin dominates the main street in the middle of Mellieħa. Here you'll find plenty of young and old Euro-travellers (especially Germans, as Maritim is a German company) enjoying the stylishly appointed rooms and suites, each with balcony, minibar, coffee and tea facilities, satellite TV and internet connection. Hotel facilities are first-rate and include restaurants, a health spa, rooftop pool and sun terrace, and lovely lush gardens with a large pool. A sophisticated choice.

MELLIEĦA BAY

Hotel Riu Seabank (☎ 2152 1460; www.seabankhotel .com; Triq Marfa; B&B per person from Lm9/23 low/high season; ✖ ☐ ☎) It has to be said, the fairly basic rooms here come as a disappointment after the opulent Moorish-style entry and lobby (complete with bird aviary). Still, the rooms are clean, comfy and well equipped, and the hotel itself is a fine family choice with something for everyone – a health spa for mum, pub for dad, 10-pin bowling alley for kids and a playroom for the littlies. Plus, with the huge onsite pool and the beach across the road, it comes as no surprise that plenty of package-tour holidaymakers call this place home. Winter rates are dirt cheap.

Mellieħa Holiday Centre (☎ 2289 3000; www.mellieħaholidaycentre.com; Triq Marfa; bungalows per person Lm11/18 low/high season, children under 12, 50% discount; ☐ ☎) As you enter this attractive, well-maintained 'village', the signs in Danish, not to mention the wholesome blonde families surrounding the pool, should leave you in little doubt you've entered Scandinavian holiday country. The large complex sits opposite the beach (to which it's connected by an underground walkway) and is set back off the main road in landscaped grounds. There are loads of family-friendly facilities, including a choice of restaurants, sports facilities, internet café, laundry, supermarket, and a large pool and sun terrace. Kids will be stoked with the games room, kids' pool and playground; parents will be pleased by the fully equipped two-bedroom bungalows. The fuss-free décor of these is simple and comfy, and each sleeps up to six and has a private, sheltered courtyard; a handful of smaller, cheaper studios is also available. The centre is sometimes booked out by Danish tour operators in the high season, but it's well worth inquiring after vacancies.

Eating & Drinking

MELLIEĦA

Pizzeria al Ponte (☎ 2152 0923; cnr Triq Ġorġ Borg Olivier & Triq Adenau; snacks & meals Lm2-6; 🕑 lunch & dinner) The food here won't set anyone's world on fire (especially given the culinary masterpieces on offer up the road – read on), but the menu is vast and crowd-pleasing and the décor is nicely done. You'll get a pretty predictable list of pizzas, pasta, sandwiches and burgers, plus a kids' menu and good desserts.

Il-Mitħna (☎ 2152 0404; 45 Triq il-Kbira; mains Lm4-7; 🕑 dinner nightly, lunch Sun) This atmospheric eatery is housed in a 400-year-old windmill, the only survivor of three that used to sit atop Mellieħa Ridge. There are outdoor tables in a pretty courtyard, and a menu of local dishes with a twist – a starter of Maltese sausage, tomato and Brie tartlet, or a main of casseroled rabbit in a bacon, sweet pepper, tomato and cream sauce. Servings are generous. There's a great-value set menu for early diners – Lm5.50 for three courses, from 6pm to 7.45pm.

Giuseppe's Restaurant & Wine Bar (☎ 2157 4882; cnr Triq Ġorġ Borg Olivier & Triq Sant'Elena; mains Lm4-8; 🕑 dinner Tue-Sat) Run by Malta's favourite TV chef, Michael Diacono, this inviting place has a winning formula of stylishly rustic décor, a relaxed atmosphere and a great menu of creative treats that changes regularly according to seasonal produce. The fresh fish is reliably good, and regulars recommend the king prawns. Bookings are recommended.

Arches (☎ 2152 3460; 113 Triq Ġorġ Borg Olivier; mains Lm4-11.50; 🕑 dinner Mon-Sat) This acclaimed restaurant is another main-street favourite. It's large and elegant, with a menu, prices and service befitting the chic décor and formality. The food is accomplished and delicious – try venison fillet on roasted asparagus or roasted spiced monkfish on a chive risotto. Frock up, and book ahead.

For the self-caterers, there are a couple of supermarkets on the main street, Triq Ġorġ Borg Olivier; note that they are all closed on Sunday.

MELLIEĦA BAY

Adira Sailing Centre & Lido (☎ 2152 3190; dinner mains Lm3-6; 🕑 lunch & dinner) Inside the sailing centre's Greek Islands–inspired exterior is an alluring café-bar. Enjoy your meal inside the sky-blue interior or preferably alfresco, with water views everywhere you look. The lunchtime menu is small, with a few baguette and burger selections; dinner-time options are greater, with appealing fish and pasta dishes.

At the southern edge of the bay, near the roundabout where the bypass rejoins the coast, is the Tunny Net Complex, home to some good dining options with outdoor terraces and water views. The casual **Café Latino Punta Rena** (☎ 2152 3254; mains Lm2-7.50; 🕑 lunch & dinner) has outdoor seating over the water and a Tex-Mex menu, with selections like nachos, fajitas and steaks any which way you please. For sweet-tooths there are also cakes and sundaes, a kids' menu and a wide choice of cocktails. Next door, the more formal **Trattoria de Buono** (☎ 2152 1332; mains Lm6-8.50; 🕑 dinner nightly, lunch Sun) serves up high quality Italian and local dishes, including rabbit casserole, flambéed king prawns or roasted chicken roulade stuffed with dried apricots, pistachios and spinach. The set menu (Lm8.50) is excellent value.

Self-caterers should head to the **supermarket** (Triq Marfa; 🕑 7.30am-7pm Sun-Fri, to 11pm Sat) inside the Mellieħa Holiday Centre (opposite), one of the few places selling groceries on a Sunday.

Getting There & Away

Buses 43, 44 and 45 from Valletta pass through Mellieħa. Bus 43 terminates here, while buses 44 and 45 continue to Mellieħa Bay (bus 45 goes on to Ċirkewwa); the fare from Valletta is Lm0.25.

To/from Sliema, catch bus 645; to/from Buġibba, you need bus 48. Both these routes run to Mellieħa town and Mellieħa Bay; the fare is Lm0.50.

There are a number of car-rental places lining the main street in town – shop around and you should find a good price, especially given the competition along here.

AROUND MELLIEĦA

The crest of Mellieħa Ridge offers some good walking to the southeast and southwest of the town. To the east, the fortress-like **Selmun Palace** (Map p102) dominates the skyline above St Paul's Bay. It was built in the 18th century for a charitable order called the Monte di Redenzione degli Schiavi (Mountain of the Redemption of the Slaves), whose business was to ransom Christians who had been taken into slavery on the Barbary Coast. The palace, which now houses a hotel and restaurant, mimics the style of Verdala Palace south of Rabat (p131).

A right turn just before you get to Selmun Palace leads in just over 1km to the derelict **Fort Campbell** (Map p102), an abandoned coastal defence built by the British between WWI and WWII. The headland commands a fine view over St Paul's Islands, and you can hike down to the coastal salt pans of Blata il-Bajda and around to Mistra Bay, or westwards along the clifftop to the ruined **tower of Għajn Ħadid** (Map p102) above the little beach at Mġieba Bay.

A left turn at the foot of the hill leading down to Mellieħa Bay puts you on the road to Anchor Bay about 1.5km away on the west coast. This steep-sided, pretty little bay was named after the many Roman anchors that were found on the sea bed by divers, some of which can be seen in the Maritime Museum at Vittoriosa (p76).

However, in 1979 Anchor Bay was transformed into the ramshackle fishing village of **Sweethaven** (Map p98; ☎ 2152 4782; www.popeye malta.com; adult/child Lm3/2; ♡ 9.30am-4.30pm Oct-Apr, to 5.30pm May-Sep) and was used as the set for the 1980 Hollywood musical *Popeye*, starring Robin Williams. The set still stands and is a family-targeted tourist attraction, but the theme park is about as interesting as, well, an abandoned film set. Adults may not be too taken by the heavy cheese factor, but younger kids in particular should find some entertainment value from the animation shows, puppets, small fun park (where you pay extra for rides) and play pool. If you're not keen to hand over your cash, you can get a good view of the village for free from the southern side of the bay (drive on past the car park entrance).

Bus 441 runs hourly from Mellieħa Bay to Anchor Bay between 10am and 5pm Monday to Saturday (one way Lm0.50).

MARFA PENINSULA

The Marfa Peninsula is Malta's final flourish before dipping beneath the waters of the Comino Channel. Some of Malta's best diving spots are found along its northern coast (see Map p47). For information on requirements, dive schools and the best locations, see the Diving & Snorkelling chapter, p44.

The peninsula is a barren ridge of limestone, steep on the south side and dipping more gently north and east from the high point of Ras il-Qammieħ (129m). A minor road leads west from the top of the hill up from Mellieħa

Bay, passing the **Red Tower** (☎ 2121 5222; adult/child Lm0.50/free; ♡ 10am-4pm Mon-Sat, to 1pm Sun), built in 1649 for Grand Master Lascaris as part of the chain of signal towers that linked Valletta and Gozo. The view from the tower's flat roof is stunning. The road continues west to the wild headland of **Ras il-Qammieħ**, with more incredible views north to Gozo and south along the western sea cliffs of Malta.

Opposite the Red Tower road, another road leads east along the spine of the peninsula, with side roads giving access to various small coves and beaches. These places are very popular with locals and best avoided on weekends, when the crowds can be enormous.

First up is **Ramla Bay**, with its small, sandy beach monopolised by the resort of the same name. Immediately to its east is **Ramla Tal'Qortin**, which has no sand and is surrounded by an unsightly sprawl of Maltese holiday huts amid a forest of TV aerials and telephone cables.

The next two roads lead down to the scrappy sandy beaches at **Armier Bay**, the most developed beach on the peninsula, with sun lounges, kiosks and a handful of cafés. The fourth road leads to Malta's only camping ground, while the next reaches **White Tower Bay**, which has another seaweed-stained patch of sand and a rash of holiday huts combining to form a small, unattractive shanty town. A track continues past the tower to the low cliffs of Aħrax Point, from which a pleasant coastal walk leads 1km south to a statue of the Madonna on Daħlet ix-Xilep. You can also reach the Madonna statue and a small chapel by following the main road east across the Marfa Peninsula.

The main road running the length of the island of Malta ends at **Ċirkewwa**, which consists of little more than a desalination plant, a hotel and the Gozo ferry terminal. A left turn just before the Paradise Bay Hotel leads to **Paradise Bay**, a narrow patch of sand below cliffs with a private lido, restaurant and a grand view of the ferry slip. It's a popular swimming spot and stages the occasional open-air clubbing event in summer.

Sleeping & Eating

Given the remote location of the three resorts in this area (not within easy walking distance of any restaurants – except for those at other hotels), half- and full-board options are available to guests at each hotel, normally at an additional cost of around Lm6 for half board per person per night. Some of Malta's best diving is found in this area, so all the resorts have diving schools, plus good water-sports facilities and regular boat trips to nearby Comino.

Adventure Campsite (☎ 2152 1105; www.malta campsite.com; 2-/4-person site with own tent Lm3.90/5.90, furnished tent per adult/child Lm5/1.50; 🖳) Kudos to these guys for opening Malta's first official camping ground – it's just a pity about the shadeless grounds and remote location. You'll need your own set of wheels: the turn-off to the camping ground is 2.5km from the main road to Ċirkewwa, and then it's a further 1km from the turn-off to the site. Once here, the facilities are reasonable and include erected, furnished tents for hire and large, clean bathrooms, along with loads of other items for rent (including bikes, barbecues and fridges). Still, you'll pay for everything, including shower tokens and picnic tables – once all that is factored in, a bed in a guesthouse may work out cheaper.

Paradise Bay Resort Hotel (☎ 2152 1166; www .paradise-bay.com; s/d from Lm16/24 low season, Lm24/42 high season; 🕸 🖳 🗪) Squeezed onto the tip of Marfa Point, opposite the Gozo ferry terminal, is this large (234-room) hotel, showing its age in comparison to its competitors but with generously proportioned rooms, corridors and common areas. Unless you don't mind dingy, dated décor, opt for the superior rooms, which have better furnishings and a fresher feel. All rooms have a balcony with good water views – the sea view takes in the ferry terminal and Comino, while bay views overlook the pool area and Paradise Bay. It's popular with divers and an older clientele.

Ramla Bay Resort (☎ 2281 2281; www.ramlabay resort.com; r low/high season from Lm23/53; 🖳 🕸 🗪) A recent face-lift has turned this once humdrum hotel into a great holiday option, typified by the swanky new lobby and lounge area. Check out the colourful *luzzu* (traditional fishing boat) permanently moored near the bar en route to the expansive seafront pool area. Family-friendly distractions on offer include a health spa, water sports, private beach, bike hire and what the industry refers to as 'animation' – activities to occupy different age groups, from a kids' club to salsa-dancing lessons. Needless to say, there are the requisite food and drink providers. The well-equipped rooms feature a cheery colour scheme, and all have a balcony; cheaper rooms have views to Armier Bay to the west (not as appealing as Ramla Bay itself, but a sea view nonetheless).

Superior rooms have more bells and whistles, including a plasma TV, a minibar and tea and coffee facilities (they're worth the extra outlay). Get off the bus at the Barceló Riviera Resort & Spa and walk along the waterfront to reach Ramla Bay.

Barceló Riviera Resort & Spa (☎ 2152 5900; www .riviera.com.mt; s/d from Lm35/45 low season, Lm45/70 high season; 🕸 🖳 🗪) Just off the main road, about 1.5km east of the Ċirkewwa ferry terminal, is this bright attractive option, with cheerful staff, fresh colourful décor and the requisite facilities, including a health spa, restaurants (a bistro, pizzeria and more formal restaurant), two bars and three pools. It's particularly popular with French travellers and Spaniards in summer.

The Marfa Peninsula is a culinary wasteland, with few eating options outside the three hotels. **Ray's Lido** (☎ 2152 0469; mains Lm1.50-6; 🕑 breakfast, lunch & dinner) at Little Armier Bay (the eastern side of Armier Bay) serves OK meals at its restaurant-pizzeria, and also offers sun lounges, canoes for hire and extensive water-sports facilities (including fun jet-ski tours out to Comino). On Friday nights in summer a live band plays, and there's a popular barbecue buffet.

Getting There & Away

Buses 45 and 145 run regularly between Valletta and Ċirkewwa, and the journey takes about an hour (one way Lm0.25). By car, you can make the trip in about 40 to 45 minutes. Bus 48 runs between Ċirkewwa and Buġibba (Lm0.50), and bus 645 services the Ċirkewwa–Sliema route (Lm0.50). Bus 50 runs from Valletta to Armier Bay daily from July to early September only (Lm0.25). A taxi from Malta International Airport to Ċirkewwa costs Lm13.50.

For details of ferry services to Gozo and Comino, see p189. As well as the boat service operated by the Comino Hotels, there are a couple of operators in this area. **Midas Shuttle Service** (☎ 2155 2432, 9947 4142) operates year-round from beside the Gozo ferry terminal, charging Lm4/1 adult/child for a return trip. Services run hourly from 9am to around 6pm or 7pm (according to demand) from June to September, 10am to 4pm in the shoulder season (April, May and October). Call for winter schedules. **Royal Cruises** (☎ 2155 3092, 9940 6529) has a similar schedule and arrives and departs from the Marfa jetty opposite the Barceló Riviera Resort & Spa, charging Lm4/1.50 for a return journey per adult/child.

NORTHWEST MALTA

Central Malta

This small region is a grab-bag of all that's good about Malta, minus the sprawling seaside resorts. In the heart of the country you can drive through tiny villages that see few tourists on your way between traffic-clogged urban conurbations. You can visit remarkable medieval frescoes in ancient underground catacombs, marvel at one of Europe's largest church domes, then spend the night worshipping the dance gods at a huge open-air nightclub. Natural attractions include stark cliffs that are the perfect place to watch a sunset, a scenic bay ideal for swimming (if only you can find it) and the only decent patch of greenery on this rather barren island. There are sleeping and eating options ranging from luxurious five-star hotels that host dignitaries and movie stars to university residences and rustic village restaurants where locals come for their weekend feasts of rabbit.

But the jewel in the crown, and an absolute must-see, is Mdina, once the ancient walled capital of Malta. It's a stunning town perched loftily on a crag, and its quiet streets ooze history and refinement (particularly after the day-tripping busloads clear out). In the early morning and especially in the evening, this is the kind of place that has you talking in whispers so as not to disturb the peace.

Most visitors to Malta base themselves in either the capital or by the coast, but if you're after a tranquil holiday that's a little off the well-worn path, there are a few top-notch choices here.

HIGHLIGHTS

- Enjoying the almost-spooky evening silence of beautiful **Mdina** (opposite)
- Going underground to admire the frescoes of **St Agatha's Catacombs** (p128) in Rabat
- Lunching among the locals at Bobbyland Restaurant, followed by a stroll along the top of the **Dingli Cliffs** (p130)
- Tucking into rabbit or cheering on the donkey races at the annual **L-Imnarja festival** (p131) in Buskett Gardens
- Questioning divine intervention while marvelling at the unexploded bomb in **Mosta Dome** (p131)
- **Partying** (p129) in an open-air club into the early morning to the soundtrack of an international DJ

CENTRAL MALTA

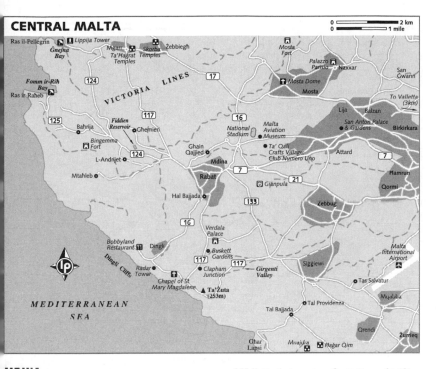

MDINA

pop 385

Mdina is, without question, historic Malta at its most photogenic. The hidden laneways offer exquisite architectural detail and some respite from the day-tripping crowds, who largely stick to the main street. Don't be surprised if you encounter, as we did, an Italian TV crew or German fashion shoot trying to capture the town's loveliness.

The citadel of Mdina was fortified from as long ago as 1000 BC when the Phoenicians built a protective wall here and called their settlement Malet, meaning 'place of shelter'. The Romans built a large town here and called it Melita. It was given its present name when the Arabs arrived in the 9th century – *medina* is Arabic for 'walled city'. They built strong walls and dug a deep moat between Mdina and its suburbs (known as *rabat* in Arabic).

In medieval times Mdina was known as Città Notabile – the Noble City. It was the favoured residence of the Maltese aristocracy and the seat of the *universitá* or governing council. The Knights of St John, who were largely a sea-based force, made Grand Harbour

and Valletta their centre of activity, and Mdina sank into the background as a retreat of the Maltese nobility. Today, with its massive walls and peaceful, shady streets, it is often referred to as the Silent City – it's well worth visiting at night, when the day-trippers have left, to experience the peace and quiet.

Orientation & Information

Mdina is the walled city; Rabat is the town outside the walls. Mdina's main street, Triq Villegaignon, runs north from the Main Gate in the south to Pjazza tas-Sur (Bastion Square), passing St Paul's Cathedral on the right. The Greek's Gate, at the west corner of Mdina, is opposite the Domus Romana in Rabat.

The bus terminus is outside Mdina on Is-Saqqajja, 200m south of the Main Gate. Visitors' cars are not allowed into Mdina, but there is parking outside the Main Gate and on Triq il-Mużew.

You'll find banks and ATMs in Rabat, opposite the bus stop, and an ATM (nicely camouflaged) on Pjazza tas-Sur. **Point de Vue** (p127; per hr Lm1) has internet access. There are public toilets outside the Main Gate.

CENTRAL MALTA

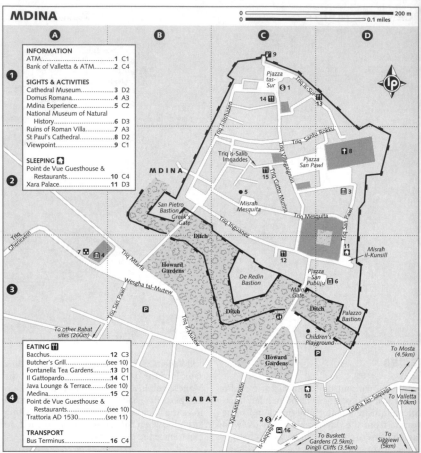

MDINA

INFORMATION
ATM.................................1 C1
Bank of Valletta & ATM........2 C4

SIGHTS & ACTIVITIES
Cathedral Museum................3 D2
Domus Romana....................4 A3
Mdina Experience.................5 C2
National Museum of Natural
  History..........................6 D3
Ruins of Roman Villa.............7 A3
St Paul's Cathedral...............8 D2
Viewpoint.........................9 C1

SLEEPING
Point de Vue Guesthouse &
  Restaurants.....................10 C4
Xara Palace........................11 D3

EATING
Bacchus............................12 C3
Butcher's Grill..................(see 10)
Fontanella Tea Gardens............13 D1
Il Gattopardo......................14 C1
Java Lounge & Terrace...........(see 10)
Medina.............................15 C2
Point de Vue Guesthouse &
  Restaurants....................(see 10)
Trattoria AD 1530...............(see 11)

TRANSPORT
Bus Terminus.......................16 C4

Sights

ST PAUL'S CATHEDRAL

The **cathedral** (Pjazza San Pawl; admission free, donations welcome; 9.30-11.45am & 2-5pm Mon-Sat, 3-4.30pm Sun) is said to be built on the site of the villa belonging to Publius, the Roman governor of Malta who welcomed St Paul in AD 60.

The original Norman church was destroyed by an earthquake, and the restrained baroque edifice you see today was built between 1697 and 1702 by Lorenzo Gafa. Note the fire and serpent motifs atop the twin bell-towers, symbolising the saint's first miracle on Malta (see the boxed text, p101).

Echoing St John's Co-Cathedral in Valletta, the floor of St Paul's is covered in the polychrome marble tombstones of Maltese nobles

and important clergymen, while the vault is painted with scenes from the life of St Paul. The altar painting *The Conversion of St Paul* by Mattia Preti survived the earthquake, as did the apse above it with the fresco *St Paul's Shipwreck* and the beautifully carved oak doors to the sacristy on the north side.

CATHEDRAL MUSEUM

Housed in a baroque 18th-century palace originally used as a seminary is the **Cathedral Museum** (2145 4697; Pjazza San Pawl; adult/child Lm1/free; 9.30am-4.30pm Mon-Fri, to 3.45pm Sat). It contains important collections of coins, silver plate, vestments, manuscripts and religious paintings, as well as a series of woodcut and copperplate prints and lithographs by the

German Renaissance artist Albrecht Dürer. There is an interesting collection of weird and wonderful olive-wood carvings by Maltese artist Anton Agius.

NATIONAL MUSEUM OF NATURAL HISTORY

The displays of the **National Museum of Natural History** (☎ 2145 5951; Pjazza San Publiju; adult/child Lm1/0.25; ✆ 9am-5pm), though housed in the elegant Palazzo de Vilhena, look a tired and the era when museums were simply full of stuffed animals in dusty glass cabinets. The most interesting section is the geology exhibit, which explains the origins of Malta's landscape and displays the wide range of fossils that can be found in its rocks. The tooth belonging to the ancient shark *Carcharodon megalodon*, found by Agassiz, is food for thought – measuring 18cm on the edge, it belonged to a 25m monster that prowled the Miocene seas 30 million years ago. Also on display (in the Seashells Room) is the pickled body of a 16kg squid found at Xemxija in St Paul's Bay. The dusty collection of stuffed mammals and birds can be safely ignored.

AUDIOVISUAL SHOWS & EXHIBITIONS

A worthwhile 25-minute audiovisual show, the **Mdina Experience** (☎ 2145 4322; Misrah Mesquita; adult/child Lm1.65/0.80; ✆ Mon-Sat) does for Mdina's history what the Malta Experience in Valletta (p65) does for Malta's. The show begins roughly every half-hour from 10.30am to 4pm Monday to Friday, and 10.30am to 2pm Saturday.

Unfortunately, the Silent City appears to be succumbing to a rising tide of tawdry tourist traps, all hitching a ride on the back of the successful Mdina Experience show. You can soak up enough history from the streets and stones without paying to see endless gory tableaux of dying knights and tortured prisoners. Don't be forced into buying tickets to other 'visual attractions' by the pushy staff at the Mdina Experience.

Walking Tour

Enter Mdina by the **Main Gate (1)**, built in 1724 and bearing the arms of Grand Master Manoel de Vilhena. The outline of the original gate can be seen in the wall to the right of the bridge. Immediately inside the gate on the right are the **Mdina Dungeons (2**; ☎ 2145 0267; www .dungeonsmalta.com; Pjazza San Publiju; adult/child/family Lm1.60/0.80/3.80; ✆ 9.30am-4pm), which house a series of gruesome tableaux depicting torture and dismemberment, accompanied by a rather wearing soundtrack of screaming, groaning, chopping and choking noises. It's a last resort for a wet day or as entertainment for bored kids.

An imposing gateway on the right leads into the courtyard of the **Palazzo de Vilhena (3)**, built as a summer residence for the Grand Master in the early 18th century. The palace served as a hospital from 1860 until 1956, and since the 1970s has housed the **National Museum of Natural History (4**; left). Go left onto Triq Inguanez and then right onto Triq Villegaignon. On the right-hand corner of the street is **St Agatha's Chapel (5)**, which dates from the early 15th century. The entire block on the right here is occupied by the **Nunnery of St Benedict (6)**, whose members live in strict

THE MDINA UPRISING

After the French invasion of Malta in June 1798, Napoleon stayed on the island for only six days before continuing his journey to Egypt, where his fleet was defeated by the British Navy at Aboukir. He left behind a garrison of only 4000 troops under the command of General Vaubois.

With revolutionary fervour, the French tried to impose their ideas on Maltese society. They abolished the nobility, defaced their escutcheons, persecuted the clergy and looted the churches. But on 2 September 1798, when they attempted to auction off the treasures of Mdina's Carmelite Church – on a Sunday – the Maltese decided that enough was enough. In a spontaneous uprising, they massacred the French garrison at Mdina, throwing its commander, Capitaine Masson, off a balcony to his death.

The French retreated to the safety of Valletta, where the Maltese, under the command of Canon Caruana of St Paul's Cathedral, besieged them. Having learnt of Napoleon's misfortune in Egypt, the Maltese asked for help from the British, who imposed a naval blockade on Malta under the command of Captain Alexander Ball. The Maltese forces suffered two hard years of skirmishing and stand-off until the French finally capitulated on 5 September 1800.

CENTRAL MALTA

WALK FACTS

Start Main Gate
Finish Misraħ il-Kunsill
Distance approx 750m
Duration 30 minutes

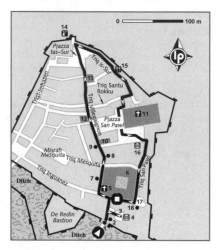

seclusion. No man is permitted to enter the convent and the sisters are not allowed to leave.

On the left is the **Casa Inguanez (7)**, the ancient seat of Malta's oldest aristocratic family, who have lived here since the 14th century. Further along Triq Villegaignon on the right, the **Casa Testaferrata (8)** is the residence of the Marquis of San Vincenzo Ferreri, another member of the Maltese nobility; the title was created by King Philip V of Spain and donated to the family in 1716. Across the street on the left is the **House of Notary Bezzina (9)**. It was from Bezzina's balcony that the French commander Masson was lobbed to his death in 1798 (see the boxed text, p125).

Next up on the right is the beautiful baroque façade of the **Banca Giuratale (10)**, built in 1730, which once housed Mdina's city council and is now home to the National Archives. Beyond that, Pjazza San Pawl opens out, dominated by the elegant baroque façade of **St Paul's Cathedral (11**; p124). Facing it is the **Palazzo Santa Sophia (12)**, which bears a stone tablet with the date 1233. Though this year is probably inaccurate, the building is still the oldest in Mdina.

Keep on along Triq Villegaignon past the Carmelite Church and monastery to the **Palazzo Falzon (13)**, also called the Norman House. The building dates from 1495 and was used for a time by Grand Master de L'Isle Adam when the Knights first arrived in Malta in 1530. Look up to see the beautiful medieval windows. The ground floor houses a private museum; at the time of research it was closed as the palazzo (mansion) undergoes extensive restoration and modernisation. The much-delayed reopening is now scheduled for late 2006; read about the restoration at www.patrimonju.org.mt.

Triq Villegaignon ends at Pjazza tas-Sur. The **views (14)** from the city walls take in all of northern and central Malta, including St Paul's Bay, Mosta Dome and the Valletta bastions. On an exceptionally clear day, you might even see the peak of Mt Etna in Sicily, 225km away to the north-northeast (scan the horizon just to the left of Mosta Dome).

Follow the walls to the right along Triq is-Sur, pausing for a cuppa and cake at the **Fontanella Tea Gardens (15)** if you wish, and bear right at Triq Santu Rokku into Pjazza San Pawl. The entrance to the cathedral is on the far side, and opposite the entry is the **Cathedral Museum (16)**, housed in the former seminary.

Go to the left of the Cathedral Museum along Triq San Pawl, which leads to the pretty little square of **Misraħ il-Kunsill (17)**. Facing the Xara Palace Hotel is the **Corte Capitanale (18)**, the former Court of Justice – note the

THE TRAGEDY OF ST AGATHA

St Agatha was a 3rd-century Christian martyr from Sicily – Catania and Palermo both claim to be her birthplace – who fled to Malta to escape the amorous advances of a Sicilian governor. On returning to Sicily she was imprisoned and tortured, and her breasts were cut off with shears – a horrific punishment gruesomely depicted in many paintings and statues in Malta. She was then burnt at the stake. There is a chapel dedicated to St Agatha in Mdina (p125) and catacombs in Rabat (p128) that are said to have been her hiding place in Malta.

figures on the balcony representing Justice and Mercy. Once back on Triq Inguanez, turn right to return to the Main Gate, or continue to the end of Triq Inguanez and exit through the Greek's Gate, and the 'ditch', to visit the Domus Romana (p128).

Sleeping

There are only two sleeping options in Mdina (and none in neighbouring Rabat); both are excellent.

Point de Vue Guesthouse & Restaurants (☎ 2145 4117; www.pointdevuemalta.com; 5 Is-Saqqajja; B&B per person Lm10-12; ▢) This guesthouse scores goals with a combination of affordable rates and a privileged position, just metres from the walled city. The large, spotless twin and double guest rooms are simply furnished, with tiled floors, whitewashed walls and recently modernised private bathrooms. They're comfy enough, although the new managers (a South African-Maltese couple) have plans to rejuvenate the décor in the not-too-distant future, now that the renovations of the property's lower levels are complete. And it's here where the Point de Vue's new persona is shining through: after stripping back the walls to their original stonework, some quirky African accents have been added (see above).

our pick Xara Palace (☎ 2145 0560; www.xarapalace .com.mt; Misraħ il-Kunsill; r from Lm85; ▨) If money is no object and your splurge inclinations lean towards history and refinement rather than modern-day glitz, the five-star Xara Palace is for you. Not only is the building (a 17th-century palazzo) superb, but the location is beyond compare. That it has only 17 individually designed suites and is filled with antiques and original artworks should give you an idea of the hotel's exclusivity, and regular guests include well-heeled Americans, Europeans, honeymooners and the odd celeb. You can choose to unwind in your warm, soft-toned duplex room or suite (all have a generous sitting area), in the sunny atrium courtyard, or at the rooftop fine-dining restaurant (mains Lm10 to Lm11), which takes in sweeping views across Malta. This is without doubt Malta's most elegant hotel.

Eating

Fontanella Tea Gardens (☎ 2145 4264; Triq is-Sur; snacks & meals Lm0.20-3; ⊠ 10am-6pm winter, to 11pm summer) Fontanella – a Maltese institution – has a wonderful setting on top of the city walls. It serves delicious home-baked cakes (Lm0.80

per piece), sandwiches and light meals and passable coffee, and you'll have ample time to admire the sweeping views from its terrace – service is ordinary.

our pick Il Gattopardo (☎ 2145 1213; 20 Triq Ville-gaignon; light meals Lm1.50-4; ⊠ lunch Mon-Sat year-round, dinner Fri & Sat summer) The name may be Italian ('the Leopard', after the famous Italian novel by Giuseppe di Lampedusa), but this charming gallery-café serves up a Greek-inspired menu in its shady courtyard, accompanied by classical music. Great choices include soups, dahl, salads and a mean baklava.

Point de Vue Guesthouse & Restaurants (☎ 2145 4117; 5 Is-Saqqajja; meals Lm1.20-6; ⊠ lunch & dinner) Just outside the city walls, Point de Vue offers an unexpected 'aristocratic-Malta-meets-Africana' experience. The casual Java Lounge & Terrace features soft leather lounges and zebra- and leopard-print cushions. At the rear, the more formal Butcher's Grill has a team of Tanzanian chefs preparing local standards and more exotic fare from a huge menu. Sure, it sounds kinda out of place, but it seems to work.

Trattoria AD 1530 (☎ 2145 0560; Misraħ il-Kunsill; mains Lm2.50-7; ⊠ lunch & dinner) Next door to the entrance to Xara Palace, this stylishly casual trattoria offers outdoor seating on the pretty square, and warm, yellow-washed walls inside. There's a kids' menu, and the grown-ups can choose from pizza and pasta choices, plus more substantial mains of fish and meat.

Bacchus (☎ 2145 4981; Triq Inguanez; snacks & lunch Lm2-3.50, dinner mains Lm3-7; ⊠ 10am-11.30pm) The property (and gardens) of this impressive restaurant and function centre takes up one-twelfth of the town of Mdina! The main restaurant is built into a vault beneath the De Redin Bastion and retains a medieval atmosphere in its vaulted ceilings and stone floors. The menu reads like a glossy magazine, with pics of each dish. Snacks and lunch dishes such as minestrone or a Maltese platter are good and reasonably priced; at dinner time choose from carefully presented French-influenced meals.

Medina (☎ 2145 4004; 7 Triq is-Salib Imqaddes; mains Lm3.50-8; ⊠ dinner Mon-Sat) The Medina (not to be confused with Caffè Medina on the main street) is a pretty-as-a-picture romantic venue – a medieval townhouse with vaulted ceilings and fireplaces for cooler evenings, and a leafy garden-courtyard for alfresco dining in warmer months. The menu offers a mix of Maltese, Italian and French dishes, with good vegetarian selections.

CENTRAL MALTA

Getting There & Away

See opposite for information on getting to Rabat. The bus terminus in Rabat is on Is-Saqqajja, 200m south of Mdina's Main Gate.

You're best off ignoring the guys touting rides in a *karrozin* (traditional horse-drawn carriage) at Mdina's Main Gate – a 35-minute spin costs a steep Lm12 to Lm15. You'll soak up far more atmosphere on foot.

RABAT

pop 11,450

The town of Rabat sprawls to the south of Mdina and is worth a wander to check out the numerous sites of historical interest. Triq San Pawl is the street to follow – it begins opposite Mdina's Greek's Gate and runs south to St Paul's Church and the town square.

Sights

Domus Romana (Map p124; ☎ 2145 4125; Wesgħa tal-Mużew; adult/child Lm2.50/0.75; ☺ 9am-5pm) This site, also called the Roman Domus, was built in the 1920s to incorporate the excavated remains of a large Roman townhouse from the 1st century BC. The centrepiece is the original peristyle court (formerly an open courtyard surrounded by columns). The mosaic floor has a geometric border around an image of two birds perched on a water bowl, known as the *Drinking Doves of Sosos*; a cistern in one corner collected rainwater. There are additional mosaic fragments and artefacts from Malta's Roman period, including sculptures, amphorae, pottery fragments and oil lamps.

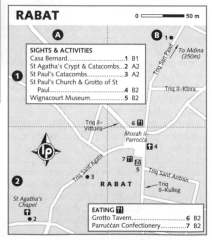

RABAT
0 —————— 50 m

SIGHTS & ACTIVITIES
Casa Bernard...............................1 B1
St Agatha's Crypt & Catacombs...2 A2
St Paul's Catacombs....................3 A2
St Paul's Church & Grotto of St
 Paul......................................4 B2
Wignacourt Museum...................5 B2

To Mdina (350m)

Triq Sant Pawl
Triq Il–Kbira
Triq Il–Vittoria
Misraħ il-Parroċċa
Triq Sant Agata
Triq Sant Antnin
Triq Il–Kulleg
RABAT
St Agatha's Chapel

EATING
Grotto Tavern..............................6 B2
Parruċċan Confectionery.............7 B2

From the Domus Romana, walk south along Triq San Pawl for around 200m to reach **Casa Bernard** (☎ 2144 4373; 46 Triq San Pawl; admission Lm3; ☺ morning tours Mon-Sat). You'll be personally guided through this privately owned 16th-century *palazzo* by one of the home's charming owners, who will explain the history of the mansion and the impressive personal collection of art, *objets d'art*, furniture, silver and china. Phone ahead for tour times.

Another 200m along the street you'll encounter **St Paul's Church**, built in 1675. Beside the church, stairs lead down into the **Grotto of St Paul** (Misraħ il-Parroċċa; admission free, donations welcome; ☺ 9.30am-5pm Mon-Sat), a cave where the saint is said to have preached during his stay in Malta. The statue of St Paul was gifted by the Knights in 1748, while the silver ship to its left was added in 1960 to commemorate the 1900th anniversary of the saint's shipwreck. Come in the early morning or late afternoon to avoid the tour groups that congest the narrow space.

From the church, numerous signposts point the way across the parish square and along Triq Sant'Agata towards two groups of early Christian underground tombs. First up, on the left, are **St Paul's Catacombs** (☎ 2145 4562; Triq Sant'Agata; adult/child Lm2/0.50; ☺ 9am-5pm), which date from the 3rd century AD and were rediscovered in 1894. There's not a lot to see in the labyrinth of rock-cut tombs, narrow stairs and passages, but it's fun to explore (note that there are a number of uneven surfaces, so mind your step). Admission includes a self-guided, 45-minute audio tour available in a handful of languages.

Another 100m down the street and on the right are **St Agatha's Crypt & Catacombs** (☎ 2145 4503; Triq Sant'Agata; adult/child Lm1/free; ☺ 9am-5pm Mon-Fri, to 1pm Sat). These catacombs are more interesting than St Paul's as they contain a series of remarkable frescoes dating from the 12th to the 15th centuries. According to legend, these catacombs were the hiding place of St Agatha when she fled Sicily (see the boxed text, p126). Tours of the catacombs are conducted regularly explain the history of the site and point out features of the artwork. Back at ground level is a quirky little museum containing everything from fossils and minerals to coins, church vestments and Etruscan, Roman and Egyptian artefacts. Note that from October to June the complex is closed between noon and 1pm.

OPEN-AIR CLUBBING

There are lots of reasons to visit this part of Malta, and refined pastimes such as museum-going and architecture-admiring are major drawcards. After dark, however, it's another story. In summer (June to September), the area around Rabat is home to some of Malta's best nightlife.

The Ibiza-styled **Gianpula** (☎ 9947 2133; www.gianpula.com), a few kilometres east of Rabat (signposted en route to Żebbuġ), is a huge open-air club that kicked off in 1980 and is still going strong. It hosts big-name events showcasing top international DJs, as well as tours from megaclubs such as Cream, Godskitchen and Ministry of Sound. As well as staging these one-off nights and the odd music festival, Gianpula is open every Friday and Saturday night from June to September. Join up to 4000 others in a huge field complete with swimming pool and seven bars.

Club Numero Uno is another open-air hot spot, found near the Ta'Qali Crafts Village. It's open on Saturday and Sunday nights in summer and its Sunset Sunday sessions are legendary, drawing over 2000 clubbers each week (check out www.pureruby.com for details).

Flyers around town advertise one-off and regular events, and keep an eye on websites mentioned here, as well as sites like www.clubbinmalta.com and www.manicmalta.com for word on the latest happenings.

Signposted from the main square is the **Wignacourt Museum** (Triq il-Kulleg; adult/child Lm1/free; 10am-3pm Mon-Sat), a real hotchpotch collection that's worth a browse. It encompasses more Christian catacombs from around the 4th century, a WWII air-raid shelter, a baroque chapel, religious icons and vestments, and changing art exhibitions.

Sleeping & Eating

See p127 for details of hotels and restaurants in Mdina.

There are some authentic hole-in-the-wall café-bars at the top of Triq San Pawl, frequented by local characters. If the smell tempts you, pick up a fresh-from-the-oven *pastizza* (ricotta- or pea-filled flaky pastry) as you wander past. You might also like to peruse **Parruċċan Confectionery** (Misraħ il-Parroċċa; closed Sun) on the main square and pick up samples of Maltese specialities like nougat, nut brittles and fig rolls.

Grotto Tavern (☎ 2145 5138; Misraħ il Parroċċa; lunch mains Lm2-5, dinner Lm4-8; lunch daily, dinner Tue-Sat), owned by a friendly French-Maltese couple, offers wining and dining on the main square. The menu waves the *tricolore* with dishes such as frogs' legs or duck à l'orange, plus fondues and raclettes perfect for sharing (Lm5 to Lm7 per person). Leave room for crêpes, chocolate fondue or *tarte aux pommes* (apple tart).

Getting There & Away

From Valletta, take bus 80 or 81 (one way Lm0.20); from Sliema and St Julian's take the direct bus 65 (Lm0.50); and from Buġibba and St Paul's Bay take bus 86 (Lm0.50).

By car, the road from Valletta is well signposted. From St Paul's Bay, begin by following signs to Mosta.

AROUND RABAT
Ta'Qali Crafts Village

The scruffy arts and crafts workshops at Ta'Qali are housed in the old Nissen huts on this WWII RAF airfield. Thankfully, the village is scheduled for a long-overdue makeover, which should make it a more attractive place to visit and browse. Despite the obvious signs of neglect, the workshops here are worth a look. You can watch glass-blowers at work, and shop for gold, silver and filigree jewellery, paintings by local artists, leather goods, Maltese lace, furniture, ceramics and ornamental glass.

The opening hours of the individual workshops vary, but most are open from 9am to 4pm Monday to Friday. Try to get here early (before 10am) if you want to avoid the coach-tour crowds.

Take bus 80 or 81 from Valletta (Lm0.20 one way). Bus 65 operates between Sliema and Rabat and calls in at Ta'Qali, as does bus 86 between Buġibba and Rabat (Lm0.50). It's about 2km from the bus terminus in Rabat to the crafts complex.

Malta Aviation Museum

Tucked away in an unassuming shed between Ta'Qali Crafts Village and the National Stadium is the **Malta Aviation Museum** (☎ 2141 6095; www.maltaaviationmuseum.com; adult/child Lm1.75/0.50; 9am-5pm), 2km northeast of Mdina. It's a

CENTRAL MALTA

real enthusiast's museum, with bits of engines, airframes and instruments lying around, and numerous restoration projects underway – including a WWII Hawker Hurricane IIa, salvaged in 1995 after 54 years at the bottom of the sea off Malta's southwest coast. You can watch locals working on the aircraft and other exhibits. Star of the show here is a WWII Spitfire Mk IX; other aircraft on display include a vintage Flying Flea, a De Havilland Vampire T11, a Fiat G91R and a battered old Douglas Dakota DC-3. To visit the museum, catch a bus to the neighbouring Ta'Qali Crafts Village (see above for route numbers).

Fomm ir-Riħ

Fomm ir-Riħ (meaning 'mouth of the wind') is the most remote and undeveloped bay on Malta. During rough weather it can be a drab and miserable place, the grey clay slopes and limestone crags merging with the grey clouds and the wave-muddied waters. But on a calm summer's day it can be a beautiful spot, with good swimming and snorkelling in the clear blue waters off the southern cliffs, and few other people to disturb the peace.

It's a long hike to get here – and locals will marvel at any nonlocals who manage to find it! From central Rabat, follow Triq Għeriexem (passing to the left of Domus Romana) to the roundabout on the edge of town; this can also be reached via the bypass from the roundabout on the Rabat–Mosta road. Follow signs for Baħrija (they can be a bit hard to spot). After the roundabout, head left at the first fork and right at the next (Fiddien Bridge), passing Fiddien Reservoir on the right. Continue straight and after about 3km bear left towards Baħrija (signed). After passing through the centre of Baħrija village, fork right, then right again.

About 1.2km from Baħrija's town square the road drops into a valley; you need to turn right into a potholed road indicated by low brick gateposts (but no gate), labelled RTO. This track ends 600m downhill above the

---

FOMM IR-RIĦ BY BOAT

If the directions to Fomm ir-Riħ sound far too complicated, you can take the easy option and view the bay from the water, on a boat trip out of Golden Bay (see p115 for more details).

---

southern cliffs of Fomm ir-Riħ. This is best accessed by car – on foot it's an 8km hike (about 1¾ hours) from the bus terminus in Rabat.

But you're not there yet! To reach the head of the bay, you need to follow a precarious footpath across a stream bed and along a ledge in the cliffs. Locals say that former Maltese prime minister Dom Mintoff used to ride his horse along this path – today posts have been cemented in place to prevent horses and bicycles using it.

From here, you can hike north to the wild cape of Ras il-Pellegrin and down to Għejna Bay (p116), or west to Ras ir-Raħeb and south along the top of the coastal cliffs to the tiny village of Mtaħleb and back into Rabat. Be aware that this area is a favourite haunt of bird-hunters – you'll spy their stone shacks all over the countryside. See p171 for tips on dealing with them.

The village of Baħrija is perfect if you're looking for somewhere well off the tourist trail in which to participate in the true Maltese Sunday lunch ritual, dining with the locals on authentic dishes (including horse meat and rabbit). Be aware, however, that unfamiliar faces in town may cause a bit of a stir! There are a handful of unassuming options on the village square, including **Ta'Gagin** (☎ 2145 0825) and **North Country Bar & Restaurant** (☎ 2145 6688).

Dingli Cliffs

Named after the famous Maltese architect Tommaso Dingli (1591–1666) – or possibly his 16th-century English namesake Sir Thomas Dingley, who lived nearby – Dingli is an unremarkable little village. But less than a kilometre to the southwest the land falls away at the spectacular 220m-high **Dingli Cliffs**. A potholed tarmac road runs along the top of the cliffs. There are also some great walks south, past the incongruous radar tower to the lonely little **Chapel of St Mary Magdalene**, built in the 17th century, and onwards to Ta'Żuta (253m) the highest point in the Maltese Islands. Here, you'll enjoy excellent views along the coast to the tiny island of Filfla.

Heading northwest along the cliffs you'll find **Bobbyland Restaurant** (☎ 2145 2895; mains Lm4-7.50; ✆ closed Mon year-round, also closed dinner Sat summer & dinner Sun winter), where you can chow down with the locals before walking off your meal with a postprandial clifftop stroll. This friendly, rustic place is 500m from the Dingli

THE FESTIVAL OF L-IMNARJA

L-Imnarja (sometimes spelt Mnarja), held on 28 and 29 June (the feast day of Sts Peter and Paul), is Malta's biggest and most boisterous festival. Its origins lie in a harvest festival dedicated to St Paul – the name is probably a corruption of the Italian *luminaria*, meaning 'illuminations', after the traditional bonfires that once lit up Rabat during the festival.

The festivities begin on 28 June with a huge party in Buskett Gardens, complete with folk music, singing and dancing. Vast quantities of rabbit stew are consumed, washed down with plenty of local wine. The carousing continues well into the small hours and many people end up spending the entire night in the gardens.

The following day, a public holiday, continues with an agricultural show at Buskett Gardens, where farmers and gardeners exhibit their produce, accompanied by local band performances. In the afternoon, bareback horse and donkey races are held at Telgħa tas-Saqqajja (Saqqajja Hill) in Rabat, attended by crowds from all over the island. The winners are awarded with *palji* (colourful brocade banners), which are taken home to adorn the victor's village.

junction; on Sundays in particular the indoor and outdoor tables are crowded with diners munching contentedly on house specialities like rabbit pan-fried in garlic, onions and herbs, or roast fillet of lamb, wrapped in puff pastry and served with garlic and rosemary sauce. Vegetarians will struggle here.

Bus 81 runs every half-hour or so from Valletta to Dingli (one way Lm0.20) via Rabat.

Buskett Gardens & Verdala Palace

The fertile valley about 2km south of Rabat (east of Dingli) harbours the only extensive area of woodland in Malta. Known as **Buskett Gardens** (from the Italian *boschetto*, meaning 'little wood'), the gardens were planted by the Knights as a hunting ground. Today they are a hugely popular outing for the Maltese and the groves of Aleppo pine, oak, olive and orange trees provide shady picnic sites in summer and orange-scented walks in winter. Buskett Gardens is the main venue for the L-Imnarja festival, held on 28 and 29 June (see the boxed text, above). The gardens are open at all times and entry is free. Bus 81 from Valletta to Dingli via Rabat stops at the entrance. Buskett is well signposted from Rabat.

En route to Buskett you'll pass the grand **Verdala Palace**, built in 1586 as a summer residence for Grand Master Hugues Loubeux de Verdalle. It was designed by Gerolamo Cassar in the form of a square castle with towers at each corner, but only for show – it was intended to be a hunting retreat, not a defendable, fortified position. The British used Verdala Palace as the Governor of Malta's summer residence and today it's the summer residence of the Maltese president. It's not open to the public.

Clapham Junction

Continue past the entrance to Buskett Gardens and follow the signs to reach a rough track signposted 'Cart Tracks'. To the right (west) of this track is a large area of sloping limestone pavement, scored with several sets of intersecting prehistoric 'cart ruts' (see the boxed text p133). The ruts are about 1.5m apart and up to 50cm deep. The name Clapham Junction – a notoriously complicated railway junction in London – was given to the site by British visitors.

MOSTA

pop 17,700

Mosta is a busy and prosperous town spread across a level plateau atop the Victoria Lines escarpment. It is famous for its Parish Church of Santa Maria, better known as the Rotunda or **Mosta Dome** (☎ 2143 3826; Pjazza Rotunda; admission free, donations welcome; ⊗ 9-11.45am & 3-5pm), which was designed by the Maltese architect Giorgio Grognet de Vassé and built between 1833 and 1860 using funds raised by the local people. A visit is worthwhile to admire the stunning blue, gold and white interior, and also to check out the bomb that fell through it in 1942 (see the boxed text, p132); be sure to dress appropriately for a place of worship.

The church's circular design with a six-columned portico was closely based on the Pantheon in Rome, and the great dome – a prominent landmark (its external height is 61m) that is visible from most parts of Malta – is said to be one of the broadest unsupported domes in Europe. Its diameter of 39.6m is exceeded only by the Pantheon (43m) and St Peter's (42.1m) in Rome. But dome comparison

---

THE MIRACLE OF MOSTA

On 9 June 1942, during WWII, three enemy bombs struck the Mosta Dome while around 300 parishioners waited to hear Mass. Two bounced off and landed in the square without exploding. The third pierced the dome, smashed off a wall and rolled across the floor of the church. Miraculously, no one was hurt and the bomb failed to detonate. A replica of the bomb can be seen in the church sacristy, to the left of the altar.

---

is a tricky business open to dispute. The parishioners of Xewkija on Gozo claim that their church has a bigger dome than Mosta's – although the Gozitan Rotunda has a smaller diameter (25m), it is higher and has a larger volumetric capacity. So there!

Apart from the church, there's not much else to see in Mosta, but it does make a good starting point for exploring the Victoria Lines (see the boxed text, p99). To reach **Mosta Fort** (not open to the public) from the Rotunda, head northwest on Triq il-Kostituzzjoni (to the left of the church, facing the portico), cross the bridge over Wied il-Għasel, and turn right along Triq il-Fortizza and walk through this quite industrial area. At the end of the street go straight ahead at the roundabout – the distance from the church to the fort is about 2.5km.

At the elevated **Pjazza Café** (☎ 2141 3379; 1st level, Pjazza Rotunda; snacks & meals Lm0.65-6; ☺ breakfast, lunch & dinner) you can enjoy good views of the dome from a table by the window, while downing a light lunch or snack. The nearby **Tal-Koppla** (☎ 2142 2880; Pjazza Rotunda; snacks & meals Lm1-6; ☺ breakfast, lunch & dinner) is a colourful, casual café-restaurant with something for everyone, including pies with various fillings (octopus, tuna and spinach, chicken and mushroom), salads, pizza, a kids' menu, and local dishes such as rabbit in garlic or octopus stew.

A few doors up from Tal-Koppla is **Ta'Marija Restaurant** (☎ 2143 4444; www.tamarija.com; Triq il-Kostituzzjoni; mains Lm5-9.50; ☺ lunch daily, dinner Mon-Sat), a worthwhile option if you're keen to try traditional Maltese cuisine and don't mind a bit of (dare we say?) cheesy entertainment with your meal. Three-course set menus (priced from Lm5.50 to Lm9.50) are a good deal, as is the buffet offered on Saturday night and Sunday lunchtime (Lm7.25); there's also

plenty of choice on the à la carte menu. The food is highly rated by locals – in the 2006 *Definitive(ly) Good Guide to Restaurants in Malta and Gozo,* Ta'Marija wins the gong for best Maltese food and best local wine list. And the entertainment? Wednesday and Friday see traditional Maltese folk dancing and singing; Thursday is country music night (complete with line dancing!), and Saturday is 'party night' with a DJ and local singer. Sunday lunch is family-oriented, with kids' toys and games.

A number of buses pass through Mosta. From Valletta take bus 47, 49 or 58. From Sliema and St Julian's you can reach Mosta on bus 65, and from Buġibba and St Paul's take bus 86.

NAXXAR
pop 10,600

Naxxar, a couple of kilometres northeast of Mosta (and more or less joined by the urban sprawl), is another bustling town worthy of a visit for its few interesting attractions, the highlight of which is the lavish **Palazzo Parisio** (☎ 2141 2461; www.palazzoparisio.com; Pjazza Vittorja; adult/child Lm3.50/1.75; ☺ tours on the hr 9am-3pm Mon-Fri). Originally built in 1733 by Grand Master Antonio Manoel de Vilhena, it was acquired by a Maltese noble family in the late 19th century. The new owners set about refurbishing and redecorating, and the end result was a stately home unique in Malta – the magnificent interior and baroque gardens have been described as a 'miniature Versailles'.

The entrance to the palazzo is directly opposite the **Parish Church of Our Lady**, one of the tallest baroque edifices on Malta. Construction was started in the early years of the 16th century according to the designs of Vittorio Cassar (son of the more famous Gerolamo Cassar, who designed Verdala Palace, p131).

To get to Naxxar, take bus 55 or 56 from Valletta (one way Lm0.20), or bus 65 from Sliema (Lm0.50).

THE THREE VILLAGES

The main road from Valletta to Mosta passes through the town of **Birkirkara** (population 22,000), one of the biggest population centres on the island and part of the huge conurbation that encircles Valletta and the Three Cities. Birkirkara's **Church of St Helen** is probably the most ornate of Malta's churches, a late flowering of baroque exuberance built in the mid-18th century. On the strength of his performance here, the designer, Domenico Cachia, was given the job of remodelling the façade of the Auberge de Castille in Valletta.

Just west of Birkirkara is an upmarket suburban area known as the Three Villages, centred on the medieval settlements of **Attard**, **Balzan** and **Lija**. Although modern development has fused the three into a continuous urban sprawl, the old village centres still retain their parish churches and narrow streets, and there are some interesting historical sites to visit.

Triq il-Mdina, the main road that skirts the southern edge of Attard, follows the line of the **Wignacourt Aqueduct**, built between 1610 and 1614 to improve the water supply to Valletta. Substantial lengths of the ancient structure still stand beside the road. The **Church of St Mary** (Pjazza Tommaso Dingli) in Attard, designed by Tommaso Dingli and built around the same time as the aqueduct, is one of the finest Renaissance churches on the island (see the boxed text, p38). Lija's **Church of St Saviour** (Misraħ it-Trasfigurazzjoni), designed in 1694, is the focus of one of Malta's liveliest festas (feast days), famed for its spectacular fireworks, on 6 August.

The main attraction in this area is the **San Anton Palace & Gardens** (palace closed to public; gardens admission free; ☉ dawn-dusk), which lies between Attard and Lija. The palace was built in the early 17th century as the country mansion of Grand Master Antoine de Paule. It later served as the official residence of the British Governor of Malta, and is now the official residence of the Maltese president. You can cop a lungful of cleanish air inside the lovely walled gardens that stretch between the palace and the main entrance on Triq Birkirkara; they contain groves of citrus and avocado, as well as a bird aviary. The Eagle Fountain, just inside the main gate, dates from the 1620s. The Mask Fountain is surrounded by unusual floss-silk trees with thick, thorn-studded trunks and beautiful pink flowers.

A plethora of buses runs to this area. To get to the San Anton Gardens, take bus 40 from Valletta (Lm0.20); this service passes through Attard, Balzan and Lija. Birkirkara is best reached on bus 71 from Valletta.

THE RIDDLE OF THE RUTS

One of the biggest mysteries of Malta's prehistoric period is the abundance of so-called 'cart ruts' throughout the islands. In places where bare limestone is exposed, it is often scored with a series of deep parallel grooves, looking for all the world like ruts worn by cartwheels. But the spacing of the ruts varies, and their depth – up to 60cm – means that wheeled carts would probably get jammed if they tried to use them.

A more likely explanation is that the grooves were created by a travois – a sort of sled formed from two parallel poles joined by a frame and dragged behind a beast of burden, similar to that used by the Plains Indians of North America. The occurrence of the ruts correlates quite closely to the distribution of Bronze Age villages in Malta.

This still leaves the question of what was being transported. Suggestions have included salt and building stone, but it has been argued that whatever the cargo was, it must have been abundant, heavy and well worth the effort involved in moving it. The best suggestion to date is that the mystery substance was topsoil – it was carted from low-lying areas to hillside terraces to increase the area of cultivable land, and so provide food for a growing population.

In some places the ruts are seen to disappear into the sea on one side of a bay, only to re-emerge on the far side. In other spots they seem to disappear off the edge of a cliff. These instances have given rise to all sorts of weird theories, but they are most convincingly explained as the results of long-term erosion and sea-level changes due to earthquakes – the central Mediterranean is a seismically active area and Malta is riddled with geological faults.

An ongoing study (entitled 'The significance of cart ruts in ancient landscapes') is endeavouring to document and interpret the ruts at Malta's Clapham Junction and at a second site in Spain. Perhaps one day soon we'll better understand the how, when and why of the ruts... In the meantime, documents explaining the methods and aims of this study can be found at www .heritagemalta.org/significance_of_cart_ruts.html.

Good places to see the ruts and come up with your own theories include Clapham Junction near Buskett Gardens and the top of the Ta'Ċenċ cliffs on Gozo (see p154).

Sleeping & Eating

University Residence (☎ 2143 6168 or 2143 0360; www.university-residence.com.mt; Triq R M Bonnici, Lija; dm from Lm3/5 low/high season; 🖳 🖳) About 200m north of the San Anton Gardens is the official student residence for the University of Malta, 4km away and connected by a free bus service. It's a well-equipped, well-run facility, and a good place to meet local and international students – beware, though, that securing short-term accommodation here can be tough (especially from June to September). The residence sleeps a few hundred students and is in a residential area. There are self-catering facilities, tennis courts, large grounds, a minimarket, a café-bar and a laundrette. There's a three-night minimum on stays and a variety of good accommodation available, including hotel-standard rooms from Lm16. To get here, catch bus 40 from Valletta.

Corinthia Palace Hotel (☎ 2144 0301; www.corinthia hotels.com; Vjal de Paule, Attard; r from Lm80; 🔀 🖳 🖳) On the other side of the San Anton Gardens, and at the other end of the accommodation spectrum to the uni residence, the five-star Corinthia Palace is popular with conference organisers and official delegations, and appeals to an older crowd who enjoy the discreet location, lush gardens, health spa and upmarket onsite restaurants. That the complimentary shuttle bus calls regularly at Malta's only golf course should give you some idea of the clientele. All rooms have a decent-sized balcony – request a pool view. There are often good deals available on room rates – it pays to ask, or check the website.

Melita Gardens (☎ 2147 0663; Triq id-Dmejda; mains Lm2-7.50; 🕓 lunch & dinner) Taking the effort out of deciding where to dine is this all-pleasing option, right by the entrance to the San Anton Gardens. The complex houses an atrium café, large courtyard, restaurant, wine bar, pizzeria and even an internet café (and everything on the menu is available to take away). You're bound to find something here to suit your fancy.

You can buy drinks and ice creams for your garden stroll from the kiosk beside the entrance to the San Anton Gardens.

A good option of an evening is to frock up a little and visit one of the highly regarded restaurants at the Corinthia Palace Hotel – the elegant **Corinthia Room** (🕓 dinner nightly) for fine dining; **Rickshaw** (🕓 dinner Mon-Sat) offering pan-Asian cuisine, and **Pizza, Pasta e Basta** (🕓 dinner nightly May-Oct), a seasonal alfresco pizza and pasta eatery. There's also an all-day café in the hotel's lobby, where a decent lunch buffet costs Lm3.75.

Southeast Malta

For all the industrial grit and general shabbiness that characterise parts of southeast Malta, visitors should think carefully before dismissing the region entirely and concentrating their sightseeing efforts elsewhere. Several of Malta's most significant historical sites are in the southeast, including two impressive temples (Ħaġar Qim and Mnajdra) dating back over 5000 years, and the Għar Dalam cave, full of fossilised remains of prehistoric animals. There is some excellent coastal scenery with boat trips available to visit grottoes, plus enticing swimming spots well off the tourist trail. A genuine highlight is the old fishing village of Marsaxlokk, with a photogenic harbour full of colourful boats and a waterfront lined with restaurants specialising in fresh fish, patronised by discerning locals and camera-toting day-trippers. These small honey pots of tourist activity are easily accessed by bus from Valletta.

Still, few holiday-makers choose to stay in these parts, and it's getting harder for them to do so. While luxurious new five-star hotels are popping up all over Malta's more prosperous northern region, it was announced in 2006 that the largest and flashest hotel in the southeast would soon be demolished. This no doubt leaves the south as the working-class poor relation to the north; after copping an eyeful of the unavoidable heavy industry dotted around this region, visitors may well get the impression that, aside from a few notable exceptions, tourism is a dirty word down here.

HIGHLIGHTS

- Questioning who, when, how and why at the mysterious **Ħaġar Qim** and **Mnajdra temples** (p142)
- Devouring local seafood specialities with a view of the photogenic harbour in **Marsaxlokk** (p137)
- Taking a midmorning boat trip to the **Blue Grotto** (p141) out of Wied iż-Żurrieq
- Sunning yourself, snorkelling and enjoying some sustenance at **Għar Lapsi** (p143)

Għar Lapsi ★
Ħaġar Qim & Mnajdra temples ★
Marsaxlokk ★
★ Blue Grotto

SOUTHEAST MALTA

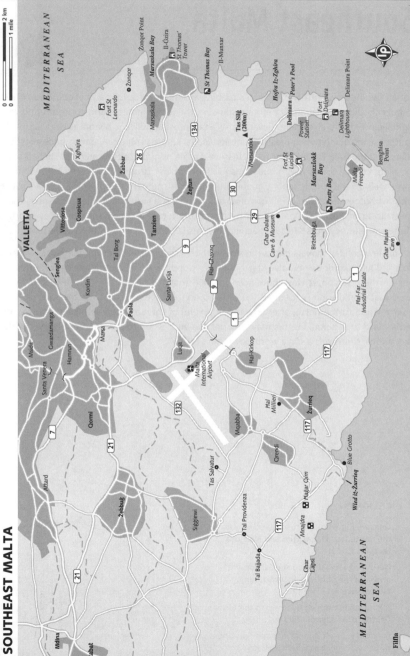

SOUTHEAST MALTA

MEDITERRANEAN SEA

Mdina
Rabat
Attard
Żebbuġ
Santa Venera
Msida
Gwardamanga
Ħamrun
Qormi
Marsa
VALLETTA
Senglea
Cospicua
Vittoriosa
Tal Borg
Kordin
Paola
Tarxien
Żabbar
Xgħajra
Marsaskala

Siġġiewi
Tal Providenza
Tal Bajjada
Tas Salvatur
Luqa
Santa Luċija
Ħal-Għaxaq
Żejtun

Mqabba
Ħal Millieri
Ħal-Kirkop
Żurrieq

Qrendi
Mnajdra
Ħaġar Qim
Għar Lapsi
Wied iż-Żurrieq
Blue Grotto

Malta International Airport

Ghar Dalam Cave & Museum
Birżebbuġa
Ħal-Far Industrial Estate
Għar Ħasan Cave

Marsaxlokk
Fort St Lucian
Marsaxlokk Bay
Pretty Bay
Malta Freeport
Benghisa Point

Tas Silġ (200m)
Delimara
Power Station
Fort Delimara
Delimara Lighthouse
Delimara Point
Hofra Iż-Żgħira
Peter's Pool

St Thomas Bay
St Thomas' Tower
Il-Munxar
Il-Gżira

Marsaskala Bay
Zonqor
Zonqor Point
Fort St Leonardo

Filfla

MEDITERRANEAN SEA

MEDITERRANEAN SEA

134
26
30
29
9
9
1
132
7
21
21
117
117
117
1

0   1 mile
0   2 km

MARSAXLOKK

pop 3000

Despite the encroachment of modern industry, the ancient fishing village of Marsaxlokk (marsa-shlock; from *marsa sirocco*, meaning 'southeasterly harbour') at the head of Marsaxlokk Bay remains resolutely a slice of real Maltese life.

Old low-rise houses ring the waterfront, and a photogenic fleet of brightly coloured *luzzu* (fishing boats; see below) dance in the harbour. Men with weathered faces sit by the waterside mending nets and grumbling about the tax on diesel, while others scrape, paint and saw as they ready their boats for the sea. The town is home to around 70% of the Maltese fishing fleet, and is – not surprisingly – renowned for its top-notch seafood restaurants, making a magnet for long-lunching locals and busloads of day-trippers.

It makes a relaxed place to base yourself. If you're after nightlife into the wee small hours you'll be disappointed, but if you're looking to chill out (and regularly chow down on all manner of fishy morsels), you'll be happy. Once the lunchtime tourist buses depart, it'll just be you and the locals.

History

Marsaxlokk Bay is Malta's second natural harbour. It was here that the Turkish fleet was moored during the Great Siege of 1565 (p21), and Napoleon's army landed here during the French invasion of 1798 (p26). In the 1930s the calm waters of the bay were used as a staging post by the huge, four-engined Short C-Class flying boats of Britain's Imperial Airways as they pioneered long-distance air travel to the far-flung corners of the Empire. During WWII Marsaxlokk Bay was the base for the Fleet Air Arm, and in 1989 the famous summit meeting between Soviet and US presidents Mikhail Gorbachev and George Bush (senior) was held on board a warship anchored in Marsaxlokk Bay. Today the harbour is framed by the fuel tanks and chimney of a power station and the huge cranes of the Kalafrana Container Terminal – eyesores that will probably prevent any serious tourist development.

Sights & Activities

The daily **market** on the waterfront sells mainly tourist tat aimed at the tour groups, who regularly sally forth from their buses for a lunchtime shopping break. Far more interesting is the **Sunday Fish Market**, where you can admire the riches of the Med before they're whisked off to Malta's top hotels and restaurants (but rest assured, you'll still find the tourist tat here too). The market starts early in the morning and the best stuff is long gone by afternoon.

Delimara Point, southeast of Marsaxlokk, is blighted by a huge power station whose chimney can be seen for miles around, but there are a few good swimming places on the eastern side of the peninsula. **Peter's Pool** is the best, a natural lido in the rocks with large areas of flat slab for sunbathing between swims. Follow the narrow, potholed road out towards Delimara Lighthouse until you are just past the power station chimney (about 1.5km from the main road), and you'll see a low building on the left with 'Peter's Pool' signposted on it. A sump-crunchingly rough track leads down

---

MALTESE BOATS

The brightly coloured fishing boats that crowd the harbours around the coast have become one of Malta's national symbols. Painted boldly in blue, red and yellow, with the watchful 'Eyes of Osiris' on the bows to ward off evil spirits, they are unmistakably Maltese. The harbour at Marsaxlokk is famous for its colourful vista of moored fishing boats.

There are different kinds of traditional Maltese vessels. The *luzzu* (*loots*-zoo) is a large double-ended fishing boat (for nonsailors, that means it's pointed at both ends). The *kajjik* (*ka*-yik) is similar in appearance, but has a square transom (it's pointed at the front end only). The *dgħajsa* (*dye*-sa) is a smaller and racier-looking boat, with very high stem and stern-posts – a bit like a Maltese gondola. These are not solid, seaworthy fishing boats, but sleek water-taxis. A small flotilla of *dgħajsa* is now carrying tourists back and forth between Valletta and the Three Cities. They were powered by oars, but today's *dgħajsas* generally carry an outboard engine. Local enthusiasts maintain – and race – a small fleet of oar-driven vessels. The waterfront at Vittoriosa and Senglea is the best place to admire these classic boats.

ANY WAY THE WIND BLOWS

In Malti, the points of the compass are mostly named for the winds that blow from that direction. These are versions of the old Latin names used by Roman sailors.

north	*tramuntana*
northeast	*grigal*
east	*lvant*
southeast	*xlokk*
south	*nofs in-nhar*
southwest	*lbiċ*
west	*punent*
northwest	*majjistral*

Xlokk is the Maltese equivalent of the Italian sirocco, both of which derive from the Arabic word *sharg*, meaning 'east.' The *xlokk* is a hot, humid and oppressive wind that blows from the southeast, usually in spring, bringing misty conditions to the island. It derives its heat from the Sahara and picks up its humidity passing over the sea. The *tramuntana*, from the Italian for 'across the mountains', is the cold northerly wind from the direction of the Alps. The northeasterly *grigal* is the typical winter wind that batters the rocky coast of Malta, and makes for an uncomfortable ferry crossing to Gozo, while the northwesterly *majjistral* is the stiff sailing breeze of summer afternoons, the equivalent of the Turkish *meltem*.

to a parking area. Don't leave anything in your car – this is a favourite spot for thieves.

The road to Delimara passes **Tas Silġ**, where archaeologists have uncovered a Punic-Roman temple. This may be the famous Temple of Juno that was plundered by Verres, the Roman Governor of Sicily and Malta in 70 BC, as recorded in the writings of Cicero. Due to on-going excavations, the site is not open to the public.

South of Marsaxlokk, on the road to Birżebbuġa, is **Fort St Lucian**, built in 1610 to protect the bay. Today it houses a naval college and the offices of a government fish farm.

Sleeping

There's only one accommodation option in Marsaxlokk, and thankfully it's a ripper.

ourpick Duncan Guesthouse (☎ 2165 7212; http:// duncanmalta.com; 33 Xatt is-Sajjieda; d from Lm14; ⚒) Friendly, family-run Duncan's is hands-down the sweetest accommodation deal in southern Malta. It's above Duncan Bar & Restaurant on the waterfront, and the spacious guest rooms come in family-friendly configurations. They're well kitted out for lengthy stays, each with sitting area, TV, small balcony, spic-and-span modern bathroom and kitchenette. Air-con is an optional extra. There's a washing machine for guest use (a rare beast in Malta), plus plans for turning the empty roof area into

a sun terrace – the perfect vantage point for sundowner drinks and harbour-watching.

Eating

It's all about the seafood in Marsaxlokk. Restaurants line the harbour, most offering alfresco dining. There are some casual places geared to tourists, plus more upmarket selections. Marsaxlokk is a favourite location for the Maltese to enjoy a long Sunday lunch among family and friends – if you wish to join them in this weekly ritual, bookings for the following restaurants are advised.

Pisces (☎ 2165 4956; 86 Xatt is-Sajjieda; mains Lm3-6.50; ⚒ lunch & dinner Thu-Tue) Don't be too disheartened if you can't get in to Ir-Rizzu. Down the road, Pisces has an equally fine-looking menu with house specialities including warm octopus salad or mussels stewed in spicy tomato sauce. And there are meat and pasta dishes that cater to non-fish-lovers too.

Ir-Rizzu (☎ 2165 1569; 52 Xatt is-Sajjieda; mains Lm3-7; ⚒ lunch & dinner) Ir-Rizzu has a large and bustling dining room devoid of airs and graces. The fish do the talking here – check out the mind-boggling list of local piscatorial specimens, everything from *lampuki* (dolphin fish) and octopus to king prawns or a hearty bowl of *aljotta* (Maltese fish soup). Lots of locals trust Ir-Rizzu for its quality; the downside is no outdoor seating.

Ron's Restaurant (☎ 2165 0382; 54 Xatt is-Sajjieda; mains Lm2-6; lunch & dinner) Ron is a welcoming host offering outdoor tables for a casual drink or light snack, or a more formal upstairs dining area with funky blue walls, stylish décor, a great view over the boat-filled harbour and a no-surprises menu of reliable seafood favourites.

Getting There & Away

Bus 27 runs every half-hour from Valletta to Marsaxlokk from around 6.30am to 9pm (services are more frequent on Sunday morning for the fish market). Tickets cost Lm0.20 one way. Bus 627 runs hourly until 3pm from Buġibba via Sliema and St Julian's to Marsaxlokk (one way Lm0.50).

BIRŻEBBUĠA

pop 7650

Birżebbuġa (beer-zeb-*boo*-ja, meaning 'well of the olives') lies on the western shore of Marsaxlokk Bay. It began life as a fishing village, but today it's a dormitory town for workers from the nearby Malta Freeport. The misleadingly named **Pretty Bay** lies at the southern end of town. Although it has a very pleasant sandy beach, it also has a not-terribly-pretty view of the Kalafrana Container Terminal, only 500m away across the water.

There's little to see in town, but 500m north on the main road from Valletta is the **Għar Dalam Cave & Museum** (☎ 2165 7419; adult/child Lm1.50/0.50; 9am-5pm). Għar Dalam (aar-da-lam; the name means 'cave of darkness') is a 145m-long cave in the Lower Coralline Limestone (for more on this formation see p40). It has yielded a magnificent harvest of fossil bones and teeth belonging to dwarf elephants, hippopotamuses and deer – an estimated total of over 7000 animals – which lived between 180,000 and 18,000 years ago. The animals are all of European type, suggesting that Malta was once joined to Italy, but not to northern Africa.

The revamped museum at the entrance contains an exhibition hall with displays on how the cave was formed, and how the remains of such animals came to be found here, plus how these animals adapted to new conditions. In the older part of the museum are display cases mounted with thousands and thousands of bones and teeth. It's not hugely interesting unless you're a palaeontologist, but impressive in terms of sheer numbers. Beyond the museum a path leads down through gardens to the mouth of the cave, where a walkway leads 50m into the cavern. A pillar of sediment has been left in the middle of the excavated floor to show the stratigraphic sequence. For geology and prehistoric history buffs only.

On the cliff-bound coastline south of Birżebbuġa lies another cave, **Għar Ħasan Cave** (admission free; 24hrs). Follow the road towards Żurrieq, then turn left on a minor road that ends at an industrial estate (there are plenty of signposts). The cave entrance is down some steps in the cliff-face to the left; there is usually an enterprising local in the car parking area out the front with torches for hire for around Lm0.30 to help you find your way inside the cave. The 'Cave of Ħasan' is supposed to have been used as a hide-out by a 12th-century Saracen rebel. With a torch you can follow a passage off to the right to a 'window' in the cliff-face. Note that at the time of research access to the cave wasn't possible thanks to roadworks, but it should be accessible again by the time you read this.

To get to Għar Dalam and Birżebbuġa, take bus 11 from Valletta. The cave museum is on the right-hand side of the road at a small, semicircular parking area 500m short of Birżebbuġa – look out for it as it's not well signposted. There is no public transport to Għar Ħasan – it's a 2.5km walk south of Birżebbuġa.

MARSASKALA

pop 5420

Marsaskala, gathered around the head of its long, narrow bay, was originally a Sicilian fishing community (the name means 'Sicilian Harbour'; note that you will also see it spelt Marsascala). Today it is an increasingly popular residential area and seaside resort among the Maltese; save for a couple of reasonable restaurants, the town has little appeal for travellers. It rarely rates a mention in guidebooks to Malta and is well off the tourist trail compared with northern resorts (especially now that the town's major hotel has announced its impending closure). Marsaxlokk makes a considerably more interesting and picturesque southern base.

Sights & Activities

No-one could accuse Marsaskala of being over-endowed with sights or tourist attractions. The main activities are hanging out in cafés and bars along the waterfront, strolling along the promontory and fishing in the harbour.

The Triq ix-Xatt promenade is the focus of the town and where most of the restaurants and cafés can be found. On the north side of the bay, Triq iż-Żonqor goes past the Church of St Anne, with its distinctive Italianate campanile, to Żonqor Point, where a swimming pool and water polo stadium are located. Triq is-Salini, on the south side of the bay, leads to the headland of il-Gżira and St Thomas' Tower.

St Thomas' Tower, on the southern point of the bay, is a small fort that was built by the Knights of St John after a Turkish raiding party landed in Marsaskala Bay in 1614 and plundered the nearby village of Żejtun.

St Thomas Bay is a deeply indented – and deeply unattractive – bay to the south of Marsaskala, lined with concrete and breeze-block huts and a potholed road. There's a sandy beach of sorts, and the place is popular with local people and windsurfers. It's about a 10-minute walk from Marsaskala along Triq Tal-Gardiel (past the Sun City Cinema complex). From St Thomas Bay you can continue walking along the coast to Marsaxlokk (about 4km).

Sleeping

Accommodation options in Marsaskala are shrinking following the announcement in late 2006 that the huge, four-star Corinthia Jerma Palace Hotel (the largest hotel in Malta's southeast) will be demolished to make way for upmarket apartments. This leaves only a couple of uninspiring, if affordable, options if you're looking for a bed.

Summer Nights Guesthouse (☎ 2163 7956; m.cut ajar@ondnet.net; Triq ix-Xatt; d Lm10/12 low/high season) Basic, good-value rooms are on offer at this central guesthouse in the heart of the town's action (there's a restaurant and pub downstairs). Rooms have private bathroom, fan, TV and fridge (some have kitchenette), and all have a balcony with sea view.

Charian Hotel (☎ 2163 6392; www.charianhotel.com; Triq is-Salini; d incl breakfast Lm14/16 low/high season) A small, unremarkable, family-run hotel about 600m from the centre. Rooms here are small and a tad dingy but well equipped, with ceiling fan, TV and balcony (most with sea view), and there's a rooftop terrace with Jacuzzi.

Eating & Drinking

Marsaskala's redeeming feature is its restaurants. There are some good options here, popular with locals who are happy to travel across Malta to enjoy a well-prepared meal.

Jakarta (☎ 2163 3993; Triq Tal-Gardiel; dishes Lm3-6; ☽ dinner Wed-Mon) Despite its name, Jakarta offers mostly Malaysian and Chinese cuisine from an extensive menu of meat, poultry and seafood dishes (and decent selections for vegetarians). Rabbit in five-spice sauce (or served with pancakes, Peking-duck style) lend a local flavour – and we've never seen Thai wine on any European menus before! There are good-value set menus from Lm7 per person. Takeaway available.

Tal-Familja (☎ 2163 2161; Triq Tal-Gardiel; mains Lm3-7; ☽ lunch & dinner Tue-Sun) A particular local favourite is the friendly and relaxed Tal-Familja, away from the town centre (about 300m past the cinema). You'll need some time to choose from the huge menu and daily specials, at the heart of which are fresh fish, seafood and classic Maltese cuisine (kids are well looked after too). The excellent service and massive portions will have you heading home well sated.

Grabiel (☎ 2163 4194; Pjazza Mifsud Bonnici; mains Lm5.50-7.50; ☽ lunch & dinner Mon-Sat) Elegant Grabiel is popular with the expense-account brigade, no doubt because of the hefty prices it charges for its renowned fish and seafood dishes. Less cashed-up patrons can dine alfresco at the attached (downmarket) kiosk-style café, with less interesting food and more reasonable prices (eg omelettes, pasta or roast chicken priced from Lm0.50 to Lm4).

For fast food, try **Country Style** at the southern end of the promenade. The food is certainly nothing to write home about – it has a simple selection of soups, sandwiches, doughnuts and cakes, and pizza of an evening – but internet access is available, and there's a playground outside where you can keep an eye on the kids.

There are a number of options on the promenade for sitting with a beer and just watching the world go by. There are kebab and pasta places for a quick bite, and café-bars that liven up of an evening. **Summer Nights** (☎ 2163 7956; Triq ix-Xatt) has a bustling restaurant and English-style pub, plus a big screen for televising sports matches.

Getting There & Away

Buses 17, 19 and 20 run regularly from Valletta to Marsaskala (one way Lm0.20). The bus terminus is on Triq Sant'Antnin at the southern end of the waterfront promenade.

ŻURRIEQ

pop 9000

The village of Żurrieq sprawls across a hillside on the south coast, in a sort of no-man's-land to the south of the airport. This part of Malta feels cut off from the rest of the island, and although it's only 10km from Valletta as the crow flies, it seems much further. Signage from Żurrieq to neighbouring towns is poor, but this region is small and it shouldn't take long to find the direction you need (ask locals for guidance if you get stuck).

The **parish church of St Catherine** was built in the 1630s and houses a fine altarpiece of St Catherine – painted by Mattia Preti in 1675, when the artist took refuge here during a plague epidemic – and there are several 17th- and 18th-century windmills dotted about the village. On a minor road between Żurrieq and Mqabba is the **Chapel of the Annunciation** (☎ 2122 5952) in the deserted medieval settlement of Ħal Millieri. This tiny church, set in a pretty garden, dates from the mid-15th century and contains important 15th-century frescoes – the only surviving examples of medieval religious art in Malta. Both church and garden are normally locked, but are open to the public from 9.30am to noon on the first Sunday of each month. Telephone to confirm these times or to possibly arrange an alternative time for viewing; read more about the chapel on the website of **Din l-Art Ħelwa** (National Trust of Malta; www.dinlarthelwa.org).

About 2km west of Żurrieq lies the tiny harbour of **Wied iż-Żurrieq**, set in a narrow inlet in the cliffs and guarded by a watchtower. Here boats depart for enjoyable 30-minute cruises to the **Blue Grotto**, a huge natural arch in the sea cliffs 400m to the east.

The boat trips take in about seven caves, including the Honeymoon Cave, Reflection Cave and Cat's Cave. The best time is before midmorning, when the sun is shining into the grotto. **Boat trips** (☎ 2164 0058, 9945 5347; adult/child Lm3/1.50) on small boats (up to eight passengers) depart from 9am to around 5pm daily, weather permitting (trips are less likely to run from December to February). If there is any doubt about the weather or sea conditions, call to check.

You can see the Blue Grotto without a boat from a viewing platform beside the main road, just east of the turn-off to Wied iż-Żurrieq.

It's a souvenir-shop ghetto above the harbour in Wied iż-Żurrieq, alongside much-of-a-muchness restaurants serving up snacks, fish, rabbit, pasta etc.

Browse and see if anything takes your fancy. **Congreve Channel Restaurant** (☎ 2164 7928; snacks & mains Lm1.50-6; ☯ closed Wed) is a down-to-earth option with king prawns, shellfish and swordfish at the higher end of the price range, and simple pasta and burger meals at the lower end.

Buses 38 and 138 run from Valletta to Żurrieq and Wied iż-Żurrieq (on a circular route that also includes Ħaġar Qim and Mnajdra temples) every 30 minutes or so from 9.20am to 4.15pm. Tickets are Lm0.50 one way.

ĦAĠAR QIM TEMPLE

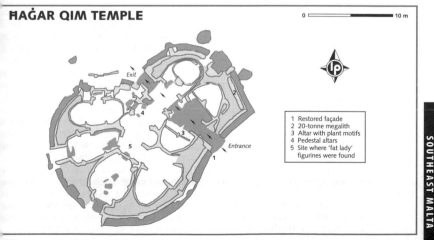

0 ——————— 10 m

Exit

Entrance

1 Restored façade
2 20-tonne megalith
3 Altar with plant motifs
4 Pedestal altars
5 Site where 'fat lady' figurines were found

MEGA-ATTRACTIONS

The megalithic temples of Malta, which date mainly from the period 3600 to 3000 BC, are the oldest freestanding stone structures in the world. They predate the pyramids of Egypt by more than 500 years.

The oldest surviving temples are thought to be those of Ta'Ħġrat (p116) and Skorba near the village of Mġarr on Malta. Ġgantija (p161) on Gozo, and Ħagar Qim and Mnajdra (see below) on Malta are among the best preserved. Tarxien (p81) is the most developed, its last phase dating from 3000 to 2500 BC. The subterranean tombs of the Hypogeum (p80) date from the same period as the temples and mimic many of their architectural features below ground.

The purpose of these mysterious structures is the subject of much debate. They all share certain features in common – a site on a southeasterly slope, near to caves, a spring and fertile farmland; a trefoil or cloverleaf plan with three or five rounded chambers (apses) opening off the central axis, which usually faces between south and east; megalithic construction, using blocks of stone weighing up to 20 tonnes; and holes and sockets drilled into the stones, perhaps to hold wooden doors or curtains made form animal hide. Most temple sites have also revealed spherical stones, about the size of cannonballs – it has been suggested that these were used like ball bearings to move the heavy megaliths more easily over the ground.

No burials have been found in any of the temples, but most have yielded statues and figurines of so-called 'fat ladies' – possibly fertility goddesses. Most have some form of decoration on the stone, ranging from simple pitting to the elaborate spirals and carved animals seen at Tarxien. There are also 'oracle holes' – small apertures in the chamber walls which may have been used by priests or priestesses to issue divinations. The temples' southeasterly orientation has suggested a relationship to the winter solstice sunrise, and one amateur investigator has put forward a convincing theory of solar alignment (see www.geocities.com/maltatemples/).

ĦAĠAR QIM & MNAJDRA

The megalithic temples of Ħaġar Qim (*adge-ar eem*; 'standing stones') and Mnajdra (mm-*nigh*-dra) are perhaps the best preserved and most evocative of Malta's prehistoric sites, especially at dawn or sunset when the ancient stones are tinged pink and gold. The temples are fenced off and the gates are locked at these times but it's worth the effort, especially around the winter solstice (21 December) at some of the supposed solar alignments.

It costs a steep Lm2 to visit just one temple, Lm3 to visit both. Once inside it's disappointing that there is limited information explaining the story of these temples and what makes them so remarkable. At the time of research, Heritage Malta was conducting free guided tours of the site daily at 11am and 3.30pm – recommended if you want to come away with some sort of understanding. A guided tour of the displays of the National Museum of Archaeology in Valletta (p62) is also highly recommended.

Happily, things are set to change in the near future. EU funding is being channelled into a project with two goals – the conservation of the temples, and a better interpretation of the site. The temples will each receive a temporary tentlike shelter to protect them from the elements (while searching for a permanent so- lution), and a new visitors centre will be buil here, offering a small café and bookshop, an all-important information panels detailing th cultural and natural significance of the area If all goes according to plan, the covering should be in place by late 2007 and the visitor centre completed sometime in 2008.

Ħaġar Qim (☎ 2142 4231; adult/child Lm2/0.50; 9am-5pm) is right next to the parking area. The **façade** with its trilithon entrance, has been restored rather too obviously, but gives an idea of wha it may once have looked like. The temple were originally roofed over, but the woode structures have long since rotted away.

Before going in, look round the corner t the right – the **megalith** here is the largest i the temple, weighing over 20 tonnes. The tem ple consists of a series of interconnected, ova chambers with no uniform arrangement, an differs from other Maltese temples in lackin a regular trefoil plan. In the first chamber o the left is a little altar post decorated with **plar motifs**, and in the second there are a couple c **pedestal altars**. The '**fat lady**' statuettes and th so-called *Venus de Malta* figurine that wer found here are on display in the Nationa Museum of Archaeology in Valletta (p62).

Mnajdra (☎ 2142 4231; adult/child Lm2/0.50; ☻ 9am-pm), a 500m walk downhill from Ħaġar Qim, is more interesting. There are three temples side by side, each with a trefoil plan and a different orientation. The oldest temple is the small one on the right, aligned towards the southwest and Filfla island. The central temple, pointing towards the southeast, is the youngest. All date from between 3600 and 3000 BC.

It has been claimed that the southern temple is full of significant solar alignments. At sunrise during the winter solstice, a beam of sunlight illuminates the altar to the right of the inner doorway. At sunrise during the summer solstice, a sunbeam penetrates the window in the back of the left-hand apse to the pedestal altar in the left rear chamber. In the right-hand apse there is a separate chamber entered through a small doorway, with a so-called 'oracle hole' to its left. The function of this is unknown.

On the cliff top to the southeast of Mnajdra is a 17th-century watchtower and a memorial to Sir Walter Congreve (Governor of Malta 1924–27) who was buried at sea off this point. You can hike east along the cliffs towards Wied iż-Żurrieq and the Blue Grotto (p141), or west to Għar Lapsi (p143). The tiny uninhabited island **Filfla**, 8km offshore, is clearly visible. It suffered the ignominy of being used for target practice by the British armed forces until it was declared a nature reserve in 1970. It supports important breeding colonies of seabirds, including an estimated 10,000 pairs of storm-petrels, and a unique species of lizard. Landing on the island is forbidden.

Ħaġar Qim Restaurant (☎ 2142 4116; mains Lm2 5; ☻ lunch daily year-round, dinner Tue-Sun summer, Fri-Sun winter), above the car park, serves the usual suspects (pizza, pasta, Maltese specialities). There's a large open-air terrace and an uninspiring view of the scruffy garden and the car park – you're better off at Blue Grotto or Għar Lapsi for more variety and better panoramas.

Buses 38 and 138 run from Valletta to Ħaġar Qim and Mnajdra (on a circular route that also includes Wied iż-Żurrieq) every 30 minutes or so from 9.20am to 4.15pm. Tickets cost Lm0.50 one way.

GĦAR LAPSI

On the road west of the temples is a turn-off (signposted) to Għar Lapsi. The name means 'Cave of the Ascension', and there was once a fishermen's shrine here. The road winds steeply to the coast and ends at a car park beside a couple of restaurants and boathouses. The main attraction here is the swimming – a little cove in the low limestone cliffs has been converted into a natural lido, with stone steps and iron ladders giving access to the limpid blue water. It's a popular spot for bathing and picnicking among locals, and also well frequented by divers and fishermen.

If swimming has given you an appetite, there are two contrasting restaurants above the cove. The 1950s-style **Lapsi View** (☎ 2164 0608; meals Lm0.50-6; ☻ lunch & dinner Tue-Sun) is housed in a crumbling blue building that looks a little worse for wear, but inside is a taste of retro-Malta, with much of the original furniture still in place. As you'd expect, old-fashioned home-cooking is the order of the day, and the menu caters to tourists and locals, with burgers, sandwiches and pizzas, plus rabbit, steak, *lampuki* (dolphin fish) and stewed octopus.

The primary-coloured interior of **Blue Creek** (☎ 2146 2786; snacks & meals Lm2-11.50; ☻ lunch & dinner Wed-Mon) has more polish but less local character, and the tables on the sunny outdoor terrace (directly above the water) are hotly contested. The menu has something for all-comers, from snacks and sandwiches to pasta and seafood, and some surprising main dishes of meats far from home (eg ostrich medallions, grilled kangaroo loin). Come for lunch rather than dinner, in order to enjoy the setting.

Getting to Għar Lapsi without a car is tricky. For hikers, there is a footpath along the 3km stretch of cliff top between Għar Lapsi, Ħaġar Qim and the Blue Grotto. For public transport users, the town of Siġġiewi is about 4km north of Għar Lapsi; and bus 94 shuttles infrequently between the two points on Thursday and Sunday from July to September only. The alternative is to hike each way from Siġġiewi. Bus 89 runs from Valletta to Siġġiewi (one way Lm0.20).

Gozo & Comino

For the holidaymaker, Gozo has an air of exclusivity about it, no doubt helped by the surfeit of upmarket hotels, luxuriously converted farmhouses and high-quality restaurants, and the lack of package-holiday crowds such as those found on bigger, brasher Malta to the south.

Gozo, called Għawdex (*aow*-desh) in Malti, provides soothing respite from the bustling, noisy resorts and manic drivers of Malta. Although it is more than one-third the size of its larger sister island, it has less than one-tenth of the population – only about 30,000 Gozitans live here (and they are Gozitans first, Maltese second). The land is more fertile, the scenery is greener, the pace of life is much slower and the locals seem friendlier.

The island offers all the attractions of Malta but in a more compact package: good walking, a superb coastal landscape and excellent scuba diving and snorkelling, plus history in the form of megalithic temples and medieval citadels. If you're looking for action-packed nightlife you'll be disappointed, but if you're interested in a chance to enjoy warm hospitality and see how the rest of Malta must have been before the advent of mass tourism, you're in luck. A day trip won't allow enough time to sample this tiny island's treasures, however. It's worth scheduling at least a few days here, or, indeed, making Gozo the primary focus of your trip.

And while you're in the neighbourhood, consider slipping across to Malta's third island, tiny Comino. You've seen the image of the stunning Blue Lagoon on enough postcards – it's time to check out the real thing. An afternoon here provides ample time for top-class swimming and snorkelling.

HIGHLIGHTS

- Exploring Victoria's historic charm in both **Il-Kastell** (p146) and the laneways of **Il-Borgo** (p148)

- Getting red sand in your shorts at lovely **Ramla Bay** (p163)

- Taking in the impressive 360-degree views from tiny **Comino** (p164), then going for a dip in crystal-clear waters

- Renting a **converted farmhouse** (p150) in a sleepy Gozitan village and spending a blissful week unwinding

- Learning to **dive** (p44) with the experts in Xlendi or Marsalforn

- Enjoying a fine meal at one of Gozo's top restaurants, including **Restaurant Ta'Frenċ** (p160) outside Marsalforn; **It-Tmun Victoria** (p150) in the capital; or **Tatita's** (p157) in San Lawrenz

★ Marsalforn
★ Ramla Bay
★ San Lawrenz
★ Victoria
★ Xlendi
Comino ★

GOZO & COMINO

GOZO

VICTORIA (RABAT)
pop 6640

Victoria, the chief town of Gozo, sits in the centre of the island, 6km from the ferry terminal at Mġarr and 3.5km from the resort town of Marsalforn. Victoria's main attraction is the compact and photogenic citadel Il-Kastell.

Victoria is Gozo's main hub of shops and services. It was named for the Diamond Jubilee of Queen Victoria in 1897. Originally known as Rabat, it is still called that by many of the islanders (and by several road signs).

Orientation

Victoria is on a hill crowned by the ramparts of Il-Kastell ('the Citadel', or its Italian names of Gran Castello/the Cittadella). Telgħa Tal-Belt (Castle Hill) runs downhill from Il-Kastell to Pjazza Indipendenza (aka It-Tokk). Triq ir-Repubblika, Victoria's main street, runs east downhill from Pjazza Indipendenza. The bus station and main car park are on Triq Putirjal, running south off Triq ir-Repubblika.

Victoria's narrow streets are a labyrinthine one-way system – it may take several circuits of the town and unintentional trips to Kerċem before you find your way around.

Information
BOOKSHOPS
Bookworm (Map p146; ☎ 2155 6215; 105 Triq ir-Repubblika) Well-stocked shop with a good range of books, plus local and British newspapers.

EMERGENCY
Police station (Map p146; ☎ 2156 2040; Triq ir-Repubblika)

INTERNET ACCESS
Arkadia Shopping Centre (Map p146; Triq Fortunato Mizzi; per hr Lm1.20; ☻ Mon-Sat) There is a row of computers inside the complex, in front of the Body Shop. Machines can be used when the complex is open, but vouchers to use them can only be purchased from the lotto booth here, which is open 9am to 1pm and 4pm to 7pm Monday to Saturday.
Aurora Opera House (Map p146; ☎ 2156 2974; Triq ir-Repubblika; per 75min Lm1; ☻ 7am-1am) There are a few computers in the foyer of the opera house; to use them, buy your coupon from the bar here.

GOZO & COMINO

PRACTICALITIES

In this chapter, Gozo's main town, Victoria, is described first, followed by Mġarr, the main harbour. The rest of the island is covered in a roughly clockwise direction from Mġarr.

There are some very good websites to help with planning a visit to Gozo – try www.gozo.com, www.islandofgozo.org, www.discoveringgozo.com or www.gozo.gov.mt. See p17 for ideas on how to amuse yourself for a week on the island.

MEDICAL SERVICES

General Hospital (Map p146; ☎ 2156 1600; Triq I-Arċisqof Pietru Pace) Also known as Craig Hospital.

MONEY

Bank of Valletta (Map p146; 102 Triq ir-Repubblika) Has ATM.

Travelex (Map p147; cnr Triq ir-Repubblika & Telgħa Tal-Belt; ☿ 9am-5pm Mon-Fri, 9am-3.30pm Sat) Cashes travellers cheques and changes money.

POST

Post Office (Map p147; Triq ir-Repubblika; ☿ 8.15am-4.30pm Mon-Fri, 8.15am-12.30pm Sat)

TOURIST INFORMATION

Tourist Information Office (Map p146; ☎ 2156 1419; Tigrija Palazz, cnr Triq ir-Reppublika & Triq Putirjal; ☿ 9am-5pm Mon-Sat, 9am-12.30pm Sun & public holidays) On the ground floor of a shopping arcade, not far from the bus station. Often closed between 12.30pm and 1pm for lunch.

Sights
IL-KASTELL

All items mentioned here feature on the map on p147.

The **Cathedral of the Assumption** (Misraħ il-Katidral; adult/child Lm1.25/free; ☿ 9am-5pm Mon-Sat) was built between 1697 and 1711 to replace a church that had been destroyed by earthquake in 1693. The earthquake had struck in southern Italy yet caused damage as far away as Malta. The cathedral was designed by Lorenzo Gafa, who was also responsible for St Paul's Cathedral at Mdina (p124). The elegant façade is adorned with the escutcheons of Grand

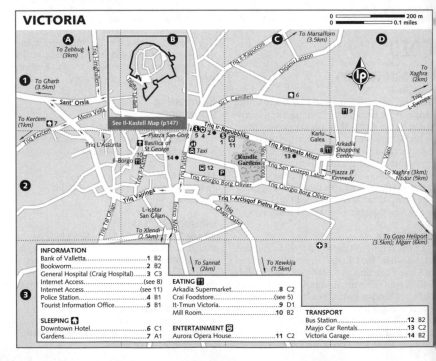

VICTORIA

```
0        200 m
0        0.1 miles
```

To Żebbuġ (3km)
To Marsalforn (3.5km)
To Gharb (3.5km)
To Xagħra (2km)
Sant' Orsla
To Kerċem (1km)
See Il-Kastell Map (p147)
To Żebbuġ
Triq L-Imgħallem
Triq It-Tafal
Triq Il-Kapuċċini
Djamu Lanzon
Sqaq L-Europa
Sqaq L-Camilleri
Mons Vella
Piazza San Ġorġ
Triq ir-Repubblika
Karlu Galea
Arkadia Shopping Centre
Triq L'Assunta
Basilica of St George
Taxi
Triq Fortunato Mizzi
To Xagħra (3km); Nadur (5km)
Il-Borgo
Triq Putirjal
Rundle Gardens
Triq San Ġużepp Labre
Piazza JF Kennedy
Triq Ġorġio Borg Olivier
Triq Ġiorgio Borg Olivier
Triq Vajringa
Triq Tal-Chain
L-Isptar San Ġiljan
Enrico Mizzi
Triq Chain Qaiet
Triq I-Arċisqof Pietru Pace
To Gozo Heliport (3.5km); Mġarr (6km)
To Xlendi (2.5km)
To Sannat (2km)
To Xewkija (1.5km)
```

**INFORMATION**
Bank of Valletta.................................**1** B2
Bookworm...........................................**2** B2
General Hospital (Craig Hospital)......**3** C3
Internet Access..............................(see 8)
Internet Access............................(see 11)
Police Station.....................................**4** B1
Tourist Information Office.................**5** B1

**SLEEPING**
Downtown Hotel................................**6** C1
Gardens.............................................**7** A1

**EATING**
Arkadia Supermarket.........................**8** C2
Crai Foodstore...............................(see 5)
It-Tmun Victoria................................**9** D1
Mill Room.........................................**10** B2

**ENTERTAINMENT**
Aurora Opera House........................**11** C2

**TRANSPORT**
Bus Station.......................................**12** B2
Mayjo Car Rentals............................**13** C2
Victoria Garage................................**14** B2
```

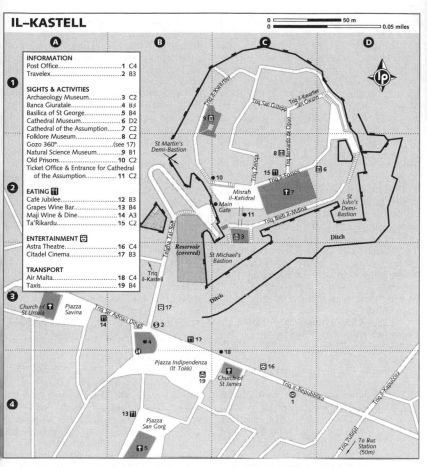

IL–KASTELL

0 — 50 m
0 — 0.05 miles

INFORMATION
Post Office.....................................1 C4
Travelex...2 B3

SIGHTS & ACTIVITIES
Archaeology Museum......................3 C2
Banca Giuratale.............................4 B3
Basilica of St George.......................5 B4
Cathedral Museum..........................6 D2
Cathedral of the Assumption.............7 C2
Folklore Museum............................8 C2
Gozo 360º.............................(see 17)
Natural Science Museum..................9 B1
Old Prisons..................................10 C2
Ticket Office & Entrance for Cathedral
  of the Assumption.....................11 C2

EATING
Café Jubilee.................................12 B3
Grapes Wine Bar...........................13 B4
Maji Wine & Dine..........................14 A3
Ta'Rikardu...................................15 C2

ENTERTAINMENT
Astra Theatre................................16 C4
Citadel Cinema.............................17 B3

TRANSPORT
Air Malta....................................18 C4
Taxis...19 B4

Master Ramon de Perellos and Bishop Palmieri. Due to lack of money the dome was never completed, but the impression of one was maintained inside by way of a clever trompe l'oeil painting. The admission price includes a self-guided audio tour (but note that you need to pay a Lm10 refundable deposit, or leave ID such as a licence, to be given the audio piece). The ticket office is in the passageway connecting Misrah il-Katidral with Triq Bieb il-Mdina.

The **Cathedral Museum** (☎ 2155 6087; Triq il-Fossos; admission included in cathedral ticket price; ♥ 9am–5pm Mon-Sat) is just northeast of the cathedral. The downstairs vault contains church gold and silver, while the upstairs gallery is devoted to religious art and includes quite a disturbing

19th-century painting depicting the martyrdom of St Agatha (see boxed text, p126, for more on her grisly end). The ground floor houses various items including a 19th-century bishop's carriage and an altar with a wax model of the Last Supper.

There are four other small museums within the Citadel. They display reasonable collections, but if you're pushed for time, don't feel as though you've missed out – the museums in Valletta are better. If you do plan to visit more than one of the four, it's worth buying a Citadel Day Ticket (Lm2), which gives entry to all four sites and is available at each of them.

The **Archaeology Museum** (☎ 2155 6144; Triq Bieb il-Mdina; adult/child Lm1/0.25; ♥ 9am-5pm) contains finds from the island's prehistoric temples at Ġgantija (p161), though the model of the temple is more interesting than the array of pottery shards. Finds from the Punic and Roman periods are displayed upstairs, including inscriptions, terracotta cremation urns, lots of amphorae and anchors, and some fascinating jewellery and amulets in the form of the Eye of Osiris – an ancient link to the symbols found on Maltese fishing boats of today. The museum has received funds for upgrading, and by the time you read this it should be displaying a number of other artefacts from Ġgantija temples and related Xagħra excavations.

The **Folklore Museum** (☎ 2156 2034; Triq Bernardo de Opuo; adult/child Lm1/0.25; ☽ 9am-5pm) is in a lovely old building that dates from around 1500, and shows Sicilian and Catalan influences; note the beautiful arched windows overlooking Triq Bernardo de Opuo. The museum is a maze of stairs, rooms and courtyards, and the building itself is more interesting than the large collection of domestic, trade and farming implements that give an insight into rural life on Gozo.

The **Natural Science Museum** (☎ 2155 6153; Triq il-Kwartier; adult/child Lm1/0.25; ☽ 9am-5pm), in another gracious old building, has low-key exhibits explaining the geology of the island and its water supply. On display upstairs is a rather sad collection of stuffed birds.

The **Old Prisons** (☎ 2156 5988; Misraħ il-Katidral; adult/child Lm1/0.25; ☽ 9am-5pm) served as a jail from the late 1500s to 1904. The cells here once held Jean Parisot de la Valette (see boxed text, p57) for the crime of 'aggressive behaviour' for a few months before he became Grand Master. The most interesting part of a visit to the prison is the extensive historic graffiti etched into the walls by the inmates, including crosses, ships, hands and the cross of the Knights.

TOWN
Pjazza Indipendenza, the main square of Victoria, hosts a daily market (from around 6.30am to 2pm) known throughout the island as **It-Tokk** (the meeting place). The semicircular baroque building at the western end of the square is the **Banca Giuratale** (Map p147), built in 1733 to house the city council; today it contains government offices.

A narrow lane behind the Banca Giuratale leads to Pjazza San Ġorġ and the **Basilica of St George** (Map p147), the original parish church

of Rabat dating from 1678. The lavish interior contains a fine altarpiece of *St George and the Dragon* by Mattia Preti. The old town, known as **Il-Borgo**, is a maze of narrow, meandering alleys around Pjazza San Ġorġ and is a lovely place to wander.

Rundle Gardens (Map p146; ☽ 6am-8pm summer, 7am-6pm winter), south of Triq ir-Repubblika, were laid out by General Sir Leslie Rundle (Governor of Malta from 1909 to 1915) in around 1914.

AUDIOVISUAL SHOWS & EXHIBITIONS
Although they've taken off in Valletta and Mdina on Malta, audiovisual shows and exhibitions have yet to hit Gozo to the same extent. Perhaps it's just a matter of time before there are dungeons and assorted gory tableaux around every corner inside the Citadel.

For now, you can take in **Gozo 360°** (Map p147; ☎ 2155 9955; entrance on Telgħa Tal-Belt; adult/child Lm1.75/0.85; ☽ every half-hr 10.30am-3.30pm Mon-Sat, 10.30am-1pm Sun & public holidays), shown at the Citadel Cinema. It's a 30-minute audiovisual show on the history of Gozo, along the lines of the Malta Experience in Valletta (p65). Commentary is available in eight languages.

Walking Tour
From Pjazza Indipendenza, cross the main street and climb up Telgħa Tal-Belt to the Citadel's main gate. There are two gates into Il-Kastell – enter through the **Old Main Gate (1)** on the right (the larger new gate was opened in 1957), noting the Roman inscription on the left-hand inner wall from the 2nd century AD.

On your right after you enter is the **Archaeology Museum (2**; p147). Pass the museum and go up the stairs on the right into **St Michael's Bastion (3)**, and continue along the top of the city wall to **St John's Demi-Bastion (4)**. There is a good panorama from here. Look for the huge dome of the Rotunda at Xewkija, with Comino and Malta in the background; the distant Gothic spire of the church above Mġarr harbour; the watchtower of Nadur, and the dome and twin clock-towers of its parish church; and the view of Xagħra on its hilltop to the east, capped by Ta'Kola Windmill and the Church of Our Lady of Victory. Off to the left you can see the white apartment blocks around Marsalforn Bay. The **Gozo Craft Centre (5**; ☽ 8am-around 4.30pm Mon-Sat) is in the old prison building behind the bastion; stop in to admire the lace and other local handiwork.

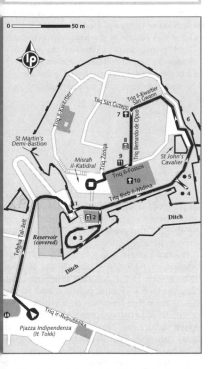

Climb the stairs below St John's Cavalier to reach the upper battlements, with more good views to the north and west. The **fortifications (6)** were built at the beginning of the 17th century to guard against further Turkish attacks following the Great Siege of 1565. Until 1637, when the Turkish threat receded, all Gozitans were bound by law to spend each night within the city walls. After that date people drifted back to the countryside, and many of the abandoned houses were ruined in the huge earthquake of 1693 (which rocked southern Italy and did considerable damage in Malta). Their tumbled remains can still be seen.

Walk down Triq il-Kwartier San Ġwann. Beyond the archway, at the little **Chapel of St Joseph (7)**, turn left down Triq Bernardo de Opuo, past a beautifully restored medieval building that houses the **Folklore Museum (8**; opposite), and then right on Triq il-Fossos. Stop in at **Ta'Rikardu (9**; below) to sample some fine local produce, then continue along Triq il-Fossos to arrive in the little square in front of the cathedral. In the passageway south of the square is the entry to the early-18th-century **Cathedral of the Assumption (10**; p146), worth a look for the painted ceiling. From here, make your way back to Victoria to continue your explorations of the town, and be sure to take time to wander the peaceful alleys of Il-Borgo.

Festivals & Events
See p172 for details of some of the country's foremost festivals, some with events held on Gozo. **Mediterranea** (www.mediterranea.com.mt) is a Gozo-specific festival of culture held every November.

Sleeping
Gardens (Map p146; ☎ 2155 7737, 2155 3723; www.casal goholidays.com; Triq Kerċem; B&B per person with shared bathroom Lm6) Found west of the main square, this building has a small, difficult-to-spot sign at the front. The warm, hospitable owners rent out simple, comfortable rooms for affordable prices, over three floors (connected by lift). Facilities include guest kitchens and garden terraces. It's a very good budget option in a good location. The owners also have self-catering apartments and farmhouses for rent, scattered around Gozo; see the website for more information.

Downtown Hotel (Map p146; ☎ 2210 8000; www .downtown.com.mt; Triq L-Ewropa; B&B per person Lm7-16; ▢ ▣ ▩) Victoria's only hotel opened in mid-2005 and offers bright, fuss-free rooms with good amenities (cable TV, hairdryer, minibar). Prices are slightly higher on the weekends, giving an indication of the main clientele – visitors over from Malta. There's a family-friendly feel, with a rooftop pool (with magic views), kids' club, a nightclub that rocks from October to May and a restaurant and café.

Eating & Drinking
IL-KASTELL
Ta'Rikardu (Map p147; ☎ 2155 5953; 4 Triq il-Fossos; platter for 2 Lm3.60; ☿ 10am-6pm) An institution in Victoria, Rikardu's sells souvenirs and paintings as well as local produce such as honey, cheese

---

GOZITAN FARMHOUSES

One of the best accommodation options for a stay on Gozo, especially if you're looking for a little local colour and rustic charm, is to rent a farmhouse. Dozens of these old, square-set farm buildings have been converted into accommodation, and many retain the beautiful stone arches, wooden beams and flagstone floors of their original construction (some are up to 400 years old). Most rental properties now have all the facilities you'll need for an easy holiday, including full kitchen, swimming pool, outdoor terrace and barbecue, laundry and cable TV. They can sleep anywhere from two to 16 people, so are perfect for families or groups of friends, and the costs are very reasonable – from around Lm350 per week for two people in the high season (most high-season rentals are weekly), or from Lm30 per night for two people in the low season. The farmhouses are usually inland in pretty, slow-paced villages like Xagħra and Għarb. Almost anyone with a guesthouse or hotel on the island can arrange a farmhouse for visitors; check the following websites for details of properties for rent (note that many agencies offer cheaper apartments and villas on Gozo, as well as vintage farmhouses):

www.farmhousegozo.com
www.gozo.com/gozodirectory/farmhouses.php
www.gozofarmhouses.com
www.gozorentals.com
www.gozogreatescapes.com

---

and wine. Take a seat and order a cheap, delicious platter, which includes cheese, bread, locally grown fresh tomatoes, sundried tomatoes, capers and olives. Vegie soup or homemade ravioli is also available; wash it all down with a glass or two of Gozitan wine.

TOWN

Café Jubilee (Map p147; ☎ 2155 8921; Pjazza Indipendenza; snacks & meals Lm0.40-2.25; ☿ 8am-1am) This lovely old-fashioned bar (the sister establishment of Café Jubilee in Valletta, p69) has a classy interior featuring a marble counter, brass rails, lots of dark wood and waiters in black waistcoats. It serves an affordable all-day menu of snacks and light meals, which you can also enjoy at the outdoor tables on the main square. Of an evening it becomes a popular wine bar and serves good local drops.

Mill Room (Map p146; ☎ 2155 5323; 94 Triq Il-Karita; snacks & meals Lm0.50-3.20; ☿ 9am-6pm Mon-Sat) Take the narrow street to the left of the Basilica of St George (facing the church) to find this intriguing café, with a fab snacky menu of sandwiches and salads served in all sorts of wonderful indoor-outdoor, upstairs-downstairs rooms and terraces. In the past it's also been a wine bar – it's worth heading here to see if it has extended its hours again (note that the sign above the gate reads Tickety-boo).

Grapes Wine Bar (Map p147; ☎ 7947 3503; Pjazza San Ġorġ; snacks & meals Lm1-3; ☿ lunch & dinner) One of a new breed of wine bars springing up all over

Malta. For a memorable Gozitan experience, sit at the old sewing machine tables with views of the basilica, choose a good local (or foreign) wine, and graze on a platter of regional cheese/sausage/seafood.

It-Tmun Victoria (Map p146; ☎ 2156 6667; Triq L-Ewropa; mains Lm3.50-6.50; ☿ dinner Fri-Wed, lunch Sun) Take a turn at the Arkadia shopping complex to reach It-Tmun, polished and professional from the linen-covered tables to the extensive wine list and menu of fusion dishes. Asian influences, New Zealand beef, fresh local fish and creative pasta options come together wonderfully in an elegant blue and white dining room. There's a lounge and bar available for nightcaps and chilling out, too. This place has won a number of local awards; it's worth booking ahead.

Maji Wine & Dine (Map p147; ☎ 2155 0878; 6 Triq Sir Adrian Dingli; mains Lm4-7; ☿ lunch & dinner Thu-Tue) Foodies on Gozo are rejoicing at the opening of another top-quality restaurant in Victoria. Maji smoothly combines bar, lounge and restaurant with stylish contemporary décor and an impressively modern menu (wild mushroom risotto, coconut-crusted halibut, macadamia nut meringue). There's great local art on display (and for sale). Bookings advised.

SELF-CATERING

There are fruit and vegetable vendors around It-Tokk and at the car park beside the bus station. The well-stocked **Arkadia supermarket**

(Map p146; Triq Fortunato Mizzi; 8am-7pm Mon-Sat) is on the basement level of the Arkadia shopping centre; closer to the bus station there's **Crai Foodstore** (Map p146; Tigrija Palazz, cnr Triq ir-Reppublika & Triq Putirjal; 7am-1pm & 4.30-7pm Mon-Sat).

Entertainment
Despite its diminutive size, Victoria has two theatres to Valletta's one. The **Aurora Opera House** (Map p146; 2156 2974) is the home of the Leone Philharmonic Society, and the **Astra Theatre** (Map p147; 2155 6256) is home to La Stella Philharmonic Society. Both are on Triq ir-Repubblika and stage opera, ballet, comedy, drama, cabaret, pantomime and celebrity concerts. Check the local press for details of performances.

Victoria also has the two-screen **Citadel Cinema** (Map p147; 2155 9955; www.citadelcinema.com; Telgħa Tal-Belt; ticket per adult/child Lm1.85/1.35), which shows mainstream films. Check the website or local newspapers to see what's showing.

Getting There & Away
A regular helicopter service operates between Malta International Airport and Gozo. For details see p185. The main ferry service between Malta and Gozo has frequent crossings during the day and also operates throughout the night during summer (see p189 for more information).

Air Malta (Map p147; 2299 9624; 13 Pjazza Indipendenza; 8.30am-5pm Mon-Fri) has a central office in Victoria.

Getting Around
TO/FROM THE HELIPORT
Gozo's heliport is just south of St Cecilia's Tower, about 3.5km southeast of Victoria and signposted off the main road to Mġarr. Most hotels will offer to pick you up from the heliport, and rental agencies can organise transfers; otherwise, you could phone and arrange for a taxi to meet your flight. Alternatively, you can walk 200m up to the main road and catch bus 25 into Victoria (Lm0.20).

BUS
Victoria's **bus station** (Map p146; Triq Putirjal) is just south of Triq ir-Repubblika, about 200m from Il-Kastell. All the bus routes are circular, starting and finishing at Victoria. Except for bus 25, which shuttles regularly between Victoria and Mġarr and connects with the ferries to Malta, the buses are slow and run

according to the needs of the local schools and shoppers – so the schedule is not often convenient for sightseeing. There's a flat fare of Lm0.20, except for summer tourist routes to Dwejra and Ramla Bay (Lm0.35). Schedule inquiries can be made on 2156 2040.

CAR & BICYCLE
If you want to see as much of the island as possible, then it makes sense to rent a car. It's also quite cheap – even cheaper than on Malta. You'll also find that the quieter roads and shorter distances make cycling a more attractive option on Gozo than on Malta.

Victoria Garage (Map p146; 2155 6414, 2155 3741; Triq Putirjal), opposite the bus station, rents out bicycles (Lm2 per day, or Lm1.50 per day for longer rentals) and cars (daily rate of around Lm10, or Lm8 for longer periods).

Mayjo Car Rentals (Map p146; 2155 6678; www.mayjo.com.mt; Triq Fortunato Mizzi) has a large range of vehicles and good rates (from Lm6/8 per day in the low/high season for the smallest vehicle – for rentals of a week or longer). Prices vary with length of rental, size of car and time of year.

TAXI
Taxis hang around at the bus station and at Pjazza Indipendenza (Map p147). Approximate taxi fares from Victoria: to Marsalforn Lm4; to Mġarr Lm5.50; to Xagħra Lm3.50; and to Xlendi Lm3. To book a taxi, try phoning **Belmont Garage** (2155 6962) or **Mario's Taxis** (2155 7242).

WALKING
Gozo is so small that you could walk from Mġarr to Marsalforn in two hours. Away from the relatively busy road between Mġarr and Victoria the roads are pretty quiet and there are lots of attractive hikes around the coast.

MĠARR
Mġarr is Gozo's main harbour and the point of arrival for ferries from Malta. When we visited, the waterfront was a mess – a new ferry terminal was under construction. The tourist information office and bank that once welcomed visitors had closed; hopefully they will return in a new home when the new terminal opens.

The 20th-century neogothic **Church of Our Lady of Lourdes** (Triq Lourdes) appears almost to hang over the village. Begun in 1924, lack of funds meant that its construction was

GOZO & COMINO

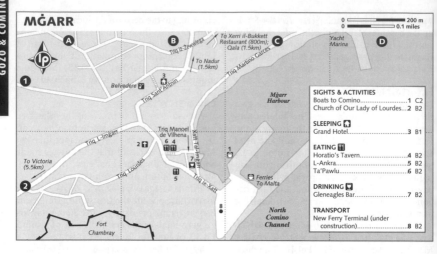

not finally completed until the 1970s. The hilltop above it is capped by the ramparts of **Fort Chambray**, built by the Knights of St John in the early 18th century. It was originally intended to supplant Victoria's Citadel as Gozo's main fortified town, and the area within the walls was laid out with a grid of streets similar to that of Valletta. But with the decline of the order in the late 18th century the plan came to naught. Instead, the fort served as a garrison and later as a mental hospital; it's rumoured that the on-again off-again developments to turn the fort into a hotel and residential complex are back on, but it's hard to keep up…

Activities

A right turn at the top of the harbour hill leads to a **belvedere** with a grand view over the harbour to Comino and northern Malta. Triq iż-Żewwiega leads to an even better **viewpoint** just south of Qala (it's worth the effort to get here – it's 1.8km uphill from the harbour to the viewpoint, and once here you can enjoy the magnificent panorama from Xerri Il-Bukkett restaurant (opposite).

Xlendi Pleasure Cruises (☎ 2155 9967; www.xlendi cruises.com) offers half- and full-day boat trips around Gozo and/or Comino from April to October. A full-day trip taking in Gozo and Comino costs Lm13.50/7.50 per adult/child and includes swimming stops and free use of snorkelling equipment. A half-day trip around Gozo is Lm10/5 per adult/child; around Comino and the Blue Lagoon is

Lm8.50/4.75. And you're not too far away to take in some of the highlights of the big sister down south – a full day visiting Valletta and Grand Harbour costs Lm16.50/8. On all trips an optional buffet lunch costs an extra Lm3.20/2. Trips depart from Mġarr harbour, but there's free transport for participants from Xlendi and Marsalforn to the departure point (and transfers can be arranged from other points of the island). You can book trips through most travel agents in the resort towns on Gozo.

Ticket-sellers selling tickets to Comino sit by the kerb of the main road through town – the going rate is Lm3 return, and boats generally leave Mġarr hourly from around 10am to 4pm. **Anselma** (☎ 9945 9389) is one such ferry service; it's worth telephoning ahead to check if and when the boats are operating.

Sleeping

Grand Hotel (☎ 2156 3840; www.grandhotelmalta.com; Triq Sant'Antnin; B&B per person Lm8.50-17.50 low season, Lm12-23 high season; ⊠ � □) With the recent closure of L-Imġarr Hotel, there's only one accommodation option left in Mġarr. The four-star Grand Hotel has a fine position overlooking the harbour, with bright, airy rooms and extensive facilities including a sauna, gym, games room, restaurant and cocktail bar. Its least expensive rooms have no view; from these it's a small step up to a 'country view' room; sea-view rooms are naturally at the top of the scale, and are a very worthy investment.

Eating & Drinking

Xerri il-Bukkett (☎ 2155 3500; Triq iż-Żewwiega; snacks & meals Lm1-5.50) Who cares about the menu when the view is this good? Xerri il-Bukkett is just south of Qala, about 1.8km uphill from Mġarr harbour, and has a terrace with a stupendous view across the channel to Comino and northern Malta. There's a pub area for a casual drink and snack, and a restaurant serving traditional dishes such as fried rabbit, swordfish, *braġioli* (thin, rolled slices of beef stuffed and then braised in a red-wine sauce) and so on. And it's great to see that this place appeals as much to locals as to view-impressed tourists – at the front of the restaurant is an area where local men gather to play bocce.

L-Ankra (☎ 2155 5656; Triq ix-Xatt; mains Lm1.50-6; ⏱ lunch & dinner) Up the hill from the ferry terminal and opposite Gleneagles Bar, L-Ankra has a brightly coloured dining room and a menu full of the usual suspects (pasta, fresh fish, fried rabbit, king prawns) – which it executes very well. Of an evening there are also pizza selections, including the Gozitan, a great introduction to the local produce – it's groaning under the weight of anchovies, capers, black olives, potatoes, onion, basil, tuna and fresh tomato.

Horatio's Tavern (☎ 2156 6669; 9 Triq Manoel de Vilhena; platters for 2 Lm3-4; ⏱ noon-late) Triq Manoel de Vilhena is lined with restaurants. Horatio's, at the top of the hill, is a cosy, casual midrange option. It's a nautically themed tavern with outdoor seating and a menu of sandwiches, salads and platters. Try a platter of local treats (including Gozitan cheeses and sausage), fish (marinated swordfish and salted tuna), Italian hams and salamis, or imported cheeses.

Ta'Pawlu (☎ 2155 8355; 4 Triq Manoel de Vilhena; mains Lm5-7; ⏱ dinner Wed-Mon) Next door to Horatio's, this restaurant raises the bar with a more elegant dining room and more-upmarket selections. Mains might include sautéed calamari or king prawns; duck breast with honey and orange sauce; or veal with cognac sauce. Leave room for the crème caramel, homemade ice cream or 'surprise' crepes for dessert.

Gleneagles Bar (Triq ix-Xatt) This is the place to head for a cold beer at the end of the day. It commands a view over the harbour, and is the social hub of the village, filling up in the early evening with a lively mix of locals, fishermen, yachties and tourists looking for some Maltese colour.

Getting There & Around

Gozo Channel (☎ 2155 6016; www.gozochannel .com) operates the car ferry that shuttles between Malta's Ċirkewwa and Gozo's Mġarr every 45 to 60 minutes from 6am to around 8pm (and roughly every two hours throughout the night). Return tickets are purchased in Ċirkewwa, so there's no need to buy a ticket in Mġarr.

Bus 25 meets ferry arrivals and runs from the harbour to Victoria (Lm0.20). Taxi drivers tout for business among the crowds disembarking from the ferry; a taxi to Victoria will cost around Lm5.50, to Xagħra it's Lm5, to Xlendi it's Lm7 and to Marsalforn expect Lm7.50.

GĦAJNSIELEM
pop 2480

Mġarr merges uphill into the town of Għajnsielem (ayn-*see*-lem, meaning 'spring of peace'). The huge, modern **Church of Our Lady of Loreto**, built in neogothic style, looms over the village square.

On the western edge of the village, on the main road from Mġarr to Victoria, is **Gozo Heritage** (☎ 2156 1280; Triq l-Imġ ⏱ 9am-4.30pm Mon-Sat), which advertises itself as a 'walk through 7000 years of living history'. It's a pretty lame series of historical tableaux – the legend of Calypso, Ġgantija temples, the Romans, the Great Siege, WWII – accompanied by special light and sound effects (*why are there so many of these attractions in Malta?*).

Another 100m along the road to Victoria is **St Cecilia's Tower**. The level area around the tower served as a temporary airfield in 1943 during the invasion of Sicily. A left turn at the tower leads to Gozo heliport (see p185 for details on the Malta–Gozo helicopter service).

MĠARR IX-XINI

The narrow, cliff-bound inlet of Mġarr ix-Xini (Port of the Galleys) was once used by the Knights of St John as their main harbour on Gozo – one of their watchtowers still guards the entrance. It was also used by Turkish admiral Dragut Reis, who raided Gozo in 1551 and took most of the island's population into slavery.

There's a tiny shingle beach at the head of the inlet, and a paved area where tourists and locals stake out their sunbathing territories. The swimming and snorkelling along the rocks is very good, and the little cove near the western headland of the bay is a private lido that belongs to Hotel Ta'Ċenċ

The road from Sannat and Xewkija down to Mġarr ix-Xini is quite steep and narrow, and wouldn't be much fun on a day with lots of beach traffic. You can walk here from Victoria in just over an hour.

XEWKIJA

pop 3280

The village of Xewkija – and most of southern Gozo – is dominated by the vast dome of the Parish Church of St John the Baptist, better known as the **Rotunda** (🕙 5am-noon & 3-8pm). Work on the new church began in 1951 and was finally completed in 1971; it was built mainly with the volunteer labour of the parishioners, and paid for by local donations. Its vast size – the 75m dome is higher than St Paul's Cathedral in London, and the nave can seat 4000 people – is said to be due to rivalry with Mosta on Malta, whose rotunda was also funded by the local people.

The rotunda was built around the old 17th-century church, which was too small for the community's needs – the new one can seat around three times the village's population. The interior is plain, but impresses through sheer size. Paintings of scenes from the life of St John the Baptist adorn the six side-chapels. To the left of the altar is a museum where baroque sculptures and other relics salvaged from the old church are displayed. The wooden statue of St John was fashioned in 1845 by Maltese sculptor Paul Azzopardi.

TA'ĊENĊ

pop 1735

The quiet village of Sannat, once famed for its lace-making, lies 2km south of Victoria, and gives access to the Ta'Ċenċ plateau. Signs from the village square point the way to Hotel Ta'Ċenċ, one of Gozo's best hotels. The track to the left of the entrance to the walled hotel grounds leads to the high plateau of Ta'Ċenċ – the **views** north to Victoria, Xewkija and Xagħra are good, especially towards sunset. Wander off to the left of the track, near the edge of the limestone crag, and you will find a prehistoric **dolmen** – a large slab propped up on three smaller stones like a table. Keep your eyes peeled – the dolmen is not signposted and is a little tricky to spot.

The best walking is off to the right, along the top of the huge Ta'Ċenċ **sea cliffs**. These

spectacular limestone crags, more than 130m high, were once the breeding ground of the Maltese peregrine falcon (see boxed text, p41). Near the cliff top you can see traces of prehistoric 'cart ruts', origins unknown (see boxed text, p133). At the time of research concerned locals were involved in a fight to protect the area from planned development, which included a five-storey hotel, bungalows and a golf course – read about it at www .savetacenc.com.

The ritzy, five-star **Hotel Ta'Ċenċ** (☎ 2155 6819; www.vjborg.com/tacenc; Triq Ta-Ċenċ 🔀 🖳 🖵) hides in 160 hectares on a remote cliff-top plateau just east of Sannat and has an attractive low-rise design that makes good use of local stone. Rooms are surprisingly modest, but the location and facilities do much to compensate. The main building has a beckoning array of sofa-filled living spaces, and beyond these are landscaped gardens and two outdoor pools. If these don't appeal, head to the indoor-outdoor pool at the relaxation-inducing 'wellness spa', or catch the courtesy bus to the hotel's private rocky beach, complete with bar and restaurant. And when you've checked out your surrounds, retire to a sought-after table under the carob tree of the hotel's highly regarded Italian restaurant, Il-Carrubo (open for lunch and dinner).

Buses 50 and 51 run between Victoria and Sannat (Lm0.20).

XLENDI

Development has turned the fishing village of Xlendi into a popular resort town. Sure, it's busier now, but there's no denying that the bay is still beautiful – considerably more so than at Marsalforn, Gozo's other popular resort town. It's a favourite place for locals (Maltese crossing over to the quieter island for a weekend break) and tourists to chill out by the sea, with good swimming, snorkelling and diving, and plenty of rocks for sunbathing.

By the bus stop and car park, a block back from the waterfront, is an ATM and currency exchange machine. Nearby, **Herbees Diner** (opposite; per hr Lm1) offers internet access.

Sights & Activities

At the head of the bay, steps lead up the cliff above the little fishing-boat harbour to a tiny cove in the rocks where you can swim. Alternatively, you can keep walking up the hillside above and then hike over to Wardija Point and

Dwejra Bay. On the south side of Xlendi Bay, a footpath winds around to the 17th-century watchtower, **Torri ta'Xlendi**, on Ras il-Bajjada. From here you can hike east to the Sanap cliffs, and on towards Ta'Ċenċ.

Xlendi Pleasure Cruises (☎ 2155 9967; www.xlendi cruises.com) is set up beside the water and offers motorboats, canoes and paddleboats for hire, as well as fishing trips, water-skiing, snorkelling and cave tours. The company also has a menu of cruises leaving from Mġarr harbour – see p152 for itineraries and prices. Note that there are free transfers from Xlendi to Mġarr for cruise passengers.

There are a couple of dive operators in town that can help you explore the excellent nearby dive sites (see p48), offering 'taster' dives, beginner courses, and excursions for those who already know what they're doing. They can also help arrange accommodation.

Moby Dives (☎ 2155 1616; www.mobydivesgozo.com; Triq il-Gostra)

St Andrews Divers Cove (☎ 2155 1301; www.gozo dive.com; Triq San Ximun)

Sleeping

San Antonio Guesthouse (☎ 2156 3555; www.clubgozo .com.mt; Triq it-Torri; B&B per person Lm6.50-13; ☒ ☒) This guesthouse is perfectly located, a fair climb up the hill on the south side of the bay. It's close enough to Xlendi's harbour-front activity when you want it, yet far enough to allow a relaxing holiday. The rates provide marvellous value and get you one of 13 rooms – all large, bright and spotless, decked out in chunky pine furniture. Surprisingly, air-con, cable TV, big private bathrooms and balconies/terraces are standard, and there's a garden, swimming pool and kiddies' pool. For optimum views, request a pool-facing room on the 1st floor. The accommodating owners can help arrange transfers, car hire and various extras; they also have self-catering apartments and farmhouses – check the website for more information.

St Patrick's Hotel (☎ 2156 2951; www.vjborg.com /stpatricks; Xatt ix-Xlendi; B&B per person Lm9-25; ☒ ☐) Bang in the middle of the Xlendi waterfront is the four-star St Patrick's, with attractive, well-equipped rooms that are popular with weekending Maltese. The cheaper rooms face a nice internal courtyard; the next step up sees rooms with a balcony and view over the town car park and valley beyond. You'll pay more for a room with balcony and sea view, but

the view is indeed lovely. There's a rooftop terrace with spa, and a ground-level waterside restaurant.

Also recommended:

Serena Aparthotel (☎ 2155 3719; www.serena.com .mt; Triq Puniċi; B&B per person from Lm10/14 low/high season; ☒ ☒) A large, well-equipped complex on the south side of the bay, with self-catering suites and a heavy dose of '70s décor.

San Andrea Hotel (☎ 2156 5555; www.hotelsan andrea.com; Xatt ix-Xlendi; B&B per person Lm8-17; ☒) Smaller than St Patrick's Hotel but in an equally lovely location and with similar facilities. Rooms are undersized but comfy.

Eating

Herbees Diner (☎ 2155 6323; meals from Lm1.50; ☽ 6am-11pm Mon-Thu, to 4am Fri, 11am-2.30pm & 6pm-4am Sat, 11.30am-11.45pm Sun) This late-night fast-food joint by the car park (back from the waterfront) has a cheap menu of fried or roasted chicken, kebabs and burgers. It also has internet access (Lm1 for 70 minutes).

Stone Crab (☎ 2155 6400; Xlendi Bay; mains Lm2-7; ☽ lunch Mar-Oct, dinner Jun-Oct) This cheerful, family-friendly restaurant has a winning combination of waterside tables and a huge menu of well-priced pasta, pizza and seafood favourites. The regular special of crab-filled ravioli is delicious; other dishes include spaghetti with octopus, clams or shellfish; pizzas heavy with fishy morsels; or Maltese specialities including octopus cooked in garlic.

Ic-Cima Restaurant (☎ 2155 8407; Triq San Xmun; mains Lm3-6; ☽ lunch & dinner Wed-Mon) High up over the village, away from the waterfront hubbub, this friendly place has an outstanding view over the bay and the coastal cliffs from its large outdoor terrace (across the road from the restaurant itself). It's an excellent choice for Gozitan and Italian cuisine, with the emphasis on seafood, but there's also a variety of inexpensive pizzas to choose from.

It-Tmun (☎ 2155 1571; 3 Triq il-Madonna Tal-Karmnu; mains Lm5-7; ☽ lunch & dinner Wed-Mon) There are plenty of waterfront restaurants in Xlendi but the best culinary hot spots can be found along Triq il-Madonna Tal-Karmnu, back from the seaside. Judging by the crowds, It-Tmun (predecessor of It-Tmun Victoria, p150) is clearly the Sunday-lunch favourite. A sure bet is the fresh catch of the day, or you might opt for calamari, Barbary duck or roast chicken. Round things off nicely with cherry cheesecake or tiramisu.

Entertainment

La Grotta (☎ 2155 1583; www.lagrottaleisure.com; Triq ix-Xlendi; ☾ 10pm-dawn Fri & Sat May-Oct) On the road to Victoria about 600m east of Xlendi, is the best nightclub in the Maltese Islands, in a unique, lovely setting. It's housed in a limestone cave in the cliffs above the valley, with two large dance areas (indoors and out). The admission price varies, depending upon the attraction that night (DJs, live music etc).

Club Paradiso (☎ 2156 0810; Triq ix-Xlendi; ☾ year-round) Found above La Grotta and run by the same people, is this smaller scale, more-traditional (indoor) club pumping out commercial tracks and R&B.

Getting There & Away

Bus 87 runs between Xlendi and Victoria. By car, follow signs from the roundabout at the southern end of Triq Putirjal in Victoria. Or, it's a 3km walk from Victoria bus station.

GĦARB

pop 1050

The village of Għarb (pronounced aarb, meaning 'west') in the northwest of Gozo has one of the most beautiful churches in the Maltese Islands. The baroque **Church of the Visitation** was built between 1699 and 1729, with an elegant curved façade and twin bell-towers. Three female figures adorn the front: Faith, above the door; Hope, with her anchor, to the right; and Charity. Inside, there is an altarpiece, *The Visitation of Our Lady to St Elizabeth,* which was gifted to the church by Grand Master de Vilhena.

The attractive **village square** was the location for the classic postcard, on sale throughout Malta and Gozo, showing a traditional British red telephone box beside a red letter box and a blue police station lamp (unfortunately the red letter box has since been removed).

Next door to the police station is **Għarb Folklore Museum** (☎ 2156 1929; Triq il-Knisja; adult/child Lm1.50/free; ☾ 9.30am-4pm Mon-Sat, 9.30am-noon Sun). This early-18th-century house has 28 rooms crammed with a fascinating private collection of folk artefacts. The exhibits, assembled by the owner over the past 20 years, include an early-18th-century printing press, a child's hearse, farming implements, fishing gear, jam-making equipment and much more.

A drive or pleasant walk of about 30 minutes (just over 2km) from Għarb leads to the tiny **Chapel of San Dimitri** (signposted on the road to the left of the church). This small, square church with its baroque cupola dates originally from the 15th century, though it was rebuilt in the 1730s. It stands in splendid isolation amid terraced fields. You can continue the walk down to the coast, and return via the hilltop of **Ġordan Lighthouse**, or the Basilica of Ta'Pinu.

The **Basilica of Ta'Pinu** (Triq ta'Pinu; ☾ 7am-12.30pm & 1.30-7pm) is Malta's national shrine to the Virgin Mary and is an important centre of pilgrimage. It was built in the 1920s on the site of a chapel where a local woman, Carmela Grima, heard the Virgin speak to her in 1883. Thereafter, numerous miracles were attributed to the intercession of Our Lady of Pinu, and it was decided to replace the old church with a grand new one. Built in a Romanesque style, with an Italianate campanile, the interior of pale golden stone is calming and peaceful. Part of the original chapel, with Carmela Grima's tomb, is incorporated behind the altar. The basilica's name comes from the man, Filippino Gauci, who used to tend the old church – Pinu is the Malti diminutive for Filippino. The track leading to the top of the hill of Ta'Għammar opposite the church is punctuated by marble statues marking the Stations of the Cross. Visitors to the basilica should note that no shorts, miniskirts or sleeveless dresses are allowed.

Where the road to Għarb from Victoria forks (400m after the turning to Ta'Pinu) you'll find **Jeffrey's Restaurant** (☎ 2156 1006; 10 Triq il-Għarb; mains Lm4-6.50; ☾ dinner Mon-Sat Apr-Oct). Set in a converted farmhouse with a pretty courtyard, Jeffrey's offers home-style cooking that makes good use of local produce, and you can sample Maltese specialities such as *braġioli* (p52), stuffed marrow and the highly rated rabbit in wine and garlic.

Buses 1, 2 and 91 go to Għarb; bus 91 will take you to Ta'Pinu (Lm0.20).

SAN LAWRENZ

pop 570

A left turn at Jeffrey's restaurant in Għarb (see above) leads to the village of San Lawrenz, where novelist Nicholas Monsarrat (1910–79) lived and worked for four years in the early 1970s. His love for the Maltese Islands is reflected in his novel *The Kappillan of Malta,* which grew out of his experiences here.

En route from Għarb to San Lawrenz you'll pass the **Ta'Dbieġi Crafts Village** – a miniature clone of Malta's Ta'Qali (p129) – selling handicrafts, lace, glass and pottery. The stalls have variable hours, generally from around 10am to 4pm, but it's best to go in the morning. A left turn just after the crafts village leads to the **Kempinski Hotel San Lawrenz** (☎ 2211 0000; www .kempinski-gozo.com; Triq ir-Rokon; r Lm75-95; ), a swish hideaway set in landscaped grounds. You get the feeling nothing is too much trouble for the obliging staff here, and the crowd is an interesting mix of honeymooners, families and well-heeled older Europeans. Facilities to help pass the time include a large health spa (with a huge list of de-stress treatments), tennis and squash courts, a gym, indoor and outdoor pools and pool bars. There's also a coffee lounge, trattoria and fine-dining restaurant. The spa and eateries are open to the public.

Back in San Lawrenz, right by the church on the charming town square is **Tatita's** (☎ 2156 6482; Pjazza San Lawrenz; mains Lm3-6.50; lunch & dinner Apr-Oct), which comes highly recommended by our readers. Smart modern renovations have turned this town house into a stylish restaurant, or you can dine alfresco on the postcard-perfect square. The kitchen prepares local treats such as homemade ravioli filled with Gozo cheese; grilled stuffed quail; and fresh local calamari and king prawns.

Buses 1, 2 or 91 connect San Lawrenz with Victoria (Lm0.20).

DWEJRA

Geology and the sea have conspired to produce some of Gozo's most spectacular coastal scenery at Dwejra on the west coast. Two

vast, underground caverns in the limestone have collapsed to create two circular depressions now occupied by Dwejra Bay and the Inland Sea.

The **Inland Sea** is a cliff-bound lagoon connected to the open sea by a tunnel that runs for 100m through the headland of Dwejra Point. The tunnel is big enough for small boats to sail through in calm weather, and the Inland Sea has been used as a fishermen's haven for centuries. Today the fishermen supplement their income by taking tourists on **boat trips** (per person Lm1.50) through the cave.

A few minutes' walk from the Inland Sea is a huge natural arch in the sea cliffs, known as the **Azure Window**. In the rocks in front of it is another geological freak called the **Blue Hole** – a natural vertical chimney in the limestone, about 10m in diameter and 25m deep, that connects with the open sea through an underwater arch about 8m down. Understandably, it's a very popular dive site. The snorkelling here is excellent, too. Between the Inland Sea and the Azure Window is the little **Chapel of St Anne**, built in 1963 on the site of a much older church.

FUNGUS ROCK

Known in Malti as Il-Ġebla tal-Ġeneral (The General's Rock), Fungus Rock takes both of its names from the fact that the Knights of St John used to collect a rare plant from the rock's summit. The plant (*Cynomorium coccineus*) is dark brown and club-shaped, and grows to about 18cm in height. It is parasitic and has no green leaves, which is why it was called a fungus or, in Malti, *gherq tal-Ġeneral* (the General's root). It's native to North Africa, and Fungus Rock is the only place in Europe where it's found.

Extracts from the plant had powerful pharmaceutical qualities, and were said to stem bleeding and prevent infection when used to dress wounds. The plant cured dysentery and ulcers, and was used to treat apoplexy and venereal diseases. It was long known to the Arabs as 'the treasure among drugs', and when a general of the Knights of St John discovered it growing on a rock on Gozo, he knew he had struck gold. A rope was strung between the mainland and the rock, and harvesters were shuttled back and forth in a tiny, one-man cable car. Qawra Tower was built to guard the precious resource. The plant extract was much in demand in the Knights' hospitals; it was sold at a high price to the various courts of Europe.

The broad horizontal shelf of rock to the south of Dwejra Point has been eroded along the geological boundary between the Globigerina Limestone and the Lower Coralline Limestone – the boundary is marked by a layer of many thousands of fossilised scallop shells and sand dollars (a kind of flattened, disc-shaped sea urchin). See p40 for more on these limestone layers. Just offshore is **Crocodile Rock** (seen from near Qawra Tower it looks like a crocodile's head) between Dwejra Point and Fungus Rock (see below).

Qawra Tower overlooks **Dwejra Bay**. This collapsed cavern has been completely invaded by the sea, and is guarded by the brooding bulk of **Fungus Rock** (see boxed text, p157). A path below the tower leads to a flight of stairs, cut into the rock, which leads down to a little slipway on the edge of the bay. There is good swimming and sunbathing here, away from the crowd of day-trippers who throng the rocks around the Azure Window. For even more peace you can hike right around to the cliff top on the far side of the bay, where the view back over Fungus Rock to Dwejra Point is spectacular.

You can get snacks from a **café** by the car park at Dwejra, and there are a couple of **kiosks** here selling drinks and ice creams to the day-trippers.

Bus 91 runs infrequently between Victoria and Dwejra (Lm0.35) from March to October. Alternatively, catch bus 1, 2 or 91 to San Lawrenz (Lm0.20) and walk the 1.5km down to the bay.

MARSALFORN

Marsalforn is Gozo's main holiday resort, but tourist development has ensured that it is not an especially lovely town. The bay of this former fishing village (the name is possibly derived from the Arabic for 'bay of ships') is now lined with an ugly sprawl of hotels and apartment buildings, gradually spreading northwest along the coast towards Qbaijar. Still, it's a low-key resort compared with the fleshpots of Sliema and Buġibba on Malta, and offers some good out-of-season deals on accommodation.

Most of the restaurants, hotels and guesthouses are clustered around the waterfront. You can change money at the Bank of Valletta on the promenade, which has an ATM and a 24-hour moneychanging machine. **Extreme Sports Internet Café** (☎ 2155 0983; Triq il-Munġbell; per 70min Lm1; ⏱ noon-midnight), adjacent to the Extreme Sports bar (p160), offers internet.

Sights & Activities

There's not much worth seeing in the town itself. One reader wrote 'please mention the Christ statue just outside Marsalforn. It is the only thing there worth seeing'. She is referring to the large statue of Jesus you'll see on the small hill (Rio de Janeiro–style) to the left as you enter town from Victoria. It was erected in the 1970s, replacing earlier statues and a wooden cross from around the 1900s. The 96m-high hill is known as Tas-Salvatur, or 'the Redeemer'.

At the head of the bay is a tiny scrap of sand, but better swimming and sunbathing

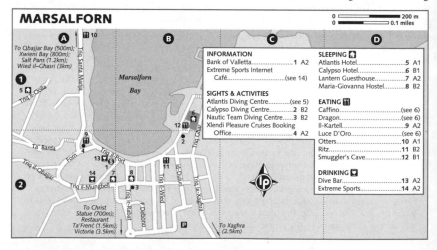

MARSALFORN

0 _____ 200 m
0 _____ 0.1 miles

To Qbajjar Bay (500m);
Xwieni Bay (800m);
Salt Pans (1.2km);
Wied il–Ghasri (3km)

Marsalforn Bay

INFORMATION
Bank of Valletta....................1 A2
Extreme Sports Internet
Café.............................(see 14)

SIGHTS & ACTIVITIES
Atlantis Diving Centre..........(see 5)
Calypso Diving Centre............2 B2
Nautic Team Diving Centre.....3 B2
Xlendi Pleasure Cruises Booking
Office.............................4 A2

SLEEPING
Atlantis Hotel.......................5 A1
Calypso Hotel.......................6 B1
Lantern Guesthouse................7 A2
Maria-Giovanna Hostel..........8 B2

EATING
Caffino.............................(see 6)
Dragon.............................(see 6)
Il-Kartell............................9 A2
Luce D'Oro.......................(see 6)
Otters.............................10 A1
Ritz.................................11 B2
Smuggler's Cave.................12 B1

DRINKING
Dive Bar.............................13 A2
Extreme Sports....................14 A2

To Christ
Statue (700m);
Restaurant
Ta'Frenċ (1.5km);
Victoria (3.5km)

To Xaghra
(2.5km)

can be found on the rocks out to the west. You could also hike eastward over the hill a couple of kilometres to Calypso's Cave and Ramla Bay.

If you walk west from town along the nicely updated promenade (with a handful of restaurants en route) you'll reach the tiny sand beaches at **Qbajjar Bay** and **Xwieni Bay**, separated by a headland with a small fort. Beyond Xwieni the rocky shore has been carved into an impressive patchwork of **salt pans**, which are still worked in summer.

Another 20-minute hike beyond the salt pans will bring you to the narrow, cliff-bound inlet of **Wied il-Għasri**. Here a narrow staircase cut into the rock leads down to a tiny shingle beach at the head of the inlet. It's a gorgeously picturesque place and there is good swimming and snorkelling when the sea is calm, but it's best avoided in rough weather when the waves come crashing up the narrow defile. You can also drive or walk to Wied il-Għasri from the village of Għasri, about 2km south, but it's a bit tricky to find – you'll need a decent map if you're coming from this direction. If you're coming from Marsalforn, there is an unsigned turn-off on the right about 300m after the coastal road heads inland.

Check out p152 for information about Xlendi Pleasure Cruises out of Mġarr that offer free transfers to/from Marsalforn. There are a number of dive operators in town that can help you explore Gozo's great dive sites (p48), including:

Atlantis Diving Centre (☎ 2156 1826; www.atlantis gozo.com; Atlantis Hotel, Triq il-Qolla)

Calypso Diving Centre (☎ 2156 1757; www.calypso divers.com; Triq il-Port) Near the Calypso Hotel.

Nautic Team Diving Centre (☎ 2155 8507; www .nauticteam.com; cnr Triq il-Munġbell & Triq ir-Rabat)

Sleeping

our pick **Maria-Giovanna Hostel** (☎ 2155 3630; www .gozohostels.com; cnr Triq il-Munġbell & Triq ir-Rabat; B&B per person Lm6-8) No-one else in Malta caters to independent, budget-minded travellers like this wonderful hostel. And hostel is perhaps a misleading term – this is more like a guesthouse, with rooms rented out individually (no dorm beds, no room-sharing necessary). From the pretty town-house exterior to the fish tank, plants and piano in the communal lounge, this place is clearly well looked after. There are only five guest rooms (two with en suite), each decorated in rustic style, with funky cast-iron beds and colourful linen and rugs. Guests have use of the hostel's kitchen, dining area and TV lounge, and breakfast is included. The friendly owners live across the road and can arrange all sorts of extras (for a small fee): laundry, home-cooked local meals, taxi service, a water taxi to Comino. Nothing seems too much trouble. The owners can also help with self-catering apartments and farmhouses – check the website for more information.

Lantern Guesthouse (☎ 2156 2365; www.gozo.com /lantern; Triq il-Munġbell; B&B per person Lm6.50-8) Not a bad fall-back budget option, the Lantern has clean, homely rooms, all with en suite, cable TV and fridge. The owners can also hook you up with reasonably priced apartments around town.

Atlantis Hotel (☎ 2156 1826; www.atlantisgozo.com; Triq il-Qolla; B&B per person from Lm10/15 low/high season; ▨ ▣) Above the west side of the bay is this large hotel complex, which extends to both sides of the street and has loads of facilities. The dated exterior and lobby don't inspire a lot of confidence but the well-equipped rooms are decent for the price. It's particularly popular with the diving crowd.

Calypso Hotel (☎ 2156 2000; www.hotelcalypsogozo .com; Triq il-Port; B&B per person from Lm11.50/18 low/high season; ▨ ▣) After recent renovations the Calypso boasts fresh, stylish décor and excellent facilities. The large modern guest rooms are clean and contemporary, in warm blue tones. An international and Maltese crowd makes good use of the handful of on-site restaurants and café, plus the lovely pool, bar and sun terrace on the roof. Sea-view rooms cost an additional Lm4 per person.

Eating & Drinking

The majority of restaurants in Marsalforn have reduced hours in winter – it pays to call ahead to check somewhere is open before setting off.

Il-Kartell (☎ 2155 6918; Triq il-Port; mains Lm2-5.50; ☯ lunch & dinner) Sit right by the water or inside the rustic dining rooms at this bustling place, housed in a couple of old boathouses in the southwestern corner of the bay. The menu includes pasta dishes around the Lm2 mark, along with fresh fish, traditional dishes and daily specials chalked up on the blackboard.

Otters (☎ 2156 2473; Triq Santa Marija; mains Lm3.50-6; ☯ lunch & dinner) Waterfront Otters, on the western edge of the bay, has stylishly reinvented itself and now boasts a tasteful charcoal interior with white and yellow accents, and a fusion menu to match the new surrounds. Choose from mains along the lines of seared yellow-fin tuna; braised lamb and date *tajine*; or pork chops topped with pineapple and lime salsa.

Restaurant Ta'Frenċ (☎ 2155 3888; Triq ir-Rabat; mains Lm5-13; ☯ lunch & dinner Wed-Mon) For a special occasion and to see what the fuss is about, head to this *très élégant* restaurant, about 1.5km south of Marsalforn on the road to Victoria. It's in a beautiful setting (a 200-year-old converted farmhouse surrounded by garden) and is polled as the best and the most popular eatery in the country. There's an impressive menu of French, Italian and Maltese dishes, with rabbit-filled ravioli or traditional *aljotta* (fish soup) to start, followed by slow-cooked lamb shank, fresh fish or steak Diane. Crêpes suzette, flambéed at the table, are quite a show-stopper. Vegetarians are catered to, as are children, surprisingly. There's also an extensive, award-winning winelist – take a taxi home. Bookings advised.

The Calypso Hotel is home to a very good Chinese restaurant, the **Dragon**, plus **Luce D'Oro**, an elegant rooftop restaurant. Fashionable **Caffino**, at ground level, is the best choice for a snack or drink, with loads of savoury pastries, toasted sandwiches and mouthwatering cakes.

The **Ritz** (☎ 2155 8392; Triq il-Wied; snacks Lm0.30-1) is far from ritzy – it's a cheap-and-cheerful café-bar selling snacks and sandwiches (a steak sandwich is Lm0.65). **Smuggler's Cave** (☎ 2155 1005; Triq il-Port mains Lm2.50-5.50), by the Calypso Hotel, has cheap pizzas and burgers (plus the usual pasta, meat and fish), but feels more like a British seaside restaurant than a Maltese one, and you can get a traditional roast pork or beef.

Dive Bar (☎ 2155 9931; Triq il-Port) is a great nighttime watering hole – stop by for pizza in its bright, nautically themed interior, which is reminiscent of a ship's galley. **Extreme Sports** (☎ 2155 0983; Triq il-Munġbell), a block back from the waterfront, is another popular drinking den, with a restaurant upstairs, and big screens televising sporting events in an extremely big way.

Getting There & Away

Bus 21 runs regularly between Marsalforn and Victoria (Lm0.20).

XAGĦRA
pop 3850

The pretty village of Xagħra (shaa-ra) spreads across the flat summit of the hill east of Victoria, seemingly lost in a dream of times past. The early-19th-century Church of Our Lady of Victory looks down benignly on the tree-lined village square, Pjazza Vittorja, where old men sit and chat in the shade of the oleanders.

Orientation & Information

The main road from Mġarr and Victoria zigzags up the hill from the south and passes the site of the temples of Ġgantija before joining the village square in front of the church. A left turn here leads back towards Victoria on a rough, steep, minor road (affording fabulous views of Victoria and Il-Kastell). A right turn leads past the school and post office to the Marsalforn road. The Bank of Valletta (no ATM) is at the western end of the square.

Sights

A narrow lane beside the school leads to the restored **Ta'Kola Windmill** (☎ 2156 1071; il-Bambina; adult/child Lm1/0.25; ☯ 9am-5pm). Built in 1725, the windmill is now something of an attraction, housing a museum of country life with exhibits of woodworking tools, farm equipment and period bedroom and living quarters. Best of all is the climb up the narrow stairs to see the original milling gear, complete with millstones.

Visitors can also purchase a **Xagħra Day Ticket** (Lm2), which includes entry to the Ġgantija temples and Ta'Kola Windmill on the same day. This ticket is available at both the temples and windmill.

In the back streets to the north of the village square lie **Xerri's Grotto** (☎ 2155 6863; l'Għar ta'Xerri; adult/child Lm0.75/0.30) and **Ninu's Cave** (Triq Jannar; admission Lm0.50). These underground caverns,

---

EDWARD LEAR ON GOZO

Edward Lear (1812–88), an English landscape painter and nonsense poet (Lear popularised the limerick as a form of comic verse), spent much of his life travelling around the Mediterranean. He visited Gozo in 1866, and described the scenery as 'pomskizillious and gromphiberous, being as no words can describe its magnificence'.

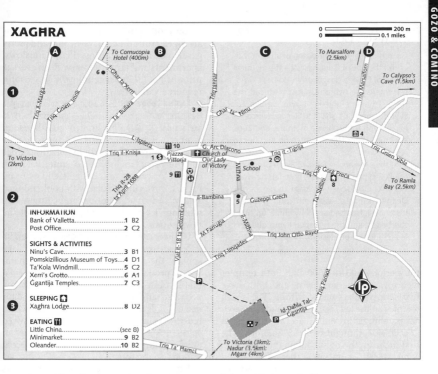

XAGHRA

complete with stalactites and stalagmites, are unusual in that they are both entered through private houses. Having discovered the caves beneath their homes, the owners decided to cash in on the tourist potential. Xerri's Grotto was discovered in 1923 when Antonio Xerri was digging a well. It's the bigger, deeper and more interesting of the two. Opening times are at the discretion of the owners, but are generally from 9.30am to 5pm in summer (with shorter hours outside the peak tourist months).

At the eastern end of town the road forks – left for Marsalforn, right for Ramla Bay. A few metres along the Ramla road on the left is the **Pomskizillious Museum of Toys** (☎ 2156 2489; Triq Gnien Xibla; adult/child Lm1/0.50; ☻ 10am-noon & 3-6pm Mon-Sat May-Oct, 10am-1pm Thu-Sat Apr, 10am-1pm Sat & public holidays Nov-Mar), popular with kids (and kids at heart) for its impressive array of dolls houses, toy soldiers, dolls and various other old toys.

Signposts near the Pomskizillious Museum of Toys point the way through the maze of minor roads east of Xaghra down to **Calypso's Cave**, overlooking the sandy beach of Ramla Bay – it's a 30-minute walk from the village square. The cave itself is hardly worth the

hike – it's just a hollow under an overhang at the top of the cliff – but the view over Ramla Bay is lovely. On a calm day visitors can usually see the remains of an artificial reef extending into the sea off the eastern headland of the bay. This was part of the defences built by the Knights of St John to prevent attackers landing on the beach. In theory, the enemy ships would run aground on the reef, where they would be attacked using primitive mortar like weapons.

ĠGANTIJA

Located on the crest of the hill to the south of Xaghra, the megalithic **Ġgantija temples** (☎ 2155 3194; access from Triq l-Imqades; adult/child Lm1.50/0.50; ☻ 9am-5pm) command a splendid view over most of southern Gozo and beyond to Comino and Malta. As the name implies (ġgantija – dje-*gant*-ee-ya – means 'giantess'), these are the largest of the megalithic temples found in the Maltese Islands – the walls stand over 6m high, and the two temples together span over 40m.

Along with Ta'Ħaġrat (p116) and Skorba (p116) on Malta, the Ġgantija temples are thought to be Malta's oldest, dating from

CALYPSO'S ISLE

Gozo is one of the half-dozen or so contenders for the title of Calypso's Isle – the mythical island of Ogygia described in Homer's *Odyssey* where the nymph Calypso seduced the hero Odysseus and kept him captive for seven years. But she could not overcome his longing for his home in Ithaca, and Zeus eventually sent Hermes to command her to release him.

If the cave above Ramla Bay on Gozo was really Calypso's hideaway, then it is no wonder that Odysseus was keen to get home. Despite the nice view and pretty island, it's a long, hot and scratchy climb up from the beach, and the cramped living quarters leave a lot to be desired.

the period 3600 to 3000 BC. Both temples face towards the southeast, and both have five semicircular niches within. The south temple (on the left) is the older, and is entered across a huge threshold slab with four holes at each side, thought to be for libations. The first niche on the right contains an altar with some spiral decoration – there was once a pillar here with a snake carved on it, but the pillar now lives in Victoria's Archaeology Museum (p147). The left-hand niche in the inner chamber has a well-preserved trilithon altar; on the right is a circular hearth stone and a bench altar.

There is little of interest in the north temple, but the outer wall of the temple complex is impressive in scale. The largest of the megaliths measures 6m by 4m and weighs around 57 tonnes, and the wall may originally have stood up to 16m tall.

Heritage Malta has set up a small 'info pod' giving a short audio narration on the temples in a half-dozen different languages. But, as with other temple sites in Malta, it has a ways to go to ensure that visitors leave the site with an understanding of what makes these piles of stones so special.

Sleeping & Eating

Cornucopia Hotel (☎ 2155 6486; www.vjborg.com/cornucopia; Triq Gnien Imrik; s/d Lm11.25/22.50 low season, Lm26/39 high season, bungalows, villas & apt Lm15-60; 🗙 🗷) Cornucopia and its accommodation options are set in and around a converted farmhouse about 1km north of the village square. Four-star

accommodation is available in hotel rooms arranged around a courtyard, pool and pretty garden, or in self-catering villas, bungalows, apartments and farmhouses (with an average price of Lm25/50 per unit low/high season); request a valley view.

Xagħra Lodge (☎ 2156 2362; www.gozo.com/xagħra lodge; Triq Dun Gorġ Preca; s/d Lm16/21 low season, Lm19/25 high season; 🗙 🗷) This homely guesthouse in a quiet neighbourhood is run by a friendly English couple. There are excellent facilities for the price, including en suite, balcony, cable TV and tea and coffee facilities in all rooms; flowering garden with pool and bird aviary; and an adjacent bar and Chinese restaurant. It's a five-minute walk east of the town square.

Oleander (☎ 2155 7230; Pjazza Vittorja; mains Lm3.50-6; 🕒 lunch & dinner Tue-Sun) On the pretty village square, the popular Oleander has a menu you've probably seen before (pastas, *braġioli*, rabbit, fresh fish, local lamb), but it's all well prepared and regulars rave over the rabbit dishes – 'Oleander fried rabbit' is glazed with a red-wine sauce and fried with garlic and mixed spices. It's a pleasant place to while away an evening, and there are a couple of other decent options on the square.

Little China (☎ 2156 2362; Triq Dun Gorġ Preca; dishes Lm2-6, set menu from Lm6; 🕒 dinner Mon-Sat) If you're tired of perusing menus full of pizza, pasta and rabbit, head to Little China, adjacent to the Xagħra Lodge. On offer is a huge range of meat, vegetable, noodle and seafood dishes – favourites like sweet and sour pork, beef with black bean sauce, lemon chicken and crispy duck. There are lots of soups and starters, and vegetarian options.

For those who prefer to picnic or self-cater, there's a handy **minimarket** (Vjal it-18 Ta'Settembru; 🕒 6.30am-7pm Mon-Sat) just south of the square.

Getting There & Away

Buses 64 and 65 run between Victoria and Xagħra (Lm0.20).

NADUR

pop 4230

Nadur is Gozo's 'second city', spreading along a high ridge to the east of Victoria. In Malti, Nadur means 'lookout', and a 17th-century watchtower overlooks the Comino sea lanes from the western end of the ridge.

Nadur's ornate **Church of Sts Peter & Paul** (Pjazza San Pietru u San Pawl) was built in the late 18th century – the entrance is framed by white statues of the two saints, giving the church its local nickname of *iż-Żewġ* (the pair). The interior is richly decorated with marble sculptures, and the vault is covered with 150 paintings. See the boxed text, p38, for more about the church.

A block south of the church (well signposted from the square) is the **Kelinu Grima Maritime Museum** (☎ 2156 5226; Triq il-Kappillan; adult/child Lm1/0.50; ☯ 9am-4.45pm Mon-Sat), a private collection of ship models, relics and maritime memorabilia.

On the square directly behind the church is **Anthony's Bar & Restaurant** (☎ 2156 5369; 20 Triq Madre Ġ Camilleri; pizzas Lm1.25-2.35; mains Lm2-5.50; ☯ dinner Tue-Sun), a small, friendly place with well-priced meals.

To get to Nadur, take bus 42 or 43 from Victoria (Lm0.20).

AROUND NADUR

Narrow country roads radiate northward from Nadur to three beaches, all signposted. **Ramla Bay** (also called Ir-Ramla) is the biggest and best sandy beach on Gozo, and one of the prettiest in the islands – the strand of reddish-gold contrasts picturesquely with the blue of the sea and white statue of the Virgin Mary. As such, it is usually heaving with people in summer, when cafés, souvenir stalls and water-sports facilities abound. It is much quieter and more pleasant in spring and autumn, and in winter you can have the place almost to your (goose-pimpled) self. The minimal remains of a **Roman villa** are hidden among the bamboo behind the beach, and Calypso's Cave (p161) looks down from the hilltop to the west. Ramla Bay is also easily accessed (on foot or by car) from Xagħra, and bus 42 runs between the bay and Victoria from July to September (Lm0.35).

The next beach to the east is **San Blas**, a tiny, rock-strewn bay with some patches of coarse rust-coloured sand backed by steep, terraced fields with prickly pear hedges. It's a lovely place to take a picnic lunch and a good book, and perhaps a mask and fins for snorkelling – the water is quite shallow and very clear. There are no facilities here, and there's parking space

---

GOZO AGRITOURISM

At the time of research an excellent new initiative had just been created. It caters to eco-minded travellers interested in experiencing first-hand the island's renowned hospitality and rural customs.

The nonprofit **Ager Foundation** (☎ 2156 4378; www.agerfoundation.com) has launched the Gozo Experience, a project with the noble aims of promoting responsible, sustainable tourism on Gozo and safeguarding the natural environment. It offers visitors (locals and tourists alike) the chance to get back to nature – milk a goat, go fishing, cook up a traditional feast – alongside Gozitans and according to Gozitan traditions. Options for one-day outings include:

- experiencing the life of a local shepherd, and being shown how ġbejniet (p51), the traditional cheese, is made
- preparing and tasting natural Gozitan food
- fishing onshore or from a boat with a local fisherman
- learning about local wine-making practices
- bird watching with local birders
- exploring Gozo's archaeology and heritage

The experiences are designed with families in mind (especially with parents who'd like their kids to have some understanding of where supermarket produce comes from) and are a hit with city slickers enamoured with the romance of rural life. Other back-to-basics outings may include herb-picking or wildflower identification, or a visit to a local festa. Groups are kept small (with a maximum of eight participants) and costs are very reasonable (eg a day spent meeting a local shepherd, with the chance to milk a sheep and make cheese, costs adult/child Lm8/4, including lunch). Tailored outings can be arranged. This is a unique project that deserves to do well; check the website and contact the Ager Foundation for more information.

for only a handful of cars on the very narrow track above the bay. You can walk here from Nadur in about 30 minutes (take Triq San Blas off Triq it-Tiġrija, two blocks north of Nadur's church; it's just over 2.5km from town).

Attractive **Dahlet Qorrot**, the third bay, is popular with local weekenders. There's a tiny sandy stretch, but most of the swimming is off the rocks beside the rows of little boathouses (carved out of the rock, and with brightly painted doors). There's usually plenty of space to park; you can buy drinks and snacks in summer only. A turn-off en route to San Blas leads to Dahlet Qorrot.

QALA

The village of Qala (a-la) has little to see except for a couple of 18th-century **windmills**. The road east of the village square (Triq il-Kunċizzjoni) leads down to the coast at **Hondoq ir-Rummien**, a cove with a scrap of sand, bathing ladders on the rocks, and benches with a view across the water to Comino. There are toilets here, and a kiosk catering to sunbathers.

COMINO

pop 4

It's stretching the truth to say that you'll be getting away from it all here. Comino (Kemmuna in Malti) was once reportedly the hide-out of pirates and smugglers, but now regularly plays host to boatloads of sunseeking invaders. Home to the Blue Lagoon, one of Malta's most hyped natural attractions, the island itself is a small, barren chunk of limestone wedged smack-bang between Malta and Gozo. Almost the only inhabitants are the guests and staff of the island's single hotel, but hordes of day-trippers from Malta and Gozo put paid to any desert-island fantasies. In winter, when the hotel is closed, only a handful of people remain.

Classified as a nature reserve and bird sanctuary, and free of cars, Comino is only 2.5km by 1.5km in size, and away from the hotel and the Blue Lagoon the island is peaceful and unspoiled. A walk along the rough tracks affords some great views of northern Malta or of Gozo. It's impossible to get lost here, given the island's tiny size and the fact that St Mary's Tower, the only landmark of note, is visible from almost everywhere on the island.

The main part of the Comino Hotel is on San Niklaw Bay, and the Comino Hotel Bungalows are on Santa Marija Bay, 500m to the east. A rough track lined with oleander trees, rather grandly named Triq Congreve, runs from Santa Marija Bay south to St Mary's Tower. Side tracks lead to the Blue Lagoon and San Niklaw Bay.

SIGHTS

The only manmade sights of note on Comino are the little **Chapel of Our Lady's Return from Egypt** at Santa Marija Bay and **St Mary's Tower**, built by the Knights in 1618. It was once part of the chain of signal towers between Gozo and Mdina but today is just an observation post used by the Maltese military. Climb the steps and enjoy the views.

The island's biggest attraction is the **Blue Lagoon**, a sheltered cove between the western end of the island and the uninhabited islet of Cominotto (Kemmunett in Malti). This immensely photogenic cove has a white-sand sea bed and clear turquoise waters – it's an image repeated on countless souvenir postcards from Malta.

In summer the bay gets inundated with people daily between around 10am and 4pm; if you're staying at the hotel, of course, you can enjoy the lagoon in relative peace in the early morning and late afternoon. The southern end of the lagoon is roped off to keep boats out; there is top-notch swimming and snorkelling here, plus you can swim over to Cominotto.

Take care in the unrelenting summer heat – there is no shade here, and most sunbathing is done on the exposed rocky ledges surrounding the cove. There are public toilets and a few kiosks selling cool drinks, ice creams and snacks (eg burgers, hot dogs and sandwiches). Deckchairs (per day Lm1.25) and umbrellas (Lm1) can be hired for extended luxurious lazing about.

SLEEPING & EATING

An international crowd of sunseekers, scuba divers and those who prefer to holiday without too many distractions make a regular pilgrimage to the well-equipped **Comino Hotels** (☎ 2152 9821; www.cominohotels.com; half board per person Lm17-28; ❘❘ ❘ ❘), the only place to stay on the island. (Note that the hotel is open only from April to October.) The four-star hotel has 95 rooms at San Niklaw Bay and 46 bungalows at Santa Marija Bay, but no self-catering options. Bungalows are a larger option than the hotel rooms, with a sitting area; these are open from May to October.

Pack a good book – there are no museums or shops to distract you, and only the hotel's café, restaurant and bar (and your fellow guests) keep you fed, watered and entertained. A garden-view room costs Lm17 per person per night for half board in the low season (April, May and October), Lm23 in the mid-season (June and from mid- to late September) and Lm28 in the high season (July to mid-September). Full board costs an additional Lm6. The buffet meals are of a good standard.

By day there are hotel-organised activities (at additional cost) to occupy your time – the most popular is scuba diving, taking advantage of Comino's excellent dive sites (see p49). Instruction and courses for beginners, experienced divers and kids are available through the hotel's dive school, **Comino Dive Centre** (☎ 2157 0354; www.cominodivecentre.com).

Other diversions include a private beach (in San Niklaw Bay), swimming pools, tennis courts and bikes, waters sports (including rental of windsurfing equipment, sailing and motor boats, and canoes) and boat excursions. Or you can simply recharge your batteries in your bright, bland but perfectly adequate room (featuring air-con, phone, cable TV, fridge and balcony).

Day-trippers can use the hotel's facilities for a stiff fee of Lm14 a day, but this must be booked in advance through the hotel. The price includes lunch, a return boat ticket and use of the pool and private beach. Casual visitors might like to escape the Blue Lagoon and dine at the café or buy a drink at the bar.

GETTING THERE & AWAY

The hotel runs its own boat service, with around seven crossings a day from Ċirkewwa in Malta's north (between 7.30am and 11.30pm) and Mġarr in Gozo's south (between 6.15am and 10pm). Arriving and departing hotel guests are given priority on the boats, and the return ticket price per adult/child is Lm3.50/1.75; the ferry can also be used by nonresidents of the hotel for the same price. The boats do not run from November to March, when the hotel is closed. To get to Ċirkewwa from Valletta, take bus 45.

Independent water taxis also operate regularly to the island from the two ports – from Mġarr it's usually Lm3 return, and from Ċirkewwa it's Lm4 return. Sightseeing trips operate to the Blue Lagoon from tourist areas like Sliema, Buġibba and Golden Bay in Malta, and Xlendi and Marsalforn in Gozo.

Directory

CONTENTS

ACCOMMODATION

There is a wide range of accommodation available in the Maltese Islands, though much of it is in fairly uniform resort hotels and apartments. The authorities are attempting to drive Malta's

---

BOOK ACCOMMODATION ONLINE

For more accommodation reviews and recommendations by Lonely Planet authors, check out the online booking service at www.lonelyplanet.com. You'll find the true, insider lowdown on the best places to stay. Reviews are thorough and independent. Best of all, you can book online.

ACCOMMODATION PRICES

In this book, we have classified sleeping options as follows:

Budget A bed in these establishments (usually hostels, two-star hotels and guesthouses) will cost under Lm10 per person.

Midrange Lm11 to Lm25 per person in high season (based on two people sharing a room).

Top End Lm26 or more per person in high season (based on two people sharing a room).

---

tourist industry upmarket, and almost all the new hotels and developments are at the luxury end of the spectrum (and a number of budget guesthouses have closed in recent times). However, there are still plenty of good budget options and accommodation bargains in the low season (from November to March, excluding the Christmas and New Year period).

Camping

There is only one camping ground in Malta, on the Marfa Peninsula in northwest Malta (see p120), but its shadeless grounds and remote location render it unappealing.

Guesthouses

Guesthouses in Malta are usually small (six to 10 rooms), simple, family-run places and are often good value at around Lm6 to Lm8 per person (and there is often no single supplement). Most rooms will have a washbasin, but showers and toilets are mostly shared. A simple breakfast is normally included in the price. Facilities will usually not include air-con or a swimming pool, but there are a few exceptions to this rule. Bear in mind that some guesthouses in resort areas close in the low season (all guesthouses in Valletta are open year-round).

Hostels

The **National Student Travel Service** (NSTS; Map p58; ☎ 2558 8000; www.nsts.org; 220 Triq San Pawl, Valletta) is an associate member of Hostelling International (HI), and operates the very good Hibernia Residence & Hostel, in Sliema (Malta's only true hostel, p88). It has arrangements with a few guesthouses scattered throughout the country to provide cheap accommodation to hostellers.

Hotels

Hotels in Malta range from crumbling but character-filled old townhouses in Valletta, to modern gilt-and-chrome palaces of five-star luxury overlooking a private marina. The majority (especially somewhere like Buġibba) are bland, faceless tourist hotels, block-booked by package tour companies in summer, and either closed or eerily quiet in winter. However, there are a few places that have real character, like the Castille Hotel in Valletta, housed in an old mansion; the Xara Palace in Mdina; and the Kempinski San Lawrenz Resort & Spa or Hotel Ta'Ċenċ on Gozo, but the latter three hotels are among the most expensive in the islands.

The are plenty of glitzy new five-star hotels on Malta, but also a disturbing number of neglected three-star places crying out for renovations. Most of the large four- and five-star places offer the kind of holiday where you may not need to leave the hotel's grounds – they're fully equipped with cafés, bars and restaurants (most hotels include breakfast in their rates, and some offer half-board and full-board arrangements). At these places you'll usually find indoor and outdoor pools, a gym and/or sporting facilities, plus a program of children's activities; and quite possibly a health spa, a dive company, and perhaps a beachside lido offering pool and water sports (water-skiing, boat trips, canoe or boat hire, ringo rides etc).

Typical high-season hotel rates are Lm12 to Lm25 per person, but they rise to as high as Lm50 for the four- and five-star places. Prices may well halve in the low season. You should also be aware that many hotels and guesthouses quote their prices per person, not per room.

There are loads of internet sites offering information on hotels and other accommodation options in Malta, including:

Holiday Malta (www.holiday-malta.com)
Malta Hotel (www.maltahotel.net)
Malta Hotels (www.malta-hotels.com)
Visit Malta (www.visitmalta.com/en/where_to_stay)

PRACTICALITIES

- English-language daily newspapers include *the Times* (online at www.timesofmalta.com) and *the Independent* (www.independent.com.mt). The former has a good mix of local, European and world news, the latter has good coverage of domestic social issues. *Malta Today* (www.maltatoday.com.mt) is published weekly (on Sunday) and includes a useful supplement with listings of TV, cinema and events for the coming week.

- There are more than 20 local radio stations broadcasting mostly in Malti but occasionally in English. There are two state-run TV stations and half-a-dozen small commercial channels broadcasting in Malti. Most of the main Italian TV stations can be received in Malta. Satellite and cable TV are widely available in hotels and bars, providing a wide range of stations from Europe and the US.

- Malta, like most of Europe and the UK, uses the PAL video system.

- Malta's electricity supply is 240V/50Hz and the plugs have three flat pins as in the UK. Continental European appliances (plugs with two round pins) will need an adaptor (many accommodation providers supply these).

- Like the rest of Europe, Malta uses the metric system. The British legacy persists in the use of pint glasses in some pubs.

DIRECTORY

Rental Accommodation

There are hundreds of self-catering apartments with little to choose between them. Most have a private bathroom, a balcony and a kitchen area with fridge, sink and two-ring electric cooker. Though lacking a little in charm, they are often very good value at under Lm12 per person, even in high season.

If you're looking for something with a little local colour, get in touch with a tour operator or agency that specialises in Gozo farmhouses (see the boxed text, p150).

High & Low Seasons

The cost of accommodation in Malta can vary considerably with the time of year, and low-season rates are often a bargain. Low season is almost always November to March. High season generally refers to the period April to October, but some accommodation providers have a 'shoulder' or 'mid' season covering April, May and October, with high-season prices restricted to June, July, August and September. Many hotels count the Christmas and New Year period as high season too. The high- and low-season prices quoted in this book are generally the maximum and minimum rates for each establishment.

Bear in mind that some places (small guesthouses and cheaper hotels) in some resort areas close in the low season – as does the Comino Hotel, making a stay on Comino impossible from November to March.

ACTIVITIES

One of the most popular activities for holiday-makers in Malta is diving – see the Diving & Snorkelling chapter (p44) for details.

The Marsa Sports Complex is used by various national sport associations. The complex, about 4km southwest of Valletta, includes a horse-racing course, the Marsa Sports Club (below) and the National Athletic Stadium. Facilities include five turf pitches, a rugby pitch, a baseball pitch, two netball courts, two basketball courts and one full-size football ground.

The **Marsa Sports Club** (☎ 2123 3851; www.marsasportsclub.com) includes an 18-hole golf course (the only one in Malta – see Golf below), 19 tennis courts, five squash courts, a swimming pool, cricket ground and gymnasium. Visitors may use these facilities; a day membership costs Lm2, a week Lm10.

The website of the **Malta Tourism Authority** (www.visitmalta.com) has loads of information on the different types of activities possible in Malta, and organisations that can help you pursue them. Click on the 'What to Do' pages.

Bird Watching

Although barely a dozen species of bird are permanent residents on Malta, the islands sustain important breeding colonies of seabirds, including storm-petrels and Cory's shearwaters. Malta also lies on an important migration route between Africa and Europe, and in spring (September to November) and autumn (April and May) vast numbers of migrating birds can be seen – as can numerous bird hunters (p42), unfortunately.

Where to Watch Birds & Other Wildlife in the Maltese Islands, written by Alex Casha and published by BirdLife Malta, is a comprehensive guide.

BirdLife Malta (☎ 2134 7646; www.birdlifemalta.org) is the best contact for birders visiting Malta. It manages the Għadira Nature Reserve (p118) at Mellieħa Bay and the Is-Simar Nature Reserve (p114) at Xemxija, plus monitors activity that threatens wild birds and has a website detailing recent sightings.

Golf

The **Royal Malta Golf Club** (☎ 2123 9302; www.maltagolf.org; 9/18 holes Lm13.50/20) is a private members' club established in 1888, located at the Marsa Sports Club at Marsa, southwest of Valletta. Visitors are welcome to play the 18-hole, par-68 course, but reservations are essential (it's best to avoid Thursday and Saturday morning, as these days are reserved for members' competitions). Club facilities include a pro shop, bar, restaurant and driving range.

Horse Riding

Horses have long played an important part in Maltese life, and you can often see owners out exercising their favourite trotting horses. The quieter back roads offer enjoyable riding – instruction and horse hire can be organised through most major hotels.

Riding schools in Malta include:

Bidnija Horse Riding School (☎ 2141 0010; www.bidnijahorseriding.com; Triq il-Bdiewa, Mosta)

Golden Bay Horse Riding (☎ 2157 3360; Għajn Tuffieħa) See p115 for more details.

Pandy's Riding School (☎ 2134 2506; Triq Tobruk, Pembroke)

Wagon Wheel Horse Riding School (☎ 2155 6254; Triq Marsalforn, Victoria, Gozo)

Rock Climbing

There are more than 1200 established rock-climbing routes in the Maltese Islands (most on limestone), with some of the most popular sites for climbers below the Dingli Cliffs in the west, at Għar Lapsi, and near the Victoria Lines below Naxxar. **Malta Rock Climbing** (☎ 2148 0240; www.malta-rockclimbing.com) offers four-hour taster sessions (Lm15) – perfect for the indecisive types – guided climbing excursions (half day Lm15, full day Lm25) and climbing courses.

Running

Several major running events are held each year in Malta, including triathlons and half-marathons, culminating in the **Malta Marathon** (www.maltamarathon.com) and half-marathon, held in late February/early March (you really wouldn't want to be running too far in the heat of summer!). Application forms are available from the website; the entrance fee is €35.

Sailing

Malta is a major yachting centre, with a large marina at Msida, a smaller one at Gozo's Mġarr harbour, and two slick modern marinas – one at the Portomaso development in St Julian's, the other, called the Grand Harbour Marina, at Vittoriosa. Many yacht owners cruise the Med in summer and winter their vessels in Malta.

A full program of races and regattas is held between April and November each year (great for participants and spectators). The popular **Rolex Middle Sea Race** (www.rolexmiddle searace.com) is a highly rated offshore classic staged annually in October. The race is 607 nautical miles, from Malta, sailing anticlockwise around Sicily before returning to Malta. For details of events and opportunities for crewing, contact the **Royal Malta Yacht Club** (☎ 2133 3109; www.rmyc.org; Manoel Island) or check the website.

Qualified sailors are able to hire a yacht by the day or the week from one of several charter companies. If you don't have a RYA Coastal Skipper qualification you'll need to pay extra for a skipper (around Lm35 per day). Try:

Captain Morgan Yacht Charter (☎ 2346 3333; www.yachtcharter.com.mt; per week from Lm1100/1350 low/high season, including tax) Rates quoted are for an eight-berth Oceanis Clipper 411 sailing yacht.

S & D Yachts (☎ 2133 1515; www.sdyachts.com; per week from Lm900)

Yellow Fun Watersports (☎ 2373 4366; www .yellowfunwatersports.com) Offers a range of sailing and motor yachts, for day or overnight charters.

If a yacht seems a little too much to handle, sailing dinghies can be rented by the hour at most tourist resorts for around Lm5 an hour.

Swimming

Don't go to Malta expecting miles of sandy beaches – there are only a handful of sandy stretches, and these get very busy. There are a number of rocky bays and coves that offer swimming in crystal-clear waters (take a snorkel along). See p14 for our favourite places to take a dip.

Walking

There is some good walking to be enjoyed on the winding back roads and cliff-top paths of Malta and Gozo, although fences, dogs and bird-shooters can occasionally prove to be a nuisance. Distances are small and you can easily cover much of the islands on foot. A circuit of Gozo is a good objective for a multiday hike.

A great source of information is the **Ramblers' Association of Malta** (www.ramblersmalta.joint comms.com), which organises informal guided country walks for likeminded folk from October to early June (the best time for walking). This organisation is dedicated to safeguarding public access to the Maltese countryside in the face of threats such as hunting and commercial development; read about their campaigns on the comprehensive website.

Windsurfing

Windsurfing is enjoyed year-round in Malta. Equipment hire and instruction are available at the main tourist resorts. Mellieħa Bay, St Paul's Bay and St Thomas Bay are popular venues. A good place for information is the website at www.holidays-malta.com/wind surf.

BUSINESS HOURS

The following indicates the standard opening hours for businesses and services in Malta. In this book we have only listed opening hours where they differ significantly from these broad guidelines.

DIRECTORY

Banks

Banking hours can vary from branch to branch, but they are all generally open 8.30am to 12.30pm Monday to Friday (some banks will stay open until 2pm, or even slightly longer on Friday) and 8.30am to around noon Saturday. The summer hours (from mid-June to September) see branches opening at 8am but with very few banks open into the afternoon.

Museums

The standard opening hours for all Heritage Malta–administered museums and historic sites are now 9am to 5pm daily (last entry is at 4.30pm); these museums are closed on major public holidays. Privately run museums have varying hours.

Pharmacies

Pharmacies are generally open from 9am to 1pm and 4pm to 7pm Monday to Saturday. Duty pharmacists that open late and on Sunday or public holidays are listed in local newspapers.

Restaurants & Cafés

See p53 in the Food & Drink chapter to have an overview of opening hours for eating establishments.

Shops

Shops are generally open between 9am and 1pm, and again between 4pm and 7pm Monday to Saturday. In tourist areas in summer they will often be open all day. Almost all shops are closed on Sunday and public holidays.

CHILDREN
Practicalities

Malta is quite a good destination for a family holiday. As in other Mediterranean countries, children are made welcome almost everywhere, and there is a mountain of activities to keep them busy. Pharmacies are also well stocked with baby products such as formula, bottles, dummies (pacifiers) and nappies (diapers). Most hotels have cots available and safety seats can be arranged through most car-rental companies (though it's best to arrange this in advance to be sure). Large resort hotels have so-called 'animation' programs (ie activities and kids' clubs) that will keep most kids (and their parents) happy and amused.

Many restaurants have highchairs and kids' menus (see p54 for advice on eating out with kids in tow).

Lonely Planet's *Travel with Children* is packed with useful advice for travelling families.

Sights & Activities

Kids might enjoy the Malta Experience and other audiovisual shows and exhibitions in Valletta (p65) and Mdina (p125). An option for older kids (who are not easily frightened) is a visit to the Mdina Dungeons (p125), which are fitted out with spooky sound effects and gory torture scenes.

The whole family can enjoy a boat trip out of Wied iż-Żurrieq (p141), Buġibba (p101), Golden Bay (p115) or Sliema (p87). Some more expensive distractions for older kids include jeep safaris (p87) and horse riding (p168).

The Splash & Fun Park, with its water-slides and playground, is at Baħar iċ-Ċagħaq; and its neighbour, Mediterraneo Marine Park, puts on dolphin and sea-lion shows for the public. You can also swim with the dolphins here. See p98 for details. Popeye Village at Anchor Bay (also known as Sweethaven; p120) is always popular with younger children, even if they've never heard of Popeye.

In summer you can hire snorkelling gear, canoes, dinghies etc at most tourist resorts. Golden Bay and Mellieħa Bay are sandy beaches with safe paddling and swimming for kids.

CLIMATE CHART

For a European destination, Malta has agreeably warm weather year-round, with temperatures rising to uncomfortably hot in July and August. The climate chart below is for Valletta, Malta's capital. For more detailed information on climate and the best times for travel to Malta see p12.

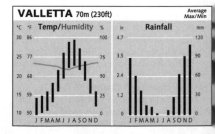

COURSES

Malta is one of the few places where people wanting to learn or improve their English can combine a language course with a Mediterranean holiday. There are around 50 English-language schools in Malta, ranging from one-person operations to the Berlitz Language Centre, and together they cater to around 60,000 students a year from over 50 countries.

Sliema and St Julian's have the greatest concentration of schools, and most can organise accommodation for course participants in homestays, student residences, apartments or hotels.

For details of vacation and business courses, contact:

Federation of English Language Teaching Organisations Malta (FELTOM; www.feltom.com) Works with the Ministry of Education's monitoring board in overseeing professional standards in language schools.

Malta Tourism Authority (www.visitmalta.com) This website has loads of information in various languages and a full list of schools.

National Student Travel Service (NSTS; ☎ 2558 8000; www.nsts.org)

CUSTOMS

Duty-free goods are not sold to those travelling from one EU country to another. If you're entering Malta from outside the EU, the duty-free allowance per person is 1L of spirits, 1L of wine and 200 cigarettes or 100 cigarillos or 50 cigars or 250g of tobacco, 60mL of perfume and 250mL of *eau de toilette*. Duty will be charged on any gifts over Lm50 that are intended for local residents.

DANGERS & ANNOYANCES
Hunting

If you go walking in the countryside, beware of the national obsession with shooting and trapping birds – the little stone shacks that pepper the cliff tops are shooters' hides. You will hear the popping of shotguns before you see the shooters – and they are not at all welcoming. The close season for shooting is from late May to August (the shortest in Europe), but even these dates are routinely ignored by hunters, and the law is poorly enforced. See p42 for more information on this issue.

If you do encounter hunters, the best thing is to greet them and keep walking – certainly don't confront them if you disapprove of their activities (hunters won't take kindly to this, and things could get ugly). By all means express your opinions elsewhere – letters of support to BirdLife Malta (p168), or of disapproval to the local newspapers or government departments can't hurt.

Rip-off Merchants

There are regular complaints in the letters to the editor sections of Maltese newspapers from holiday-makers who have been ripped off in some way, and we've had first-hand experience of this. Beware of locals short-changing those unfamiliar with the currency (although this will likely decrease after the euro is introduced), and anywhere without a written price overcharging non-locals (we've experienced this in restaurants without menus, and from kiosks that do not post their prices).

In the past there have been complaints of taxi drivers ripping off travellers, but the authorities have attempted to remedy this – official taxis were fitted with meters in mid-2006. If you arrive at the airport or port, there are kiosks where you pay the set taxi tariffs up front.

Road Conditions & Driving

Much of the road network in Malta is badly in need of repair, which means that driving is often an uncomfortably bumpy experience. Rules of the road are rarely observed, which adds to the stress of driving in unfamiliar territory, especially during rush hour conditions around Sliema and St Julian's.

There is something of a macho, devil-may-care culture among young male drivers, and the accident rate is correspondingly high. This attitude extends to bus drivers too.

Theft

Malta has a low rate of violent crime, and crimes against visitors are a rarity. Incidents involving pickpockets and purse-snatchers are uncommon, but in past years there have been increasing reports of thieves breaking into cars parked in quiet areas like Marfa and Delimara Point. The only real defence is to lock the car and not leave anything of value in it.

Although Valletta is far safer than most European capitals, it's sensible to exercise a degree of caution, especially in the quieter side streets late at night.

DIRECTORY

DISCOUNT CARDS

Senior Cards

In Malta, people over 60 are entitled to discounted admission to all government-owned museums.

Student & Youth Cards

A valid ISIC card is worth taking along. The **National Student Travel Service** (NSTS; ☎ 2558 8000; www.nsts.org) issues a small booklet listing shops, restaurants, attractions and other establishments in Malta offering discounts of 15% to 40% to ISIC card-holders. Admission to state-run museums is also discounted for students.

EMBASSIES & CONSULATES

Full lists of Maltese embassies abroad and foreign embassies in Malta can be found at www.foreign.gov.mt.

Maltese Embassies & Consulates

Diplomatic representation abroad includes the following:

Australia (☎ 02-6290 1724; 38 Culgoa Circuit, O'Malley ACT 2606)

Canada (☎ 416-207 0922; Clarica Centre, 3300 Bloor St, West Suite 300 – Mezzanine Level, Etobicoke, Ontario M8X 2X2)

France (☎ 01 56 59 75 90; 92 Ave des Champs Elysées, 75008 Paris)

Germany (☎ 030-26 39 110; Klingelhöferstrasse 7, 10785 Berlin)

Ireland (☎ 01-676 2340; 17 Earlsfort Tce, Dublin 2)

Italy (☎ 06-687 99 90; 12 Lungotevere Marzio, 00186 Rome)

Netherlands (☎ 070-356 1252; Scheveningseweg 2, 2517 KT, The Hague)

UK (☎ 020-7292 4800; Malta House, 36-38 Piccadilly, London W1J 0LE)

USA (☎ 202-462 3611/2; 2017 Connecticut Ave NW, Washington, DC 20008)

Embassies & Consulates in Malta

Countries with representation in Malta include the following:

Australia (Map p84; ☎ 2133 8201; Villa Fiorentina, Rampa Ta'Xbiex, Ta'Xbiex)

Canada (Map p58; ☎ 2552 3233; 103 Triq I-Arċisqof, Valletta)

France (Map p58; ☎ 2123 3430; 130 Triq Melita, Valletta)

Germany (Map p86; ☎ 2133 6531; www.valletta.diplo .de; Il-Piazzetta, Entrance B, 1st fl, Triq it-Torri, Sliema)

Italy (Map p73; ☎ 2123 3157/8/9; 1 Triq Vilhena, Floriana)

Netherlands (Map p84; ☎ 2131 3980; www.nether landsembassy.org.mt; Whitehall Mansions, Ix-Xatt Ta'Xbiex, Ta'Xbiex)

UK (Map p84; ☎ 2323 0000; www.britishhigh commission.gov.uk/malta; Whitehall Mansions, Ix-Xatt Ta'Xbiex, Ta'Xbiex)

USA (Map p73; ☎ 2561 4000; http://valletta.us embassy.gov; 3rd fl, Development House, Triq Sant'Anna, Floriana)

FESTIVALS & EVENTS

The festa (feast day) is a hugely important event in Maltese family and village life. During the past 200 years festas have developed from simple village feast days into extravagant five-day spectacles, lasting from Wednesday to Sunday.

Every village has a festa, usually on a Sunday, to celebrate the feast day of its patron saint, and most villages try to outdo each other – the more spectacular (and costly) the show, the 'better' the parish and the stronger the saint will become. The church is decorated with coloured lights, its treasures and relics are cleaned and polished and placed proudly on display, and the village is dressed up with banners, flags and lights.

Most festas are held from May to September. If a festa is held while you're visiting, do yourself a favour and go along to join in the outdoor festivities (the church services themselves will hold little appeal to nonreligious travellers). Tour operators often organise evening trips to a local festa. The timing of church services and events is usually as follows: on the eve of the feast day, vespers and Mass are at 6pm, followed by band club concerts and the main fireworks display at around 10pm; on the Sunday, pontifical High Mass is celebrated at 9am and 7pm, with the evening Mass followed by the procession. This is the climax of the festa, when the life-size statue of the patron saint is paraded through the streets accompanied by brass bands, fireworks, petards and church bells. People then retire to the bars to drink, chat and sample traditional snacks or sweets such as *qubbajt* (nougat) sold from mobile kiosks that make the rounds of the festas.

But festas aren't the only excuse to throw a party in Malta, and the website of the Malta Tourism Authority has a comprehensive list of what's on, where and when (including links to festa dates and locations) – check out www.visitmalta.com/en/whats_on.

Other noteworthy annual events include the following:

FEBRUARY/MARCH

Carnival (www.maltafestivals.com) A week of vibrant celebrations preceding Lent, with a traditional procession of floats, fancy dress and grotesque masks. It's celebrated throughout the islands but the main procession is in Valletta.

EASTER WEEK

Good Friday Pageants are held in several towns and villages. Lifesize statues depicting scenes from the passion and death of Jesus Christ are carried shoulder high in procession along the main streets of the town, accompanied by men and women dressed as biblical characters.

Easter Sunday A day of joy (in contrast to the solemnity of Good Friday). Early in the morning there are processions bearing the statue of the Risen Christ. Particularly interesting are those held at the three harbour towns of Vittoriosa, Senglea and Cospicua, where the statue bearers actually *run* with the statue. It's customary for children to have their *figolla* (an almond-based Easter cake) blessed by the Risen Christ during these processions.

MAY

Fireworks Festival (www.maltafestivals.com) A noisy and colourful festival of fireworks, folk music and entertainment, set against the awesome views of Grand Harbour's bastions. Prime viewing is at Pinto Wharf.

Powerboat Grand Prix (www.powerboatp1.com) Grand Harbour hosts the first grand prix of the annual Powerboat P1 World Championship. It's a spectacular sight against a great backdrop – join the revhead crowds lining the Sliema waterfront for a glimpse.

JUNE

L-Imnarja Harvest festival with an agricultural show and traditional horse races; festivities are centred on and around Rabat (see the boxed text, p131).

JULY

Malta Jazz Festival (www.maltajazzfest.com) An increasingly popular event, with outdoor performances for jazz cats held beneath the bastions of Valletta. Held on the third weekend in July.

Farsons Great Beer Festival (www.farsons.com/beer festival/) Ten days of family fun (despite the adult-oriented name) at Ta'Qali in the centre of the island. Local artists performing, plenty of food options, and a focus on local and international beer.

Malta Arts Festival (www.maltaculture.com) A three-week summer festival from late July into August, incorporating music, dance, theatre and literature performances, as well as art exhibitions, at various venues in and around Valletta.

CHRISTMAS IN MALTA

The festive season is celebrated with style in Malta. The strong Catholic tradition of the islands means that the religious aspect of Christmas is still very strong and the parish church, decorated with colourful lights, is the focus of the festivities. Candlelit carol services are held in the days leading up to Christmas, and midnight Mass on Christmas Eve is the high point of the proceedings.

Every town and village has its crib (called *presepju* in Malti, and often signposted), showing the nativity scene. The tradition of the crib or nativity scene dates back to the 5th or 6th century, as shown by surviving sketches in the catacombs of St Agatha in Rabat (p128). Villages compete to construct the most impressive nativity scenes, complete with motorised mechanical figures, elaborate lighting and even waterfalls. Some travel agents offer guided tours of the best cribs.

The commercial aspect of Christmas is fully celebrated too, with street lights and decorations, window displays, band club concerts and a frenzy of evening shopping in the streets of Valletta in the week before Christmas Day. It's a good time to visit: the weather in December is pleasantly mild and not too wet, the islands are quiet and at their greenest, and red poinsettias – a traditional Christmas sight – brighten many a garden and windowsill.

SEPTEMBER

Malta International Air Show (www.maltairshow .com) Held over a weekend in late September at the Luqa airfield, by the airport. Exhibition of visiting aircraft and aerial displays.

OCTOBER

Historic Cities Festival (www.maltafestivals.com) Ten days of cultural activities including music, dance and pageantry in Malta's main historic cities (Valletta, Vittoriosa and Mdina), culminating in the Malta Military Tattoo (www.maltamilitarytattoo.org).

Rolex Middle Sea Race Offshore sailing classic big with the Royal Malta Yacht Club (p169).

NOVEMBER

Mediterranea (www.mediterranea.com.mt) A 10-day festival of culture on Gozo, celebrating the history, art, crafts, opera and music of the island.

DIRECTORY

FOOD

See the Food & Drink chapter (p51) for details of *fenkata* (communal rabbit dish), *lampuki* (dolphin fish), Kinnie (a soft drink) and other quirks of Maltese cuisine, plus information on what to eat in Malta and where to eat it.

GAY & LESBIAN TRAVELLERS

Homosexual sex was legalised in Malta in 1973, and the age of consent for males and females is 16. Attitudes towards homosexuality in Malta are much the same as in most of southern Europe. Younger people and women are usually more tolerant than older people and straight men – and remember that it's a very Catholic country, and public affection (straight or gay) is generally frowned upon.

Still, although Malta is not a very 'out' destination, it is gay-friendly. Although there are only a handful of gay venues, a few clubs have the occasional gay night. The best way to find out more on the local scene is to visit www.gaymalta.com.

Malta Gay Rights Movement (www.maltagayrights .org) staged its first Gay Pride march in Valletta in July 2004, and has staged one annually since then. Although the march and surrounding festivities are tiny in comparison to the large Euro gatherings, they're a chance for Malta's LGBT community to gather, celebrate diversity and push for an end to discrimination. Check out www.gaymalta.com for more.

HOLIDAYS

Malta observes 14 national public holidays. Few restaurants and sights are open on major holidays (eg Good Friday, Christmas Day, New Year's Day), and buses runs to a limited schedule.

New Year's Day 1 January
St Paul's Shipwreck 10 February
St Joseph's Day 19 March
Good Friday March/April
Freedom Day 31 March
Labour Day 1 May
Commemoration of 1919 independence riots 7 June
Feast of Sts Peter and Paul (L-Imnarja festival) 29 June
Feast of the Assumption 15 August
Victory Day 8 September
Independence Day 21 September
Feast of the Immaculate Conception 8 December
Republic Day 13 December
Christmas Day 25 December

INSURANCE

A travel insurance policy to cover theft, loss and medical problems is a good idea. Worldwide coverage to travellers from over 44 countries is available online at www.lonelyplanet .com/travel_services.

Some policies specifically exclude 'dangerous activities', which can include scuba diving (a popular holiday activity in Malta). If 'risky' activities are on your agenda, as they may well be, you'll need the most comprehensive policy.

You may prefer to have an insurance policy that pays doctors or hospitals directly rather than you having to pay on the spot and claim later. If you have to claim later, make sure you keep all documentation. Some policies ask you to call back (reverse charges) to a centre in your home country, where an immediate assessment of your problem is made. Check that the policy covers ambulances or an emergency flight home.

For details of health insurance see the Health chapter (p192) and for more details on car insurance see the Transport chapter (p189).

INTERNET ACCESS

Malta is a well-wired destination – most hotels and tourism-related organisations have a web page. There are also numerous internet cafés in Malta, while many hotels and cafés have at least one computer available for guest use; a number of establishments (top-end hotels, primarily) now offer wi-fi hotspots – use a wi-fi directory site such as www.jiwire.com to locate these.

Typical charges for internet access are around Lm1 an hour. Many computers belong to the **MelitaNet** (www.melita.net) or **Yellow Blue** (www.yellowblue.net) network of machines for public use – if you purchase a voucher for one network, you receive a password allowing the voucher to be used at any of their computers throughout the country. The websites for

---

THE COMPUTER ICON

Throughout this guide, hotels and other types of accommodation that have a computer that guests can use to access the internet are flagged with a computer icon like this: 🖳 ; those that are wi-fi friendly, but have no computer, are not.

each network list computer locations; major MelitaNet cybercafés (in Paceville, Sliema and Buġibba) also offer good-value rates for overseas telephone calls.

If you're travelling with your laptop, check that it is compatible with the 240V current in Malta; if not you will need a converter. You'll also need a telephone plug adaptor. Having a reputable global modem will prevent access problems that can occur with PC-card modems brought from home. For tips on travelling with a laptop and getting connected, see the business traveller section of www teleadapt.com.

For useful travel websites, see p14.

LEGAL MATTERS

All towns and most villages have their own police station, the smaller ones are manned by a single officer and often marked by a traditional British-style blue lamp.

If you are arrested or detained by the police you have the right to be informed, in a language that you understand, of the reasons for your arrest or detention, and if the police do not release you they must bring you before a court within 48 hours. You also have the right to inform your consulate and to speak to a lawyer.

For an emergency requiring help from the police (*pulizija* in Malti), call ☎ 112. Useful addresses include:

Gozo's main police station (Map p146; ☎ 2156 2040; Triq ir-Repubblika, Victoria)

Malta police headquarters (Map p73; ☎ 2294 2190; Pjazza San Kalcidonju, Floriana)

MAPS

There is a wide selection of maps of the Maltese Islands to choose from. A general one that is good value and hard-wearing is the *Malta FlexiMap* (Lm3) from Insight Maps. It shows Malta and Gozo at 1:50,000 scale, and has street maps of Valletta, Sliema & St Julian's, Buġibba, Mdina and Victoria, with useful town and street indexes. Also laminated, the Berndtson *Malta & Gozo* map (Lm3) is another good option, at 1:45,000 with town plans covering Sliema, Mdina, Victoria, Valletta and Buġibba.

The mAZe by Frans A Attard is a comprehensive street atlas covering every town and village on Malta and Gozo; it costs around Lm6 from bookshops in Malta. Although the text is in English, street names are usually given in Malti only.

> ### ARE YOU OLD ENOUGH?
>
> In Malta the legal drinking age is only 16; you can drive from age 18 and the age of consent (for both heterosexual and homosexual sex) is 16.

MONEY

The Maltese lira, plural liri (Lm) is divided into 100 cents (c). There are 1c, 2c, 5c, 10c, 25c, 50c and Lm1 coins, and Lm2, Lm5, Lm10 and Lm20 notes. When speaking in English, locals often refer to the local currency as the pound, and a £ symbol is also sometimes used. Prices quoted in this book are in lira, unless otherwise stated.

See the inside front cover for a table of exchange rates, or log on to www.oanda.com. The Getting Started chapter has information on costs.

There are convenient ATMs and 24-hour foreign exchange facilities at Malta International Airport, and some ATMs and a bank at Pinto Wharf, next to the Sea Passenger Terminal.

ATMs

There are ATMs at Malta International Airport, Pinto Wharf and in all the main towns in Malta, where you can withdraw Maltese cash using a credit or debit card and PIN. These transactions may incur a 'handling charge' of around 1.5% of the amount withdrawn – check with your bank before departing (and bear in mind that if you're withdrawing from a credit-card account, you'll be paying interest on the cash advance until you pay off your credit card bill).

Cash

Cash can be changed at hotels, banks, exchange bureaus and some tourist shops. There are also 24-hour exchange machines at banks in the main tourist towns, including Valletta, Sliema and Buġibba, where you can feed in foreign banknotes and get Maltese currency back. The euro, British pound and US dollars are widely accepted.

Credit Cards

Visa, MasterCard and Amex credit and charge cards are widely accepted in hotels, restaurants, shops, travel agencies and car-hire agencies.

DIRECTORY

FROM LIRA TO EURO

If things go to plan, €-day for Malta is 1 January 2008. On this date, the country will adopt the euro as its national currency, doing away with the Maltese lira.

To facilitate a smooth changeover, the government has issued guidelines for businesses to follow in the lead-up to €-day. Dual pricing (ie the display of prices in both lira and euro) is mandatory from 1 July 2007 to 30 June 2008 (and voluntary in the first six months of 2007). It should be noted that prior to €-day, the display of prices in euro is for information purposes only – it doesn't indicate that a business will accept payment in euro (although an increasing number of larger businesses will allow this before the official changeover date).

There are still a number of economic criteria the government must fulfil before being permitted to enter the euro zone, and the final go-ahead of the new currency's introduction won't be given until mid-2007. There is a chance that economic indicators (eg high inflation) may force the postponement of €-day to a later date (probably January 2009).

Read more about the changeover at the official government website of the **National Euro Changeover Committee** (www.euro.got.mt).

Taxes & Refunds

VAT (value-added tax) was reintroduced to Malta in 1999, with two rates of tax: accommodation is charged at 5% (and is usually included in the rates quoted) and the rate for other items is 18%. Food, medicine, education, maritime services, air, sea and public transport are exempt from VAT.

Visitors to Malta can reclaim VAT provided they satisfy certain regulations. Repayment of VAT applies only to purchased goods valued at not less than Lm25 and bought from a single registered outlet, as shown on the receipt, and when the total value of the items is not under Lm100. If you wish to get a VAT refund, you should fill out an application form, available at the custom exit points at the airport or sea port. The next steps on how to obtain your refund are provided on the form and at the customs offices at the airport and sea port.

Tipping & Bargaining

Tipping etiquette is like mainland Europe's (ie tipping is not expected, but appreciated). In restaurants where no service charge is included in the bill, leave 10% for good service. Baggage porters should get about Lm0.15 per piece of luggage, car park attendants Lm0.20 to Lm0.50. Taxi drivers don't expect a tip, but it's nice to round up a fare in order to leave a small tip (up to 10%) if warranted.

Bargaining for handicrafts at stalls or markets is essential, but most shops have fixed prices. Hotels and car-hire agencies often bargain in the off season between October and mid-June – stays/rentals of a week or more will often get a 10% discount.

Travellers Cheques

The main brands of travellers cheques can be easily exchanged at hotels, banks and bureaus de change. You'll find that pounds sterling, euro and US dollars are the favoured denominations. Banks give better rates than hotels, but they often levy a charge of Lm0.20 to Lm0.25 per transaction.

PHOTOGRAPHY & VIDEO

Film, camcorder cassettes and camera equipment are easily obtained at dozens of photographic shops in all the main towns in Malta. Print film is also available from souvenir shops and hotels in the main tourist areas.

For the best results in your travel photos, shoot your pictures early and late in the day with dusk and dawn sun – before 10am and after 4pm. The blazing sun of a Maltese summer will give a flat and washed-out look to pics taken in the middle of the day. If you want to capture that 'tropical turquoise' look of the water in Comino's Blue Lagoon, you will need to use a polarising filter.

For tips on taking the perfect holiday snaps, look out for Lonely Planet's *Travel Photography* book.

POST

Malta Post (www.maltapost.com) operates a reliable postal service. Post office branches are found in most towns and villages (in some towns the local newsagent/souvenir shop acts as a branch agent).

Local postage costs Lm0.08; a 20g letter or postcard sent airmail to the UK or Europe costs Lm0.16, to the USA Lm0.22 and to Australia Lm0.27. Stamps are frequently available from hotels and souvenir shops as well as from post offices.

SHOPPING

Traditional handicrafts include lace, silver filigree, blown glass and pottery, and are available throughout the country. Hand-knitted clothing is produced in the villages and can be quite cheap, but remember to shop around before you make a purchase – the Malta Crafts Centre in Valletta (p71) or the Ta'Qali Crafts Village (p129) are good places to start. The best bargains (and often the most authentic pieces) are to be found on Gozo; inside Il-Kastell are a few options for purchasing handmade lace. Also check out the Ta'Dbieġi Crafts Village (p156) near Għarb. Note that bargaining for handicrafts at stalls or markets is essential, but most shops have fixed prices.

Valletta and Sliema are where local fashionistas go shopping. Here you'll find UK high-street labels, Italian footwear and a few unique boutiques.

SOLO TRAVELLERS

Solo travellers are not terribly common in Malta. Most people travel here on short-term summer package holidays with partners/family/friends, or make an annual pilgrimage from northern Europe for winter sun and meet up with people doing the same (at this time of year the average age of visitors to Malta increases significantly!).

Obviously many solo students head here to study English, but they invariably socialise with fellow students. If you are a solo traveller and looking for company, try staying at the University Residence (p134) in Lija or Hibernia Residence & Hostel (p88) in Sliema.

Still, there is no real stigma attached to lone travellers. Many guesthouses rent rooms at a set rate per person and do not charge a single room supplement. Others may charge a supplement of 50% of the per-person rate. Five-star hotels usually have a set rate per room and it doesn't matter whether there's one or two people staying in it – the rate remains the same. You may feel a little conspicuous dining solo in restaurants, surrounded by large groups of locals or travellers, but the service you receive shouldn't be affected.

Solo female travellers should refer to the tips for Women Travellers (p179).

TELEPHONE
Mobile Phones

More than 80% of Malta's population has a mobile phone, and mobile-phone numbers begin with either 79 or 99. Malta uses the GSM900 mobile phone network which is compatible with the rest of Europe, Australia and New Zealand, but not with the USA and Canada's GSM1900. If you have a GSM phone, check with your service provider about using it in Malta and beware of calls being routed internationally (expensive for a 'local' call).

You may consider bringing your mobile phone from your home country and buying a Maltese SIM card, which gives you a Maltese mobile number. (Your mobile may be locked-in to the local network in your home country, so ask your home network for advice before going abroad.) There are two mobile phone companies in Malta: **Vodafone** (www.vodafone.com.mt) and **Go Mobile** (www.go.com.mt) offer local SIM cards for Lm5, plus prepaid vouchers for a minimum of Lm5 worth of calls. Prepaid vouchers for topping up credit are available at many stores and kiosks throughout Malta. Both Vodafone and Go Mobile have stores inside the Embassy Complex on Triq Santa Luċija in Valletta, and Go Mobile also has an outlet in the arrivals hall at the airport to help new arrivals get connected to the Maltese network.

You can rent a mobile phone from **Telecom Electronics** (☎ 2137 6050; www.telecom.com.mt; Naxxar Rd, San Ġwann; rental 1 day/1 week/2 weeks Lm5/23/38, plus a refundable deposit) Phone delivery and pick-up can be arranged.

Phone Codes

The international direct dialling code is ☎ 00. To call Malta from abroad, dial the international access code, ☎ 356 (the country code for Malta) and the number.

There are no area codes in Malta. In late 2001 Malta moved from six-digit local phone numbers to eight-digit numbers.

Public Phones & Phonecards

Public telephones are widely available, and most are card-operated (there are also coin-operated phones, but these are not as common). There are over 1500 public cardphones installed in various localities – including public outdoor areas and indoor premises such as the airport, hospitals and restaurants. You can

DIRECTORY

buy phonecards at many kiosks, post offices and souvenir shops. Telecards are available in denominations of Lm2, Lm3, Lm4 and Lm5. Easyline cards can be used from any line (including payphones and mobiles, even from hotels) and can be used in a range of overseas destinations. They are available in denominations of Lm2, Lm5, Lm6, Lm10 and Lm15.

Local calls from public phones cost Lm0.10 to landlines (minimum Lm0.25 to mobiles).

International calls are discounted by around 20% between 8pm and midnight Monday to Friday, all day Saturday and Sunday (offpeak rate), and by up to 36% between midnight and 8am (night rate) every day.

TIME

Malta is in the same time zone as most of Western Europe (one hour ahead of the UK). The country is two hours ahead of GMT/UTC from the last Sunday in March to the last Sunday in October (the daylight saving period) and one hour ahead for the rest of the year. For more on international timing and to work out when it is best to phone home, see the map of world time zones on p206.

TOILETS

Malta is well-equipped with public toilets, often at the entrance to a public garden or near the village square. They are usually (but not always) clean and in good order, but it's a good idea to have a small packet of tissues stashed in your handbag or daypack as public toilets are often short of loo paper.

If there is an attendant, it is good manners to leave a tip of a few cents in a dish by the door.

TOURIST INFORMATION
Local Tourist Offices

The head office of the **Malta Tourism Authority** (☎ 2291 5000; www.visitmalta.com; Auberge d'Italie, Triq il-Merkanti, Valletta) is for postal and telephone inquiries only. Your best source of information is the comprehensive website, with directories, interactive maps and loads of holiday and practical information.

There are local tourist information offices at Valletta and Malta International Airport (for their contact details and opening hours see p57), St Julian's (p85), and Victoria on Gozo (p146).

Tourist Offices Abroad

The **Malta Tourism Authority** (www.visitmalta.com) has overseas representation that can help with inquiries from potential holidaymakers (information on the official website is available in 10 languages). Contact the following:

Australia (☎ 02-9321 9154; office.au@visitmalta.com; World Aviation Systems, 403 George St, Sydney NSW 2000)
France (☎ 01 48 00 03 79; info@visitmalte.com; Office du Tourisme de Malte, 9 Cité Trévise, 75009 Paris)
Germany (☎ 069-285890; info@urlaubmalta.com; Fremdenverkehrsamt Malta, Schillerstrasse 30-40, D-60313 Frankfurt-am-Main)
Ireland (☎ 01-678 1460; info@plunkettcommunications.com; Plunkett Communications, 16 Morehampton Rd, Dublin 4)
Italy (☎ 011-66 87 550; info@adam.it; Ente per il Turismo di Malta, Corso Marconi, 33-10125 Torino)
Netherlands (☎ 020-6207 223; info@malta.nl; Verkeersbureau Malta, Leliegracht 20, 1015 Dg Amsterdam)
UK (☎ 020-8877 6990; office.uk@visitmalta.com; Malta Tourist Office, Unit C, Park House, 14 Northfields, London SW18 1DD)
USA (☎ 973-884-0899; office.us@visitmalta.com; Malta Tourist Office, 300 Lanidex Plaza, Parsippany, New Jersey NJ 07054)

TRAVELLERS WITH DISABILITIES

Maltese government policy is to improve access for people with disabilities, but many of Malta's historic places – notably the steep, stepped streets of Valletta – remain difficult, if not impossible, to negotiate in a wheelchair or for those with restricted mobility. Several sites are accessible, however, including the Malta Experience and the Museum of Archaeology in Valletta. A good number of the more expensive hotels have wheelchair access and some have rooms specially designed for disabled guests.

The **Malta Tourism Authority** (www.visitmalta.com) can provide information on hotels and sights that are equipped for wheelchair users; its website uses a wheelchair icon to indicate whether a venue has easy access or facilities for the disabled.

The **National Commission for Persons with Disabilities** (☎ 2148 7789; www.knpd.org; Centru Hidma Soċjali, Triq Braille, Santa Venera) can provide information on facilities and access for disabled travellers in Malta.

VISAS

When Malta joined the EU in 2004, the country opened to all EU nationals for study or residence purposes, but movement for work purposes may still face restrictions. It's worth contacting the Maltese embassy or consulate in your home country for more information.

Visas are not needed for visits of up to three months by nationals of most Commonwealth countries (including UK, Australia, New Zealand, Canada, but excluding South Africa, India and Pakistan), most non-EU European countries (excluding Russia), the USA and Japan. The complete list of countries whose nationals don't need a visa is online at the website of the **Ministry of Foreign Affairs of Malta** (www.foreign.gov.mt). Other nationalities must apply to the Maltese embassy, high commission or consulate in their country, or directly to the immigration police in Malta if there is no official Maltese representation. Application forms are on the ministry's website.

If you wish to stay for more than three months you should apply for an extension at the **immigration office** (Map p73; ☎ 2122 4001; sb.police@gov.mt; Pjazza Vicenzo Buġeja, Floriana) in the police headquarters in Floriana before your three months are up. You will need four recent passport photographs and proof that you have enough money to support yourself and not be a burden on the state. Extensions are usually granted without a problem. Applications for temporary residence should also be made at police headquarters.

Visit Lonely Planet's website at www .lonelyplanet.com for links to up-to-date visa information.

WOMEN TRAVELLERS

Malta remains a conservative society by Western standards, and women are still expected to be wives and mothers; however, an increasing number of women are now joining the workforce. Young males have adopted the Mediterranean macho style, but they are not usually aggressive.

Malta presents no unusual dangers for women travelling alone. Normal caution should be observed, but the chance of being the victim of crime in Malta is quite low. If you are alone, Paceville – the nightclub zone at St Julian's – is hectic and sometimes testosterone-fuelled (especially on weekends) but not particularly unsafe.

Transport

CONTENTS

GETTING THERE & AWAY

ENTERING THE COUNTRY
Passport

Citizens of EU member states can travel to Malta with their national identity cards. Travellers from countries that don't issue ID cards, such as the UK, must carry a valid passport. All non-EU nationals must have a full valid passport. See p179, for visa requirements.

AIR

Malta is well connected to Europe and North Africa, with daily direct flights to/from Amsterdam, Brussels, Catania (Sicily), London (Gatwick, Heathrow and Luton), Manchester, Milan, Munich, Paris, Rome and Tripoli (Libya); and at least two direct services weekly to/from Athens, Berlin, Birmingham, Budapest, Cairo, Dubai, Dublin, Düsseldorf, Frankfurt, Glasgow, Hamburg, Istanbul, Larnaca (Cyprus), Lisbon, London (Stansted), Lyon, Madrid, Marseille, Moscow, Oslo, Prague, Stockholm, Tunis, Vienna and Zürich.

There are no direct flights into Malta from places further afield. If you're flying from elsewhere, it's best to get to Dubai (from Asia, Australia and New Zealand) or a major European city such as Rome, London, Paris or Frankfurt, then join a direct connecting flight to Malta.

> **THINGS CHANGE...**
>
> The information in this chapter is particularly vulnerable to change. Check directly with the airline or a travel agent to make sure you understand how a fare (and ticket you may buy) works, and be aware of the security requirements for international travel. Shop carefully. The details given in this chapter should be regarded as pointers and are not a substitute for your own careful, up-to-date research.

Airports & Airlines

All flights arrive and depart from **Malta International Airport** (MLA; ☎ 2124 9600; www.maltairport .com) at Luqa, 8km south of Valletta. The airport has good facilities, including ATMs and currency exchange, internet access, a tourist office (open daily), left luggage, and a regular, inexpensive bus service to and from Valletta (see p71).

Gozo has a **heliport** (GZM; ☎ 2156 1301) with a helicopter link (see p185) to Luqa.

The Maltese national airline is **Air Malta** (code KM; ☎ 2166 2211; www.airmalta.com), a small airline with a good safety record. It has a number of overseas sales agents (see the website for details).

AIRLINES FLYING TO & FROM MALTA

Alitalia (code AZ; ☎ 2123 7115; www.alitalia.com) Hub Rome.

British Airways (code BA; ☎ 2124 2233; www.ba.com) Hub London.

BritishJet (code BJC; ☎ 2157 9350; www.britishjet .com) Low-cost airline operating between Malta and various British regional airports.

Egyptair (code MS; ☎ 2132 2256; www.egyptair.com .eg) Hub Cairo.

Emirates (code EK; ☎ 2557 7255; www.emirates.com) Hub Dubai.

Germanwings (code 4U; ☎ UK +44 870-252 1250; www.germanwings.com) Hub Cologne/Bonn. Low-cost German carrier beginning flights to/from Malta in 2007.

JAT Yugoslav Airlines (code JU; ☎ 2133 2814; www .jat.com) Hub Belgrade.

KLM Royal Dutch Airlines (code KL; ☎ 2133 1010; www.klm.com) Hub Amsterdam.

Libyan Arab Airlines (code LN; ☎ 2122 2735) Hub Tripoli.
Lufthansa (code LH; ☎ 2125 2020; www.lufthansa .com) Hub Frankfurt.
Ryanair (code FR; ☎ Ireland +353 1 249 7791; www .ryanair.com) Various hub cities.
Swiss International Air Lines (code LX; ☎ 2180 2777; www.swiss.com) Hub Geneva/Zürich.
Tuninter (code UG; ☎ 2132 0732) Hub Tunis.

Tickets

High season in Malta is June to September and ticket prices are at their highest during this period. A month or two either side is the shoulder season (April, May, October), while low season is November to March. Holidays such as Christmas and Easter also see a jump in prices. Check the 'special fares' section of the Air Malta website to see if there any good deals going for the period you are travelling.

Calling around, checking internet sites, comparing the airline and travel agent prices, and scouring major newspapers' travel sections can result in significant savings on your air ticket. Start early – some of the cheapest tickets have to be bought well in advance.

Well-known travel agents are listed later in this chapter under individual country headings. Good online agencies for cheap tickets:

Cheap Tickets (www.cheaptickets.com)
Ebookers (www.ebookers.com)
Expedia (www.expedia.com)
Last Minute (www.lastminute.com)
Priceline (www.priceline.com)
Travel Cuts (www.travelcuts.com)
Travelocity UK (www.travelocity.co.uk); US (www .travelocity.com); Asia-Pacific (www.zuji.com.au)

Asia

Bangkok, Singapore and Hong Kong are the best places to shop around for discount tickets. **STA Travel** (www.statravel.com/worldwide .htm) has offices in Hong Kong, Singapore, Japan, China, Malaysia, Taiwan and Thailand. Major Asian airlines (eg Thai Airways and Singapore Air) serve most of Western Europe, and also connect with Australia and New Zealand. Similarly, discounted fares can be picked up from Qantas, which usually transits in Kuala Lumpur, Bangkok or Singapore.

Australia & New Zealand

For flights from Australia and New Zealand to Europe there are a number of competing airlines and a variety of fares. It can sometimes work out cheaper to purchase a round-the-world ticket than to do a U-turn on a return ticket.

CLIMATE CHANGE & TRAVEL

Climate change is a serious threat to the ecosystems that humans rely upon, and air travel is the fastest-growing contributor to the problem. Lonely Planet regards travel, overall, as a global benefit, but believes we all have a responsibility to limit our personal impact on global warming.

Flying & Climate Change

Pretty much every form of motorised travel generates CO_2 (the main cause of human-induced climate change) but planes are far and away the worst offenders, not just because of the sheer distances they allow us to travel, but because they release greenhouse gases high into the atmosphere. The statistics are frightening: two people taking a return flight between Europe and the US will contribute as much to climate change as an average household's gas and electricity consumption over a whole year.

Carbon Offset Schemes

Climatecare.org and other websites use 'carbon calculators' that allow travellers to offset the level of greenhouse gases they are responsible for with financial contributions to sustainable travel schemes that reduce global warming – including projects in India, Honduras, Kazakhstan and Uganda.

Lonely Planet, together with Rough Guides and other concerned partners in the travel industry, support the carbon offset scheme run by climatecare.org. Lonely Planet offsets all of its staff and author travel.

For more information check out our website: www.lonelyplanet.com

Cheap flights from Australia/New Zealand to Europe generally go via Southeast Asian capitals, involving stopovers at Kuala Lumpur, Bangkok or Singapore. Some flights go via the Middle East, so another option might be to fly to Dubai and then direct to Malta with Emirates. Roughly speaking, a return ticket to Europe will set you back A$2000/2400 from Australia in the low/high season.

Some travel agents, particularly small ones, advertise cheap air fares in travel sections of weekend newspapers, such as the *Age* in Melbourne and the *Sydney Morning Herald*. The *New Zealand Herald* has a travel section where travel agents advertise fares. Book online at www.travel.com.au and www.travel.co.nz.

Two well-known agents for cheap fares are STA Travel and Flight Centre, with branches throughout Australia and New Zealand. Contact details are:

Flight Centre Australia (☎ 133 133; www.flightcentre .com.au); New Zealand (☎ 0800 243 544; www.flight centre.co.nz)

STA Travel (Australia ☎ 1300 733 035; www.statravel .com.au; New Zealand ☎ 0800 474 400; www.statravel .co.nz)

Canada

Travel Cuts (☎ 1-866-246-9762; www.travelcuts.com) is Canada's national student travel agency. For online bookings try www.expedia.ca and www.travelocity.ca.

Both Alitalia and Air Canada have direct flights from Toronto and Montreal to Rome, where you can connect with flights to Malta. Roughly speaking, expect to pay C$1100/2000 for a return ticket to Rome from the Canadian east coast in the low/high season, and C$1400/2200 from the west coast.

Continental Europe

Malta is well connected by air to many European cities.

DENMARK

Kilroy Travels (☎ 70 80 80 15; www.kilroytravels.com; Skindergade 28, Copenhagen)
STA Travel (☎ 33 14 15 01; www.statravel.dk; Fiol-straede 18, Copenhagen)

FRANCE

Nouvelles Frontières (☎ 0825 000 747; www .nouvelles-frontieres.fr)
Voyageurs du Monde (☎ 01 40 15 11 15; www.vdm .com)

GERMANY

STA Travel (☎ 030-310 0040; www.statravel.de; Hardenbergstrasse 9, Berlin)

ITALY

CTS Viaggi (☎ 06 462 043 116; www.cts.it; Via Genova, Rome)

THE NETHERLANDS

ISSTA (☎ 020-618 80 31; 226 Overtoom Straat, Amsterdam)
Kilroy Travels (☎ 020-524 51 00; www.kilroytravels .com; Singel 413, Amsterdam)

NORWAY

Kilroy Travels (☎ 81 55 96 33; www.kilroytravels.com; Nedre Slottsgate 23, Oslo)
STA Travel (☎ 81 55 99 05; www.statravel.no; Karl Johansgate 8, Oslo)

SWEDEN

Kilroy Travels (☎ 0771-545769; www.kilroytravels .com; Kungsgatan 4, Stockholm)
STA Travel (☎ 0771-611010; www.statravel.se; Kungs-gatan 30, Stockholm)

SWITZERLAND

STA Travel (☎ 022-818 02 00; www.statravel.ch; rue de Rive 10, Geneva)

The Middle East

Emirates has around five flights a week between Dubai and Malta, with connections to/from destinations in Australia, India, Asia and other parts of the Middle East. Air Malta flies twice a week between Malta and Istanbul.

Recommended agencies in the region include:

Al-Rais Travels (www.alrais.com) In Dubai.
Israel Student Travel Association (ISTA; ☎ 02-625 7257) In Jerusalem.
Orion-Tour (☎ 212-232 6300; www.oriontour.com) In Istanbul.

North Africa

There are frequent flights between Malta and various North African cities, including Cairo, Tripoli, Tunis and Casablanca. One recommended travel agency in the area is **Egypt Panorama Tours** (☎ 2-359 0200; www.eptours .com) in Cairo.

The UK & Ireland

Roughly speaking, a return fare to Malta will cost you UK£160/320 in the low/high season from the UK, and there are some good winter prices (around UK£120) if you're prepared to shop around. Charter flights are usually much cheaper than scheduled flights, especially if you don't qualify for the under-26 and student discounts. You could also check out websites like www.bargain holidays.com (with scheduled and charter flights, plus package holiday offers) or www .lastminute.co.uk.

From October 2006, low-cost carrier Ryan air plans to fly daily between London, Luton and Malta; and from February 2007 the airline will fly three times a week between Malta and Dublin.

Look for special deals in the travel pages of the weekend broadsheet newspapers, as well as in *Time Out*, the *Evening Standard* and the free magazine *TNT*.

Recommended travel agencies and online ticket sites include the following:

Cheap Flights (www.cheapflights.co.uk)
Cheapest Flights (☎ 0870-428 6204; www.cheap estflights.co.uk)
Ebookers (☎ 0800-082 3000; www.ebookers.com)
Flight Centre (☎ 0870-499 0040; www.flightcentre .co.uk)
Online Travel (☎ 0870-887 0100; www.onlinetravel .com)
Quest Travel (☎ 0871-423 0135; www.questtravel .com)
STA Travel (☎ 0870-163 0026; www.statravel.co.uk)
Trailfinders (☎ 0845-058 5858; www.trailfinders.co.uk)
Travel Bag (☎ 0800-082 5000; www.travelbag.co.uk)
Usit (☎ Ireland 01-602 1904; www.usit.ie)

The USA

There are no direct scheduled flights from the USA to Malta. The best option is to fly into a busy European hub, such as London, Frankfurt, Paris or Rome, and catch a connecting flight from there to Malta. Flight options across the North Atlantic, the world's busiest long-haul air corridor, can be bewildering and fares can vary wildly in price. For example, a return flight to a major European city like Rome will cost you US$500/1000 in the low/high season.

The following agencies are recommended for online bookings:

Cheap Tickets (www.cheaptickets.com)
Expedia (www.expedia.com)
Lowest Fare (www.lowestfare.com)
STA Travel (☎ 1800-781-4040; www.sta.com)
Travelocity (www.travelocity.com)

LAND
Bus

You can travel by bus from most parts of Europe to a port in Italy and catch a ferry from there to Malta. **Eurolines** (www.eurolines.com) is a consortium of coach companies that operates across Europe with offices in all major European cities. Bear in mind that a discounted air fare will probably work out cheaper than the long bus trip once you allow for food and drink to be bought en route.

As the saying goes, all roads lead to Rome; from there you will have to continue to Malta by bus or train to one of the ferry ports in southern Italy or Sicily (see p184).

Car & Motorcycle

With your own vehicle, you can drive to southern Italy and take a car ferry from Salerno, Pozzallo or Catania (Sicily) to Malta (see p184). From northern Europe the fastest road route is via the Simplon Pass to Milan, from which Italy's main highway, the Autostrada del Sole, stretches all the way to Reggio di Calabria. From London the distance is around 2200km.

Car drivers and motorbike riders will need the vehicle's registration papers, a Green Card, a nationality plate and their domestic licence. Contact your local automobile association for details about necessary documentation.

Train

Rail travel from major European cities to southern Italy and Sicily is convenient and comfortable, but if Malta is your only destination then you may want to rethink your plans, as the train will prove considerably more expensive than a discounted flight. For the latest fare information on journeys to Italy from the UK, contact the **Rail Europe Travel Centre** (☎ 0870-837 1371; www.raileurope.co.uk). Another source of rail information for all of Europe is **Rail Choice** (www.railchoice.com).

If you're touring Europe on a Eurail or Inter Rail Pass, you can take the train to Reggio di Calabria or Catania to catch a ferry to Malta.

SEA
Departure Tax

All passengers leaving Malta by sea are required to pay a Lm11 departure tax, which should be added by the travel agent when you buy your ticket. Maltese nationals and foreigners residing in Malta also pay an incredibly steep 'travel levy' of Lm21.

TRANSPORT

Ferry

Malta has regular sea links with Sicily (Pozzallo and Catania), southern Italy (Salerno) and northern Italy (Genoa). You can also sail from Tunis to Malta (but not, strangely, from Malta direct to Tunis). Ferries dock at the Sea Passenger Terminal beside Pinto Wharf in Floriana, underneath the southeast bastions of Valletta.

Virtu Ferries (www.virtuferries.com) Malta (☎ 2122 8777); Catania (☎ 095-535 711); Pozzallo (☎ 0932-954 062) offers the shortest, fastest Malta–Sicily crossing with its catamaran service (carrying cars and passengers) to/from Pozzallo and Catania. In the past, Virtu has operated a service between Malta and Reggio di Calabria, but at the time of research this wasn't operating. The company also operates day excursions to Sicily (see p191).

The Pozzallo–Malta crossing takes a mere 90 minutes and operates year-round (seven times a week in June, up to 10 times a week in July and August, dropping to three times a week from November to April, weather permitting). The high-season fares are as follows:

From Pozzallo

passenger	one way/return	€81/99
car	one way/return	€110/140
motorcycle	one way/return	€60/75

From Malta

passenger	one way/return	Lm26/35
car	one way/return	Lm35/41
motorcycle	one way/return	Lm17/25

The Catania–Malta crossing takes three hours and operates from March to October (five times a week in August, down to once a week in March). Fares are:

From Catania

passenger	one way/return	€81/99
car	one way/return	€130/155
motorcycle	one way/return	€85/110

From Malta

passenger	one way/return	Lm26/35
car	one way/return	Lm40/59
motorcycle	one way/return	Lm25/31

Departure taxes are not included in the prices listed above, nor are fuel surcharges (add Lm2 each way from Malta, €4 from Sicily, subject to change). Children under four travel free of charge; children aged four to 15 pay 50% of the adult fares. Bikes travel free. If you're travelling from Malta to Sicily, when booking ask about transfers from your accommodation to the ferry terminal by Pinto Wharf – it's worth paying the extra charge (Lm3 per person) as there is no public transport to the wharf, and taxis can prove expensive.

Ma-Re-Si Shipping (☎ 2123 3127; www.ma-re-si.com) has a ro-ro (roll-on/roll-off) car ferry operating three overnight return trips weekly between Catania and Malta (12 hours). The service operates year-round; cabins are available (one way/return from Lm30/45 per cabin, not per person). Prices (excluding taxes) are as follows:

From Catania

passenger	one way/return	€55/90
car	one way/return	€95/145
motorcycle	one way/return	€35/65
bicycle	one way/return	€18/35

From Malta

passenger	one way/return	Lm20/35
car	one way/return	Lm35/55
motorcycle	one way/return	Lm12/24
bicycle	one way/return	Lm6/12

SMS Travel & Tourism (Map pp58-9 ☎ 2123 2211; www.smstravel.net; 311 Triq ir-Repubblika, Valletta) is the local agent for Virtu and Ma-Re-Si services.

Grimaldi Ferries (☎ 2122 6873; www.grimaldi-ferries.com) operates a weekly service year-round from Salerno, south of Naples, calling in at Tunis en route to Malta (ie Salerno–Tunis–Malta–Salerno). There is no direct service from Malta to Tunis; travellers must sail to Salerno and wait for a service to Tunis. From Salerno, it is possible to sail on to Valencia in southern Spain. The Maltese agent for this service is **Sullivan Maritime** (☎ 2122 6873; 21/22 Triq Santa Barbara, Valletta).

Grandi Navi Veloci (☎ 2569 1600; www.gnv.it) has a similar weekly Genoa–Tunis–Malta–Genoa service. Again, you can sail directly from Tunis to Malta, but there is no service from Malta to Tunis. The local agent is **Gollcher & Sons** (☎ 2569 1604; 19 Triq San Zakkarija, Valletta).

Ferry schedules tend to change from year to year, and it is best to confirm the information given here, either with the ferry company or with a travel agent.

Travellers should be aware that the Malta–Sicily catamarans do not have exchange facilities and there are none available at the Sea Passenger Terminal. Pinto Wharf, a short walk from the terminal, has a Bank of Valletta with an ATM and an **exchange bureau** (☑ 8.30am-10pm) open long hours.

At the time of research, public transport links with the ferry terminal in Floriana were poor. With luggage, you'll probably need to catch a taxi to your destination. Set fees are established – head to the information booth at Pinto Wharf (to Valletta is Lm4, to Sliema/St Julian's is Lm7). To reach Valletta with a lighter load, you could try the following: take bus 98 from the eastern end of Pinto Wharf to Valletta's City Gate (runs hourly, Lm0.15); climb up the steep hill opposite Pinto Wharf (It-Telgha Tal-Kurcifiss) and keep an eye out for the set of stairs that will take you up to the war memorial, close to City Gate; or follow the waterfront northeast, under the Lascaris Bastion, then veer left and climb the steps up at Victoria Gate.

Yacht

Malta's excellent harbour and its strategic location at the hub of the Mediterranean has led to its development as a major yachting centre. There are berths for 700 yachts (up to 18m length overall) in Msida Marina near Valletta; and Mgarr Marina on Gozo has space for over 200 boats. There are also two upmarket marinas – at the **Portomaso complex** (www.portomaso marina.com) in St Julian's, and the **Grand Harbour Marina** (www.ghm.com.mt) in Vittoriosa.

For more information on these marinas and details of the logistics and formalities of sailing to Malta, contact the **Malta Maritime Authority** (MMA; ☎ 2133 2800; www.mma.gov.mt; Yachting Centre Directorate, Ta'Xbiex Seafront, Ta'Xbiex).

Malta's popularity with the yachting fraternity means that it is possible to make your way there as unpaid crew. Yachts tend to leave Gibraltar, southern Spain and the Balearics in April and May to head towards the popular cruising grounds of the Greek Islands and the Turkish coast. It's possible to just turn up at a marina and ask if there are any yachts looking for crew, but there are also agencies that bring together yacht owners and prospective

crew (for a fee). Check out one such agency, UK-based **Crewseekers** (☎ 01489-578 319; www .crewseekers.co.uk), which charges £60/85 for a six-/12-month membership.

TOURS

There are dozens of tour operators in the UK, Europe and North America that offer package holidays and organised tours to Malta. Package holidays, which include flights and accommodation, can offer some real bargains, particularly in winter – Malta is a year-round charter destination.

There are also many tour operators catering to a wide range of special interest groups, including walking, diving, history, archaeology, architecture and religion, and others offering holidays designed for senior travellers. The comprehensive website of the **Malta Tourism Authority** (www.visitmalta.com) allows you to search for tour operators based on country and speciality. Click on 'Getting Here', then 'Tour Operators'.

GETTING AROUND

AIR

Malta's only internal air service is the regular **helicopter link** (☎ 2156 1301; www.airgozo.com) between Malta International Airport and the heliport on Gozo at Xewkija. The flight takes only 15 minutes and services operate year-round, with between four and seven flights daily in both directions. The regular adult fare is Lm30/50 one way/return. Children, students and senior citizens (aged 61 and over) receive generous discounts on the regular fare. There's a baggage allowance of 20kg.

Reservations should be made at least 48 hours in advance through the website, Air Malta offices or any IATA travel agent. Check-in time is 45 minutes before departure, or 1¼ hours if you are flying from Gozo to connect with an international flight at Malta.

BICYCLE

Malta is not a good option for a cycling holiday. Cycling on Maltese roads can be nerve-racking – the roads are often narrow and potholed, and drivers show little consideration for cyclists. Things are considerably better on Gozo – the roads are still rough, but there's far less traffic.

TRANSPORT

You can rent bikes for around Lm2 per day from **Magri Cycles & Spares** (☎ 2141 4399; 135 Triq il-Kungress Ewkaristiku, Mosta) and **Victoria Garage** (Map p146; ☎ 2155 6414; Triq Putirjal, Victoria, Gozo).

BUS

There is an extensive network of buses in Malta (over 500 buses and around 85,000 passengers daily). Almost all bus routes on Malta originate from the chaotic City Gate bus terminus (Map p188) in Valletta and radiate to all parts of the island, which makes certain cross-country journeys (eg Marsaxlokk to Marsaskala) a bit inconvenient, as you have to travel via Valletta. There are also a few direct services enabling tourists based in Sliema and Buġibba to do day trips to major sightseeing destinations (eg from Sliema, St Julian's and Buġibba to Marsaxlokk, Ċirkewwa for the Gozo ferry, Mdina or the northern beaches of Golden Bay and Għajn Tuffieħa) that do not go through Valletta. In towns and villages the bus terminus is usually found on or near the parish church square.

Services generally run from around 5.30am to 11pm, and fares range from Lm0.20 to Lm0.50 one way, depending on route and distance. Late-night buses (operating after 11pm till about 1.30am) cost Lm0.50 and link the nightlife area of Paceville with Sliema, Valletta and Buġibba. Pay the driver when you get on for your ticket; hold on to this for the duration of the journey, as you may need to present it to an inspector. Have small change available for your ticket purchase – the driver is unlikely to give change of more than Lm1.

BIG YELLOW BUSES

Malta's buses are a tourist attraction in themselves. Many of them are classic Bedfords, Thames, Leylands and AECs dating from the 1950s, '60s and '70s, brightly painted in a livery of yellow, white and orange; the Gozo buses have a more restrained colour scheme of grey, white and red. Although the old buses are undeniably picturesque, the downside is that they can also be noisy and uncomfortable, with clattering diesel engines and creaky-squeaky suspension that can rattle the fillings out of your teeth. *The Malta Buses* by Michael Cassar and Joseph Bonnici is an illustrated history of the island's celebrated public transport.

The buses display their route numbers, but not their destinations, in the windscreen. You can find details of routes and fares at the booths of the **Public Transport Association** (PTA; ☎ 2125 0007/8; www.atp.com.mt) at City Gate bus terminus, or online. A free map of route, schedule and fare information is available on most buses, from bus terminals and from tourist information offices. Routes of interest to travellers are shown on the Main Bus Routes map (Map opposite).

On Gozo, all the bus routes except the bus 25 Victoria–Mġarr service are circular, starting and finishing at the Victoria Bus Terminal, off Triq Putirjal. The flat fare is Lm0.20. Services are less frequent than on Malta and are geared more to local needs than tourist requirements – buses are less frequent in the afternoon, and most stop running by early evening. Route numbers and destinations are clearly displayed on a notice board at the bus station in Victoria.

Bus Passes

The PTA issues one-/three-/five-/seven-day bus passes costing Lm1.50/4/5/6, which give unlimited travel on Malta's buses between 5.30am and 11pm. They can be purchased from the PTA offices at City Gate bus terminus, Sliema ferry terminus and Buġibba terminus. Be aware that you'll need to use the bus system quite heavily to get any value from the (in our opinion) overpriced tickets. For example, fares to/from Valletta cost no more than Lm0.25 – so you'd need to use the one-day pass more than six times to consider it anywhere worthwhile! If you're based in Sliema, St Julian's or Buġibba it's a slightly better investment – direct bus routes from these towns to major tourist attractions cost Lm0.50.

CAR & MOTORCYCLE

The Maltese love their cars. On weekends (Sunday in particular) they take to the road en masse, visiting friends and family or heading for the beach or a favourite picnic site. This means that there is often serious congestion on the roads around Valletta, Sliema and St Julian's. Friday and Saturday night in Paceville is one big traffic jam.

Distance isn't a problem – the longest distance on Malta is 27km and the widest point is around 15km. On Gozo the longest distance is about 14km, the widest only 7km.

MAIN BUS ROUTES

From Valletta (except to Sliema & St Julian's)

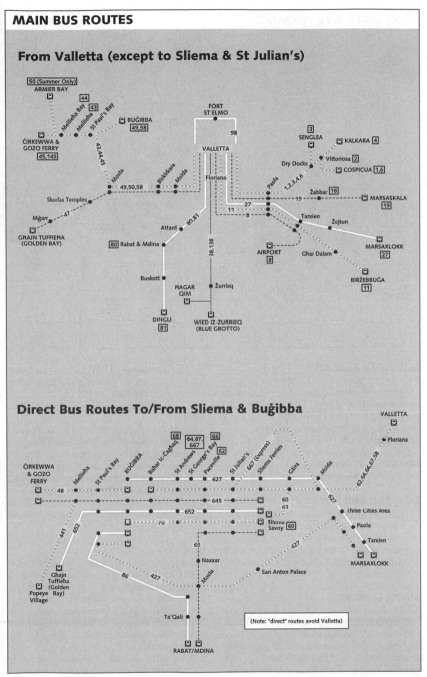

TRANSPORT

Direct Bus Routes To/From Sliema & Buġibba

(Note: "direct" routes avoid Valletta)

TRANSPORT

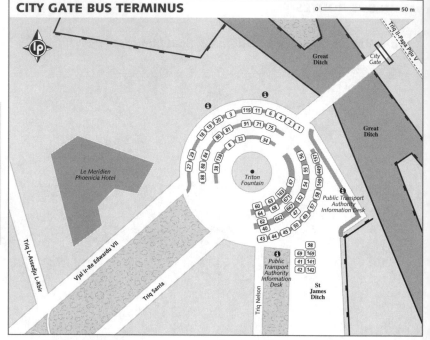

CITY GATE BUS TERMINUS

Automobile Association

If you're renting a car, you'll be provided with a telephone number to contact in the event of mechanical difficulties or breakdown. If you are bringing your own vehicle, it's a good idea to take out European breakdown cover (offered in the UK by both the RAC and the AA). For roadside assistance in Malta, contact **RMF** (☎ 2124 2222; www.rmfmalta.com) or **MTC** (☎ 2133 3033; www.mtctowingmalta.com).

Bring Your Own Vehicle

Tourists are permitted to use their vehicles for a maximum of six months in any given year without the need to apply for a permit. A motor vehicle entering a foreign country must display a sticker identifying its country of registration.

Driving Licence

All EU member states' driving licences are fully recognised throughout Europe. For those with a non-EU licence, an International Driving Permit (IDP) is a useful adjunct, especially if your home licence has no photo or is in a foreign language. Your local automobile as-

sociation can issue an IDP, valid for one year, for a small fee. You must carry your home licence together with the IDP.

Fuel

The price of fuel is set by the government and at the time of research was Lm0.50 a litre for unleaded petrol. Petrol stations are generally open from 7am to 7pm Monday to Saturday; most are closed on Sunday and public holidays, but some larger stations have a self-service, cash-operated pump (Lm2 or Lm5 notes accepted) for filling up outside opening hours.

Hire

Car rental rates in Malta are among the lowest in Europe, and hiring a car allows you to see a lot more of the island if your time is limited. If you hire a car on Malta you can take it over to Gozo on the ferry without a problem. However, rental rates on Gozo are lower and there's also the cost of a ferry ticket for the car to consider.

Most of the car-hire companies have representatives at the airport, but rates vary so it's worth shopping around. Make sure you know what is included in the quoted rate – many of the local agencies quote very low rates that do not include full insurance against theft and collision damage.

Obviously rates will vary with season, length of rental period and the size and make of car (plus extras like air con). Daily rates for the smallest vehicles start from around Lm8 a day (for rental of seven days or longer) in the low season.

The age limit for rental drivers is generally 21 to 70, but drivers between 21 and 25 may be asked to pay a supplement of up to Lm4 a day. You will need a valid driving licence that you have held for at least two years. Rental rates often include free delivery and collection, especially in the Valletta–Sliema–St Julian's area.

International agencies with offices in Malta include:

Avis (☎ 2124 6640; www.avis.com.mt)
Budget (☎ 2123 3669; www.budget.com)
Europcar (☎ 2138 8516; www.europcar.com)
Hertz (☎ 2131 4636; www.hertz.com.mt)
Sixt (☎ 2182 1416; www.e-sixt.com)
Thrifty (☎ 2148 7030; www.meligroup.com)

There are dozens of local car-hire agencies and many accommodation providers also offer car rental arrangements – it pays to ask when you're making a booking. The following have been recommended as being reliable; most will drop off and collect cars (usually for a small fee):

Billy's (☎ 2152 3676; www.billyscarhire.com; 113 Triq Ġorġ Borg Olivier, Mellieħa)
Mayjo Car Rentals (Map p146; ☎ 2155 6678; www .mayjo.com.mt; Triq Fortunato Mizzi, Victoria, Gozo)
Wembleys (Map pp88-9; ☎ 2137 0451/2; www .wembleys.net; Triq San Ġorġ, St Julian's)
Windsor Car Rentals (☎ 2137 8671; 10 Triq San Franġisk, Sliema)

Insurance

Car-hire companies offer CDW (collision damage waiver) and/or theft damage protection insurance with rental vehicles at extra cost (usually charged per day). Be sure to read the fine print and understand what you're covered for, and what excess charges you'll be up for in the case of an accident.

Normally cars registered in other European countries can circulate freely in Malta; check with your local insurance company before you leave to make sure you are covered.

Parking

Parking can be hell in the Sliema–St Julian's and Buġibba–Qawra areas. Don't even think about taking a car into Valletta – only residents are allowed to park within the city walls. Use the large underground car park near the City Gate bus terminus.

Local traffic police are swift and merciless in the imposition of Lm10 on-the-spot fines. Most main towns, tourist sites and beaches have a car park, with an attendant dressed in a blue shirt and cap and usually wearing an official badge. These attendants will expect a tip of around Lm0.25 upon your departure.

Road Rules

Like the British, the Maltese drive on the left. Speed limits are 80km/h on highways and 50km/h in urban areas, but are rarely observed. Wearing a seat belt is compulsory for the driver and front-seat passenger. Any accidents must be reported to the nearest police station (and to the rental company if the car is hired); don't move your vehicle until the police arrive, otherwise your insurance may be nullified.

Road signs and regulations are pretty much the same as the rest of Europe, with one important difference – in Malta no-one seems to pay the least attention to any of the rules. Be prepared for drivers overtaking on the inside, ignoring traffic lights, refusing to give way at junctions and hanging on your rear bumper if they think you're going too slowly. All rental cars have registration numbers ending in K, so tourists can be spotted easily. Vehicles coming from your right are supposed to have right of way at roundabouts, but don't count on vehicles on your left observing this rule.

You should also be aware that many of the roads are in pitiful condition, with cracks and potholes, and there are very few road markings. In winter, minor roads are occasionally blocked by wash-outs or collapsed retaining walls after heavy rain. Signposting is variable – some minor sights are easy to find, while major towns remain elusive. Get yourself a good road map (see p175).

The maximum blood-alcohol concentration allowed in drivers in Malta is 0.08%.

FERRY
Malta to Gozo

Gozo Channel (☎ 2155 6016; www.gozochannel.com) operates the regular ro-ro car ferry services between Malta and Gozo.

TRANSPORT

KARROZZIN

The *karrozzin* – a traditional horse-drawn carriage with seats for four passengers – has been in use in Malta since 1856. Many of the carriages are treasured family possessions passed down from father to son, and are cared for with obsessive pride.

You can catch a *karrozzin* in Valletta at City Gate, Pjazza San Ġorġ and Fort St Elmo, at Pinto Wharf, and at Mdina's Main Gate. There are regular reports of greedy drivers overcharging unwitting tourists. Haggle with the driver and be sure to agree on a fare before getting in. About Lm5 per person (maximum Lm10 for a carriage) is average for a tour of the local sights.

There is a cargo ferry that departs at 1pm Monday, Tuesday and Thursday from the Sa Maison wharf at Pieta Creek (below the Floriana fortifications) sailing to Mġarr. The crossing takes about 1½ hours and this service is used predominantly by heavy commercial vehicles.

The main ferry service runs between Ċirkewwa (Malta) and Mġarr (Gozo), with crossings every 45 to 60 minutes from 6am to around 8pm (and roughly every two hours throughout the night). The journey takes 25 minutes, and the return fare is Lm2/0.50 per adult/child, Lm6.75 for a car (including driver), Lm0.50 for a bicycle. Fares are marginally discounted on sailings after 8pm.

Bus 45 runs regularly between Valletta and Ċirkewwa (one way Lm0.25), and bus 25 operates between Mġarr and Victoria on Gozo (Lm0.20).

To Comino

Comino Hotel (☎ 2152 9821; www.cominohotels.com) runs its own ferry service, with around seven crossings a day from Ċirkewwa on Malta (between 7.30am and 11.30pm) and Mġarr on Gozo (between 6.15am and 10pm). Arriving and departing hotel guests are given priority on the boats and their return fare is Lm2/1 per adult/child. The ferry can also be used by nonresidents of the hotel (at a return fare of Lm3.50/1.75 per adult/child). The boats do not run from November to March, when the hotel is closed.

Independent water taxis also operate regularly to the island from these two ports – from

Mġarr (Lm3 return), and Ċirkewwa (Lm4 return). These services may run on demand in the low season.

Day trips operate to the Blue Lagoon from tourist areas like Sliema, Buġibba and Golden Bay in Malta, and Xlendi and Marsalforn in Gozo.

Valletta to Sliema

The **Marsamxetto ferry service** (☎ 2346 3862) crosses frequently between Valletta and Sliema. The crossing takes only about five minutes and there are departures every hour (every half-hour from 10am to 4pm), beginning at around 8am and finishing around 6pm. Ferries depart from Sliema on the hour and half-hour, and leave from Valletta at quarter past and quarter to the hour. The fare one way is Lm0.40.

TAXI

Official Maltese taxis are white (usually Mercedes, with a taxi sign on top). To combat regular complaints of overcharging, from mid-2006, taxi drivers must by law use the meter to determine the fare (except from the airport and seaport, where there are set fares).

Details of the fixed fares from the airport are available at the taxi desk in the arrivals hall, where you can pay in advance and hand a ticket to the driver. The fares are as follows:

destination	fare from the airport	fare from the seaport
Valletta/Floriana	Lm6.50	Lm4
Three Cities area	Lm7.50	Lm7
Mdina/Rabat	Lm8.50	Lm8
Sliema/St Julian's area	Lm8.50	Lm7
Buġibba/St Paul's Bay	Lm10.50	Lm10
Golden Bay area	Lm12.50	Lm10
Mellieħa	Lm12.50	Lm12
Ċirkewwa	Lm13.50	Lm13
Airport	Lm6	n/a

There are taxi ranks at City Gate and outside the Grand Master's Palace in Valletta, and at bus stations and major hotels in the main tourist resorts.

As an alternative to the white taxis, black taxis (with no sign on top) are owned by private companies and usually offer cheaper set fares (similar to the UK's minicabs). To order a taxi, it's best to ask at your hotel reception for the name and number of their preferred service, or try one of the following 24-hour companies:

Belmont Garage (☎ 2155 6962) Gozo
Freephone Taxis (☎ 8007 3770)
Wembley Motors (☎ 2137 4141)

TOURS

There are loads of companies offering tours around the islands, by boat/bus/4WD or a combination of the three. Prices vary (as do what's included), so shop around. If you're pushed for time these trips can be a good way to see the highlights, but itineraries can often be rushed with little free time. Day trips to Gozo and Comino are also common.

There are dozens of tours on offer, from half-day tours to the Blue Grotto or Valletta's Sunday market, to full-day trips to the Three Cities, Mosta and Mdina, and Gozo, or evening trips to take in festa celebrations. Tours can be arranged through most hotels and travel agents.

Captain Morgan Cruises (☎ 2346 3333; www.captain morgan.com.mt) is the biggest tour operator in the Maltese Islands and offers a wide range of boat excursions. There's a popular tour of Grand Harbour, which departs five or six times daily from March to October and costs Lm6.75/5.25 per adult/child. There is also an all-day cruise around Malta and Comino (six times a week from May to October, three times a week in March, April and November), which will set you back Lm16/10.75 per adult/child (buffet lunch included). Other options include day trips to the Blue Lagoon on Comino (from adult/child Lm7.75/5.75), a sunset cruise (adult/child Lm20.50/10.75 including buffet dinner), or a full day sailing on a catamaran (adult/child Lm26.75/16.50 including lunch). These trips depart from the Ferries area in Sliema; some trips include transfers to/from your accommodation in the price. There are also 'underwater safari' cruises (adult/child Lm5.95/4.50) out of Sliema and Buġibba, on boats with underwater viewing areas.

From March to November, Captain Morgan also offers popular chauffeur-driven jeep safaris of remote parts of Malta (adult/child Lm23/19) and Gozo (adult/child Lm26/22). Lunch is included, as is the Malta–Gozo return ferry ticket for Gozo tours. Book ahead as places are limited. For a bird's-eye view, consider a 10-minute helicopter sightseeing trip (Lm40/35, including transfers to the airport).

Alliance Cruises & Tours (☎ 2133 2165; www.al liancecruises.com) offers a program of boat tours similar to Captain Morgan, also out of Sliema. A day trip around Malta and Comino leaves four times weekly and costs Lm11.95/6.95 per adult/child, while a 1½-hour harbour cruise costs Lm6.50/4.50 (also available of an evening for the same price).

Alliance also runs bus tours taking in Gozo (adult/child Lm16.95/13), Mdina (adult/child Lm12.50/11), and the highlights of the south (Marsaxlokk, the prehistoric temples and the Blue Grotto, adult/child Lm12.50/11). Prices include transport and guide, admission fees to museums if applicable, and lunch. Alliance also have a jeep safari to out-of-the-way locations on Malta (adult/child Lm15.95/12.95) or Gozo (adult/child Lm22.50/18).

Hera Cruises (☎ 2133 0583; www.herayachtmalta.com) offers sailing trips on its two twin-mast yachts, built in Turkish *gulet* style. Sailings are from Sliema, with a half-day cruise from Sliema to Selmun Bay (including a sightseeing sail around Grand Harbour) at Lm12/7 per adult/child. A full day sailing around Malta and Comino is Lm24/13.50, including buffet lunch. Hera's 'snorkelling adventure' involves sailing from Sliema to Comino as well as snorkelling instruction from a PADI divemaster; the cost is Lm26/17.50; there's a similar tour offering diving instruction to beginners (Lm45).

Excursions to Sicily

Virtu Ferries (☎ 2122 8777; www.virtuferries.com) runs high-speed passenger catamaran services to Pozzallo and Catania (see p184) that enable travellers a day trip to Sicily. Two itineraries are possible: the first takes you on a guided tour to the active volcano, Mt Etna, and to visit the chichi town Taormina, with its ancient Greco-Roman ruins (Lm39); the second takes in Mt Etna and the baroque city Modica (Lm36).

For both tours, you join the 7am ferry from Malta, arriving in Pozzallo 1½ hours later. The return journey is at 9.30pm, getting you back to Malta at 11pm. Prices include taxes but exclude the cost of lunch. Transfers from your hotel to the port (and back again at the end of the tour) cost Lm3. You can book a trip through most hotels and travel agents in Malta.

YACHT

If you'd like to tour the Maltese Islands in class, consider chartering a yacht. See p169 for details on charter companies.

TRANSPORT

Health

CONTENTS

Travel health depends on your predeparture preparations, your daily health care while travelling and how you handle medical problems that do develop. Malta is a healthy place. Your main risks are likely to be sunburn, foot blisters, insect bites and mild stomach upsets.

BEFORE YOU GO

Prevention is the key to staying healthy. Planning before departure, particularly for pre-existing illnesses, will save trouble later. See your dentist before a long trip, carry a spare pair of contact lenses and glasses, and take your optical prescription. Bring medications in their original, clearly labelled, containers. A signed and dated letter from your physician describing your medical conditions and medications, including generic names, is also helpful. If carrying syringes or needles, be sure to have a physician's letter documenting their medical necessity.

INSURANCE

Citizens of the EU, plus Iceland, Liechtenstein, Norway and Switzerland, receive free or reduced-cost state-provided health care with the European Health Insurance Card (EHIC) for medical treatment that becomes necessary while in Malta. The EHIC will not cover you for nonemergencies or emergency

repatriation home. Each family member will need a separate card. The EHIC replaced the E111 in 2006; full details are online at http://ec.europa.eu/employment_social/healthcard/.

Malta has reciprocal health agreements with Australia and the UK. Australians are eligible for subsidised health care for up to six months from their date of arrival in Malta; UK residents for up to 30 days. Details of these arrangements, the EHIC in Malta and various health services can be found on the website of the Maltese **Ministry of Health** (www.sahha.gov.mt).

If you need health insurance, strongly consider a policy covering the worst possible scenario, such as an accident requiring an emergency flight home. Find out in advance if your insurance plan will make payments directly to providers or reimburse you later for overseas health expenditures.

RECOMMENDED VACCINATIONS

No vaccinations are required to travel to Malta. However, the World Health Organization (WHO) recommends that all travellers should be covered for diphtheria, tetanus, measles, mumps, rubella and polio, regardless of their destination.

INTERNET RESOURCES

The WHO's publication *International Travel and Health* is revised annually and is available online at www.who.int/ith/. Other useful websites include www.mdtravelhealth.com (travel health recommendations for every country; updated daily) and www.fitfortravel.scot.nhs.uk (general travel advice).

IN TRANSIT

DEEP VEIN THROMBOSIS (DVT)

Blood clots may form in the legs during plane flights, chiefly because of prolonged immobility. The main symptom of DVT is swelling or pain of the foot, ankle or calf, usually but not always on just one side. When a blood clot travels to the lungs it may cause chest pain and breathing difficulties. Travellers with any of these symptoms should immediately seek medical attention.

To prevent the development of DVT on long flights, walk about the cabin, contract the leg muscles while sitting, drink plenty of fluids and avoid alcohol and tobacco.

JET LAG & MOTION SICKNESS

To avoid jet lag (common when crossing more than five time zones) try drinking plenty of nonalcoholic fluids and eating light meals. Upon arrival, get exposure to natural sunlight and readjust your schedule (for meals, sleep and so on) as soon as possible.

Antihistamines such as dimenhydrinate (Dramamine) and meclizine (Antivert, Bonine) are usually the first choice for treating motion sickness. A herbal alternative is ginger.

IN MALTA

AVAILABILITY OF HEALTH CARE

High-standard health care is readily available in Malta and for minor illnesses pharmacists can give valuable advice and sell over-the-counter medication. They can also advise when more specialised help is required and point you in the right direction. There are pharmacies in most towns; these are generally open from 9am to 1pm and 4pm to 7pm Monday to Saturday. On Sundays and public holidays they open by roster in the morning – the local Sunday newspapers print details of the roster.

Malta's public general hospital is **St Luke's Hospital** (Map p84; ☎ 2124 1251, emergency 112; www .slh.gov.mt; Triq San Luqa, Gwardamanġa), near Pietà (southwest of Valletta) and accessible by bus 75 from the capital. The long-delayed opening of Malta's large new hospital, Mater Dei, is now scheduled for July 2007 (but many believe there will be further delays). Mater Dei is in Tal-Qroqq, near the University of Malta. Gozo's smaller **General Hospital** (Map 146; ☎ 2156 1600; Triq I-Arċisqof Pietru Pace, Victoria) may also be of use. GP service is also available at a network of health centres (at Floriana, Gżira, Qormi, Paola, Cospicua, Mosta, Rabat and on Gozo).

The standard of dental care is usually good; however, it is sensible to have a dental checkup before a long trip.

TRAVELLER'S DIARRHOEA

Simple things like a change of water, food or climate can cause stomach upsets. If you develop diarrhoea, make sure to drink plenty of fluids, preferably with an oral rehydration solution (eg dioralyte). If diarrhoea is bloody, persists for more than 72 hours or is accompanied by fever, shaking, chills or severe abdominal pain you should seek medical attention.

ENVIRONMENTAL HAZARDS
Heat Exhaustion & Heatstroke

Take care in the fierce heat of a Maltese summer. Heat exhaustion follows excessive fluid loss with inadequate replacement of fluids and salt. Symptoms include headache, dizziness and tiredness. Dehydration is already happening by the time you feel thirsty – aim to drink sufficient water to produce pale, diluted urine. To treat heat exhaustion, replace lost fluids by drinking water and/or fruit juice, and cool the body with cold water and fans.

Heatstroke is much more serious, resulting in irrational and hyperactive behaviour, and eventually loss of consciousness and death. Rapid cooling by spraying the body with water and fanning is ideal. Emergency fluid and electrolyte replacement by intravenous drip is recommended.

Insect Bites & Stings

Mosquitoes are found in most parts of Europe; they may not carry malaria but can cause irritation and infected bites. Use a DEET-based insect repellent.

Bees and wasps cause real problems only to those with a severe allergy (anaphylaxis). If you have a severe allergy to bee or wasp stings carry an 'epipen' or similar adrenaline injection.

Sandflies are found around Mediterranean beaches. They usually cause only a nasty, itchy bite but can carry a rare skin disorder called cutaneous Leishmaniasis.

HEALTH

Water

Malta's tap water is safe to drink but heavily chlorinated, so stick to the bottled variety if you don't like the taste. Any water in the countryside, whether from a stream or spring, is best left alone.

TRAVELLING WITH CHILDREN

If you are travelling with children you should know how to treat minor ailments and when to seek medical treatment. Make sure children are up-to-date with routine vaccinations, and discuss possible travel vaccines well before departure, as some vaccines are not suitable for children under a year.

In hot moist climates any wound or break in the skin is likely to let in infection. The area should be cleaned and kept dry. If your child has vomiting or diarrhoea, lost fluid and salts must be replaced. It may be helpful to take rehydration powders for reconstituting with boiled water.

WOMEN'S HEALTH

Emotional stress, exhaustion and travelling across time zones can all contribute to an upset in the menstrual pattern. Some antibiotics, diarrhoea and vomiting can interfere with the effectiveness of oral contraceptives and lead to the risk of pregnancy – remember to take condoms just in case. Time zones, gastrointestinal upsets and antibiotics do not affect injectable contraception.

Travelling during pregnancy is usually possible, but always consult your doctor before planning your trip. The most risky times for travel are during the first 12 weeks of pregnancy and after 30 weeks.

Language

CONTENTS

Malti – the native language of Malta – is a member of the Semitic language group, which also includes Arabic, Hebrew and Amharic. It's thought by some to be a direct descendant of the language spoken by the Phoenicians, but most linguists consider it to be related to the Arabic dialects of western North Africa. Malti is the only Semitic language that is written in a Latin script.

Both Malti and English are official languages in Malta, and almost everyone is bilingual. Travellers will have no trouble at all getting by in English at all times. However, it's always good to learn at least a few words of the native language, and the sections that follow will provide a basic introduction to Malti.

If you want to learn more about the language, look out for *Teach Yourself Maltese* by Joseph Aquilina or *Learn Maltese – Why Not?* by Joseph Vella. Lonely Planet's *Europe Phrasebook* has a useful Maltese section. A small range of pocket dictionaries and phrasebooks is available in bookshops in Malta. They are of variable quality and usefulness, so it's worth checking the content carefully before buying.

PRONUNCIATION

There are 29 letters in the Maltese alphabet. Individual letters aren't too diffcult to pronounce once you learn the rules, but putting them together to make any kind of sense is a major achievement. Most are pronounced as they are in English. The following list highlights the trickier stuff.

ċ	as the 'ch' in 'child'
g	as in 'good'
ġ	soft, as the 'j' in 'job'
għ	silent; lengthens the preceding or following vowel
h	silent, as in 'hour'
ħ	as the 'h' in 'hand'
j	as the 'y' in 'yellow'
ij	as the 'ai' in 'aisle'
ej	as the 'ay' in 'day'
q	a glottal stop; it's like the missing 't' in the cockney pronunciation of 'bottle' (bo'ul)
x	as the 'sh' in 'shop'
z	as the 'ts' in 'bits'
ż	soft, as in 'zero'

ACCOMMODATION

Do you have any rooms available?	Ghad fadlilkom xi kmamar vojta?
Can you show me a room?	Tista' turini kamra?
How much is it?	Kemm hi?
I'd like a room ...	Nixtieq kamra ...
with one bed	b'sodda waħda
with two beds	b'żewġ sodod
with en suite	bil-kamra tal-banju

CONVERSATION & ESSENTIALS

Hello.	Merħba.
Good morning/day.	Bonġu.
Good evening.	Bonswa.
Goodbye.	Saħħa.
Yes/No.	Iva/Le.
Please.	Jekk jogħġbok.
Thank you.	Grazzi.
Excuse me.	Skużani.
How are you?	Kif inti?
I'm fine, thank you.	Tajjed, grazzi.
Do you speak English?	Titkellem bl-ingliż?
What's your name?	X'ismek?
My name is ...	Jisimni ...
I love you.	Inhobbok.

DIRECTIONS

Where is a/the ...?	Fejn hu ...?
Go straight ahead.	Mur dritt.
Turn (left/right).	Dur fuq (ix-xellug/il-lemin).
near/far	il-viċin/il-bogħod

LANGUAGE

SIGNS

Miftuħ	Open
Magħluq	Closed
Dħul	Entrance
Ħrug	Exit
Vjalq	Avenue
Sqaq	Lane/Alley
Twaletta	Toilet
Rġiel	Men
Nisa	Women

NUMBERS

0	*xejn*
1	*wieħed*
2	*tnejn*
3	*tlieta*
4	*erbgħa*
5	*ħamsa*
6	*sitta*
7	*sebgħa*
8	*tmienja*
9	*disgħa*
10	*għaxra*
11	*ħdax*
12	*tnax*
13	*tlettax*
14	*erbatax*
15	*ħmistax*
16	*sittax*
17	*sbatax*
18	*tmintax*
19	*dsatax*
20	*għoxrin*
30	*tletin*
40	*erbgħin*
50	*ħamsin*
60	*sittin*
70	*sebgħin*
80	*tmienin*
90	*disgħin*
100	*mija*
1000	*elf*

SHOPPING & SERVICES

How much is it?	*Kemm?*
What time does it open/close?	*Fix'ħin jiftaħ/jagħlaq?*
... embassy	*ambaxxata ...*
bank	*bank*
chemist/pharmacy	*ispiżerija*
hotel	*hotel/il-lukanda*
market	*suq*

EMERGENCIES

Help!	*Ajjut!*
Call a doctor!	*Qibgħad ghat-tabib!*
Police!	*Pulizija!*
I'm lost.	*Ninsab mitluf.*
ambulance	*ambulans*
hospital	*sptar*

post office	*posta*
public telephone	*telefon pubbliku*
shop	*ħanut*

TIME & DATES

What's the time?	*X'ħin hu?*
today	*illum*
tomorrow	*għada*
yesterday	*il-bieraħ*
morning	*fil-għodu*
afternoon	*wara nofs in-nhar*
Monday	*it-tnejn*
Tuesday	*it-tlieta*
Wednesday	*l-erbgħa*
Thursday	*il-ħamis*
Friday	*il-gimgħa*
Saturday	*is-sibt*
Sunday	*il-ħadd*
January	*Jannar*
February	*Frar*
March	*Marzu*
April	*April*
May	*Mejju*
June	*Ġunju*
July	*Lulju*
August	*Awissu*
September	*Settembru*
October	*Ottubru*
November	*Novembru*
December	*Diċembru*

TRANSPORT

When does the boat leave/arrive?	*Meta jitlaq/jasal il-vapur?*
When does the bus leave/arrive?	*Meta titlaq/jasal il-karozza?*
I'd like to hire a car/bicycle.	*Nixtieq nikri karozza/rota.*
left luggage	*hallejt il-bagalji*
I'd like a ... ticket.	*Nixtieq biljett ...*
one-way	*'one-way'*
return	*'return'*

Glossary

See also the Language chapter (p195) for an introduction to the Malti language and some useful phrases for travellers, and the Food & Drink chapter (p51) for an explanation of delicious and intriguing Maltese specialities.

AFM – Armed Forces of Malta
auberge – the residence of an individual langue of the Knights of St John

bajja – bay
bastion – a defensive work with two faces and two flanks, projecting from the line of the rampart
belt – city
bieb – gate

cavalier – a defensive work inside the main fortification, rising above the level of the main rampart to give covering fire
ċimiterju – cemetery
curtain – a stretch of rampart linking two bastions, with a parapet along the top

daħla – creek
dawret – bypass
demi-bastion – a half-bastion with only one face and one flank
dgħajsa – a traditional oar-powered boat

festa – feast day
fortizza – fort
foss – ditch

għajn – spring (of water)
għar – cave
ġnien – garden

kajjik – fishing boat
kappillan – parish priest
karrozzin – traditional horse-drawn carriage
kastell – castle
katidral – cathedral

kbira – big, main
knisja – church
kwartier – quarter, neighbourhood

langue – a division of the Knights of St John, based on nationality
luzzu – fishing boat

marsa – harbour
medina – fortified town, citadel
mina – arch, gate
misraħ – square
mitħna – windmill
mużew – museum

palazzo – Italian term for palace or mansion
parroċċa – parish
passeggiata – evening stroll (Italian term)
pjazza – square
plajja – beach, seashore
pont – bridge
pulizija – police

rabat – town outside the walls of a citadel
ramla – bay, beach
ras – point, headland
razzett – farm, farmhouse

sqaq – alley, lane
sur – bastion
suq – market

taraġ – stairs, steps
telgħa – hill
torri – tower, castle
triq – street, road

vedette – a lookout point, watchtower
vjal – avenue

wied – valley

xatt – wharf, marina

Behind the Scenes

THIS BOOK

This is the 3rd edition of *Malta & Gozo*. Neil Wilson wrote the first edition and Carolyn Bain wrote the 2nd edition. This guidebook was commissioned in Lonely Planet's London office, and produced by the following:

Commissioning Editor Paula Hardy
Coordinating Editor Phillip Tang
Coordinating Cartographer Andy Rojas
Coordinating Layout Designers Pablo Gastar, Carlos Solarte
Managing Editor Imogen Bannister
Managing Cartographer Alison Lyall
Assisting Editors Elisa Arduca, Adrienne Costanzo, Joanne Newell
Assisting Cartographer Corey Hutchison
Cover Designer Rebecca Dandens
Project Manager Craig Kilburn
Language Content Coordinator Quentin Frayne

Thanks to David Connolly, Sally Darmody, Kate McDonald, Trent Paton, Celia Wood

THANKS
CAROLYN BAIN

Once again, my thanks to the LP folk behind this book, and to the various locals, expats and tourists in Malta who gave freely of their time, answered questions, gave directions, offered opinions or just generally helped out. I'm grateful to all of them, especially Charlie Busuttil and his family in Valletta. Big thanks to everyone back home and to family and friends dotted around the globe, especially (on this trip) to the very fabulous Graham Harris and Kate Johns.

OUR READERS

Many thanks to the travellers who used the last edition and wrote to us with helpful hints, useful advice and interesting anecdotes:

John Abela, Mick Adams, Tracey Colletti & Steven Adams, Paul Affleck, Joseph Aquilina, Caroline Ash, Peter Bonnici, Stuart Brain, Andrew Brash, S Brooker, Norman Cain, Silvana Cardona, John Clark, Verdon Coucom, Nicola Coxon, Ian & Gill Cuthbertson, Roland de Jong, Erna Dils, Stane Droljc, Anna Earles, Mario Falzon, Mark Farrugia, Carole Feldman, Marvin Feldman, Annmaria Forbes, Ben Forder, Joanne Fox, Kay Fraser, Doug Gardiner, Nur Garriga-Segura, Anne Greig, Erik Griep, Jiaxin Guan, Katy Guest, Melissa Harrison, Martina Holgersson, Rok Jarc, Heath Kelly, Maurice Kime, Thorsten Koehler, Jackie Leardi, Pedro Lopez, Chris Louie, Doris & Gunnar Lundh, Duncan Martin, Antonio Martinez, Brett McBain, Gregory McElwain, Tormod & Bratt Mediaas, Liina Meiusi, Mark Miceli-Farrugia, K Millard, Elizabeth Myers, Godfrey Newman, Francis Reiss, Toby Ritchie, Peter Sammit, Christine Sandaas, William Sherlock, Robert Spiteri, Eric Stokkink, Katya Stroud, Andrea Trapani, Ralph Vick, Anna Walker, Anke Walzebug, Joshua Welbaum, Ken Westmoreland

---

THE LONELY PLANET STORY

The story begins with a classic travel adventure: Tony and Maureen Wheeler's 1972 journey across Europe and Asia to Australia. There was no useful information about the overland trail then, so Tony and Maureen published the first Lonely Planet guidebook to meet a growing need.

From a kitchen table, Lonely Planet has grown to become the largest independent travel publisher in the world, with offices in Melbourne (Australia), Oakland (USA) and London (UK). Today Lonely Planet guidebooks cover the globe. There is an ever-growing list of books and information in a variety of media. Some things haven't changed. The main aim is still to make it possible for adventurous travellers to get out there – to explore and better understand the world.

At Lonely Planet we believe travellers can make a positive contribution to the countries they visit – if they respect their host communities and spend their money wisely. Every year 5% of company profit is donated to charities around the world.

SEND US YOUR FEEDBACK

We love to hear from travellers – your comments keep us on our toes and help make our books better. Our well-travelled team reads every word on what you loved or loathed about this book. Although we cannot reply individually to postal submissions, we always guarantee that your feedback goes straight to the appropriate authors, in time for the next edition. Each person who sends us information is thanked in the next edition – and the most useful submissions are rewarded with a free book.

To send us your updates – and find out about Lonely Planet events, newsletters and travel news – visit our award-winning website: **www.lonelyplanet.com/contact**.

Note: we may edit, reproduce and incorporate your comments in Lonely Planet products such as guidebooks, websites and digital products, so let us know if you don't want your comments reproduced or your name acknowledged. For a copy of our privacy policy visit www.lonelyplanet.com/privacy.

Index

INDEX

INDEX

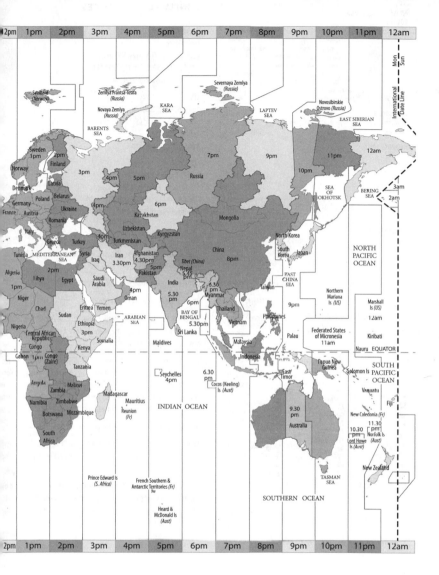

12pm 1pm 2pm 3pm 4pm 5pm 6pm 7pm 8pm 9pm 10pm 11pm 12am

Mon/Sun
International Date Line

Svalbard (Norway)
Zemlya Frantsa-Iosifa (Russia)
Severnaya Zemlya (Russia)
Novosibirskie Ostrova (Russia)
Novaya Zemlya (Russia)
KARA SEA
LAPTEV SEA
EAST SIBERIAN SEA
BARENTS SEA

Sweden 1pm 2pm
Norway
Finland
Denmark
Latvia
3pm
Russia
7pm
9pm
11pm
12am
Germany
Poland
Belarus
4pm
10pm
France
Austria
Ukraine
4pm
6pm
SEA OF OKHOTSK
BERING SEA
3am
2am
Italy
Romania
Kazakhstan
Mongolia
Greece
Turkey
4pm
Uzbekistan
Kyrgyzstan
China
8pm
North Korea
Tunisia MEDITERRANEAN SEA
Syria
Turkmenistan
South Korea
Japan
NORTH PACIFIC OCEAN
Algeria
Iraq
Iran 3.30pm
Afghanistan 4.30pm
Tibet (China)
EAST CHINA SEA
Libya
Egypt
Saudi Arabia
Pakistan 5pm
Nepal 5.45pm
Taiwan
Northern Mariana Is (US)
Marshall Is (US)
Niger
Oman
India 5.30 pm
6.30 pm
Myanmar
9pm
Chad
Sudan
Eritrea Yemen
6pm
Thailand
Philippines
Nigeria
Ethiopia 3pm
ARABIAN SEA
BAY OF BENGAL
Vietnam
Palau
Federated States of Micronesia 11am
Kiribati
12am
Central African Republic
Sri Lanka 5.30pm
Malaysia
Nauru EQUATOR
Congo
Kenya
Maldives
Indonesia
SOUTH PACIFIC OCEAN
Gabon 1pm
Congo (Zaire)
Tanzania
East Timor
Papua New Guinea
Solomon Is
Vanuatu
Angola
Malawi
Zambia
Seychelles 4pm
6.30 pm
Cocos (Keeling) Is (Aust)
New Caledonia (Fr)
Fiji
Namibia
Zimbabwe
Madagascar
Mauritius
Reunion (Fr)
INDIAN OCEAN
9.30 pm
Australia
10.30 pm
Norfolk Is (Aust)
Lord Howe Is (Aust)
11.30 pm
Botswana
Mozambique
South Africa
New Zealand
Prince Edward Is (S. Africa)
French Southern & Antarctic Territories (Fr)
TASMAN SEA
SOUTHERN OCEAN
Heard & McDonald Is (Aust)

12pm 1pm 2pm 3pm 4pm 5pm 6pm 7pm 8pm 9pm 10pm 11pm 12am

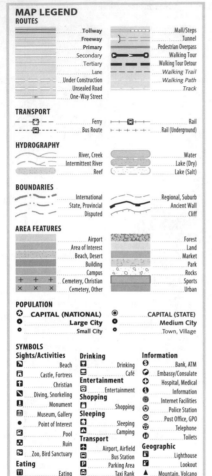

MAP LEGEND

ROUTES

Tollway
Freeway
Primary
Secondary
Tertiary
Lane
Under Construction
Unsealed Road
One-Way Street

Mall/Steps
Tunnel
Pedestrian Overpass
Walking Tour
Walking Tour Detour
Walking Trail
Walking Path
Track

TRANSPORT

Ferry
Bus Route

Rail
Rail (Underground)

HYDROGRAPHY

River, Creek
Intermittent River
Reef

Water
Lake (Dry)
Lake (Salt)

BOUNDARIES

International
State, Provincial
Disputed

Regional, Suburb
Ancient Wall
Cliff

AREA FEATURES

Airport
Area of Interest
Beach, Desert
Building
Campus
Cemetery, Christian
Cemetery, Other

Forest
Land
Market
Park
Rocks
Sports
Urban

POPULATION

○ **CAPITAL (NATIONAL)**
● **Large City**
● Small City

◉ CAPITAL (STATE)
● **Medium City**
○ Town, Village

SYMBOLS

Sights/Activities
Beach
Castle, Fortress
Christian
Diving, Snorkeling
Monument
Museum, Gallery
Point of Interest
Pool
Ruin
Zoo, Bird Sanctuary

Eating
Eating

Drinking
Drinking
Café

Entertainment
Entertainment

Shopping
Shopping

Sleeping
Sleeping
Camping

Transport
Airport, Airfield
Bus Station
Parking Area
Taxi Rank

Information
Bank, ATM
Embassy/Consulate
Hospital, Medical
Information
Internet Facilities
Police Station
Post Office, GPO
Telephone
Toilets

Geographic
Lighthouse
Lookout
Mountain, Volcano

LONELY PLANET OFFICES

Australia
Head Office
Locked Bag 1, Footscray, Victoria 3011
☎ 03 8379 8000, fax 03 8379 8111
talk2us@lonelyplanet.com.au

USA
150 Linden St, Oakland, CA 94607
☎ 510 893 8555, toll free 800 275 8555
fax 510 893 8572
info@lonelyplanet.com

UK
72–82 Rosebery Ave,
Clerkenwell, London EC1R 4RW
☎ 020 7841 9000, fax 020 7841 9001
go@lonelyplanet.co.uk

Published by Lonely Planet Publications Pty Ltd
ABN 36 005 607 983

Printed by SNP Security Printing Pte Ltd, Singapore